Capital and Class
in Scotland

Capital and Class in Scotland

Edited by

TONY DICKSON

Department of Sociology
Glasgow College of Technology

JOHN DONALD PUBLISHERS LTD
EDINBURGH

ISBN 0 85976 065 0

Phototypeset by Burns & Harris Limited, Dundee
Printed in Great Britain by Bell & Bain Ltd, Glasgow

Contents

List of Contributors

Tony Dickson is Head of the Department of Sociology at Glasgow College of Technology.

Tony Clarke is Lecturer in Sociology in the Department of Politics and Sociology at Paisley College of Technology.

Roddy Gallacher is a post-graduate student in the Department of Sociology at Aberdeen University. He is in the final stages of a PhD on 'Class and Class Consciousness in the Vale of Leven 1919-1980'.

Jim McGoldrick is a post-graduate student in the Department of Sociology at Glasgow University. He is in the final stages of a PhD on 'The History and Organisation of the Boilermakers' Society in Scotland'.

Joseph Melling is a Research Fellow in the Department of Social and Economic Research at Glasgow University.

Ian Watt is Lecturer in Sociology in the Department of Politics and Sociology at Paisley College of Technology.

Peter Wybrow is a post-graduate student in the Department of Sociology at Aberdeen University. He is in the final stages of a PhD on 'The British National Oil Corporation: A Study of Government Policy in the North Sea'.

Introduction

IN the introduction to *Scottish Capitalism*[1] I noted a major problem which had constrained the efforts of the contributors to that work, namely, the dearth of primary research into so many aspects of Scottish society and its history. As a result *Scottish Capitalism* was based almost exclusively on existing secondary sources, which were themselves weakened by major gaps in our knowledge. In contrast, the essays written for this volume are all based on original research by the contributors. In this sense they reflect a more general trend over the last five years towards a greater interest by academics in Scotland in the society in which they live.[2]

The essays in this book are focused on different aspects of Scottish society, and are located within different historical periods. There are, however, a number of linkages between the essays. First, and foremost, there is an underlying theoretical unity in that all the contributions are based upon those insights deriving from Marxist analysis. The specific weight given to explanatory concepts varies from one essay to another, as does the particular focus of interest. This reflects more general trends in Marxist analysis in Britain in the last twenty years, which has seen a widening of the range of focus of such work, from studies of the 'labour process' to arguments about the precise meaning and definition of the concept of 'mode of production' itself.[3] This diversity of approach is reflected in this volume as, for example, in the contrast between the piece by Jim McGoldrick, on shipbuilding on Clydeside between the wars, which has as its primary emphasis an examination of debates about the labour process in that industry, and, on the other hand, the essay by Ian Watt, which examines wider changes in the Scottish economy since 1945, with particular reference to their effects on the employment of women. Nevertheless, despite such contrasts, all the essays demonstrate a consistent emphasis on the fundamental conflict between capital and labour, and the particular forms which class struggle has taken in Scottish society.

The second theme which emerges from most of the essays contains an implicit criticism of certain tendencies in Marxist writings on the development of class consciousness and collective action. In particular they illustrate the problems raised by accounts which present an overly cohesive view of working class action and consciousness in different periods. The essays in this volume examine a number of sources of division and sectional identities within the working class. In doing so they illustrate the need for caution in assuming

1

that processes evident in one locality or region must operate in a similar fashion elsewhere.

Tony Clarke and myself, in our study of Paisley between 1770 and 1850, argue that the nature of the local economy threw up various barriers to the formation of solidaristic forms of working class action. The small-scale nature of local manufacturing concerns, their vulnerability to movements in the trade cycle, and the existence of divisions between segments of the labour force on the grounds of occupation, culture and religion (especially between the handloom weavers and the cotton spinners) hindered the emergence of cohesive working class organisation. Although there *were* periods of collective action (for example in the riots of 1819 in Paisley, and in the agitation leading up to the 1832 Reform Act), these were interspersed with times in which political action reflected divisions within the working class and instead involved alliances between different class groupings (for example between the handloom weavers and small manufacturers). On this basis we tentatively suggest that the descriptions by Thompson[4] and Foster[5] of cohesive working class action at a wider level may be qualified by more detailed accounts of particular localities.

In a related fashion the essay by Joe Melling, on Clydeside between 1880 and 1918, focuses on the significance of the locality (or community) as a base for working class action. He stresses the need for a greater sensitivity by historians to the ways in which the language of 'class' and 'community' has had different meanings in different historical contexts, and the necessity for situating this understanding within a broader analysis of social relations in capitalist society. At the same time, however, he illustrates the manner in which the linkages between different communities on Clydeside, the sector of employment on which they were dependent, and the relationships between employers and their labour force in the locality, influenced the forms and strategies of working class action. Despite these local identities, and the different conditions upon which they were based, he traces the forces which underlay those periods in which the action of different groups coalesced, as for example in the rent strike of 1915 in Glasgow. Nevertheless, the fragility of such common action is underlined in this account by his discussion of those factors which could point in a contrary direction — such as the characteristics of sexual divisions in the workforce, the different circumstances at work in specific localities, and the divisions implicit in the labour process itself (as evidenced in the failure of the Clyde Workers' Committee to generate a wider basis of support in 1916).

Roddy Gallacher's essay on the Vale of Leven after 1914 also points to both the possibilities for, and the limitations on, collective working class action.[6] He addresses himself to the disjunction between the radicalism of working class action in the Vale between the Wars, when something akin to Foster's 'labour community' in Oldham was created, and the quiescence and reformist orientation of working class action since 1945. In explaining this disjunction he focuses, like Melling, on the specificities of the locality in influencing working class action, showing how the phenomenally high rates of unemployment in the 1920s and 1930s, combined with the withdrawal of employers from the local structures of administrative control, formed a social vacuum within which working class leaders could establish a significant degree of control of these political and social apparatuses. But he also demonstrates the fragile nature of this 'labour community', both in terms of the alliance between the local branches of the ILP, Communist Party, and Labour Party, and in terms of the recurring possibilities for sectionalism implicit in the existence of significant sexual, religious, and occupational divisions in the Vale's working class. The thrust of working class radicalism was progressively eroded from the late 1930s under the impact of the revival of employment (and the control mechanisms built into employment itself), the problems for working class organisation deriving from the nature of 'branch firms' established by foreign investment, and the dominance of the idea of economic growth at all costs which encapsulated the thinking of both the Conservative and Labour Parties in the 1950s and 1960s.

One of the most important forms of division within the working class, both in historical and contemporary terms, is the subject of Ian Watt's essay, in which he examines the changes in Scotland's economic structure since 1945 with particular reference to their effects on, and implications for, the position of women in Scottish society. He illustrates the growing importance of women in the labour force in Scotland, as the traditional male-dominated 'heavy' industries have declined and the tertiary sector has grown, and as foreign investment has tended to be concentrated in sectors with a high level of female employment. He points to the failure, both of academics and of the labour movement, to come to terms with the implications of these developments. He argues that theories which ignore the nature of sexual divisions in a capitalist division of labour, by relegating women to the position of footnotes in a general theory of working class action, must be seen as, consequently, seriously inadequate. In addition the Scottish labour movement has deliberately neglected the implications of women's employment and runs the risk of remaining seriously divided in its struggle with capital unless it remedies this neglect.

Thus, implicit in these essays is the suggestion that accounts which fail to examine the specific features of particular localities, and the sources of division within the working class in different periods, run the risk of giving an over-optimistic view of working class consciousness and action. It can be argued that these accounts lead to the assumption that the 'normal' process of historical development is the growing cohesion and self-awareness of the working class. In contrast, these essays suggest in their different ways that such solidarity and class consciousness have been, and are, fragile constructs which have to be *made* through working class action. Any account which neglects the barriers to the process of forging cohesion thereby gives an unrealistic assessment of the possibilities for action.

A similar point can be made in relation to a third, though less explicit, theme in these essays. Just as certain Marxist accounts may be seen to give an overly cohesive view of *the* working class, so they also, frequently, present a similarly misleading view of *the* 'ruling class', or *the* 'bourgeoisie'. If there is no immutable 'law' of capitalist development which guarantees the trans- formation of the working class from a class in itself to a class for itself, then a similar point can be made about bourgeois consciousness and action. A number of the essays in this book point to the importance of an awareness of the divisions which may exist between different segments of capital. The essay by Tony Clarke and myself highlights significant conflicts between a group of 'small' manufacturers in Paisley, on the one hand, and the larger manu- facturers and landowners, on the other. Not only did the nature of the class origins of small manufacturers encourage an identification with the interests of the handloom weavers (as manufacturers had often begun as weavers them- selves) but, in addition, the stranglehold of Scottish landowners on political power meant that 'political reform' could weld sections of the working class into an alliance with these manufacturers *against* the landed interest (re- inforced by agitation around economic policy and the Corn Laws). Thus Thompson's view of an insurgent, organised working class confronting an alliance of landowners and industrial bourgeoisie has to be qualified in relation to Paisley. A similar point is made by Melling in the first part of his essay where he stresses the extended hold which landowners in Scotland exerted on political power, and the implications that had for delaying an alliance with an indigenous industrial bourgeoisie.

Jim McGoldrick, in his study of shipbuilding on Clydeside between the wars, makes the point in another way. He shows how the inter-war crises in shipbuilding led employers to search for ways of solving their problems. The restructuring of the labour process in shipbuilding was one obvious solution, since new mechanised techniques such as pneumatic riveting and welding were available as a means of reducing labour costs and improving productivity. Nevertheless, the introduction of such techniques did not take place for some time due, on the one hand, to divisions within the employers' ranks over the best method of solving the crisis, and, on the other, to the ability of skilled workers to resist these new methods until they had devised ways of controlling their operation and effects.

In this sense these essays point, from a number of different directions, to the need to avoid accounts of capitalist society which have a tendency to categorise relationships in terms of a simple dichotomous model of capital/labour or working class/bourgeoisie. They illustrate the necessity for detailed study of the precise forms and varieties which *both* working class *and* bourgeoisie consciousness and action have taken. This in turn involves the recognition of the major difficulties of forging, within capitalist society, a base for working class resistance which overcomes those divisions within the working class which may erect barriers to collective action.

Such a recognition points to the final linking theme in the essays to which I would wish to draw attention. An examination of the inherent difficulties in collective working class action indicates the need to recognise class struggle in both its economic and political dimensions. A number of the essays illustrate both the possibilities and the limitations of action directed beyond the confines of production itself. The essay by Tony Clarke and myself shows that, even in the late eighteenth/early nineteenth century, the limits to working class radicalism were defined by a broader political and economic system. Attempts by local manufacturers and working class activists to mitigate the disastrous human consequences of the cycle of capitalist production were ultimately destroyed by their inability to affect that system of production itself and by their dependence on the British state in 'bailing out' the local system of Poor Relief. In the absence of a wider response by the British working class and a conception of an alternative social order, the achievements of local action were distinctly limited.

Similarly Melling's account of Clydeside between 1880 and 1918 points to the growing significance of State action (for example in the areas of housing and munition production) in structuring the effects of local action. Thus action by the working class on Clydeside in the Rent Strike had a significant effect in inducing the Government to introduce housing legislation. That achievement should not be minimised. Nevertheless, the subsequent failure of the Clyde Workers' Committee demonstrated the limits of local action which could not be fused into a wider British movement based on the Shop Stewards' movement. Again, Roddy Gallacher's essay on the Vale of Leven rightly stresses the gains made by local activists in, for example, increasing rates of Poor Relief. But, once again, the essay at the same time indicates the limited scale of these gains, and the growing dependence of the locality on decisions made elsewhere — either in the head offices of foreign firms, or in the Westminster Parliament. The point is reinforced by Pete Wybrow's discussion of the progressive role adopted by the labour movement in Scotland in attempting to pressure the oil companies and the Government to protect the interests of those working in sectors relating to North Sea oil. Their difficulties in enforcing their demands stem from the organised opposition of the oil companies, and from the alliance between these companies and successive Governments in stressing the need for rapid extraction of oil at the expense of the interests of oil workers. The inability of the labour movement to bring more effective pressure to bear reinforces the need for the welding of different groups together into a more effective political movement.

The necessity for positive action in forging those alliances required to ensure collective working class opposition to its exploitation is reinforced by those trends noted in the final two essays in the book, by Ian Watt and Pete Wybrow. Both these contributors discuss, in different ways, the manner in which the Scottish economy has become increasingly dependent on foreign capital. This has been especially true after 1945 and is highlighted by the developments in North Sea oil, and counterpointed by the rapid decline of Scotland's traditional heavy industries. Two important consequences should be noted here. First, these developments have led to a marked tendency for the British state to structure its actions towards Scotland in terms of its relationship to foreign capital. As Pete Wybrow's essay illustrates, this alliance between the British state and foreign companies creates major problems for the labour movement. Second, these problems reinforce the general difficulty of attempting to influence the consequences of investment which is dependent on decisions taken outside Scotland. Ian Watt's discussion of the consequences of branch firm production in Scotland highlights such problems in terms of their effects on unemployment and divisions within the working class. The closure of the Talbot plant at Linwood in 1981 is one graphic illustration of the dependence on foreign capital. For these reasons the growing importance of foreign capital in Scotland poses major problems for working class organisation and underlines the need for united action.

Thus we hope that the essays in the book make a contribution in two main areas. First, they are intended as an addition to our knowledge of a number of aspects of Scottish history. Second, by pointing to the dangers of analyses which fail to acknowledge and explore the difficulties in collective working class opposition to the demands of capital, they stress the necessity for constant effort in overcoming sectional identities. In this sense they emphasise that the growth of working class consciousness and solidarity cannot be seen as an inexorable process within capitalist society — it has to be worked for and actively brought about by those involved.

Finally, it only remains for me to thank those who helped in different ways in preparing this book. Primarily I am grateful to all the contributors for their hard work and for putting up with my incessant nagging over deadlines. For similar reasons I am also grateful to John Tuckwell of John Donald for *his* forbearance in terms of completion dates. My special thanks are also due to Maureen Alexander for her help in typing the contributions to the book. Her efforts were as crucial as anybody's in enabling the work to be completed.

Tony Dickson
Glasgow College of Technology

NOTES

1. T. Dickson (ed.), *Scottish Capitalism* (London 1980).
2. See, for example, I. Carter, *Farm Life in North-East Scotland 1840-1914* (Edinburgh 1979); J. Scott & M. Hughes, *The Anatomy of Scottish Capital* (London 1980); and the publication in 1981 of a new journal, *Scottish Economic and Social History*.

3. The history and nature of some of these debates are discussed in P. Anderson, *Arguments within English Marxism* (London 1980).

4. E. P. Thompson, *The Making of the English Working Class* (London 1963).

5. J. Foster, *Class Struggle and the Industrial Revolution* (London 1974).

6. See also S. MacIntyre, *The Little Moscows* (London 1980) for a discussion of the Vale of Leven between the wars.

1

Class and Class Consciousness in Early Industrial Capitalism: Paisley 1770-1850

Tony Clarke and Tony Dickson

OUR intention in this chapter is to examine the formation of working class consciousness and organisation in Paisley between 1770 and 1850, against the background of the changing economic and social structure in the town. The preliminary results of our research on class formations in Paisley will be presented in the light of continuing debates regarding the impact of early industrial capitalism on class relations and working class consciousness in Britain. We consider this a potentially fruitful exercise because, at least until very recently, the work of some important Marxist historians on the formation of the English working class in the period in question has not been taken up and applied systematically to the study of the Scottish counterpart of this class.

E. P. Thompson's *The Making of the English Working Class* must still be considered an important reference point in Marxist historiography, as is indicated by the recent attempt by Perry Anderson to reassess its significance in the light of Thompson's subsequent critique of Althusserian Marxism.[1] Thompson argued that the period 1780-1830 was crucial to the development of English working class consciousness and organisation. The experience of economic exploitation and the severity of state repression of working class industrial and political organisation, particularly in the course of the Napoleonic Wars, sharpened working class perceptions of their class enemies. At the same time, the 'self-activity' of the working class, for example in early trade union activity and in Radical politics, imparted a growing confidence in their ability to organise resistance to exploitation. Forced underground by state repression, quasi-legal trade unionism and Jacobin political organisation converged in the 'illegal tradition'. The growing cohesion and Radicalism of this class helped to cement an alliance between landowners and industrial bourgeoisie which was symbolised in the 1832 Reform Act. Thus, claims Thompson:

In the years between 1780 and 1832 most English working people came to feel an identity of interests as between themselves, and as against their rulers and employers. This ruling class was itself much divided, and in fact only gained in cohesion over the same years because certain antagonisms were resolved (or faded into relative insignificance) in the face of an insurgent working class. Thus, the working class presence was, in 1832, the most significant factor in British political life.[2]

John Foster[3] draws upon and implicitly takes issue with Thompson's interpretation by arguing that the consciousness of the working class before 1832 is best characterised as a particular type of trade union or 'labour consciousness', whilst a more mature class consciousness committed to revolutionising capitalist relations of production in favour of an alternative social order developed in some locations, but only after 1832. Basing his conclusions on a comparative study of three English towns, Foster claims that a revolutionary class consciousness developed in Oldham in the late 1830s and early 1840s. This development depended on the existence of a coercive 'labour community' capable of mitigating bourgeois control of the local state and preventing the effective use of the police and the military to repress the activities of Radical leaders. The latter, seasoned by participation in Jacobin activity in the earlier period, were thus able to gain access to the factory proletariat of the local cotton industry, where conditions were such as to expose, in a particularly visible manner, the contradictions of capitalist production. However, the resulting threat to the capitalist order from a revolutionary working class which, Jenkins has recently argued,[4] extended well beyond Oldham at the time of the Chartist general strike of 1842, was countered by the British ruling class. On a local level, in Oldham, and on a national level, the latter undertook a planned process of 'liberalisation', isolating the revolutionary vanguard and, as one major component, creating a 'labour aristocracy' which functioned after the mid-century as an effective sectional wedge which helped to prevent the formation of a collective working class response to economic exploitation.

Despite differences in their analyses, both Thompson and Foster argue that the period we are examining in relation to Paisley saw the emergence in England of an increasingly solidary and class conscious working class. But when we examine the most authoritative work on Scottish social history — Smout's *A History of the Scottish People*[5] — we appear to be faced with a dramatic contrast between an insurgent English working class and a Scottish equivalent which, apart from the early 1790s and the Radical War of 1820, was relatively quiescent. A major reason for this, according to Smout, was that working people in Scotland up to 1830 failed to develop a conception of themselves which transcended the sectional identities of their respective trades or to perceive their employers and the legal authorities, who repressed their activities, as 'class enemies'.[6] Smout's argument has recently been challenged, and tends to underplay the strengths and continuity of working class consciousness and organisations in Scotland by virtue of his focus on certain highly visible, and apparently isolated, manifestations of working class consciousness to the neglect of underlying social processes.[7] Nevertheless his analysis appears to fit well with studies of Scottish Chartism, which have contrasted the pacific, 'moral force' character of the latter with the more exclusively proletarian and 'physical force' traditions of the industrial north of England.[8]

This contrast between the work of Smout and others on Scotland, and that of Thompson and Foster on England provides the broad context in which to locate our analysis of working class consciousness and organisation in Paisley. Our primary objective in an essentially local study is to locate and explain the major tendencies within, and lines of development of, the consciousness and political activity of working people in one Scottish town, and to attempt to explain these in terms of specific characteristics of local economic and social relations *and* in terms of the impact of wider forces operative within Scottish, and British, capitalist society. But by paying attention to both the specificity of industrial capitalism and class relations in Paisley and to the extent to which Paisley may have been subject to more widespread tendencies, we hope to offer some more tentative comments on the wider debates regarding the impact of early industrial capitalism on the British working class.

We shall begin by examining the phasing of capital accumulation in Paisley and the particular composition of its productive base. In the following section, the consequences of the above for the composition of the industrial bourgeoisie and working class will be examined, together with the development of inter-class relations in the town. Finally, we discuss in more detail the development of working class consciousness and action between 1790 and 1850.

The Development of Textile Production in Paisley

A central characteristic of the economy of Paisley in the period under consideration was that it exhibited, to a particularly marked extent, the importance of textile production to capital accumulation in the early phases of industrial capitalism. Even before the Union of 1707, the manufacture of fabrics was a prominent part of the town's economic activity.[9] The Poll Tax Roll for 1695 indicates the occupations of 294 inhabitants, out of a population of about 2,000. Of these the largest group are those listed as 'weavers' (66), well ahead of 'merchants and shopkeepers' (41), 'cordiners' or 'shoemakers' (32), 'tailors' (29), and 'maltmasters' (21).[10] By 1710, the trade in linen and muslin occupied many of Paisley's inhabitants, as did the production of 'Bengals', a striped cloth of linen and cotton. In 1730, checked handkerchiefs were being produced, and these were gradually elaborated on with the introduction of lighter 'lawns' and linen gauzes.[11]

Thus, with its long history of textile production and its proximity to the trade routes between Glasgow and the colonies, Paisley was well placed to participate in the upsurge in textile manufacturing, and in the Scottish economy in general which took place after 1750. The benefits of the economic alliance concluded with England in 1707 began to be apparent after the mid-century. The profits from Glasgow's dominant position in the tobacco trade were fed back into industrial enterprise such as coal and copper mining and into agricultural improvement;[12] the cattle trade with England grew rapidly, bearing witness to the increasing market orientation of Scottish agriculture; and textile production shared fully in the increasing tempo of economic activity. The output of linen stamped for sale rose from 2.1 million yards in 1728 to 13 million yards by 1770, whilst exports of plain linen to America rose from 821,699 yards in 1755 to 2,118,936 yards in 1770.[13]

The growth of manufacturing in Paisley after 1750 was, therefore, related to this wider context. However, the development of Paisley bore certain distinctive characteristics, namely, an overwhelming reliance on textile production and a marked degree of specialisation in high quality and luxury goods. Beginning with the gradual move towards finer and lighter linen goods, this specialisation was exacerbated with the introduction of silk gauze weaving in the 1750s. This branch of production was established largely on the initiative of Humphrey Fulton, a linen weaver who settled in Maxwellton, in the suburbs of Paisley, in 1749 and who derived his knowledge of silk weaving from visits to Spitalfields where he marketed his linen goods. By 1760 Fulton had 600 looms in operation in Paisley, distributing his products as far afield as London and Dublin.[14] The industry grew rapidly after 1760, aided in particular by the passing of the Spitalfields Act which established minimum wage rates for the London silk weavers. This prompted an influx of English capital into Paisley to take advantage of the absence of legislative interference in wage determination. By 1781 one-third of Paisley silk gauze manufacturers were from London,[15] a clear example of the interpenetration of capitalist development in England and in Scotland which was facilitated by the Union of 1707.

The silk gauze industry was at its most important in Paisley for about 20 years, reaching its zenith in the years 1781-4. The value of its output in 1784 was estimated to be £350,000 per annum.[16] At its height the industry employed at least 5,000 weavers in Paisley and the surrounding district, with an equal number in such dependent occupations as those of winders, warpers, draw-boys, and so on. However, by around 1789 the industry was in decline, and was virtually at an end by 1805, when the value of its output had fallen to £10,000 per annum.[17]

The decline of the silk gauze industry indicates the problems that were to affect Paisley's textile-based economy time and again between 1770 and 1850. Highly dependent on luxury markets, the trade was particularly subject to fluctuations in demand as fashion standards changed, and the export market waxed and waned. The shrinkage in the fashion market following the French Revolution, and the rising demand for muslin (cotton) goods, fuelled by the innovations introduced by Arkwright (1768) and Crompton (1779), were major factors in the decline. The large-scale production of cheap Lancashire cotton yarn, which enabled well-finished muslin to be produced, also hastened the decline of a second branch of Paisley's economy — the manufacture of linen gauze and linen thread.

The weaving of linen gauzes grew along with the silk industry, producing cloth to the value of over £160,000 per annum at its height in the 1780s.[18] But its decline also closely followed that of the silk industry, as did that of linen thread spinning. The production of linen thread was first firmly established in Paisley by Alexander McGregor in 1735.[19] In 1744 there were 93 thread mills, with output valued at around £1,000 per annum. The industry expanded rapidly thereafter, and by 1784 there were 120 mills in operation, with an annual output worth £64,000, employing between 4,000 and 5,000 workers, mainly women. The trade was shared between 23 manufacturers, an indication of the small scale of manufacturing units in the industry. The value of the total Scottish linen thread output in 1784 was between £210,000 and £220,000, so that Paisley accounted for over one-quarter of Scottish output by value. However, although in 1791 there were 137 mills in operation, the value of their output had fallen to £60,000 per annum. By 1812 there were scarcely a dozen mills left.[20]

The demise of these industries was counterbalanced by — and in part brought about by — the growing importance of cotton manufacture. Mechanised cotton spinning commenced in Renfrewshire in about 1782, when:

> . . . a number of mills, with powerful machinery for spinning cotton, were erected, at various streams in this Shire. During thirty years the number of these mills increased to 41 . . . [In 1809] the cotton works in Renfrewshire . . . employed 932 men, 2,449 women and 1,792 children; and they sent to market cotton of the value of £630,000 sterling.[21]

After 1800, then, cotton became the most important sector of Paisley's economy. In 1805 an estimated 6,750 hand loom weavers were employed in muslin manufacture. When we take into account those occupations directly related to the loom, the total of those employed in weaving-related occupations in cotton would be about 20,000.[22] In addition, there were the smaller, but still significant, numbers employed in cotton spinning. A closely related development was the emergence of a cotton thread industry in Paisley. In 1806, Bonaparte's 'Berlin Decree' dried up the supply of silk to Britain, dealing a further blow to an already failing industry. In the same year, Patrick Clark devised a technique for twisting cotton thread so as to provide an acceptable substitute for the silk and linen employed previously. By 1812 this thread was widely marketed, and there were at least 10 cotton thread manufacturers, in addition to Clark, in the town.[23]

The other major development in the Paisley textile industry which requires some consideration here was the production of the famous Paisley shawl.[24] Attempts to imitate Indian shawls had begun in the town as early as 1803, the shawls being in general woven from silk, cotton or some mixture of these. The period up to 1820 saw the laying of the foundations of the shawl trade, with its peak coming in the succeeding twenty years. The intricate nature of shawl production on harness looms ensured the maintenance in Paisley of the tradition of highly skilled handloom weaving which had been fostered earlier in the silk industry. The rise of the shawl industry also continued the tendency for Paisley textile manufacturers to specialise in luxury or fashion goods, aimed at highly volatile markets, in contrast to the cheaper, more standardised products which were the mainstay of Glasgow's cotton industry. The Paisley shawl trade remained primarily a luxury trade until the emergence of a mass market for cheap cotton 'shawls' in the 1860s.[25]

This brief account of the development of textile production in Paisley can now be employed to highlight a number of factors which are important to an understanding of class relations in the town between 1770 and 1850. The first point to note is the overwhelming reliance of the local economy on textile production. Other industries were carried on in Paisley, including soap-making, candle-making, distilling, brewing, flour-milling, two foundries and two naileries, and a growing building industry which imported Scandinavian timber via the River Cart.[26] But in terms of manufacturing output and employment, these industries pale into insignificance when compared with textiles:

Year	Total Monetary Value of Manufactures	Monetary Value of Textile Manufactures	Percentage of Manufactures Output represented by Textiles
1789	£660,386	£600,386	91%
1806	£1,340,100	£1,173,600	88%

It is clear that Paisley would be particularly vulnerable to economic fluctuations, given that the demand for textile products was highly sensitive to changes in the domestic economy and to the impact of foreign competition. But this vulnerability, in the case of Paisley, was magnified by the fact that high-quality handloom fabrics formed such a large part of the town's output, since demand for luxury goods tended to be more volatile than general demand trends for textile products.

Thus, from the 1780s onwards, manufacturers, merchants, and the workforce were subject to a very pronounced boom/slump cycle, with major trade depressions in 1783, 1786, 1793, 1811-12, 1816-22, 1826-27, 1829, 1831, 1837, 1841-3 and 1847-8.[27] The depression of 1841 onwards was especially severe, resulting in the bankruptcy of the Town Council and of 67 of the town's 112 manufacturers. We shall be returning to the consideration of the effects of this cycle later in the chapter. It is sufficient to note here that, on first examination, the perception of the contradictions of capitalist production, which Foster sees as so crucial to the development of working class consciousness in Oldham, might be expected to have been especially marked in Paisley.

One group above all others in the Paisley labour force were made particularly aware of the effects of repeated trade cycles. The prevalence of specialised handloom fabrics indicates the key role in production and in the class structure of the handloom weavers. In Scotland more generally the displacement of the latter by mechanisation in the form of powerloom factories was a relatively slow process. Not until the 1840s did the absolute number of handloom weavers in Scotland begin to decline, a delay attributed by Smout to the abundance of cheap labour, fuelled by immigration and ease of entry to the occupation.[28] This tendency was exacerbated in Paisley by its specialisation in the production of fancy goods, and in particular the shawl. Thus, in 1837, there were still an estimated 6,040 handloom weavers in the town, of whom 5,350 were harness weavers mainly engaged in shawl production,[29] out of a total population of about 60,000. At this time there was only one powerloom factory in Paisley and the surrounding area, making a striking contrast with Foster's study of Oldham where the great bulk of weaving production was mechanised well before the end of the 1830s.[30] The survival of the handloom weavers into the 1840s in large numbers had considerable significance for the development of class relations in Paisley. This significance was enhanced by the experience of deteriorating wage-rates, hours of work, security of employment and living conditions to which the weavers were subject over the period under consideration. In much the same way that Thompson indicates for England,[31] the Paisley weavers declined from their position as a privileged section of the labour force in the 1780s to one of poverty and desperation in the course of the succeeding decades. The role of the trade cycle and other factors in contributing to this decline will be discussed in the next section, together with their impact on class relations.

However, the boom/slump cycle was not restricted in its adverse effects to the weavers and other sections of the labour force. As indicated above in relation to the crisis of 1841-3, its effects were catastrophic for many manufacturers. The reasons for this indicate a final important characteristic of textile production in Paisley between 1770 and 1850, namely, the small scale and hence vulnerability to trade depressions of most of the manufacturing units. This tendency to small concerns was less marked in certain trades, notably in the silk trade before 1800 when the Fultons and their partners gained a significant hold on the market, and in cotton spinning which called for relatively large investments in fixed capital. In addition, some tendency towards the concentration and centralisation of capital can be observed over the period. For example, the cotton thread industry was shared between 11 small firms in 1812, but only 3 were still participating in this much expanded branch of production after 1850.[32] However, there were a number of factors which ensured that most Paisley manufacturing units were small concerns. Firstly, the reliance on the luxury end of the textile trade meant that the changing dictates of fashion brought frequent short-term fluctuations in demand and quite rapid shifts from one type of product to another, particularly in the shawl industry. The inability to develop a stable mass market thus made it difficult for a base to form for industrial concentration.

Secondly, the low level of mechanisation in the weaving sector made it relatively easy for individuals with small amounts of capital to enter the market as manufacturers — a point to which we shall return in the following section. It is likely that the abundance of skilled labour in handloom weaving retarded mechanisation. For example, the Jacquard loom, which dispensed with the need to employ a drawboy to facilitate the passage of the shuttle and which was introduced to England in 1810, was not widely adopted in Paisley until 1840. Prior to this date, manufacturers were content with the quality and competitiveness offered by the traditional drawloom. It is also possible, however, that the small scale of the capitals employed in the shawl trade itself militated against speculative investments in fixed capital.

This brings us to a final consideration bearing upon the small scale of Paisley manufacturing concerns, namely, the high mortality rate of businesses attendant upon intensive competition and under-capitalisation. A contributory factor here was the rudimentary character of banking and credit facilities in Paisley. The town did not have its own bank until the formation of the Paisley Banking Company in 1783. Both this and the Union Bank of 1788 were heavily dependent on the prosperity of the local merchants and manufacturers who played a large part in establishing them.[33] Thus Paisley lacked sources of funds which were independent of the fate of its own textile-dominated economy. In consequence, in periods of bad trade, small manufacturers were heavily dependent on their own accumulated profits. These features tended to accentuate still further the boom/slump cycle as periods in which small firms proliferated were followed by crises of over-production, wage-cutting and bankruptcies. A weaver of the 1780s and 90s perceptively summed up the consequences of such conditions in relation to the period of muslin manufacture in Paisley:

About this time silk-weaving was going out of fashion, and that of muslin was taking its place, which made a great change in the circumstances, and eventually in the state and character of the inhabitants. The silk manufacture was engrossed by a few great capitalists, who could set at defiance all rivalry by poorer men. They were not under the necessity of competing with one another to force the sale of goods by underselling and running the prices down to the lowest rate. The weavers' hours of labour were moderate, yet they were so well paid that they could dress like gentlemen, and many of them bought houses with their savings. The raw material of the silk weaving was brought from foreign parts, and sold for cash at the India House; but cotton yarn was spun at home in immense quantities, and could be had in sufficient abundance by any man who could command five pounds of money, or had credit to that amount. Thus hundreds became manufacturers of muslin who could never have produced a web of silk. The market became over-stocked with goods. Those who had got their yarns on credit were obliged to sell at an undervalue, or at whatever they got, in order to pay their bills. Then the prices of weaving were reduced to the lowest possible rate. Men were required to work longer hours to make a living, which increased the evil by bringing forward an extra quantity of goods.[34]

Class Relations in Paisley

The factors isolated above as characterising the structure of the local economy before 1850 had, we shall argue, significant effects on the nature of class relations in Paisley and hence on working class consciousness and political action. In this section the discussion will focus on the general lines of development of class relations in Paisley, whilst in the final part of this chapter we shall examine the development of working class Radicalism, trade unionism and Chartism in more detail and with particular reference to the debates regarding the impact of early industrial capitalism on the emergent working class.

The main consequences of the dependence of the Paisley economy on high quality textiles which we discerned above were threefold: the survival of the handloom weavers as a strategic group in the labour force into the 1840s, the prevalence of small manufacturers in key sections of the textile trade, and the subjection of both to severe cyclical fluctuations in the economy. Accordingly, in a discussion of class relations in Paisley, it is necessary to examine, firstly, the changing material conditions and experiences of the weavers, and secondly, their relation to other groups in the labour force, so as to delimit the sectional divisions which would have to be overcome if working people were to be able to think and act in class terms. Finally, we shall turn to an examination of the structure and orientation of the manufacturers, merchants and petty bourgeoisie, and their relation to the working class.

At the beginning of this period, the artisan weavers, in the silk trade in particular, could justifiably be considered the 'labour aristocrats' of the town. From the 1770s to the beginning of the 1790s, their prosperity was founded on the buoyant demand for silk gauze and fine linen, and in particular on improvements in spinning which produced yarns at low cost, enabling manufacturers to pay high rates to weavers to get the finished cloth in marketable form. In addition the increases in the weavers' own productivity, brought about by technical innovations such as the 'flying shuttle' after 1770, further enhanced their position. The author of the Paisley section of the *Old Statistical Account*, writing in 1791, commented that:

> A journeyman weaver in Paisley that is moderately industrious and economical . . . can bring up his family with ease, and live in a manner that is far above that of very decent farmers.[35]

A weaver of the period gives substance to this view of his fellows:

> They were in the habit of laying in provision of meat, coals, butter, cheese, meal and potatoes for the winter season; to a great extent they built their own houses, partly by their own savings and partly on borrowed money; they were careful to educate their children, and they never contracted marriage until they had saved up the means of beginning to keep house.[36]

Certainly there appears to be abundant evidence to support the view that the 1770s and 1780s were a 'Golden Age' for the handloom weavers in Paisley:

Sample Wage-Rates Paisley 1791[37]

Occupation	Wage	Maximum Equivalent 6-Day Weekly Wage
Weaver	25/- to 30/- per week	30/-
Mason	2/- to 2/3 per day	13/6
Day Labourer	1/4 to 1/6 per day	9/-
Maid Servant	£2 per half year	1/6½
Best Farm Labourer	£10 per year	3/10
Male Bleacher	6/- to 9/- per week	9/-
Female Bleacher	4/6 to 9/- per week	9/-

Thus the wages of the weavers marked them off as a privileged section of the workforce. But, more important, the nature of their work as semi-independent craft workers, controlling the work process in their own homes, led to the flowering of an artisan culture which confirmed their special status and 'respectability' in the eyes of contemporary observers:

> The work they had to do required great nicety of touch, patient skill and devotion, and was thus in itself an education. The result was to produce workmen who, for general intelligence, have no counterpart at the present day. We have heard it remarked by a well informed bookseller, that many of the weavers of those days had libraries equal to those of ministers or professional men.
>
> Some occupations are so noisy that an operative cannot think while they are being carried on. Others require a great amount of muscular exertion in circumstances most unfavourable for thought or reflection, such as blacksmiths or miners . . . But hand loom weaving, as practiced in Paisley at the time of which we are now writing, had not one of these disadvantages, but had many peculiar advantages which rendered it especially favourable to intellectual development. . . . The work they had to do was indoors. It was not very noisy. It was not pressingly continuous. It was even to some extent mechanical, and left the mind and the tongue free to exercise themselves even in the midst of the operation. Yet it was not an uninteresting labour. The setting up of the web and the handling of the delicate materials then used, required nicety and skill, and gave scope for much ingenuity . . .
>
> Then again, the work was paid by the piece, and not by time. The weaver generally owned the loom at which he worked, or hired it for a lengthy period. He was thus his own master. If the weather was fine, and the woods and meadows inviting, he could enjoy himself as he pleased, and make it up by overtime . . .
>
> Thus the weaver was delightfully self-contained and independent. He could lay down his shuttle at any moment, and take it up again when it suited him, and neither he nor his web was any the worse. All the conditions of his work and his surroundings were favourable to intellectual development.[38]

The weavers thus exercised a relatively high degree of control over their own labour and, in addition, a command over their own family labour. It was common for their wives to play a part in the tambouring of the cloth, whilst it was a matter of considerable pride amongst weavers that their income removed the necessity for their children to seek paid employment. The ability to ensure an education for their children before they entered employment then reinforced the literate base of the cultural world they created. This culture involved a fierce pride in their political knowledge and the ability to debate the issues of the day:

> The man who would not differ from his neighbour, and show good reasons for so doing, was no true Paisley weaver.[39]

In particular, the Paineite ideology of political democracy and the independence of the small producer was particularly appropriate to the self-conception and aspirations of the artisan weaver. The prominence of the weavers in the Jacobin agitations of the 1790s and in the Parliamentary reform movement in the aftermath of the Napoleonic Wars was, as we shall see later, important in Paisley, as elsewhere in Britain, to the development of working class political action.

Another expression of this culture was the tradition of Paisley weaver-poets which developed from this era. The most famous was Robert Tannahill but, as Smout has noted,[40] there were a large number of others in this mould. Alexander Wilson, later to achieve fame as an ornithologist in the United States, was also a noted poet. He was forced by the magistrates in 1793 to publicly burn a poem which he had written to aid the weavers in a trade dispute, on the grounds that his verse had libelled a manufacturer.[41] In addition the weavers formed a variety of clubs devoted to leisure pursuits such as golf, fishing and hunting. Alongside these were the Friendly Societies and trade associations. A weaver of the period described the way in which these associations combined both social and industrial matters:

> When met the first hour is devoted to promiscuous conversation. At eight the newspapers of that day are produced. They are read aloud by one of the company. This occupies near an hour. At nine o'clock the chairman calls silence; then the report of trade is heard. The chairman first reports what he knows, or what he has heard of such a manufacturing house or houses, as wishing to engage operatives for such fabric or fabrics; likewise the price, the number of the yarn, etc. Then each reports as he is seated; so in the period of an hour not only the state of trade is known but any difference that has taken place between manufacturers and operatives.[42]

Finally, the social world of the weavers tended to be encapsulated in particular communities, such as Maxwellton. The latter was a centre for silk weaving before 1800 and later became known for high grade shawls. The existence of such communities of skilled weavers as tight-knit social worlds with a high level of political culture appears to have been important to the development of working class political activity in Paisley. In Maxwellton we find fertile soil for the 'illegal tradition' of underground political organisation and quasi-legal trade unionism which Thompson analyses for the Midlands and North of England between the end of the 1780s and 1820.[43] In particular, Maxwellton was an important locus of the secret organisation and preparation for insurrection which preceded the 'Radical War' of 1820.

However, the working class radicalism of the period 1790-1820, to be examined later, was in large measure a response to economic distress and to the failure of the British state to provide the remedies which the weavers repeatedly requested. We now turn to the process by which the privileged position of the skilled weavers, as an affluent, literate and self-consciously independent group was increasingly undermined after 1790. In the following decade, with the decline of silk in favour of muslin manufacture, the impact of the boom/slump cycle began to have serious repercussions for the weavers. In the manner described for Scotland by Murray,[44] each downturn in trade brought cuts in wages as a host of small manufacturers endeavoured to survive in business by stockpiling goods produced at low rates which could be unloaded on the market when demand revived.

This practice on the part of the manufacturers may help to explain why the weavers' wages continued on a downward trend rather than being forced up in times of brisk trade. Although it is probable that the most skilled were able to earn more in the early days of the shawl trade than in muslin manufacture, it is reported that the *best* hands in weaving in Paisley earned a maximum of 8/- per week in 1834[45] (compared with 24/- to 30/- in 1791). It is notable that 1834 was a year of prosperity in Paisley, with little unemployment among the weavers. The effects of low wages, and periodic unemployment in addition, on their life-style and culture were devastating:

> [B]y increasing reductions in wages a great part of the weavers have been gradually ejected from their houses by the mortgagees who lent them the money wherewith to furnish them . . . [T]he weaver now rarely tastes meat, not more than once in a month, . . . he is reduced to bread and buttermilk, with butter occasionally, or with potatoes and porridge, his clothing is scant, if not rags; . . . to this he had become inured, in so far that he is not ashamed to appear among his own class in such attire, but . . . he refrains from attending Public Worship as formerly . . . [T]he Friendly Societies to which he formerly subscribed have gone down, owing to his inability to make his quarterly payments.[46]

In addition, as wages fell, work conditions deteriorated to the level of a sweated trade:

> The hours of labour are stated at 13 to 14 hours a day, and of those who earn 8/- per week, every hour of the day not devoted to meals.[47]

Two further factors may help to explain why wages in handloom weaving failed to follow the rise in demand after a depression. Firstly, both recent historians and some contemporary observers have argued that the weavers' position was undermined largely by an over-supply of labour caused by the ease of entry of migrant labour to the occupation. Though of considerable general validity, the argument requires careful qualification in dealing with the situation in Paisley. A distinction needs to be drawn between the luxury trades and the smaller plain weaving industry in the area, since the former were less susceptible to penetration by immigrants owing to the skilled nature of the harness loom work required. With this in mind we can briefly consider the impact of the successive waves of immigration which poured into Paisley — from Ayrshire and the surrounding Lowland counties, from the Highlands under pressure of the Clearances, from the demobilisation of the Napoleonic armies, and from Ireland[48] which was a major source of immigrants from about 1800 onwards. The silk and shawl trades attracted skilled weavers from Ayrshire and, in the latter case, Dunfermline. On the other hand, the native skilled weavers were much less directly in competition with the bulk of less skilled immigrants. For example, those Irish and Highland immigrants who entered weaving were largely restricted to the plainer trades and particularly to cheaper cotton fabrics, although some may have become fancy weavers by a less direct route. According to one shawl weaver in the 1830s:

> A great many Irish come here whose families are employed as draw-boys at first; they very soon get to be weavers, thus causing a redundancy of hands.[49]

However, it is likely that this argument is an exaggeration as far as the shawl trade was concerned. The argument for a persistent over-supply of labour has more credibility in plain weaving, though this would not be without repercussions for the more skilled. Rather it would make it more difficult for native weavers to switch to coarser fabrics in order to cushion the effects of recession. But the unemployment of skilled weavers before 1840 is better interpreted as a periodic consequence of the movement of the trade cycle, as it affected the demand for specialised textiles. The existence of full employment in the better years of the 1830s (notably 1834 and 1838) casts doubt on the notion of a significant excess of skilled weaving labour in Paisley in that decade. Although it might be possible to argue that the influx of skilled Ayrshire weavers contributed to downward pressure on weavers' wages in the town, there is no guarantee that — in the absence of this inflow — production would not have been relocated from Paisley or extra labour drawn in by expanding the outwork area of Paisley manufacturers in times of good trade.

The other factor to be considered was the inability of the weavers, through trade union action, to resist or reverse wage cuts. The difficulty of maintaining effective organisation amongst out-workers in trades involving many small employers is likely to have been a contributory factor here. In addition, as Thompson notes in an English context,[50] the weavers' efforts were hampered by the refusal of the Government to legislate on minimum wages, and direct repression. The failure of the 1812 strike of weavers in the West of Scotland, which was broken by the arrest and imprisonment of its leaders, indicates some of the difficulties of extra-legal trade unionism in the Napoleonic War period, and marked the removal of the last major impediment to the further degradation of the weavers.

By the end of the 1830s, then, the weavers were reduced from a position of marked privilege to one which was no better, and in some ways a good deal worse, than that of other sections of the working class. The process of proletarianisation and demoralisation was completed by mass unemployment accompanied by further wage cuts during the recession of 1841-3, and by the gradual introduction of power looms thereafter. However, although the gradual levelling of material and cultural differences between the weavers and other wage labourers might be assumed to be rendering class solidarity and the formation of political movements on class lines more likely, significant sources of sectional division persisted into the 1840s. Although these divisions did not necessarily preclude altogether the formation of such movements, as we shall see later, they nevertheless conditioned the nature of class relations and working class political activity in Paisley.

One major division in the labour force lay between the skilled weavers and the factory operatives in the cotton spinning and thread industries. This can be illustrated by quoting from a commentary written in 1805 by William Carlile, a local manufacturer who served as Provost of Paisley in 1816 and on two subsequent occasions. He described the weavers thus:

> There is another very prominent trait in the characters of our Paisley weavers: and that is a pretty general knowledge acquired from books. If you enter into conversation with many of those who are of middle age, you will find them well informed on many subjects, particularly general history, natural history and politics. They, in general, maintain a high sense of independence; they scorn the servile adulation of those who cringe to the great.

Contrast this with his comments on those employed in cotton spinning:

> The Cotton Spinning trade now established in this part of the country is highly valuable, on account of such numbers of poor children and women as are employed in its various operations, but it appears to have no tendency to improve the morals of the country. The numbers collected in large cotton-mills, from families immersed in ignorance and vice, spread the contagion among such as have been more regularly educated, and profligate conduct is the natural result.[51]

The important point here is that both the manufacturers and many of the skilled weavers themselves shared this perception of the weavers as an educated, respectable and independent group, as opposed to the brutish and proletarian character attributed to the factory 'hand'. In this respect, the native weaver in Paisley displayed many of the attitudes attributed by Thompson to the English artisan in the early stages of the development of industrial capitalism:

> If the agricultural labourers pined for land, the artisans aspired to an 'independence'. This aspiration colours much of the history of early working-class Radicalism.[52]

One of the central contradictions of this artisan Radicalism was that it drew its strength from the fear of proletarianisation and hence could be conjoined with an attitude of cultural superiority over the common labourer or factory hand. On the part of the Paisley weavers, this was manifested in their resistance to factory employment even when faced with acute hardship. The testimony of another local manufacturer in 1835 appears to have been largely accurate on this point.

> Most natives of Paisley would, I believe, sooner earn 12/- a week at weaving with their own looms, having the command of their own time, and their ingenuity exercised in their own profession, than work in a cotton factory for 20/- or 25/- per week; our weavers, however destitute, seldom think of applying for employment in cotton factories. A cotton spinner does not hold the same rank in society as a fancy weaver.[53]

Finally, a particularly striking account of the skilled weavers' sense of their own position as a 'respectable' section of the labour force is provided by the following statement from the members of a weavers' emigration society in 1840:

> The Society feels that the supply of labour, in the weaving department at least, is far too great in proportion to the demand, even to admit of adequate wages being received, far less of regular and constant employment. No person can feel more averse than they do to apply for support from the parish poors' fund. It is their wish, as independent-minded Scotsmen, to earn a livelihood honestly and industriously by their own labour. . .
>
> It is the wish of the Society to go forth to their adopted land as a moral and religious community, and that a minister, or ministers of the gospel, and schoolmasters for the education of their children, should accompany them.[54]

It could be argued that the high moral tone and religiosity expressed in this statement was more the result of actual or desired middle class patronage than the authentic voice of the weaver. Indeed, the Reverend Robert Burns, a local Church of Scotland minister of pronounced Whig inclinations, addressed the above meeting at length. However, there is sufficient evidence to conclude that the above sentiments, with respect to an avoidance of recourse to poor relief and to religion,[55] did reflect the cultural orientation of many of the weavers.

The tendency to sectionalism within the Paisley working class did not derive solely from the weavers' sense of cultural distinctiveness, rooted in real and imagined features of the 'Golden Age'. This tendency was strengthened by three further factors — the conditions of production in the early factories and their effects on the labour force, the social and geographical origins of the factory proletariat, and the attitudes of employers and the middle classes towards sectional groupings within the working class. To take the first of these considerations, in Paisley as elsewhere in the early years of the cotton industry, the cotton spinning and thread factories employed a high proportion of female and child labour, working in very harsh conditions. The authors of the Paisley section of the *Old Statistical Account* commented:

> It is painful to think, that a manufacture which gives employment to so many hands, and

which may be a source of great wealth to individuals, may be productive of very unhappy effects upon the health and morals of the children employed in it. This there is some reason to apprehend. The numbers that are brought together, especially in the larger mills, the confinement, the breathing of an air loaded with dust and downy particles of the cotton, and contaminated with the effluvia of rancid oil rising from the machinery, must prove hurtful, in a high degree to the delicate and tender lungs of children. Add to this, that mills which produce the water-twist are kept going day and night; and children must be had who are willing to work through the night, and sleep through the day. Tempted by the wages, parents send their children to this employment at a very early age, when they have got little or no education; and the close confinement deprives them of the opportunity of acquiring more. Ignorance, disease, and mortality, are but too likely to prove the effects of this manufacture, if carried on by unfeeling and selfish men.[56]

The number of adult male spinners in Paisley itself who were subject to these conditions would have been small. Cotton spinning employed only 2,700 persons in Paisley (two large and one small mill), Elderslie (one large), and Johnstone (eleven mills) combined in 1837.[57] However, the conditions of factory production proved much more fertile ground for effective trade union organisation than the circumstances of the weavers would permit. By means of their organisation, and their control over female and juvenile workers who often were members of their families, the spinners were partly successful in maintaining the level of their money wages, and were earning up to 25/- per week in the 1830s. But their material advantage over the weavers at this period was won only at the cost of the particular privations of early factory employment and of repeated clashes with the manufacturers. The regular resort of the latter to blackleg labour during strikes intensified the bitter class conflict in this sector. Thus instances of direct violence were relatively common. In 1820 four Paisley cotton spinners were tried for attempting to shoot their employer after he had led the manufacturers in cutting wages; in 1824 two spinners from Bridge of Weir were convicted for the shooting and wounding of a blackleg who had taken the job of a man dismissed by his employer. In summary, the distinctive conditions of production and forms of class struggle in the cotton mills tended in themselves to generate a divide between factory operatives and handloom weavers. Firstly, these conditions of production militated against the development of the kind of cultural and political traditions which formed a reference point for the 'fancy weavers'. But secondly, it was in cotton spinning that the opposition between the class interests of workmen and manufacturers achieved its most stark expression. As we shall argue later, despite the relationship between Radicalism and the weaving communities, class relations between weavers and their employers were by no means entirely governed by opposition. Thus, since Radicalism was not so clearly bound up with the conditions of production and social milieux of the factory hands, as it was for the weavers, the cotton spinners approximated most closely to the 'labour consciousness' which Foster attributes to the working class before 1830.

The tendency for sectional groupings to form within the working class was exacerbated by the effects of large-scale immigration. After 1760 the first major groups of immigrants came from Ayrshire and, as we suggested above, included artisan weavers who participated in the expansion of the silk and linen industries. A number of these possessed or were able to acquire sufficient capital to make the transition to manufacturer. For example, of the families who founded the two firms which came to dominate the cotton thread industry after 1850, the Coats were Ayrshire weavers whilst the Clarks, also from Ayrshire, began as weavers' wrights or furnishers. The incorporation into Paisley of this first group of migrants, who were both 'local' and, in general, not in such reduced circumstances as the Highlanders and Irish who followed them, was free of difficulty and social tension. The view of John Parkhill, the local weaver-historian, expresses this point in terms of conventional attitudes:

> [I]n a great measure, Paisley was peopled from Ayrshire, and from the high moral character of that people, the western immigration, unlike some immigrations, greatly improved the morality of the town.[58]

The Highlanders who arrived in Paisley after 1780 were more sharply differentiated, not least by language and culture, from the Lowland Scottish inhabitants. This divide was symbolised by the Gaelic chapel constructed on Oakshaw Hill in 1793. Many of the men worked as labourers, preceding the Irish in the construction of roads and canals, whilst the bleach and dye-works provided employment for the women — many of whom were unmarried, spoke no English and lived in hostels built by the employers.[59]

Irish immigration became appreciable after 1800, and was boosted by the construction work provided on the Glasgow-Paisley-Ardrossan canal, which was begun in 1807. Many of the Irish labourers so employed settled permanently in Paisley. In 1821, one-ninth of the heads of the town's 5,730 households had been born in Ireland, whilst the local Catholic clergyman calculated the number of Irish in Paisley and the surrounding district in 1843 as 10-11,000.[60] This very substantial addition to the pool of wage labourers found work as general labourers, plain weavers, and in those ancillary occupations in textile manufacturing least favoured by the native workers. But, most important for our purposes, the Irish provided a particularly high proportion of the factory operatives. For example, in 1834, Orr's spinning mill employed 279 hands, of whom 199 were Irish. The mill owner explained to the Commissioners of the inquiry into the condition of the Irish poor that the Irish were the only employees available when he commenced production in 1810, and were still in 1834 the bulk of those seeking employment.[61]

Thus the maintenance of fancy weaving as the preserve of Lowland Scots and the concentration of Irish 'hands' in the factories ensured that cultural and religious divisions tended to coincide with that between skilled weavers and cotton spinners. In addition, although we lack at present the more precise measures of residential segregation developed by Foster,[62] it is clear that Irish immigrants tended to concentrate in areas like the New Town and the Sneddon district, emphasising in geographical terms their separation from the weavers.

Despite evidence as to the Lowland Scots weavers' sense of their own cultural superiority and the tendency of some of them to blame the Irish for their economic plight, it is difficult to assess in precise terms the extent to which cultural and religious diversity contributed to sectionalism within the Paisley working class. However, by the 1820s organised anti-Catholicism had taken root in the West of Scotland. Annual Orange marches on 12 July were attempted in Glasgow from 1821 onwards, and a Paisley lodge first participated in 1822.[63] Operating, as Young has noted,[64] under the patronage of aristocratic Toryism, the Orange lodges were particularly active in Ayrshire, and at times struck a responsive chord among working people. In July 1835, miners and labourers met at Airdrie on three consecutive days, passing resolutions to expel Catholics from the mines and other workplaces.[65] In Paisley itself, active opposition to Catholicism was manifested by some ministers of the established church, and their Catholic counterpart, the Reverend John Bremner, was frequently engaged in responding to pamphlets attacking his faith. On one occasion, Bremner was prevented from using a schoolroom for religious instruction when his clerical opponents pressured the schoolmaster to withdraw his permission.[66] In addition, discrimination against Irish residents of Paisley in the administration of poor relief was prevalent, finding its most striking instance in the deportations enforced by the local Relief Committees in 1827 and 1842. As regards the popular response to anti-Catholic organisations and to the forms of discrimination mentioned above, there is little indication in Paisley of mass action in support of them, at least up to 1850. In this respect, Paisley appears to have been similar to Oldham where, in Foster's account, a mass following for anti-Catholicism developed only after the mid-century.[67] However, in Paisley at least, the attitude of native workers before 1850 seems to have been more commonly one of passive acceptance of, rather than concerted opposition to, discrimination against Irish Catholics. On this ground we would suggest that the occupational, cultural and religious divisions between Irish and Lowland Scots workers formed a significant impediment to the development of enduring forms of working class solidarity in Paisley. As we shall endeavour to show later, the occasions on which Radical and Chartist initiatives were able to bridge such divisions were relatively few and fleeting, particularly before 1840.

The third of the influences which tended to enhance the sectionalism of the Paisley working class was the response of manufacturers and members of the middle classes to the immiseration and proletarianisation of the weavers. Many employers in Paisley saw the native fancy weavers as a strategically placed group vis-a-vis their concern to maintain work discipline and social acquiescence within the labour force. In this context, the manufacturers could be seen as sponsoring or encouraging the maintenance of the sectional identity of the Lowland Scots weavers. The views of William Carlile, cited above, exemplify the manufacturers' high esteem for the weavers as contrasted with those employed in the spinning mills. In consequence, many local manufacturers evinced considerable sympathy with the weavers as their decline gathered momentum — a humanitarian concern which was fostered by the fear that this decline would have adverse effects on other sections of the labour force. At the sessions of the Select Committee on Handloom Weavers' Petitions, 1835,

> many witnesses gave it as their decided conviction that the poverty of the Weavers had been the fruitful cause of Trade Unions amongst other artisans, who, seeing the extreme destitution the weavers were reduced to by successive reductions of wages, united for their mutual protection, to avoid falling into the same wretched condition.[68]

As regards the weavers themselves, it seemed to their employers that this key group was becoming more likely to imitate the habits imputed to the cotton spinners than to raise the level of conventional morality and work discipline in the labour force as a whole. The weavers were 'less able to pay towards supporting religious establishments and therefore go less to church', 'becoming daily more and more intemperate in the use of ardent spirits', and were 'increasingly indifferent to former feelings of loyalty'.[69] Finally these concerns were extended to the likely consequences for future generations of labourers:

> The weavers' children, not now being brought up with the same care as formerly, are likely to become, in regard to moral qualities, to industrious habits, and to loyalty and attachment to the country, a very inferior description of persons.[70]

The manufacturers' concern was not limited to pious expressions of sympathy. The Select Committee which reported in 1835 was chaired by a Paisley manufacturer, heard evidence from like-minded employers, and recommended the passing of Fielden's Minimum Wage Bill. When the Westminster Parliament rejected the latter, appointing instead a Royal Commission packed with advocates of more orthodox political economy, some of the Paisley manufacturers voluntarily fixed a table of prices in an attempt to stabilise weavers' wages. This action, taken in consultation with the weavers' association and setting aside for a short period the immediate economic interest of the employers, indicates that in Paisley class antagonisms were somewhat mitigated by the particular acts of collaboration engendered by the relationship between the weavers and their employers. This can be further illustrated by reference to the administration of Poor Relief in the town.

The nature of the Scottish Poor Law was such that, even after the Poor Law Amendment (Scotland) Act of 1845, parishes were not obliged to make statutory provision for the able-bodied unemployed. Thus in many areas, including Paisley, the main responsibility for the relief of cyclical unemployment was born by *ad hoc* Relief Committees, on which, in urban areas, manufacturers were powerfully represented and which sought funds by voluntary contribution. Although the deficiencies of the Scottish Poor Law, operating in conditions of rapid movements of labour and severe fluctuations in the level of economic activity, are now well documented,[71] it was frequently defended by contemporary commentators because it was thought to have beneficial consequences for labour discipline. According to the Reverend Dr. John Snodgrass of Paisley, writing in 1793, the adoption in some parts of a poor rate to finance provision for the unemployed was a cause for alarm since:

> there is too much reason to fear that it will be productive of very bad effects. It puts charity entirely off its natural principle. It is calculated to multiply the poor, and to increase their demands, by holding out to their view a settled maintenance which they can call their own. It divests them of sensibility, by teaching them to claim it as their right, when they would be ashamed to appear in the character of beggars. Thus it is unfavourable to industry, and it will bring at length an intolerable burden on the country. It is well-known what evils are ascribed to the poor-tax in England . . .[72]

The dependence of the unemployed upon voluntary contributions — the charity applauded by Snodgrass — thus provided an opportunity for displays of employer generosity and beneficence on the part of the local authorities. For their part, the weavers' cultural norms of independence and their desire to distinguish themselves from the 'feckless' poor might have led them to agree with some of Snodgrass's sentiments. Thus, after the depression of 1826, the operatives of Paisley presented the Provost with three silver salvers 'as an expression of public gratitude for exertions in behalf of the unemployed operatives during the late period of unexampled distress'.[73] In this way the *ad hoc* system of poor relief could further mitigate the class antagonisms between manufacturers and operatives.

Thus far, we have suggested that the artisan culture of the fancy weavers and the manufacturers' perception of them as a strategically important group in the work force not only helped to strengthen tendencies to sectionalism within the working class but also influenced in important respects the relationship between capital and labour in Paisley. This relationship differed somewhat from the suggestion of a fundamental and clearly perceived opposition of interests contained in Thompson's analysis of the English handloom weavers. In arguing that the decline of the latter was not the 'inevitable' consequence of some law-like process in the development of capitalism, Thompson stresses that their immiseration had to be actively brought about. In doing so, he places great explanatory weight on the greed and rapacity of the manufacturers in reducing wages, on the actions of the political authorities in repressing trade unions and in protecting the interests of manufacturers by refusing to introduce minimum wage legislation — a course of action legitimated by the ideology of laissez-faire:

> All this 'handling and channelling' had at least two effects: it transformed the weavers into

confirmed 'physical force' Chartists, and in cotton alone there were 100,000 fewer weavers in 1840 than in 1830. No doubt Fielden's Bill would have been only partially effective, would have afforded only slight relief in the 1830s as power-loom competition increased, and might have pushed the bulge of semi-unemployment into some other industry. But we must be scrupulous about words: 'slight relief' in the 1830s might have been the difference between death and survival.[74]

The results of our more limited study of Paisley suggest certain divergences from Thompson's analysis. We shall attempt to delimit these and, in the process, to lead up to the discussion of the nature and circumstances of the Paisley manufacturers with which we conclude this section.

Much critical analysis of Thompson's work has focused on the relative weight which he attaches to agency as against structural determinants or constraints at various points in his work.[75] In relation to the decline of the hand-loom weavers, we would suggest that — by implication — Thompson is in danger of placing too much explanatory weight on the motives of those employers who were prepared to initiate wage cuts and of manufacturers and politicians who opposed minimum wage legislation. In assuming that some relief for the weavers was possible through such legislation — and thus in condemning its opponents — he neglects to consider whether the economic constraints impinging on the manufacturers would have permitted them to maintain wages without an offsetting fall in employment through the further contraction of markets and attendant bankruptcies. Although we cannot answer this question in a definite manner, it is likely that Paisley manufacturers were increasingly constrained in this respect, particularly with the increasing frequency and severity of economic depressions in the period after the Napoleonic Wars. This tendency was, we have suggested, reinforced in Paisley by the predominance of small, under-capitalised firms operating in highly volatile markets for fashion goods. The high level of bankruptcies, particularly in 1841-3, can be taken as some indication that minimum price lists would have been largely ineffective, as proved to be the case with the manufacturers' attempt at collective regulation in the 1830s.

A related point concerns Thompson's characterisation of 'laissez-faire' doctrines as 'ideological', that is, as an account of contemporary economic conditions which served to justify morally indefensible actions and to mystify the exploitative nature of capitalist relations of production. Though not disputed here, this characterisation omits a further condition for the successful functioning of the 'laissez-faire' ideology — its accordance in certain respects with the immediately visible properties of economic processes in early industrial capitalist Britain. Conditions of exchange and competition in Paisley in the first half of the last century appeared to accord closely with the assumptions of orthodox political economy — laws of supply and demand outside their control seemed to subjugate both employers and operatives to their dictates. One Paisley weaver who was struck by this appearance and who switched from Radical politics to acceptance of political economy was John Parkhill. Commenting on the continued calls for minimum wage legislation in the 1840s, he observed:

> One of the most prominent fears is obvious, namely, the great desire our operatives have had for fixing wages by boards of trade, with no knowledge of political economy. They invariably come to the conclusion, that by fixing wages they will command ordinary wages, not taking into account that when there is no demand it is perfectly useless to fix prices, and equally so when the nature of the work is such, from its fanciful kind, to be constantly fluctuating, that no prices can be fixed with safety either to the operatives or the masters.[76]

The extent to which working class consciousness in Paisley was colonised by the ideology of 'laissez-faire' will be discussed in the next section. But it is necessary to temper Thompson's analysis of the English weavers' response to their decline with that of a recent historian of Scotland:

> There were undoubtedly as many working people in Scotland who were attracted by the propaganda of the Anti-Corn Law League, as there were inspired by the violent 'physical force' speeches of Chartists like Feargus O'Connor.[77]

As we shall see, Burgess's emphasis on the fragmented character of Scottish working class consciousness after 1830 accords well with the evidence with respect to Paisley. This emphasis is also consistent with what we know of the consequences of the 1841 depression, which was disastrous for many Paisley manufacturers, shopkeepers and tradesmen, as well as for the operatives:

> Not only did this [depression] produce a resurgence of the anti-corn law movement in the town which was a classical example of the repeal case, but it re-emphasised the economic interdependence of the middle and working classes . . .[78]

Thus the tendency towards a degree of inter-class co-operation in the political life of Paisley, encouraged by working class sectionalism and by the way in which manufacturers attempted to sponsor a close relationship between themselves and the fancy weavers, was strengthened by a further factor. Given the specific character of the Paisley textile economy, the movement of the trade cycle had effects which were highly conducive to explanation in terms of the doctrines of economic liberalism and to the perception that the interests of the working and middle classes were similar.

Class collaboration in Paisley was further encouraged by the nature of the industrial bourgeoisie and middle classes. An important factor was the prevalence of small manufacturers in the local economy, many of whom derived from relatively humble social origins. Upward mobility was facilitated by the ease of entry to muslin and shawl manufacture, where artisans and packmen could attempt the transition to merchant or manufacturer on the basis of small amounts of capital. In particular, the packmen who travelled extensively in marketing their wares were often able to acquire ideas for new products or processes of production, as well as to accumulate enough capital to implement them on a small scale:

> The object of every packman's ambition ultimately was to become a settled shopkeeper, or merchant in some commercial town . . . it frequently happened, however, from their universal eagerness to fix themselves in a settled residence, that they made the attempt with too small a capital to give them a prospect of success in the greater towns; and hence they were under the necessity of settling in secondary situations. Paisley offered itself as an advantageous position, second only to Glasgow; and men experienced in the kind of goods for which a demand existed throughout the country were well qualified for directing the operations of manufacturers in a town.[79]

Thus Humphrey Fulton, who with the McKerrells gained an early hold over the silk gauze industry, was an Ayrshire weaver before becoming a packman and finally a manufacturer. Similarly James Coats (1774-1857), the founder of the firm which later became the textile giant of Paisley, was a weaver who set up in business for himself in 1796. In this sense the social and material distinctions between artisan weavers and packmen, on the one hand, and those classed as 'manufacturers', on the other, remained relatively small and quite fluid during the period under review. This fluidity was enhanced not only by upward mobility, but also by downward mobility as undercapitalised small firms were liquidated during economic depressions. The increasing severity of the latter after the Napoleonic Wars led, for example, to a drastic reduction in the number of thread manufacturers, whilst the volatility of the market for fashion goods dictated a high failure rate for firms in the weaving sector. In addition, in newly elevated families such as the Coats', it was not uncommon for some of the manufacturer's close relations to be working at a loom until well into the nineteenth century.[80] The lack of social distance between weavers and manufacturers was further strengthened by the tendency for manufacturers to live alongside their employees, sharing a tenement with weavers and their looms. Pronounced residential segregation between manufacturers and the workforce did not develop before 1850.[81]

According to Foster, there existed in the mill-town of Oldham a relatively large and cohesive 'big bourgeoisie', whose members were 'sealed off by their economic function and concomitant capital from the petty bourgeoisie and the population as a whole'.[82] By contrast, the predominance of hand-woven fancy goods in the Paisley economy meant that relatively few substantial capitalists emerged, whilst the large 'tail' of small manufacturers and merchants were by no means isolated from the rest of the middle class or from the fancy weavers. The social institutions which developed around the manufacturers and professional men of Paisley reflected this fact in that they also incorporated a healthy sprinkling of artisans. The Barony Club, founded in 1794, functioned as a social centre for these groups, meeting above one of the town's public houses, the Saracen's Head:

> The Club was instigated by a number of influential gentlemen and successful men of business, and it was considered an honourable distinction to be admitted a member.[83]

However honoured they might have felt, the more plebeian members would not have been ill at ease amid the quite ordinary surroundings and social gossip, lubricated by a strange beverage:

> The liquor used was a peculiar mixture of beer and whisky, with a little oatmeal sprinkled on top, and then called, in club language, Pap-in, and was drank out of bickers or quaighs, which are little dishes made from wood . . .[84]

The frequently precarious economic position of the members is captured in a summary of the Club's activity by a contemporary Paisley poet:

> With a bicker and with Pap-in each member sat,
> Ripe for a toast, a story, or a song;
> But that which came on every ear most pat,
> Was some sly hint of neighbours going wrong.[85]

Indeed it is a comment on the vulnerability of the industrial bourgeoisie in Paisley that the Club became virtually moribund after the economic crisis of 1841-3.

This vulnerability and the absence of a substantial 'big bourgeoisie' with a strong sense of its social identity propelled middle class politics towards the radical end of the spectrum, founded on the appeal of small manufacturers, merchants and traders to their common interests with the working class in the struggle against the political power of the landed aristocracy. Whilst the 'big bourgeoisie' silk magnates of the Fulton and McKerrell families were prominent in orchestrating Loyalism and commanded the local Volunteer regiments during the Napoleonic Wars,[86] there emerged at the same time in Paisley an 'advanced Whig' opposition staffed by the smaller manufacturers. One such was Peter Kerr, 1762-1835, who was initially apprenticed as a weaver, attended evening classes to gain an education and rose to become chief manager of a department of a local firm by 1810. In that year he left to carry on the thread business of his wife's family, and subsequently established himself as a successful manufacturer.[87] In common with the younger Whigs, notably Jeffrey and Cockburn, who gathered around the *Edinburgh Review* in the climate of political repression during the Wars, Paisley manufacturers like Kerr attempted to ally with moderate working class Radicals on the issues of Parliamentary Reform, corruption in municipal and Westminster politics, and the economic protectionism of the Tory administration. The strength of this appeal to the common interests of the 'commercial classes' and the working class in Paisley is indicated by the resolutions passed at a public meeting in 1816, called to consider how best to revive trade in the area. The meeting was attended by both manufacturers and working men, and addressed the following resolutions to the Prince Regent:

That the present distress of the agricultural, commercial and manufacturing interests of the country are to be ascribed, not to a transition from war to peace, but to excessive taxation, occasioned by an enormous debt, useless offices, exorbitant salaries for nominal services, and a standing army, all of which are clearly deducible from that unequal and insulting representation of the people in Parliament which not only deprives them of those inestimable benefits which are natural fruits of a fair representation, but condemns them to suffer all the evils which inseparably attend the mischievous legislation of a House of Commons not representing the nation . . .

That if any proof were wanting of the impolitic, partial, and unjust system of legislation produced by the present mockery of representation, the additional Corn Bill lately passed affords ample evidence. . . . it appears to have been successful only in depressing the industrious manufacturer and mechanic, in first raising the price of the staple article of consumption at home, and next in preventing our own or foreign merchants from bringing us the surplus produce of other countries in return for those articles by the manufacture of which our artisans used to earn a comfortable livelihood.

That from the present corrupt representation of the people in Parliament hath arisen that system of profusion, under the name of sinecures and rewards for public services, by which thousands wrung from the hard earnings of the industrious mechanic and labourer have been squandered upon men wholly unknown to the public . . .[88]

When working class political action took a more insurrectionary direction in 1819-20, however, the local bourgeoisie quickly distanced themselves from such activities. For example, Peter Kerr withdrew somewhat from his 'advanced' political position. However, class collaboration revived during the Reform Bill crisis of 1830-32, under the aegis of the Renfrewshire Political Union.

With the enfranchisement of the Scottish urban bourgeoisie in 1832, the activation of a class alliance became more difficult since the weavers were able to perceive that the Reform Acts and Whig administration at Westminster had done nothing to halt their decline. Thus in the Chartist period in Paisley a rather more pronounced division between Whigs and working class Radicals is visible. This crystallisation of class boundaries in the political arena was fostered by the progressive development of distinctively bourgeois social institutions in Paisley, such as the reading rooms requiring high annual subscriptions, the formation of a Philosophical society, and so on. Nevertheless, the precarious economic position of the Paisley manufacturers in the early 1840s, the continued appeal of Corn Law repeal to sections of the working class, and the strengthening of the hand of reformers amongst the middle classes as the economic situation worsened, all point to the fact that class structures and the development of the local economy continued to generate a tendency towards class alliance on particular issues in the 1830s and 40s.

In this section, we have stressed those features of class relations in Paisley which tended to retard the development of polarised class relations between employers and, in particular, the weavers. Our intention is not to deny the existence of an objective conflict of interests between manufacturers and workers at the point of production, but rather to delimit an important set of influences which affected the mode in which, and the extent to which, this conflict of interests was expressed in working class consciousness and political organisation. The development of the latter will be dealt with more directly in the following section, in the light of those influential accounts of the history of the English and Scottish working classes referred to in the introduction.

Working class consciousness and political action 1790-1832

In considering the political evolution of the Paisley working class up to the Reform Act of 1832, the historical literature presents us with the possibility of a striking contrast between a well-ordered Scottish society and a Scottish working class whose opposition to the emerging social order was sporadic and fragmented (Smout) and the development in England of an 'insurgent' working class with a more or less coherent perception of its own interests as against those of their employers and rulers (Thompson). However, as we have argued elsewhere,[89] Smout has tended to understate both the extent and continuity of working class Radicalism in Scotland and the degree to which it posed a threat to social order. On the other hand, the broad outlines of Thompson's analysis of the development of working class consciousness seem to us to apply to Scotland and, more particularly, to Paisley. Whilst Smout tends to treat early trade union activity and working class political Radicalism as distinct and largely unrelated, Thompson analyses the effects of two sets of circumstances — growing economic insecurity and proletarianisation, combined with the state repression of the war years and after — in producing a convergence of economic and political struggles in the 'illegal tradition' which was perhaps best exemplified in the northern manufacturing districts of England by Luddism. These two conditions were also to be found in Paisley, and in a particularly striking form.

If anything, the use of the law to suppress working class Radicalism was felt more harshly in Scotland than in England, as the trials, after the Conventions of the 'Friends of the People' in the early 1790s, of Thomas Muir and others demonstrate.[90] Anti-Combination legislation was employed, as in the weavers' strike of 1812, even though many Scottish lawyers doubted that it had legal force in their country. The spy system was extended to Scotland, most notably in the Radical War of 1820, as was the attempt to whip up support for and raise troops for, the war against the French.

As regards the economic preconditions for working class radicalism, we have already argued that the artisan weavers of the 1780s in Paisley were subjected to increasingly severe wage cutting and cyclical unemployment from the early 1790s onwards. Although the thread industry was, to some extent, insulated against fluctuations in the home economy — for example, by 1840, 75% of Coats' cotton thread trade was with America — a depression in the weaving sector had a dramatic impact on unemployment through its multiplier effect on secondary occupations and the finishing trades. As weavers found themselves unemployed, so did their family labour, and thence the drawboys, dyers, tambourers etc. who were dependent on the loom. In the depression of 1820, for example, over 1,000 weavers were estimated to be out of work.[91] If one wishes to include their dependents and dependent occupational groups, one must multiply by at least 8 to gauge the extent of persons deprived of economic support. In May 1826, 12,890 was estimated to be 'the number out of employment and their dependents in Paisley and neighbourhood'.[92] What is more, these depressions worsened in the 1830s, reaching their nadir in 1841-3.

The first suggestion of a serious threat to the local economy after 1790 coincided with the upsurge of Radicalism in Britain in the aftermath of the French Revolution, thus ensuring that the politically knowledgeable Paisley weavers would play an active part in this agitation. Alexander Wilson, the local weaver-poet, was prominent in the activities of the Conventions in 1792 and 1793. The latter was a year of both economic depression and working class political organisation in Paisley:

> Paisley, in 1793, made that year the advent of her future numberless political struggles . . . Numberless societies were constituted, which were soon under the management of able and active men . . . who, although mostly belonging to the working class . . . were possessed of very general knowledge on all the topics of the time.[93]

The open and constitutional activities of the local branch of the Society of the Friends of the People, which attracted some support and active participation from members of the propertied classes, were quickly replaced by secret insurrectionary organisation after the show trials of the Convention leaders in 1793. The existence of a Jacobin leadership in the weaving communities of Paisley is indicated by the presence of the United Scotsmen organisation in the town, though this has necessarily made only a shadowy impression in the records of the time.

According to Thompson, the early 1790s were of seminal importance in the 'making' of the English working class:

> The history of reform agitation between 1792 and 1796 was (in general terms) the story of the simultaneous default of the middle class reformers and the rapid 'leftwards' movement of the plebeian Radicals. The experience marked the popular consciousness for fifty years, and throughout this time the dynamic of Radicalism came not from the middle class but from the artisans and labourers. The men of the popular societies are rightly designated Jacobins.[94]

Two qualifications need to be added in applying this view to the specific case of Paisley. Firstly, the factors predisposing at least some of the manufacturers and middle classes towards 'advanced Whiggery' and Parliamentary reform were strong enough to render their default less than total. In spite of the general severity of the Tory reaction, some 'advanced Whigs' in Paisley survived with enough credibility to make possible an alliance with the more moderate plebeian reformers in the second wave of Radical activity which immediately followed the close of the Wars. The leader of this group in Paisley, William Carlile, enhanced his own credibility with the working class Radicals by supporting the right to peaceful agitation against such government measures as the suspension of *habeas corpus* in 1794. Writing of his activities in that year, he states:

> I more openly and decidedly gave my opinion concerning the War, both as to its origin and its object; and when the two famous Bills were brought into Parliament . . . whereby, in my apprehension, the rights of the people in Great Britain, secured by them by Magna Charta and the Bill of Rights, claimed by the voice of the nation, at the Revolution of 1688, were superceded, preventing the people from meeting to petition the legislature, unless certain regulations contained in this new Act were complied with; and certain alterations were proposed by the Bill presented to the House of Peers on the ancient laws of Treason. I determined, after consulting a few friends privately, to call a meeting of respectable inhabitants, who met accordingly, to the number of about forty, at which meeting we resolved to petition both Houses of Parliament against the passing of these Acts.[95]

This opposition was seen by the authorities as a dangerous adjunct to working class agitation. The Renfrewshire landowners drew up a list of 185 suspected 'traitors', including Bailie Carlile, and the County Sheriff presented this to the Town Clerk of Paisley with a view to their imprisonment. However, the Town Clerk's horrified reaction indicated the difficulty of acting directly against a large group of prominent citizens. Perceiving this, the Renfrewshire Tories then used their influence to persuade the Paisley Bank to refuse to discount the bills or drafts drawn on London banks by the 'rebellious' manufacturers and merchants, thus undermining their credit. The manufacturers responded by threatening to demand payment in gold for the banknotes they already held. Faced by this threat, from a group with growing influence in the local economy, the bank hastily backed down.[96] The 'advanced Whigs' in Paisley thus emerged from this attempt at repression remarkably unscathed.

The second qualification of Thompson's analysis of the consequences of the repression of Radicalism in the first stages of the Napoleonic Wars, which we need to make in the case of Paisley, relates to a criticism recently levelled at Thompson by Perry Anderson. The latter argues that, in fastening on the effects of economic exploitation and political repression, Thompson succumbs to:

> a minimisation of the *nationalist* mobilisation of the whole English population by the ruling class, in its tremendous struggle for supremacy with France. Yet no full picture of English popular culture after 1815 can be gained without due notice of the depth of the ideological capture of the 'nation' for conservative ends in Britain. The result is a serious oversimplification of the legacy of the wars.[97]

Whatever its merits as a generalisation, the significance of Anderson's intervention for this limited study of Paisley is that it points to the necessity of examining the impact of British nationalism on the working class during (and after) the Wars. A degree of 'nationalist mobilisation' among the working class seems to have been achieved, particularly in the latter half of the 1790s. In addition to providing many recruits for the army, particularly for the Highland Fencible Regiments, Paisley was the site of Loyalist demonstrations attended by large crowds. For example, 20,000 attended a review of all of the Renfrewshire Volunteer associations on 31st August 1799.[98] Although army recruitment probably owed as much to economic distress as to patriotic fervour, and it is hard to judge the sentiments of working people at this time, it is clear that the Radicals had lost the initiative by the later 1790s. Whilst in 1793 an attempt to hold a weavers' loyal procession had been successfully resisted,[99] the Jacobins were now powerless to prevent popular participation in Loyalist celebrations.

However, as the Wars moved into their second decade, both middle and working class opinion hardened somewhat against them — and against those held responsible for them — particularly after Bonaparte's 'Berlin Decree' of 1806 dealt a final blow to the remnants of the silk trade in Paisley. According to a contemporary inhabitant:

> There is a wonderful alteration in men's minds now. I do not think that a regiment of a thousand strong could be raised in seven years, such is the growing intelligence of the people and their antipathy to the war . . .[100]

To the effects of war-weariness in preparing for a fresh upsurge of the Parliamentary Reform movement in 1816 were added two additional influences — periodic economic distress and the inability of the weavers to reverse their decline by achieving minimum wage legislation.

The weavers' discontent was exacerbated by the food shortages and higher prices which followed the poor harvests of 1799 and 1800. Towards the end of 1800, this dissatisfaction erupted into rioting, directed by the posting of placards which exhorted the people to assemble at specified times and places. The disturbances were sufficiently pronounced for the authorities to issue a proclamation offering a reward for the discovery and arrest of the ringleaders.[101] It is very likely that working class Radicals were active in these disturbances.

It is indicative of the economic situation of the Paisley weavers during the Wars that the nineteenth century should commence with that most traditional form of popular protest, the food riot. As Smout has noted, the money wages of fancy muslin and shawl weavers remained significantly higher than those of plain weavers at this time, but real wages nevertheless came under pressure from wartime price inflation.[102] Weavers throughout the West of Scotland petitioned Parliament for minimum wage legislation on two occasions in the early nineteenth century. When rebuffed for the second time in 1812, in the aftermath of a severe trade depression in the preceding year, the weavers formed a network of combinations extending across Scotland, northern

England and the north of Ireland. The Glasgow weavers took their case to law, attempting to induce the magistrates to activate their powers to enforce a table of prices. A seven-week strike ensued in the West of Scotland when the magistrates refused to fix minimum rates. Paisley weavers were solid in support of the strike. The Sheriff of Renfrewshire and the magistrates at Paisley took the step of issuing a proclamation which claimed the illegality of combinations, advised all weavers to return to work or be prosecuted, warned against the intimidation of other workers, and informed the friendly societies that the use of their funds to support the strikes was illegal.[103]

The strike was broken after seven weeks by the arrest and imprisonment of the leaders of the Glasgow Weavers' Committee in February 1813. The failure to gain redress of grievances by petitioning, by recourse to the law, or by strike action, and the use of the law to break the strike, served to convince the weavers of the need to reform the process by which laws were made. In addition, the committee structure constructed by the weavers to link local unions was another important legacy of the 1812 strike. The organisational experience provided by the strike and the connections established between the weaving communities in the West of Scotland helped to prepare the ground for the insurrectionary general strike of April 1820.

In some important respects, the Reform agitation which recommenced in Paisley in 1816 followed the same trajectory as that of the 1790s. Initially the initiative lay with the more moderate working class Reformers, who stressed constitutional protest and petitioning, and who were loosely supported by the 'advanced Whig' section of the local bourgeoisie. This was met by the state trials of Radical leaders in 1817, closely following the pattern set in 1793-4. Thereafter, the Reform movement took on a more plebeian and insurrectionary slant in 1819-20. However, the activity of 1816-20 appears to have been on a larger scale, as regards the West of Scotland, when compared to that of the 1790s, as a result of the failure of the weavers to check their decline and of the severity of the post-war depression.

In Paisley, the public meeting in October 1816, which savagely condemned government policy and the system of political representation, was called as a direct response to the level of unemployment in the town. A further public meeting in 1817 expressed the central assumption of the Radicals that:

> . . . the continued and increasing calamities of the time arose from the want of a proper representation of the people in Parliament, and that they should be put in possession of their undoubted rights — universal suffrage and annual Parliaments.[104]

Support for these demands was bolstered by the tours of the Scottish manufacturing districts by Cobbett and Cartwright, who stressed the fellowship between English Radicals and their Scottish counterparts.

The continuing failure of the Radicals' efforts in petitioning Parliament and the State trials of 1817, and the increasing economic distress, led to a significant shift in the direction of working class political action during 1819. At a meeting in July on Meikleriggs Moor, just outside Paisley, an estimated 30,000 people demonstrated their impatience with the lack of progress towards Reform by rejecting a petition to the Prince Regent drawn up by the organising committee and substituting instead an address to the nation — 'the House of Parliament being thought unworthy to receive a petition which contended for universal suffrage, annual parliaments and vote by ballot.[105] The turn away from the more moderate leaders of Reform in Paisley was accelerated in the aftermath of the Peterloo massacre in Manchester. A meeting to protest at these events was held on Meikleriggs Moor on 11 September 1819, a response which was widespread in England and Scotland. Despite a proclamation issued by the Renfrewshire authorities, attempting to dissuade local inhabitants from attending, and banning the carrying of flags and insignia, between fourteen and eighteen thousand gathered with a multitude of banners with mottoes such as 'Abhor the inhuman butcheries at Manchester'. Radical speakers, wearing black as a sign of mourning, were able to link the events at Peterloo to the deficiencies of the political system. One speaker stated that:

> Such proceedings clearly demonstrated the necessity of a radical reform. If the Manchester magistrates had not calculated upon the applause and support of the borough faction, this tragedy never would have been acted.[106]

The resolutions passed indicate the way in which the bulk of the Paisley Radicals saw their struggles as linked to a British context in which English reformers were called upon for leadership. One motion went beyond the strategy of petitioning in a manner which prefigures the Chartist agitations, calling for abstention from the consumption of excisable goods and inviting Cartwright, Hunt, Sir Francis Burdett and other middle and upper class 'friends of Reform in London' to name a day on which reformers throughout Britain would meet to adopt this measure and carry it into effect.[107] But although several speakers abjured the use of violence and denied charges of insurrectionary or treasonable intent, it is clear from subsequent events that many working people in Paisley no longer shared this perspective.

As the meeting on Meikleriggs Moor dispersed, a section of the crowd marched back down Paisley High Street, carrying their flags in defiance of the authorities. They were met by special constables, lining both sides of the street, the magistrates and the Provost. The latter, determined to impose control, ordered the seizure of the flags. The ensuing scuffle developed into a violent confrontation, with the police being forced to concede control of the streets, and the crowd breaking the windows of any building connected with authority. In this way began five days of conflict in which the streets were largely in the hands of the crowd, running battles developed between the military and the working people, and the authorities were forced to escalate the extent of military support in order to regain control. By the end of the trouble, troops from the 80th Regiment, the 10th Hussars and the 7th Hussars had been stationed in Paisley. The local authorities demanded that these should remain for some time, and that a permanent barracks should be built. This was accomplished within three years. The relationship between working class Radicalism and the economy was clearly perceived by the county land-owners. At meetings in October and November, they agreed to raise a troop of yeomanry cavalry, but also to petition the government for measures to relieve unemployment — a loan to complete work on the Ardrossan Canal, a donation of £30,000 to enable work to be provided in cultivating waste land and in dredging the river Clyde, money to build roads and railways, and to finance emigration, and finally for a Bill to regulate the length of apprentice-ships in weaving.[108]

Although this major breakdown of order in Paisley was unplanned and developed in a spontaneous manner, with violence directed against the clearest symbols of authority, it was not entirely devoid of direction or co-ordination. One aim of the crowd was to win the release of prisoners taken at the outset, whilst an attack on the house of Colonel Fulton of the local Volunteers is readily comprehensible in the light of Peterloo. As regards co-ordination, some of the skirmishes with the military indicated a degree of pre-planning, whilst there were eye-witness reports of large street meetings being held. However, if the Radical leaders' attempts to co-ordinate the actions of the crowd were rudimentary, the Peterloo demonstration and its aftermath gave a considerable impetus to Radical organisation in Paisley. The formation of political unions, based on workshops and neighbourhoods, gathered momentum, and there is evidence of widespread arming among the weavers. That the initiative now rested with revolutionary Jacobins was indicated at a large Radical meeting in Johnstone on 1 November 1819, where pistols were fired and battle-axes prominently displayed, along with the revival of the sym-bolism of 'caps of liberty', presented by societies of female Reformers.[109] In December, the authorities in Paisley arrested a local cutler, John Henderson, and discovered two pikes in his workshop and a number of gun barrels in the house of one of his neighbours.[110]

The organisation of armed resistance centred around the weavers' shops of Maxwellton. According to John Parkhill, who was at the centre of these events, but who later adopted a disdainful attitude towards the Radical activity of the period:

> The preparations of the unions were . . . going on with great spirit. The casting of gun bullets was, at their leisure hours, a great occupation, and the manufacture of cleggs became a great amusement . . .[111]

The Radicals undertook night drilling exercises, obtained lists of the names of the local yeomanry cavalry so that their arms could be seized, and planned for the culmination of their activity in a general rising in the West of Scotland, co-

ordinated with a similar rebellion in England. Accordingly, John Neil was sent
from Paisley as an ambassador to the English Radicals, returning with word
that

> by an agreement with the English, we were not to move until we heard that 200,000 had taken
> the field in England.[112]

That the rising, when it came in April 1820, turned into a major defeat for the
West of Scotland Radicals is well known and will not be dwelt on at any length.
A proclamation, issued by the Glasgow 'Committee for forming a Provisional
Government' in Scotland, demanded 'equality of rights (not of property)'[113]
and called for a general strike from 3rd April to further this aim. On the
appointed day, an estimated 60,000 people stopped work in the West of
Scotland. In Paisley, the weavers led the way by touring manufacturing establishments that were still working and persuading or intimidating the workforce
to join them. The Provost of Paisley summed up the situation thus:

> the working classes here are all idle and assembled in crowds in the streets. Some of the cotton
> mills began in the morning to work but have struck since breakfast.[114]

However, despite the apparent solidarity of the response to the strike call, the
Radical War was over very quickly in Paisley. One young man was killed and
another wounded during a search for arms by a party of Radicals when the
occupants of a house opened fire, and an old man died from bayonet wounds
when soldiers, also searching for weapons, sought to drive back a hostile
crowd. Faced with a strong military presence, the arrest of suspected leaders,
and the apparent absence of an English rising, the Paisley Radicals did not take
to the field in a military sense. With the exception of the cotton mills, most of
the Paisley working class were back at work within a week.

From this brief account of the period from the 1790s to the Radical War,
some tentative conclusions can be drawn regarding the development of
working class consciousness and organisation in Paisley up to 1820. The
Radicalism and insurrectionary preparations of 1819-20 can be seen as the
cumulative effect of the worsening economic position of the weavers, and of
their failure to obtain redress by peaceful protest and trade union organisation.
In the close-knit weaving communities there came to exist a close approxi-
mation to Thompson's 'illegal tradition' in which a relationship was fostered
between quasi-legal trade unionism, a high level of political culture and a
Jacobin revolutionary leadership. The latter were able to seize the initiative in
the period of the Radical War, after the tactics of the more 'moderate'
reformers had failed once more to bear fruit. Stressing the scale and tenacity of
working class Radicalism in Scotland, Young has argued that in 1820 'a major
revolutionary movement was planning to set up a Scottish republic', and has
claimed the existence of a class conscious, nationalist and republican working

class.[115] Elements of such a movement certainly existed in Paisley. However, in assessing Young's claims, and to account for the development of the working class in Paisley after 1820, it is necessary to note not only the strengths of working class Radicalism but also its unevenness and its weaknesses.

To begin with, in Paisley and — we suspect — elsewhere in the West of Scotland, it is not clear that the working class of 1820 can be portrayed as un-ambiguously nationalist and republican. A striking feature of Radical politics in Paisley, both before and after 1820, was the tendency of many working people and their local leaders to look to the English political context and to English Radicals for a lead in terms of objectives and strategy. It is at this point that Anderson's cautionary reference to the role of *British* nationalism during the Wars has most relevance for this study. But rather than leading to the out-right capture of the (British) 'nation' for conservative ends, the nationalist onslaught appears to have strengthened the tendency for many Scottish Radicals to mount their own appropriation of a supposedly British political heritage. For example, at the mass demonstrations of 1819, referred to earlier, platform speakers professed themselves 'loyal Reformers', whilst banners referred not only to Wallace and Bruce but to 'Magna Charta' and to the rights of 'Britons'.[116] Although most working people in Paisley would identify them-selves as Scots, this sense of their historical and cultural identity did not neces-sarily manifest itself in an overtly nationalist politics. In the two periods in which constitutional appeals for Parliamentary Reform held sway — the early 1790s and 1815-17 — they were prepared in large numbers to seek a reform of the British state, rather than a Scottish republic. Even in the insurrectionary phase of 1819-20, the assault on the British state was to be led by the English working class. The phasing of working class action is compatible with the view that, apart from a core of Jacobin revolutionaries whose size is difficult to estimate, the working people were firstly concerned to reform the British state in conjunction with their English counterparts, and only subsequently to over-throw it. When the latter appeared on the agenda, the notion of a Provisional Government in Scotland, in parallel with a similar development to the south, became plausible. This does not necessarily indicate that the restoration of Scottish sovereignty was a primary focus of working class consciousness. Rather, we suggest, the most stable components in this consciousness were the perception that the British state was failing in its obligations to working people, both English and Scottish. More variable were conceptions of how this deficiency was to be remedied. The return of the Scottish working class to the banner of Parliamentary Reform in the crisis of 1830-2 and in the Chartist agitations, notwithstanding the continued or periodic appeal of 'physical force' to some, serves to indicate that the Radical War may have been a short-lived highpoint in terms of mass support for a Scottish republic.

It is to the unevenness of the working class consciousness that we must turn for a partial explanation of the failure of the Radical War. In Paisley the insur-rectionary movement proved very fragile in the face of the military preparedness of the authorities. The predictable attempts of the authorities in Paisley to arrest Radical leaders caused a significant number of the latter to flee the town, often to make their way to America. As regards the West of Scotland, this 'decapitation' of the movement contributed, as Young suggests,[117] to the debacle of the Radical War. But the ease with which the authorities were able to disrupt and face down the insurrectionary organisations in Paisley might also suggest that, even in the weaving communities, the number of actively committed Jacobin revolutionaries was quite small and that they and their supporters lacked a clear understanding of the requirements of a successful insurrection. In addition, the continued strength of the sectional divisions within the labour force is indicated by the fact that the factory operatives were drawn into the conflict only when the general strike was already under way. Given the bitterness of the class conflict experienced by the spinners in their relations with their employers, the cotton spinners might have been expected to form the backbone of working class action. Indeed, having joined the strike, the spinners were the last section of the Paisley labour force to resume work. This attests to the strength of the spinners' union, assisted as it was by the centralisation of the labour force in the early factories. However, the possibility of co-ordinated working class political action was lessened by the extent to which the Radical organisations tended to be confined to artisans and out-workers. Virtually all of the the local Radical leaders whom we can identify fell into these occupational categories.[118]

In stressing the uneven development of working class consciousness and political organisation up to 1820, a major consideration to which we have referred has been the existence of alternative political leaderships within the Radical movement and the tendency for a large body of support to move quite rapidly between them. In this context the Radical War must be interpreted as a considerable defeat for the Jacobin revolutionaries, after which the proponents of a constitutional route to Parliamentary Reform regained the initiative. The events of 1820 also served to indicate the dangers of proletarian Radicalism to the propertied classes, with the result that many of the latter who were Whig-orientated took special pains to move into the forefront of the Reform agitations of 1830-1832. A striking feature of the Reform Bill crisis in Paisley was the relative ease with which members of the local bourgeoisie and some of the county landowners were able to initiate an alliance, albeit an uneasy one, with working class Radicals. Since this occurred against the background of increasing economic insecurity for the weavers and of sometimes violent conflict between the cotton spinners and their masters, it requires particular attention.

The narrowness of the Parliamentary franchise in Scotland and the domination of burgh administration by self-perpetuating oligarchies under the sponsorship of large landowners, together with the factors which rendered Paisley susceptible to middle class radicalism, ensured massive local support for Parliamentary Reform in Paisley when this appeared a real possibility in

1830. In December, a public meeting of 'the noblemen and gentlemen, free-holders, Commissioners of Supply, heritors, magistrates of towns, Justices of the Peace, merchants and manufacturers of the County of Renfrew' was held to applaud the formation of Grey's ministry, after Wellington's government had fallen. The meeting unanimously approved the following motion:

> That your petitioners view with great satisfaction the resolution of His Majesty's Ministers to adopt a system of retrenchment and economy in every branch of the public expenditure; that your petitioners also rejoice in the assurance given by His Majesty's Ministers that the state of representation in Parliament is about to be taken into consideration by the Government; . . . that the constitutions of most of the Royal Burghs and Burghs of Barony are defective; that your petitioners have not only no desire to possess political rights to the exclusion of respectable fellow-citizens in the municipal affairs of the town, but are disposed to regard with entire satisfaction any Parliamentary reform which by extending the elective franchise, shall diffuse more equal political rights amongst His Majesty's subjects . . .[119]

Prominent in formulating this motion was Sir John Maxwell, a substantial landowner who controlled a number of the Parliamentary votes in Renfrew-shire. He was also to the fore in forging a broad class alliance on Reform, since he played a considerable part in the activities of the Renfrewshire Political Union (R.P.U.), which was formed along the lines of the Birmingham Political Union in December 1830. The objects and rules of the R.P.U. are indicative of the participation of middle class Radicals, in conjunction with a number of the county gentry, in its leadership. An insistence on legality at all costs was coupled with demands for the reduction of taxes, the shortening of the duration of Parliament from seven to three years, and the extension of the franchise to male householders.[120] Householder status was thus taken as the guarantor of respectability. Working class aspirations were more radical than those of the R.P.U., whilst the Reform Bill itself retreated much further from universal male suffrage. Nevertheless, the trade unions and their members in Paisley were harnessed with some success to the campaigns of the R.P.U.

As Wilson notes, the Political Unions in Scotland at this time were heavily dependent on the trade unions for a mass turnout at large meetings and demonstrations.[121] At the same time, the trade unions' direct involvement in the Reform agitation was encouraged by the establishment of the *Herald to the Trades' Advocate*, a trade union paper published in Glasgow from September 1830. Taking its political lead from Joseph Hume, the paper adopted a moderate position on Reform, arguing the necessity of winning a limited franchise reform as a stepping stone to more radical measures. Hume visited Paisley on 17 December 1830, and his political views seem to have struck a responsive chord in the post-1820 climate of disillusion with 'physical force'. Trades delegates shared public platforms with R.P.U. leaders, including Sir John Maxwell, and the trades marched in procession with some of the manu-facturers to the great Reform meetings, which in Renfrewshire drew attendances of up to 50,000 people, with Paisley well represented.[122]

To what extent, then, can we see the massive working class presence in the Reform Bill agitations in Paisley as the culmination of a process wherein this class was 'made' by 1832? How far did there exist in Paisley a nexus of working class culture and organisations founded on the perception of an identity of interests across the working class and opposed to those of employers and political rulers? Our tentative conclusions can be located within the context of the recent reappraisal of Thompson's work on the English working class by Anderson. The latter suggests that to speak of the 'making' of this class may be inappropriate in that it implies the achievement of a certain fixity of working class culture and organisations by 1832:

> The term *making* here has an unmistakable force: it suggests that the character of the English working class was in its most essential traits formed by the time of the Reform Bill.[123]

In consequence, it becomes difficult to account for the discontinuity manifested by the development of the working class in the nineteenth century, and in particular for the dominance of moderate reformism after the Chartist climaxes of the 1840s. For his own part, Anderson suggests that a partial explanation for the passivity of the working class after 1850 might be found in the disruption of its political and cultural traditions by 'the radical long-term recomposition of the class' in the prolonged transition from workshop to factory production. Our point is a related one. Whilst sharing Anderson's concern with discontinuities in the development of the working class, we would also stress the unevenness of, and contradictory tendencies within, working class traditions as they developed between 1790 and 1830.

In combating historical interpretations which devalue the self-activity of working people or which portray the latter as a passive product of a process of industrialisation, Thompson emphasises the strength and vitality of 'the quasi-legal institutions of the underground', the Jacobin republicanism and trade unionism of the 'illegal tradition'. However, although this tradition was much in evidence in Paisley, the Jacobin republicans had to vie for working class support with a more moderate leadership, which came to the fore in periods of open political agitation. Thus in Paisley a significant number of working people tended to oscillate between legal and extra-legal tactics, and between the leadership of Jacobin revolutionaries and those Reformers whose concern to win the support of the propertied and middle classes led them to advocate conformity to 'the law' and 'the Constitution'. The point is not that Thompson is unaware of all this, but that the existence of competing leaderships and strategies with varying levels of support renders the assumption of a unitary working class tradition by 1832 misleading. In Paisley, 1820 saw a climactic defeat of the Jacobins. In 1832 moderation achieved some ascendancy in the Radical movement's leadership, so that a working class Radicalism committed to the strategy of 'The whole Bill or more than the Bill' was, at least temporarily, defused by the Scottish Reform Act.

Young echoes Thompson's conclusion regarding the English working class in arguing that there existed at the time of the 1830-32 crisis a '. . . great divide between the radical working classes on the one hand and the possessing classes, whether Whig or Tory, on the other . . .'[124] However, in Paisley during this crisis a tentative class alliance emerged against aristocratic Toryism and the Westminster authorities. The analysis so far suggests that the hand of those working class leaders and members of the propertied and middle classes seeking such an alliance was strengthened by certain features of class relations in Paisley, dealt with in the preceding section. Thus, whilst Young cites a succession of popular disturbances across Scotland as evidence of class antagonism at this time,[125] Paisley and the Reform demonstrations in its environs were peaceful by comparison. The threat of 'Reform or Revolution' was raised on occasion, and there would have been a strong possibility of a further shift to insurrectionism if the Reform Bill had failed to pass into law. However, working class action remained largely within the boundaries set by the R.P.U. which approved the Reform Bill despite acknowledging that it fell short of its aspirations.[126] The tendency for working people to confine themselves to seeking redress for economic grievances through the pursuit of political change, and thus the absence of a concerted attack on private property as such, created space for such an accommodation. In this respect it is important to endorse a qualification which Thompson makes to his general conclusion regarding class polarisation in early industrial Britain:

> [T]he main tradition of nineteenth-century working class Radicalism took its cast from Paine. There were times, at the Owenite and Chartist climaxes, when other traditions became dominant. But after each relapse, the substratum of Painite assumptions remained intact. The aristocracy were the main target; . . . but — however hard trade unionists might fight against their employers — industrial capital was assumed to be the fruit of enterprise and beyond reach of political intrusion.[127]

At the same time, Thompson argues that from 1795 political repression drove working people 'into a state of apartheid' which prevented the emergence of 'the "natural" alliance between an impatient radically-minded industrial bourgeoisie and a formative proletariat'.[128] However, we suggest that the nature of class relations in Paisley ensured that such apartheid was less than complete, and that elements of such an alliance could thus emerge. It is now necessary to examine the 'Chartist climax' in Paisley to discover to what extent the victory of the industrial bourgeoisie in 1832 destroyed this possibility.

Chartism and Class Collaboration 1833-1850

The failure of the Whig ministry to repeal the Corn Laws or to follow the Acts of 1832 and 1833 with more sweeping measures to extend the franchise undoubtedly generated working class disillusion in Paisley, and tended to widen the division between Whigs and working class Radicals. This process of dis-illusionment extended also to many of the newly enfranchised middle class electors, and was hastened by their dissatisfaction with the behaviour of their first representative in the reformed Parliament, Sir John Maxwell. His promin-ence in the Reform agitation had ensured him widespread public support and a comfortable majority over his Tory opponent. However, he had been obliged to accept a pledge, drawn up by a committee of electors, to work for further reforms, the abolition of protectionism and other measures, and had agreed to resign if ever he failed to live up to the expectations of his constituents.[129] These expectations were dashed almost immediately when the Paisley Member failed to support Hume's Bill to abolish sinecures in February 1833 and refused to oppose the Irish Coercion Bill in the same year. The electors' dissatisfaction bore fruit with the resignation of Sir John Maxwell in 1834. Attempts by the electors to render their parliamentary representatives directly accountable for their conduct continued into the mid-1830s, thus attesting to the strength of middle class Radicalism in Paisley. This pressure from sections of the elec-torate was reinforced by the intervention of working class Radicals in Parlia-mentary elections. In those of 1835 and 1836, meetings of non-electors were held in order to co-ordinate attempts to pressure shopkeepers and other electors into supporting Liberal candidates, by means of the threat of 'exclusive dealing'.[130] Thus, in Paisley in the 1830s, there existed some elements of a coercive 'labour community', although it does not seem to have estab-lished such a hold on local government as that which, according to Foster, was to be found in Oldham.[131] Nor were the actions of this community immediately inimical to the interests of the industrial bourgeoisie. Working class pressure on Tory electors in 1835 coincided with collaboration between some employers and the weavers' association in support of Fielden's Minimum Wage Bill. In these respects, the tactical alliance of the Reform Bill agitation had not yet been completely undermined by the rising tide of dissatisfaction with Whig policy.

A further consideration is that whilst the 'labour community' in Oldham was apparently strong enough to enforce the subordination of the middle classes to the political position of the working class Radicals by 1832,[132] the shopkeepers, merchants and small employers of Paisley did not lose the capacity for independent initiative. Partly for this reason, middle class Radicals were able to exert some influence on the course of the Chartist agitations in Paisley, through implacable opposition to the 'physical force' tendency. In addition, the importance of the handloom weavers as a con-stituent of the Paisley working class, together with the catastrophic impact of the trade depressions of 1837-42, implied a weakening labour movement. This tended to deprive the O'Connorite Chartists of their most effective con-stituency — an aggressive and confident trade unionism. In this context, Chartism in Paisley was characterised by a shifting balance of forces between 'physical' and 'moral force' leaderships, and did not exclude a degree of inter-class co-operation. 'Moral force' leaders and middle class advocates of Reform occupied a pivotal position, which could be employed to draw working people into tentative alliance with the industrial bourgeoisie, particularly in relation to Corn Law Repeal. Finally, two factors cited by Burgess in relation to Chartism in Scotland have particular relevance to Paisley. Firstly, the tendency for the weavers to identify the excess supply of labour, rather than their relation to capital, as the cause of their decline, continued to mitigate class antagonism between themselves and their employers, thus creating the possibility of class co-operation. Secondly,

> . . . it is important to appreciate how slow the extension of the franchise was in Scotland following the 1832 Act, especially in the recently enfranchised boroughs. This provided a real base for inter-class co-operation and was one of the reasons why Scottish Chartism tended to opt for 'moral' rather than 'physical' force tactics.[133]

In addition, the industrial bourgeoisie was slow to reap any direct economic benefit from the reforms of 1832 and 1833. To the extent that the landowning class and rentier bourgeoisie retained their hold on the British state, the possibility of class co-operation against this constellation of interests remained open.

The onset of renewed Radical agitation among working people in Paisley coincided with the severe trade depression of 1837, the cotton spinners' strike of the same year, and the establishment of an alliance between the popular Ayrshire Radical, Dr. John Taylor, and Fergus O'Connor. A groundswell of working class support for the latter and his 'physical force' policies was apparent in the early stages of the Chartist movement in Paisley, fuelled by his Scottish tour of 1836, and by the heightening of class antagonisms in the spinners' strike and the trial of some of the Glasgow spinners for murder and arson. The trial, in January 1838, resulted in the defendants being convicted only of 'illegal conspiracy to keep up wages', but produced sentences of seven years' transportation. These events, and the campaign on behalf of the defendants, considerably increased antipathy toward the Whig administration, and lent strength to O'Connor and Taylor in their advocacy of 'physical force' at this time.[134]

The most prominent spokesman for the O'Connorite faction in Paisley was Edward Polin, the secretary to the Renfrewshire Political Union. However, this faction was unable to gain a sustained ascendancy in the Chartist leadership, since throughout the period 1838-42 Polin was forced to contend with opposition from the proponents of 'moral force' and of class collaboration on the programme of the Charter and Repeal of the Corn Laws. Whilst controversy over 'physical force' was a disruptive factor in Scottish Chartism, this was particularly so in Paisley because of the particular nature of class relations and in consequence of the presence of the Reverend Patrick Brewster, minister of the second charge at Paisley Abbey. Brewster's interventions in Scottish

Chartism were dictated by his insistence that Britain was ruled by a 'free' rather than a 'despotic' government, so that 'resistance to constituted authority, however oppressive, is foolish and criminal, whenever there are any other means of redress'.[135] Although Brewster's 'moral force' crusading has been described by Wilson as marginal to the Scottish Chartist movement,[136] his constant interventions against O'Connor and Taylor were not without effect, particularly in Paisley. He had no links with the trade unions and alienated many Chartists because he functioned in such a way as to divide the movement. Nevertheless, his advocacy of 'Peace, Law and Order', temperance and Corn Law Reform was shared by other prominent Renfrewshire Radicals, including John Henderson, editor of the Radical *Glasgow Saturday Post and Paisley and Renfrewshire Reformer*, and Provost of Paisley from November 1841 to November 1844. Furthermore, Brewster's activities had the important effect of continually forcing the O'Connorites onto the defensive with regard to 'physical force', thus complementing the ideological offensive of some of the local Whigs. Moderate advocates of universal male suffrage who had achieved municipal office were particularly vulnerable to this offensive. Henderson was attacked by William Barr, a Whig magistrate, for allegedly avowing that he would refuse to call for military aid to the civil power in the event of disturbances, and was sharply questioned on the matter by the Select Committee on Distress in 1842.[137]

Initially, however, Brewster had little success in his attempt to win the bulk of the Chartists in Paisley to his side. He was instrumental in December 1838 in extracting from a delegate meeting in Edinburgh the 'Calton Hill' resolutions, which were intended to commit Scottish Chartists exclusively to 'moral force', and shortly succeeded in persuading the R.P.U. to adopt them. However, he subsequently found himself decisively rejected by many of the working class Chartists, being defeated by Dr. Taylor in a delegate election and comprehensively beaten by O'Connor, whom Brewster had challenged to a public debate.[138] The division between Brewster and the 'moral force' leaders of the R.P.U. on the one hand, and the rank-and-file, on the other, led the former to secede, forming a new Radical Association.[139] In the short run, Brewster had been eclipsed. At a Glasgow delegate conference in August 1839, called to consider the General Convention proposals for the 'Sacred Month' and 'ulterior measures', the Paisley delegate was one of those who reported a determination to arm.[140] Nevertheless, O'Connor, who was present at the Glasgow conference, found such general antipathy to 'physical force' and an even wider awareness of a lack of preparedness for armed insurrection, that he felt compelled to disown the 'Sacred Month' proposals and to suggest that 'moral force' would suffice to obtain the Charter.[141] By the following Spring, after the suppression of the Newport 'rising' in November 1839, Edward Polin wrote to the *True Scotsman*, denying the existence of a party in Paisley which was seeking to win the Charter by force of arms, and claiming that:

all that was ever advised by those considered the most extreme in their opinions, was that the people should be prepared by arming themselves with the means of repelling physical force, when it was brought forward by the government to put down the moral, peaceful, legal and constitutional agitation of the people.[142]

It thus becomes apparent that, despite the antipathy of working class followers of O'Connor towards him, Brewster's offensive had certain critical effects on Chartism in Paisley, when considered in conjunction with the nature of Scottish Chartism in general. He had helped to divide the movement in Paisley and forced Polin and the O'Connorites onto the defensive. Partly in consequence, there was little mass activity for the Charter in the town in 1840.[143]

The underlying weakness of the labour movement in Paisley, consequent on the survival of the handloom weavers and their inability to prevent wage cutting by trade union means, was particularly important in undermining the position of the O'Connorite Radicals. The Chartist orator, Robert Lowery, attending a soirée in Paisley during his Scottish tour in 1839, was struck by the despondency of the old weavers, careworn after years of hardship and fruitless struggle.[144] Given the lack of preparedness for insurrection, Chartist leaders who wished to avoid an alliance with the Whig Corn Law Repealers and middle class advocates of 'moral force' could rely only on a strong trade union movement as a source of independent working class initiative, as happened in the general strike for the Charter in 1842.[145] This strike found no echo in Paisley, whilst in the nearby mining districts of Ayrshire local Chartists were able in some locations to harness industrial action sparked off by wage cuts to political ends.[146] The labour movement in Paisley was further weakened by the continuing resonance of sectional divisions, particularly given the large Irish community in the town. The hostility of native trade unionists and followers of O'Connor to Daniel O'Connell, to whom the Irish labourers and factory hands were 'unswerving' in their allegiance,[147] was important in hindering working class unity. O'Connell was attacked for his views on combinations at the cotton spinners' meeting in 1838, whilst at a Radical meeting in Paisley on 4 September 1838 a motion was carried expressing loss of confidence in O'Connell and deprecating his support for the Whigs.[148] A *rapprochement* between the Chartists and the movement for Repeal of the Irish Union ensured Irish involvement in the Chartist disturbances and demonstrations in 1847-8, but came too late to have a strong impact on events in 1838-42.

Thus, despite considerable working class allegiance to O'Connor, the weakness of the labour movement in Paisley seriously hindered the attempts of Polin and his associates to prevent the initiative passing to advocates of class alliance and 'moral force'. In Glasgow, for a brief period between 1840 and 1842, the Universal Suffrage Central Committee pursued a policy of dominating or disrupting anti-Corn Law and other meetings so as to assert the primacy of the campaign for the Charter, succeeding largely through the ability to mobilise support quickly through links with the trade unions, workshops and factories.[149] In Paisley, however, such measures seem to have been much less systematic and less successful. Weavers' emigration societies developed in 1840 with only token Chartist intervention, and the attempts by Brewster, Henderson and others to ally with the anti-Corn Law movement began to meet with some success. In September 1840, Brewster was accompanied in the Paisley delegation to the Central Committee for Scotland by Peter Coats, a partner in the family thread mill.[150] Given the strength of working class opinion against the Corn Laws in Paisley, Brewster's choice of allies did not cause him to forfeit all plebeian support. When he met O'Connor once more in public debate in the autumn of 1841 at Paisley, Brewster was reported to have a majority of 'at least five to three'.[151]

The onset of a depression of great severity in 1841 had the effect of increasing the tendency towards class collaboration, not least because it had serious effects on the manufacturers and middle classes as well as on the operatives. On 16 October, 4,795 people in Paisley were reported to be dependent on the relief fund, and this rose rapidly to 15,000 by the following February, representing about 25% of the population. But, in addition, the Relief Committee reported in October 1841 that 400 tradesmen's houses were deserted and 100 retail shops closed.[152] This had the effect of converting more of the middle classes to the joint programme of universal suffrage and Corn Law Repeal. At a meeting to swear in special constables, Robert Cochran, a merchant and moderate Chartist, was joined by Alexander McGilvray (baker) and a Mr. Falconer (coal agent) in refusing to serve until sufficient food was provided to the unemployed to remove the likelihood of disturbances. In the following August, McGilvray seconded motions for the Charter and against the Corn Laws at a meeting called to prepare a petition on distress, and declared that:

> Their circumstances were now in such a position that he had resolved to leave the aristocracy and join the people in their endeavours to obtain the Charter, as the only cure for the evils they at present endured.[153]

This meeting, in drawing participants from a broad spectrum of the class structure and in voting down an amendment which sought to prevent the addition of Corn Law Repeal to the call for the Charter, symbolised the emerging class alliance in Radical politics in Paisley. In addition, the bankruptcy of more than half of the manufacturers and of the Town Council, and the collapse of the *ad hoc* system of relief for the able-bodied unemployed, focused the attention of the inhabitants on the wider economic and political forces which confronted them and on the appeal for Government assistance.

With the total collapse of the poor relief system in Paisley, only external voluntary contributions and State intervention prevented widespread starvation. On the initiative of Edward Twistleton, an assistant poor law commissioner in England, sent to Paisley to investigate the distress, certain members of the Government agreed to provide finance to the Relief Fund, providing that all able-bodied men submitted to a work test, and that relief should only be given through a controlled store system. The latter, in particular, was widely resented, and was opposed by Provost Henderson among others. However, the collapse of efforts to raise funds within Paisley ensured the acceptance of these conditions. The Government thus channelled assistance through the London Manufacturers' Relief Committee, which was by far the largest single source of relief funds in Paisley during the 1841-3 crisis.[154]

A significant aspect of this Government intervention was that, despite the fact that the crisis affected a large number of manufacturing centres throughout Britain, the Manufacturers' Relief Committee in London 'provided more for this one Scottish town than for all the districts of England put together'.[155] This Government concern for Paisley may have resulted from the particularly acute unemployment situation and the collapse of traditional structures of social control, in this case the system of poor relief. However, the recent history of the town had also established its reputation as a centre for working class insurgency in the face of cyclical unemployment and falling wages. Communications from the locality to the Government did not fail to point to the potential threat to social order, and Government assistance may well have helped to reduce this threat.

For a number of reasons, then, the crisis of 1841-3 served to strengthen the tendency of class collaboration in Radical politics in Paisley. Whilst the emphasis in Foster's analysis of Oldham is placed on the coercive weight of the 'labour community' in enforcing the subordination of elements of the middle classes to the politics of the working class, middle class Radicalism in Paisley appears to have been more strongly related to the particular economic conditions of the town, and to have had a considerably greater degree of autonomy. This is indicated once more by the formation of a Complete Suffrage Association, seeking a male householder franchise, in 1842, which grew to more than 570 members by October.[156] This attempt to deflect working class support from Chartism into a union with the middle classes was sponsored by Brewster, Henderson and other 'moral force' leaders. Although it evoked the bitter hostility of O'Connor's followers, those Chartists who wished to be free to support Corn Law Repeal or to make concessions in order to ally with middle class Radicals were more sympathetic. The existence of some body of working class support for Brewster in Paisley is indicative of the underlying weakness of the labour movement and of the divisions which plagued the Chartist movement. In addition, Brewster's appeal, though limited, was strengthened by those strands of religiosity and of the desire for independence and 'respectability' which rendered the weaver and artisan Radical culture a contradictory phenomenon. One reflection of this cultural tradition was the strength and persistence of the dissenting churches in Paisley, which had about 14,000 members in 1831.[157] As Smout notes of the Paisley weavers:

> In religion they were enthusiastic sectaries . . . Paisley was a centre of anti-burghers and later
> of baptists, and also had congregations of methodists and unitarians, otherwise rare kirks in
> Scotland.[158]

Brewster was fiercely critical of the Established Church, particularly for its manifest failure to adapt to the growth of an urban working class in the field of Poor Relief, and for its failure to recognise that Christian duty and biblical texts, as he read them, demonstrated the necessity of supporting the just demands of the working class. These strands in his position would appeal to working class Chartists like the anonymous pamphleteer 'Z', who addressed the Paisley operatives on the compatibility of religion and Reforming politics in 1841.[159] A Chartist Church, a distinctively Scottish phenomenon, was established in Paisley around 1839, and the *Scotch Reformers' Gazette* commented that 'the greatest curiosity in the whole mania . . . is the idea of preaching which has got amongst the Paisley Chartists'.[160] Christian Chartism usually went hand-in-hand with the temperance movement, in which Brewster was also active.

This brief discussion of Chartism and religion takes on significance in the light of Burgess's argument that Scots Calvinism, revitalised by the emergence of the Free Church from the Disruption in 1843, combined with economic liberalism to form the basis of the ideological hegemony of the industrial bourgeoisie in Scotland between the 1840s and 1870s.[161] In Paisley the secessionists of 1843 were led by the Reverend Dr. Burns, a cleric noted for his Whig sympathies. Brewster remained in the Established Church, ostensibly because the seceders 'have refused to recognise and claim the civil rights of a suffering and oppressed people'.[162] But precisely because he maintained a rhetorical hostility to 'Whiggery', whilst in practice seeking to foster class collaboration and to isolate the more radical Chartist leaders, Brewster's combination of religion and Radicalism could serve to assist in dividing Chartists in Paisley and in smoothing the transition to the Liberal hegemony which followed.

Conclusion

In summary, then, as in the pre-Chartist Radical agitations, the working class in Paisley in the 1830s and 1840s was divided in its support for alternative leaderships and strategies, and moderate Radicals were able to lead a section of this class into an alliance with elements of the middle classes and of the industrial bourgeoisie. Whilst the cotton spinners' experience of class conflict in conditions of factory production led them to adopt the position of the O'Connorite Chartists, their support tended to be restricted to periods of acute economic distress. Whilst factory operatives accounted for only a small proportion of the labour force, the political culture of the artisans and fancy weavers, which provided the basis for a more sustained commitment to

Radical politics, contained contradictory tendencies. A section of this group tended to emphasise their 'respectability' and affinity with non-proletarian Radicals in a manner which prefigured the moderate Parliamentary Reform movement of the 1850s and 1860s, which was aimed at achieving Household Suffrage.[163] We have suggested that Thompson's analysis of English working class consciousness cannot be extended to Paisley without taking into account the continuing possibility of limited forms of class alliance, both before and after 1830, and the attendant divisions within the proletarian Radical tradition. Although the local economy and attendant class relations in Paisley were in important respects particularly conducive to such a possibility, it is likely that this point is more widely applicable. Despite the fact that Thompson places most emphasis on the almost exclusively proletarian political activity which formed the 'illegal tradition', and argues that the possibility of an alliance between the industrial bourgeoisie and proletariat was thwarted in the course of the French Wars, he has also noted that the dilemma expressed in the opposition, 'moral force/physical force', 'was the dilemma of all Radical reformers to the time of Chartism and beyond'.[164] But this opposition, as Thompson notes at this point, was one which required a choice between a reliance on the insurrectionary capacity and/or industrial muscle of the working class and a strategy which required sufficient concessions from the Radicals to enable them to win the 'hearts and minds' of their social superiors.

The balance of forces favouring each possible resolution of this dilemma appears to have been a critical determinant of the fate of working class Radicalism in different localities in early industrial Britain. In this context, Paisley took a different route from that of Oldham and of other centres of large-scale cotton spinning and coal-mining which formed the backbone of the General Strike of 1842. Although capitalist crisis manifested itself in the local economy with increasing severity, the absence of a large factory proletariat and the underlying fragility of the labour movement attendant on the survival of the handloom weavers into the 1840s disarmed the more radical Chartist leaders at this key juncture in the development of working class political activity. In this respect, and increasingly as the belated emergence of power-loom competition after 1840 began to lead to the recomposition of the labour force, Paisley came to resemble, not Oldham, but Northampton. Here, according to Foster the shoe-making industry was largely un-unionised, and hence 'the lack of a labour movement base left any who were genuinely class conscious with the bleak alternative of political isolation or an unequal alliance with non-labour strata'.[165] Such an alliance was also favoured in Paisley by the prevalence of small employers and their 'social closeness' to the fancy weavers, by the effects of economic crisis on the 'non-labour strata' and by the continued exclusion of the latter from real political influence at the level of the British state. The resultant tradition of middle class and employer Radicalism cannot, in this context, be interpreted as a consequence solely of the impact of a coercive 'labour community', nor was it entirely a conscious bourgeois strategy to restabilise class relations. Nevertheless, the existence of this non-proletarian desire for reform, in conjunction with the persistence of sectional divisions within the labour force, did have the effect — notably at the beginning of the 1840s — of lessening the extent to which working class distress and Radicalism posed a threat to social order in Paisley. However, we have also attempted to stress that the extent of this threat was weakened by the unevenness of working class consciousness in Paisley, both between different sections of the workforce and in terms of the contradictory tendencies inherent in artisan and weaver Radicalism.

That Paisley did not manifest the degree of working class consciousness claimed by Foster for Oldham by 1842 does not, of course, necessarily vitiate his argument that the strength of this consciousness, particularly as manifested in the Chartist general strike, led to bourgeois initiatives aimed at restabilisation — the process of 'liberalisation' and the deliberate fostering of a 'labour aristocracy' in the context of a shift towards 'capital-export imperialism' after the mid-century. Indeed Foster suggests that pressure of liberalisation on a *national* level came from precisely those regions in which working class consciousness had been most fully developed.[166] However, as Saville suggested in an early review of Foster's study, the latter's argument that a degree of 'mass conviction' in a specifically revolutionary class consciousness had been established in Oldham within the few years before 1842 poses a major problem for explanation — how to account for the apparently dramatic shift towards class collaboration within the space of a few years.[167] It is possible that this problem might be lessened by attention to the probability of unevenness and lacunae within working class consciousness in this period:

> There were elements of revolutionary attitudes within the general class consciousness of working people and some of their leaders, both before and during the Chartist period, but this has long been recognised. What there was not was a single strand which can be defined as a 'revolutionary class consciousness' and applied as a blanket term on a single movement at any one point in time.[168]

As regards Paisley, there is little indication in the Chartist period of a concerted understanding of the nature of State power, and in particular little evidence that private property as such became a target of the political agitations. For example, the Owenite critique of the existing social and economic order worked in opposition to, rather than in harness with, the Chartist agitations of 1838-42. According to a contemporary Owenite pamphlet:

> if Universal Suffrage were obtained, Competition would trample as much as ever upon the happiness of the working man. No laws could prevent it . . .
> Now where is the remedy to this mournful state of things; Is it to be found in Chartism, or in Whiggism or in Toryism? No! it is to be found in the principle of voluntary and equal co-operation with a mutual union of interests.[169]

This Owenite alternative to Parliamentary Reform added a further dimension to the complex and shifting pattern of alliances and schisms which constituted working class political activity in the Chartist years.

In Scotland, in any case, the reorientation of class relations around the mid-century appears to have been less dramatic than that in the cotton districts of South Lancashire because what Burgess calls the 'class collaborationist character of labourist politics' was already a tendency in the Chartist years.[170] In Paisley, we have argued, the possibility of a class alliance of the 'industrious classes' against the Tory landed interest was never completely closed off by the repression of the Napoleonic Wars or — for the fancy weavers and artisans — by the experience of economic exploitation and crisis. The nature of class relations in Paisley, and the continued exclusion of the local bourgeoisie from real influence on the policies of the British state, kept this possibility open. After the defeat of the ultra-Radicals in 1820, which marked the high point of the 'illegal tradition', limited forms of class alliance emerged in the Reform Bill agitations, in 'moral force' Chartism and in Complete Suffragism. In this respect, the emphasis in studies of Scottish Chartism on the role of 'moral force' leaders and tendencies of class alliance is borne out. However, alongside this, it is necessary to stress the appeal of more exclusively proletarian Radicalism indicated by the existence of a substantial, although fluctuating, working class following for O'Connor in both major periods of Chartist activity — 1838-42 and 1847-8. But although the economic crisis of 1837-42 eliminated many of the small employers and further depressed the weavers' wages, thus developing further the objective basis of class polarisation, it also marked a further stage in the weakening of the labour movement. This was further undermined by the gradual development of power-loom competition in the 1840s and by the extended process in which cotton thread spinning replaced the production of hand-woven textiles as the town's major industry after the mid-century, necessitating a painful recomposition of the labour force. The progressive weakening of the labour movement in Paisley strengthened the hand of moderate Reformers committed to a strategy of class alliance, and ensured the dominance of this tendency in the period of Liberal hegemony after the mid-century.

NOTES

1. E. P. Thompson, *The Making of the English Working Class* (Penguin 1968) and *The Poverty of Theory* (London 1978). P. Anderson, *Arguments Within English Marxism* (Verso 1980), esp. pp. 30-49.

2. Thompson, *The Making . . .*, p. 12.

3. J. Foster, *Class Struggle and the Industrial Revolution* (London 1974).

4. Mick Jenkins, *The General Strike of 1842* (London 1980), esp. chapter 11.

5. T. C. Smout, *A History of the Scottish People 1560-1830* (Glasgow 1969).

6. Smout, *op. cit.*, pp. 419-420.

7. J. D. Young, 'The Making of the Scottish Working Class', *Society for the Study of Labour*

History, No. 28, 1974, pp. 61-8, and *The Rousing of the Scottish Working Class* (London 1979), chapters 2 and 3; T. Dickson and T. Clarke, 'The Making of a Class Society' in T. Dickson (ed.) *Scottish Capitalism* (London 1980), esp. pp. 168-177.

8. L. C. Wright, *Scottish Chartism* (Edinburgh 1953). A more satisfactory account is A. Wilson, *The Chartist Movement in Scotland* (Manchester 1970).

9. See *The Beauties of Scotland* (Edinburgh 1806), Vol. 3. pp. 42-43.

10. 1695 Poll Tax Roll, Paisley Public Library.

11. W. M. Metcalfe, *The History of Paisley* (Paisley 1909), p. 459.

12. See T. M. Devine, 'The colonial trades and industrial investment in Scotland c. 1700-1815', *Economic History Review*, 2nd series XXIX 1976.

13. For a more detailed discussion of the economic consequences of the Union of 1707 see K. Burgess, 'Scotland and the first British empire, 1707-1770s' in T. Dickson, op. cit.

14. J. Wilson, *A General View of the Agriculture of Renfrew* (Paisley 1812), p. 243.

15. Chalmers' *Caledonia* (Edinburgh 1823), Vol. VI, p. 813.

16. W. Carlile, 'Sketches of Paisley: a short sketch of the improved state of Paisley, including the Abbey Parish, for the year 1805', *Scots Magazine and Edinburgh Literary Miscellany*, July 1806.

17. Carlile, op. cit.

18. Carlile, op. cit.

19. M. Blair, *The Paisley Thread* (Paisley 1907), p. 23.

20. Chalmers, op. cit., p. 814.

21. Chalmers, loc. cit.

22. Carlile, op. cit.

23. Metcalf, op. cit., pp. 460-1.

24. See M. Blair, *The Paisley Shawl* (1904).

25. M. McCarthy, *A Social Geography of Paisley* (Paisley 1969), p. 97.

26. Chalmers, op. cit., pp. 815-6, McCarthy, op. cit., p. 72.

27. See McCarthy, op. cit., pp. 80-2; R. Brown, *The History of Paisley* (Paisley 1885), Vol. 2, pp. 218-224. Brown is a valuable source of verbatim quotations from primary sources.

28. Smout, op. cit., pp. 400-402. See also N. Murray, *The Scottish Handloom Weavers* (Edinburgh 1978).

29. *New Statistical Account of Scotland*, 1845, p. 268.

30. Foster, op. cit., p. 80.

31. Thompson (1968), op. cit., chapter 9; also Smout, op. cit., chapter XVII and Murray, op. cit.

32. McCarthy, op. cit., p. 66.

33. Brown, op. cit., Vol. 2, pp. 89-90.

34. *The Posthumous Works of William McGavin* (Paisley 1910), Vol. 1, p. 16.

35. *Old Statistical Account* 1793, Vol. VII, p. 90.

36. James Orr, weaver, in evidence to the Select Committee on Handloom Weavers' Petitions, 1835, *Parliamentary Papers*, Vol. 88, Minutes of Evidence.

37. Main source: *Old Statistical Account*, Vol. VII, pp. 90-91.

38. M. Blair (1904), op. cit., pp. 46-8.

39. Blair (1904), p. 48.

40. Smout, op. cit., p. 396.

41. R. Brown, op. cit., Vol. 2, p.46.

42. W. Taylor, 'An answer to Mr. Carlile's sketches of Paisley' (Paisley 1809), p. 9, Paisley Public Library.

43. Thompson (1968), op. cit., chapter 14.

44. Murray, op. cit.; see also Thompson (1968), op. cit., pp. 306-7.

45. Report of the Select Committee on Handloom Weavers' Petitions, 1835, *Parliamentary Papers*, Vol. 88, p. 4. See also Smout, op. cit., p. 400.

46. Ibid., p. 4.

47. Ibid., p. 4.

48. J. Handley, *The Irish in Scotland 1798-1845* (Cork 1945), esp. chapter 4.

49. Evidence of J. Parkhill to the Assistant Handloom Weavers' Commissioners (1839), *Parliamentary Papers*, Vol. 151, p. 12.

50. Thompson (1968), op. cit., p. 307 ff.

51. Carlile, op. cit., pp. 17-18.

52. Thompson (1968), op. cit., p. 289.

53. Alexander Carlile, cotton thread manufacturer, cited in Handley, op. cit., p. 99.

54. 'Report of a meeting of the Paisley New Zealand Emigration Society', in *Paisley Pamphlets*, Vol. 25, 1840, Paisley Public Library.'

55. On the refusal of poor relief, see the *Statement and Minutes of the Committee for the Relief of the Unemployed in Paisley and Renfrewshire, 12.10.1841*; papers of Sir John Maxwell, Glasgow Archives. On religion, see below.

56. *Old Statistical Account*, p. 88.

57. New Statistical Account, p. 274.

58. J. Parkhill, *The History of Paisley* (Paisley 1857), p. 32, emphasis added.

59. *Old Statistical Account*, p. 93.

60. Handley, op. cit., pp. 98, 103.

61. Cited in Handley, p. 99.

62. Foster, op. cit., p. 129, fig. 21.

63. Handley, op. cit., p. 305 ff.

64. Young (1979), op. cit., p. 80.

65. Handley, op. cit., p. 310 ff.

66. Ibid., pp. 304-5.

67. Foster, op. cit., pp. 218-220.

68. Report of the Select Committee on Handloom Weavers' Petitions, 1835, *Parliamentary Papers*, Vol. 88, p. 12.

69. Ibid., p. 4.

70. Ibid. Analysis of Evidence, p. 87.

71. I. Levitt and T. C. Smout, *The State of the Scottish Working Class in 1843* (Edinburgh 1980), chapters 7, 8 and 9.

72. *Old Statistical Account*, Vol. VII, p. 68.

73. R. Brown, op. cit., Vol. 2, p. 220.

74. Thompson, op. cit., p. 333.

75. See P. Anderson, op. cit.; also R. Johnson, 'Edward Thompson . . . and Socialist Humanist History', *History Workshop Journal* 6, 1978, pp. 79-100, and K. McClelland, 'Some Comments on Johnson', *History Workshop Journal* 7, 1979, pp. 101-115.

76. J. Parkhill, op. cit., pp. 91-2. For a very similar plea to the weavers, see 'A Short Address to the Weavers of Paisley . . . by an Inhabitant' 7.7.1819, in *Paisley Pamphlets*, Vol. 9, 1824.

77. K. Burgess, 'Workshop of the world: Client capitalism at its zenith, 1830-1870' in Dickson, op. cit., p. 205 ff.

78. A. Wilson, *The Chartist Movement in Scotland*, op. cit., p. 178.

79. *The Beauties of Scotland*, op. cit., p. 459.

80. M. Blair (1907), op. cit., p. 44.

81. See McCarthy, op. cit., chapter 5.

82. Foster, op. cit., p. 185.

83. *Local Memorabilia*, Paisley Public Library, 1885: 'Demolition of the Town's House. The Public Inn. The Saracen's Head Inn. Second Paper'.

84. Ibid.

85. Ibid.

86. R. Brown, op. cit., Vol. 2, pp. 106-116.

87. *Local Memorabilia*, Paisley Public Library: 'Demolition of an Old House Built in 1655. Second Paper'.

E

88. See R. Brown, op. cit., Vol. 2, pp. 166-8 for full text.

89. Dickson and Clarke, op. cit.

90. Thompson (1968), op. cit., p. 135 ff; W. Ferguson, *Scotland, 1689 to the Present* (Edinburgh 1968), p. 248 ff.

91. McCarthy, op. cit., p. 80.

92. R. Brown, op. cit., Vol. 2, p. 219.

93. J. Parkhill, op. cit., p. 34.

94. Thompson (1968), op. cit., p. 200.

95. *Local Memorabilia*, Paisley Public Library 1885, Section on the Napoleonic Wars.

96. Ibid.

97. Anderson, *Arguments within English Marxism*, op. cit., p. 37.

98. R. Brown, op. cit., p. 76.

99. J. Parkhill, op. cit., p. 35.

100. J. Parkhill, *Autobiography of Arthur Sneddon* (Paisley).

101. W. M. Metcalfe, op. cit., p. 370; also R. Brown, op. cit., pp. 99-100.

102. Smout, op. cit., p. 397.

103. R. Brown, op. cit., p. 148.

104. Ibid., p. 168.

105. Ibid.

106. Ibid., p. 171.

107. Ibid., p. 172.

108. Ibid., pp. 184, 186. Detailed eye-witness reports of the 1819 riots are reproduced in Brown, pp. 172-184.

109. Ibid., p. 185.

110. J. Parkhill, *History of Paisley*, op. cit., pp. 52-3.

111. Ibid., pp. 49-50. Cleggs were metal darts, flighted like shuttlecocks.

112. J. Parkhill, *Autobiography of Arthur Sneddon*, op. cit., p. 74.

113. R. Brown, op. cit., p. 192.

114. F. K. Donnelly, 'The Scottish Rising of 1820: A Re-Interpretation', *Scottish Tradition*, Vol. VI, 1976, p. 29.

115. Young (1979), op. cit., esp. pp. 60-61.

116. Brown, op. cit., pp. 170-2, 184-5.

117. Young (1979), op. cit., p. 61.

118. For example, in the trial of seven Radicals by Special Commission in Paisley in July/August 1820, the occupations of six of the accused were given. Five were weavers and the other a shoemaker. Cf. Brown, op. cit., pp. 205-7.

119. Ibid., p. 259.

120. 'Objects and rules of the Renfrewshire Political Union . . .', *Paisley Pamphlets*, Vol. 16, 1831, Paisley Public Library.

121. A. Wilson, *The Chartist Movement* . . ., op. cit., p. 28.

122. See R. Brown, op. cit., pp. 256-70.

123. Anderson, *Arguments* . . ., op. cit., p. 43; and for the following, pp. 43-49.

124. Young (1978), op. cit., p. 61.

125. Ibid., pp. 79, 81-2. However, Young groups together disparate types of crowd action, and conflates 'riots or the fear of riots' (p. 82).

126. Brown, op. cit., p. 259.

127. Thompson (1968), op. cit., p. 105. .

128. Ibid., p. 195.

129. 'Sir John Maxwell's Second Address to the . . . Electors of Paisley' 28.7.1832, *Paisley Pamphlets*, Vol. 57/2, Paisley Public Library; more generally, see Brown, op. cit., pp. 272-4.

130. See Brown, op. cit., p. 275, note 1 where a resolution of a meeting of non-electors, proposing the use of 'exclusive dealing', is reproduced.

131. Foster, op. cit., chapter 3.

132. Ibid., pp. 133-7.

133. K. Burgess, 'Workshop of the World . . .', op. cit., p. 211.

134. A. Wilson, 'The Chartist Movement . . .', op. cit., p. 36 ff; 'The Case of the Cotton Spinners Considered', report of a public meeting in Paisley 29.1.1838, *Paisley Pamphlets*, Vol. 23, 1838, Paisley Public Library.

135. P. Brewster, 'Seven Chartist and Military Sermons', *Paisley Pamphlets*, Vol. 252, 1843, p. 47.

136. A. Wilson, 'Chartism in Glasgow' in A. Briggs (ed.), *Chartist Studies* (London 1959), p. 256n.

137. *Paisley Advertiser* 30.7.1842 and 6.8.1842 for letters of William Barr; evidence of John Henderson, Report of the Select Committee on Distress (Paisley) 1843, *Parliamentary Papers*, Vol. 373.

138. *True Scotsman*, 26.1.1839; A. Wilson, *The Chartist Movement* . . ., p. 67.

139. P. Brewster, 'Address to the Radicals of Scotland', *True Scotsman*, 9.2.1839.

140. L. C. Wright, *Scottish Chartism*, op. cit., pp. 71-2.

141. A. Wilson, *The Chartist Movement* . . ., op. cit., pp. 87.

142. Cited in J. Godfrey and E. Goldie, *Chartism and Paisley* (Jordanhill College, Glasgow 1978), p. 26.

143. Letter signed 'Z' of Paisley, *True Scotsman*, 2.1.1841 — one of a series of reports from this correspondent.

144. B. Harrison and P. Hollis (eds.), *Robert Lowery: Radical and Chartist* (London 1979), p. 137.

145. See M. Jenkins, op. cit.; J. Foster, op. cit., p. 114 ff.

146. *Paisley Advertiser*, 6.8.1842, 13.8.1842, 20.8.1842. Thanks are due to Andrew Eccles for allowing us access to his materials of the 1842 strike in Scotland. This was not as widespread or well-co-ordinated as was the strike in the English north and midlands. In both countries many Chartists were opposed to a strike for the Charter during an acute depression, especially at the outset. The National Charter Association, whose delegates were involved in the English strike, had much less influence in Scotland. On the role of the N.C.A. in the strike, see Jenkins, op. cit., inc. Appendix B. On the strike in Scotland, see A. Wilson, *The Chartist Movement* . . ., op. cit., pp. 190-5.

147. Handley, op. cit., p. 317.

148. See above, note 134; Wright, op. cit., p. 38.

149. A. Wilson, op. cit., pp. 121-2.

150. Ibid., p. 119.

151. Ibid., p. 171.

152. Minutes of relief committee — see above, note 55. Also Levitt and Smout, op. cit., p. 156.

153. *Paisley Advertiser*, 30.7.1842 and 6.8.1842.

154. R. Brown, op. cit., p. 223.

155. Levitt and Smout, op. cit., p. 158.

156. A. Wilson, op. cit., pp. 174-5; *Chartist Minutes*, 21.9.1842, Paisley Public Library.

157. *New Statistical Account*, p. 228.

158. Smout, *A History* . . ., op. cit., p. 395.

159. 'To the Labouring Classes in Paisley', *Paisley Pamphlets*, Vol. 26, 1841, Paisley Public Library.

160. Cited in A. Wilson, op. cit., p. 142, and on Christian Chartism, chapter 11. See also K. Burgess, 'Workshop of the World . . ., op. cit., pp. 209-11.

161. Burgess, op. cit.

162. Appendix to 'Seven Chartist and Military Sermons', op. cit.

163. Burgess, op. cit., p. 221 ff.

164. Thompson (1968), op. cit., p. 176.

165. Foster, op. cit., p. 103.

166. Ibid., p. 250, and more generally chapter 7.

167. J. Saville, 'Class struggle and the industrial revolution', *Social Register*, 1974, p. 240.

168. Ibid., pp. 239-240.

169. 'Report of the discussion on socialism between Messrs L. Jones and C. Leckie, Glasgow 1839', *Paisley Pamphlets*, Vol. 24, 1839, Paisley Public Library.

170. See K. Burgess, 'Workshop of the World . . .', op. cit., esp. pp. 194-224.

2

Scottish Industrialists and the Changing Character of Class Relations in the Clyde Region c. 1880-1918

Joseph Melling

THE history of class relations has often suffered from the limited attention given to the activities of industrial employers, despite their acknowledged importance in the ranks of propertied interests. We know far more about the subtle gradations within the working class during the nineteenth century than the distribution of wealth and power amongst the dominant groups of Victorian Britain. Social historians have given us a sensitive awareness of historical change experienced in the lower reaches of bourgeois society, without portraying the businessman's reactions to the most significant of events. One of the more serious obstacles to an adequate understanding of class relations is our failure to concede to employers the same degree of social awareness and cultural achievement as that accredited to the common people. Unless we do so, it is impossible to account for the remarkable survival of major propertied interests in the world's oldest industrial society. By examining the contribution of industrialists to class relations we are able to define the limits as well as the importance of their activities, thereby locating the owners of factories and workshops amongst the capitalist class in Britain.

Whilst historians have usually failed to examine in any detail those constructing and controlling industrial production, there has been a somewhat exaggerated emphasis on workplace struggles and organisations in the advance of class relations. Important changes have taken place since the period when the Webbs or Thomas Johnston could depict working class movements in terms of trade union initiatives, but there is a recurring tendency towards economistic narrowness in even the most impressive accounts.[1] This deficiency is not wholly absent from the recent debates on the capitalist labour process, which initially relegated labour to a historically passive role in the forces of production whereas employers were accorded a very powerful strategic hold over industrial management.[2] Other contributions have illustrated the very positive and creative part which labour played in industrialisation, and its subsequent importance in the negotiation of key innovations.[3] Working people were only able to achieve a secure position in industry because they shared values and common organisations *beyond* the workplace, as well as in the labour process itself. Factory recruitment was painfully resisted by large groups of handicraft workers, determined to preserve their independence against strict supervision of work rhythms.[4] Even the dispossessed peasants and rural labourers who flooded into the expanding towns of industrial Britain carried their cultural traditions and working methods through the factory gates and machine shops. When the habitual resistance to rigorous discipline gave way, other forms of opposition remained — ranging from the early craft societies to the informal customs of output restriction prevalent in many trades.

In these respects, industrialisation was a process incorporating many of the skills and practices of pre-industrial society whilst imposing a rigid framework of organisation and direction on many key occupations. Increasing division of labour involved a sharper separation of workplace from domestic life, as well as creating fresh sectional barriers amongst the proletarians. But it did not extinguish the non-work experiences of employed trades, or reduce the great diversity of occupations and work outlets open to the population. In many ways the industrial revolution only extended the range of labouring tasks and the motley assortment of customs and payment systems which made up capitalist production.[5] Employers often depended on their skilled men to test and adapt the new machinery being developed, whilst in sectors like shipbuilding the inexperienced workmen directly participated in the evolution of a whole range of fresh ironworking techniques. It would be clearly inaccurate to represent the progressive division of labour as simply an immutable tendency towards the deskilling of workers, rather than a constant restructuring of different workforces as sections of employees were degraded, regraded and upgraded by the reshaping of production. Working people were able to influence this advance in production by adapting to particular processes, resisting the introduction of others and offering a creative alternative to management initiatives which implied further deskilling or tighter supervision.

This continuing negotiation of economic innovations depended on the existence of particular market conditions: not only the competitive product markets in which manufacturers operated but also labour markets which provided workers for the employers. Under certain favourable conditions and in distinct trades, industrialists were more inclined to concede a measure of autonomy to the workforce than in a harsher trading climate. Thus the 'frontier of control' established between capitalist management and labour varied between industries and shifted according to peculiar market forces. There *were* significant general advances in technical innovation, management organisation, and the scale and sophistication of enterprises during the later nineteenth century, but their impact in alternative sectors of the British economy was largely determined by the employers' subjective appraisal of costs and benefits in prevailing market conditions. Similarly, the character of industrial conflict tended to revolve around certain key issues of control: but the relative importance of these disputes and their prominence at different periods depended on the environment of distinct trades. Confrontations over entry to the work process, the control of specific areas of work, the handling of particular tools and machines, the conditions and methods of payment, and problems of disciplining and supervision, all involved the question of *control* at the workplace and were all present to some degree in quite distinct industries. But the weight and scope of the conflict varied sharply between occupations and skills as similar as those found in engineering and iron shipbuilding. Any account of the advances in production and labour resistance must be examined in terms of the objective constraints, market forces and the pattern of conflict prevalent in each industry during the nineteenth century.

The contrasting experiences of different sectors, and even in the regional development of the same industry, had important implications for the sectional awareness of working people. The same forces of innovation and change which divided work processes had contradictory tendencies towards fragmentation and consolidation amongst employers and labourers alike, partly reflected in the respective organisations created during the later half of the last century. These were more often agencies for the defence of established prerogatives in the industrial conflicts of the period, rather than serious instruments of economic reorganisation, but they often formalised the negotiation of change within each industry. Thus any broader collective action by capital or labour and any sharp delineation of class antagonisms across industries involved the accommodation of interests and groupings *within* the ranks of employers and labourers — suggesting the consciousness of a greater common interest rather than just pragmatic alliances.

The way in which such a consciousness is created may depend on the experience of relations and conflicts beyond the formal work obligations of industry. Indeed, some historians have argued that the very different economic structure of towns and cities affected the industrial and social relations to such a degree that the spatial fragmentation of industrial society must be considered a major factor in its political development.[6] Other writers have emphasised the degree to which local developments and identities limited the political horizons of the working class, making class co-operation far more common than direct conflict in such areas.[7] It is suggested that such distinctions not only fragmented class awareness and deflected collective action, but also tended to legitimise industrial authority by reproducing workplace hierarchies within local areas and allowing employers to publicise their social concern for the wellbeing of their employees.[8] Whilst areas of industrial Lancashire and the West Riding may have seen violent social protest during the 1840s, numerous settlements from Birmingham to Glossop clearly did not. Moreover, even the scenes of physical force Chartism were later to become major examples of class co-operation and social stability, indicating the temporary character of direct antagonisms.

It is frequently in this context that alternative concepts to that of 'class relations' are introduced by social historians attempting to convey and explain the importance of more intimate relationships in capitalist society. Such writers often deploy the ideas of 'community', 'paternalism' and 'deference', to depict contacts between classes as well as connections within a social class. There are a number of initial difficulties in attempting to apply such concepts as 'community', however attractive they may appear as tools of analysis. Recent debates over the term itself demonstrate the hazards of transplanting words between disciplines such as history and anthropology, when no satisfactory definitions or consistency of usage are available.[9] The concept has long been current in studies of peasant societies, although its connotations have differed as sharply here as elsewhere.[10] Marxists have been equally willing to utilise the term as conservative or liberal academics, though there is again a diversity of meanings accorded to the word in classical and subsequent Marxist writing.[11]

Rather than seeking to construct the most vital elements of 'community' in the bulk of existing literature, it is more fruitful to see words such as 'community', 'paternalism' and 'deference' as themselves the product of historical development and cultural expression rather than as neutral abstractions which we can use to encompass stages in the development of fundamentally different societies. This is all the more necessary when we can trace the widespread and changing usage of words like 'community', and the differences in meaning attached to them by alternative groups at a particular time. It is significant that the original coiners of the word 'community' were not the spokesmen of tribal or peasant society, but the self-conscious advocates of medieval bourgeois privileges. The communal obligation created within the framework of European feudalism offered a material and political alternative to the oath of fealty binding unequal parties in a chain of vertical relationships.[12] The later appropriation of the word by positivist social science took place, again significantly, following the great bourgeois advances of Enlightenment and European revolutions when the erosion of ties of personal dependence and spread of looser market or civil relations offered a fresh basis for contrast.[13] This shift in the connotation of community, from bourgeois nexus in feudal society to the supposed opposite of wider market relations as depicted by German sociology, illustrates the persistent inversion of definitions which such key words have suffered. This is hardly surprising, given the saturation of intellectual life by different currents of bourgeois ideology, and the basic importance of language itself in the construction of this ideology. Surveys of terms such as 'community' have shown the degree to which they evoke a desirable moral order whilst also claiming to depict existing relations and sentiments within society.[14]

Similar comments can be made about the concepts 'paternalism' and 'deference', since they appear to have originated in the period of intense historical change and bourgeois revolution during the seventeenth century.[15] Rather than contributing to the more liberal and individualistic trend in political philosophy, however, concepts such as 'paternalism' articulated the contrary assertion of respect for established authority and state power — without which civil society could not exist. This counterpoint to unrestrained possessive individualism partly reflected the ambiguous outcome of the struggle between traditional monarchy and the progressive forces of bourgeois revolution, resulting in the alternative vision of morality formulated by Hobbes and restated by Burke and Bagehot. Even more than the concept of community, ideas of paternalism and deference belong to the complex evolution of bourgeois ideology, embodying a prescription for correct behaviour as well as a claim to describe contemporary society.

Thus if we are to understand the origins of the language used to describe social relations in bourgeois society, we must focus initially upon the transition to that form of society and the sharpened awareness which this process stimulated. For it was in this period that language extended previous intellectual boundaries and threw up such words as 'community', 'paternalism' and 'deference' as well as the notion of class itself. As the advances in production threw up fresh social forces, so whole groups expressed their aspirations in new ways or refashioned older words and ideas to meet their own interests. Conflicting elements appropriated and translated current notions of morality to legitimate their actions against established authority, though frequently claiming to uphold lawful practices. Thompson has illustrated the way in which eighteenth century crowds of food rioters incorporated traditional notions of 'paternalist' regulation in their attacks on profiteers taking advantage of market conditions.[16] On the eve of the triumph of bourgeois political economy and the dismantling of the last relics of state control, protesting mobs of people composed their own 'moral economy' of legitimate behaviour — in which the governing class partly concurred. It is arguable that in this setting paternalism comprised more than a 'model' of traditional rights and regulations, or that it subsequently gave way to the rationalism of the classical economists. Both philosophies presented an image of society which encompassed political as well as economic imperatives, and gave an important role to state authority in the preservation of civil society. There was a significant shift towards market freedom during the birth of industrial capitalism, but the ideology of paternalism and deference survived along with numerous practices of pre-capitalist government. Similarly, the cultural traditions and inherited beliefs which formed the basis of the 'moral economy' were not completely submerged by the triumph of industrial capitalism, however retarded in the transformation from common people to proletariat.

In order to understand the growth of class relations in Scotland, and the particular contribution which employers made to these relations, we must examine the genesis of Scottish capitalism and rise of industrial production on Clydeside and elsewhere. Only then will we appreciate the context in which contemporaries used such words as 'community', and what this tells us about prevailing ideology as well as actual conditions in Scottish society. Just as industrialisation was to some degree a process of negotiation between antagonistic interests, so the creation of an urban environment and new cultural forms were part of a social terrain never wholly dominated by Scottish industrialists.

Scottish capitalism and the development of regional industry

The inherent weakness and divisions of Scottish feudal society made it a constant prey to the succession of invasions and conflicts which powerfully influenced its development.[17] Torn by internal brigandage and clan alliances and threatened by English expansion, the Scots nobility were remarkably successful in their limitation of monarchical authority and sustained defeat of Catholic Stuart pretensions. Whilst breaching the moves towards strong central government in Scotland and effectively removing religious institutions from direct dependence on the crown, the landed interests were unable to generate a strong bourgeois contingent or establish an independent trading economy capable of challenging England's growing empire in the seventeenth and eighteenth centuries.[18] The political reliance on English protection and support against Catholic absolutism was not lessened by their military defeats at the hands of Cromwellian forces, or the later trading rivalry culminating in the Darien fiasco. Union of the parliaments in 1707 really conceded the remnants of economic independence and political autonomy in return for access to the spoils of British empire, though their distribution initially flowed mainly in the form of patronage to the patrician aristocracy of Scottish society.[19]

These political developments were of fundamental importance in shaping the course of Scottish capitalism thereafter, as well as the *distribution* of wealth and power north of the border. The gradual transformation of agriculture and commerce during the eighteenth century was accomplished by larger propertied elements, who succeeded in enhancing their own accumulation without a dramatic change in the service relationships which still dominated the Scottish economy.[20] Even the shift to more advanced cultivation or sheep farming did not require an immediate departure from the land for a rural populace able to diversify in kelp, fishing and potato planting once the shepherds replaced ploughmen. Substantial progress in linen manufacturing also tended to reinforce the domestic base of the handicraft economy, rather than producing a massive movement of population and rapid urbanisation in the Lowlands. Fabulous fortunes were made in the tobacco trading districts of Glasgow whilst Edinburgh merchants were financing the urban growth which resulted in the Scottish Enlightenment, but again it was the middle class and

luxury tradesman who really reaped many of the benefits in the dawn of commercial capitalism.

The character of economic growth confirmed the dominant position of the
large landowners, whilst facilitating the precocious development of commercial, financial (particularly banking) and professional interests, with the
bulk of manufacturing carried on under the control of putting-out or mercantile capitalists. Perhaps even more so than in England and Wales, capitalist
market relations evolved out of the post-feudal stage of production without a
fundamental rupture in property holding or the distribution of wealth. Moreover, these advances took place within the economic and political structure of
British imperial mercantilism, which affected not only the emphasis given to
specific exports but also the outlook and mentality of the flourishing professional groups of bourgeois Scotland.

Scottish industrialists arrived on the scene during the last decades of the
eighteenth and first of the nineteenth centuries, to find that the owners of the
soil and of the financial and trading houses possessed a strong hold over
political influence. It is true that the Glasgow business community became
bitterly disillusioned with British colonial policy during the 1770s and 1780s,
indicated by the founding of the first mainland Chamber of Commerce in the
city.[21] Aristocratic leadership and the patrician connexions of London politics
were also questioned during the Napoleonic Wars and their aftermath, but this
was hardly an effective political challenge and involved relatively few
industrialists. It was not until the 1840s that the grievances over trading conditions, Corn Law restrictions, and growing legislative interference with
industry mobilised large numbers of industrial businessmen along with other
interests.[22]

Even at this period of active campaigning and middle class consciousness,
there were innumerable divisions within the ranks of the employers as well as
differences separating them from other forms of bourgeois property. The large
coalowner of Lanarkshire had little in common with the Paisley millocrat or
railway magnate, while each had even less connection with the small handi-
craftsman printer or the sweatshop tailor of large cities. Within individual
trades there were the problems of distance and personal competition to overcome before industrialists could correspond socially, and the physical dispersal
of manufacturing settlements made frequent contact difficult. Employers did
not form a coherent group, were rarely active in politics or wider society, and
could only be brought to act collectively with great difficulty. During the years
of industrialisation they articulated their aspirations through the medium of
the church — usually the Free Kirk — and were prepared to limit their
challenge to aristocratic patronage and London rule, to an unswerving support
for the Liberal Party in Scotland.[23]

The highly diverse and fragmented character of Scottish employers was
largely the consequence of their origins and their quite distinct experiences of
industrialisation itself. The pace of innovation and the tempo of workplace

relations differed substantially between trades, as did the labour requirements of individual industries or concerns. Scotland's natural resources and geographical situation were geared to meeting the needs of an expanding British economy and its overseas markets, although competition *with* regions in England and Wales was to become a major feature of her subsequent economic development. In some instances the growth of industries and the creation of an industrial infrastructure were actually retarded and distorted by the uneven character of the transition towards capitalism in Scotland. This was nowhere more evident than in the progress of the building industry, obviously essential to creation of manufacturing bases and the generation of economic activity in the regional economy. Here the contradictions between the existing network of property relations and the requirements of expanding production were most apparent as the Clyde rose to become a major industrial centre.[24] Interested parties in the construction of dwellings and factories were the landed interests derived feu rents in perpetuity, speculators relying on credit and the prospect of sale to middle class purchasers, financial interests holding the bond of mortgage which was usually required for acquisition, and various professional groups negotiating the transactions. In the case of dwellings for working class rental (which was the most common form of tenancy) there would be the profits accruing to the owner, the commission charged by a variety of legal agents such as house factors, and the rates levied by local authorities and police commissions — all of which would be eventually shouldered in the rents arranged by monthly or weekly lets to working class occupants.

Industrial employers and other propertied elements were themselves burdened by many of these charges and not infrequently hostile to the raising of rents and rates within a local area. Their primary concern was clearly to achieve and sustain profitability within the market conditions prevailing, but since labour markets were of keen concern to these growing enterprises they were naturally anxious that housing should be available at reasonable rents in the immediate locality. Since the housing market and building cycles operated according to a range of variable factors outwith the control of either industrialists or speculative building entrepreneurs, employers were occasionally persuaded into direct intervention in the provision of accommodation when market forces failed to meet their needs. One of the reasons for the recurring difficulties of the building industry itself being the persistent strategic hold of craftsmen over work processes, the conditions and relations of different sectors were of vital significance in the rise of the regional economy. Thus in tracing the responses of industrialists to changing business needs and problems of labour discipline, it is essential to keep this interconnection between distinct areas of production in mind as well as the links binding market conditions with productive relations in manufacturing itself.

Industrial development and workplace relations in the Clyde region

The initial responses of both employers and workpeople to the process of accelerating industrialisation were conditioned by the persistence of pre-industrial skills and practices, and the experience of mass migration during the early decades of the nineteenth century. Whilst the period saw the demise of many feudal relics, including the termination of bondage and personal service ties in mining and rural areas, this often inhibited the resistance to new industrial methods by completely disorientating those leaving the countryside for manufacturing settlements. Alternatively, the complicated pattern of industrialisation and continuation of handicraft alongside mechanised output channeled working class energies in different directions, thereby deflecting potential resistance. Thirdly, the tide of migration sweeping from Lowlands, Highlands and Ireland into the Clyde valley carried along the culture and traditions of peasants without any real conception of factory organisation or the problems of urban life in cities like Glasgow. Caught up as they were in this whirlpool of economic forces, employers frequently resorted to a harsh disciplining of their workforce whilst labourers strove to maintain a measure of resistance and some control over their bewildering situation by resorting to a variety of tactics in the workplace. Those landlords who attempted to take advantage of the booming employment in towns like Paisley, Greenock and the burghs around Glasgow to charge high rents, also experienced a similar depth of opposition from tenants with fresh memories of the bitter struggles over settlement rights.[25]

The industrialisation of the west of Scotland was dominated by the ascendancy of distinct sectors in four major stages of development from the early nineteenth century. The first period saw the transition of textiles from linen to cotton (or cotton-based) fabrics and the dramatic collapse of hand-loom manufacturing thereafter as competition with power looms increased. Whilst this decline was still in progress, there occurred the important discoveries of ironmaking techniques and the spread of coal and iron production during the 1830s and 1840s. The growth in trade and movement of population stimulated the building of railways and locomotive engineering during these middle decades of the century, which in turn generated considerable construction activity in areas hitherto isolated from the changing world of industry and trade. A fourth major stage of innovation came with the increased demand for iron steamships, in which the Clyde established an early expertise, and the third quarter of the century saw crucial local inventions in marine engineering which secured the reputation of the Scottish yards. Each stage of industrial expansion was accompanied by a division of labour in which the workpeople contributed, even if negatively, to the forces as well as the relations of capitalist production. One important consequence was the imposition of a marked sexual division of labour, not only between but also within staple industries, which contributed to the wider social divisions affecting Scottish society.

In many respects the Scottish textile industry possessed an advantage over its counterpart in Lancashire, having developed later than the English sector and thereby enjoying the fruits of improved technology and experience during the 1830s.[26] Plentiful supplies of labour and the availability of investment capital encouraged early textile masters to construct large mills in Lanarkshire, frequently more rigorously organised and supervised than in England. At the same time, however, Lancashire quickly established a hold over the bulk delivery of raw materials from America and a specialised knowledge of markets which Scottish employers found difficult to equal. During the unpredictable conditions of the 1830s and 1840s, manufacturers were compelled to concentrate on the fancy fabrics whilst resisting the pressures from labour for improved wages. When masters attempted to introduce wage cuts in a period of depression, they encountered bitter resistance from the male-dominated spinning section of the trade.[27] This challenge to management authority was defeated and then destroyed by the outlawing of the unions and ruthless replacement of skilled males by inexperienced females wherever practicable. Rather than delegating responsibilities for supervision and discipline to an autonomous stratum of manual workers, the employers insisted on a tighter control over superintending labour in both weaving and spinning departments.[28]

The inherent fragility of the cotton industry was only to become fully apparent later in the nineteenth century, when the whole British trade was being pressed by the modern factories of Germany and the U.S.A. Scotland suffered the additional disadvantages of changing fashions and diminished demand for the fancy trades in which it excelled, and from the lower workloads in the weaving sheds — partly dictated by the widespread use of younger women and the attentive care required in the completion of intricate pattern-work on fancy products. Whilst the Lancashire concerns directed their trade towards the easier imperial and neutral markets, Lanarkshire firms often shifted into the manufacture and printing of coarser calico cloth (in which again Lanarkshire competed with Lancashire on disadvantageous terms), or attempted to intensify workloads in their mills.[29] Having relied so heavily on the low wages of their female employees to sustain them in competitive periods, employers were unable to persuade either male or female workers to take on additional burdens for a plainly inadequate return during the 1870s and 1880s. By the end of the nineteenth century the manufacture of textiles was in terminal decline, with resistance again evident in the cotton districts of Bridgeton and Paisley.[30] Only where progressive manufacturers diversified into the production of thread or specialised in high quality goods could such a catastrophic descent be arrested. Even then it took all the ingenuity and determination of imported managerial talent like Phillippi of the Paisley giants, J. P. Coats, to introduce a more rational approach to production and marketing in lines such as cotton thread.

The same individual who restored the fortunes of the Coats empire was prominent amongst the new generation of managerialists and cartel advocates who set up the Calico Printers' Association trust in Scotland during the 1900s.[31] This combine controlled 85% of total British calico printing by the pre-War years, although the fourteen Scottish constituents shared their dominant position with the powerful United Turkey Red concern which had been formed in 1890 as a result of amalgamations between firms and plants in the famous Vale of Leven settlements.[32] The processes carried on by textile printers were similar to the staple industry in that they relied on cheaper female workers — frequently imported from outside the West of Scotland — to labour in their bleach plants, oily houses and colour plants at Levenside near Loch Lomond.[33] Unlike the textile firms of Glasgow or Paisley, the printing employers also relied upon a considerable contingent of skilled male workers who commanded the respect and trade recognition of their masters. The workplace elite were the talented designers and engravers who created the patterns capable of maintaining a hold over the notoriously fickle Indian markets, and who became more valuable as competition increased.[34] Less prestigious but almost as well organised were the printing machinists who gave an expert finishing to the dyed cloth and whose control of the machinery was reinforced by their national union membership. In the hazardous trading climate of the late nineteenth century their employers could only convince them of the need for greater productivity by careful negotiation and sensitive conciliation of union officials.[35] Although they enjoyed a remarkable success in this policy until the immediate pre-War period, dyeing and printing manufacturers found unrest spreading rapidly just before the outbreak of War amongst quite distinct grades of their workforce at areas like Leven.[36]

The problems of creating attractive products with distinctive design features also occupied the time of carpet manufacturers such as James Templeton of Greenhead. By employing mostly younger females in his mechanised carpet works at Glasgow, Templeton was already the largest carpet maker in Scotland by the 1860s and employed over five hundred people when he was visited by David Bremner.[37] The prospect of growing domestic demand for carpets rather than linoleum, and the effective management decisions taken by Templeton and others allowed them to make large fortunes whilst the cotton manufacturers were afflicted with contracting markets and workplace resistance. Indeed, the higher female wages and better working conditions offered by employers such as Templetons attracted many women away from the cotton sheds and hardened the opposition to intensified exploitation by staple textile manufacturers.

Another branch of Scottish textiles which enjoyed improving markets during the later part of the century was the rope and twine trades, which responded to the massive expansion of shipbuilding by diversifying into hard fibres, twine manufacture and metal ropes at centres such as Greenock and

Govan. During the 1880s there were seventy firms engaged in ropemaking at Glasgow, though the regional industry was already dominated by such large enterprises as The Gourock Company near Port Glasgow. In a favourable situation for the shipyards and Clyde docks, these employers were successful in carrying through both technical and organisational changes at their plants, whilst continuing to depend on abundant supplies of female workers. Finding that there was a shortage of women at Port Glasgow, the Gourock firm opened a fresh works at nearby Greenock where ready workers could be hired without difficulty.[38] The same flexibility and diversification enabled the Gourock management to respond quickly to the extraordinary demand for tents and camping equipment during such imperialist campaigns as the Boer War, which was only one aspect of growing benefits from overseas colonial links enjoyed by such manufacturers.[39]

Even a brief survey of the changing fortunes of the Scottish textile industry illustrates at once its heterogeneous character and its reliance upon a reasonably passive and hardworking labour force. The contrasting experiences of cotton manufacture, calico printing and dyeing, carpet making, and the hard fibre trades of rope production make any generalisations about the textiles sector extremely superficial. They shared a common requirement in cheaper female workers but each depended on male supervisory and managerial grades if not actual manual operatives to some degree. Concern was also widespread over the growth of international competition after 1870, though the employers' ability to respond varied according to material and managerial resources. Organised resistance was relatively rare before the 1890s, though a mounting tide of unrest can be traced amongst quite different grades in the staple industry and dyeing sectors during the pre-War years. The more astute employers recognised the depth of this resistance and channeled their negotiations for increasing output via recognised union bargaining, delegating responsibility for maintaining output in some degree to the offical representatives of workmen. In many other branches of textiles the business leaders failed to initiate a creative alternative to either the low-wage traditions or the deteriorating market environment, thereby running the risks of unfair competition and of provoking spontaneous, unorganised disruption amongst the workforce.

Whereas the textiles industry evolved a system of factory production based on rigorous supervision of largely female labour, the mining of coal and iron continued as a male-dominated occupation throughout the century. The Lanarkshire coalfield quickly established itself as the principal source of national coal resources and was still contributing over half Scotland's output in the 1920s.[40] As one of Britain's great inland coalfields, Lanarkshire was directly dependent on the market demand of industrialists and householders in the West of Scotland rather than on coastal or export outlets for its product. Particularly significant was the call for supplies from the iron foundries with whom many of the larger colliery owners developed close contacts after the introduction of hot-blast ironmaking techniques during the 1830s. Such substantial employers had experienced real difficulties in attracting the necessary labour after the final termination of colliery bondage in the 1790s, but the great flood of immigration during the middle decades of the century fortunately coincided with the crucial breakthroughs in heavy industries and facilitated the rapid advance of coalmining. Even the limitations on the employment of women and young persons during the 1840s was offset by the arrival of Irish peasant labour ready to spend unlimited hours beneath the surface of Lanarkshire.

Tight regulation of the collier's work was clearly impossible, given the constraints of space and manpower resources, and experienced hewers were expected to train and direct those raw recruits congregating at the mining settlements in the West of Scotland. The larger concerns were able to employ professional managers very early in the history of the industry, who were both technical consultants and directors of a pit workforce.[41] Below them were various grades of technical, maintenance and supervisory employees, including the key group of colliery deputies responsible for safety and output underground. It was the deputies who kept in daily contact with the men and discussed work problems at different seams with groups of colliers, as well as actually supervising the oncost workers employed to service the faceworkers. Since direct control over the work process, the tools used, and the training of fresh hands was virtually impossible, employers had to rely on other forms of direction and incentives. Different varieties of sub-contracting survived in many areas, though more adventurous managements tended to favour incentive systems and sliding scales later in the century. There were also gradual moves towards replacing stoop and room (or pillar and stall working) with longwall gang organisation, and the use of coalcutting machinery was introduced at the Baird and other collieries after the 1860s.[42] These advances were retarded by the natural lay of the thin seams and more general problems of diminishing returns in the old coalfield during the later decades.

The imperatives for fresh managerial strategies increased only after 1870 as pig iron production was eclipsed and new fields emerged in Fife and elsewhere to challenge the supremacy of Lanarkshire. Its virtual exclusion from export markets and disappointing rates of productivity caused anxieties amongst large and small producers alike, though the capacity of the latter for radical change was one of the most serious limiting factors weighing on the industry. The natural response of such coalowners was to search for ways of raising workloads whilst containing the wage rates paid to the hewers and ancillary labourers. Organised resistance to the masters had been effectively decimated in the 1840s-50s, when firms such as Dixons of Govan had outlawed trade unions as unChristian and a pernicious interference with the rights of 'free labour' at their pits. Yet the objective barriers to close surveillance of working methods allowed the colliers to preserve their own customs and resistance unhindered by management discipline procedures. Faced with the decline in the price of coal and a glutting of local markets, miners restricted their own output through the practice of 'darg' and refused to accept the logic of political economy or the rules of the market game as specified by management.

After 1870 this tradition of restriction and resistance was only partly modified by the spread of coherent trade unionism in the Lanarkshire coalfield.[43] The larger firms in the county were eventually persuaded into recognising and working with 'responsible' trade unions such as that led by Alexander Macdonald, later M.P. and close friend of Lord Elcho.[44] Colliery masters were themselves organising along more formal lines during the 1870s, when the Lanarkshire Masters' Association was formed — dominated by firms with large coal and iron interests, who were generally favourable to stable collective bargaining as well as progressive innovations in the industry.[45] In place of the constant friction over output and wages came the sliding scale and conciliation machinery which employers in both coal and iron sectors came to support during the late nineteenth century.[46] The recognition of miners' unions which such arrangements entailed did have its drawbacks when employers found that the productivity and rates of profit from coalmining remained disappointingly low, but the field continued to expand before 1914, and the preservation of wage rates at least protected larger firms against the unscrupulous proprietors who sought to cut wages. The problem of industrial control was only shifted to a higher and more formal stage by the growth of unionisation, but at least it rescued the employers from the uncertainties of output restriction and local stoppages.

The very effectiveness with which Macdonald and his successors promoted the cause of responsible trade unionism and continuity of agreements caused a certain amount of unrest amongst local groups of miners who found existing settlements incapable of meeting their aspirations. Their responses to the initiatives of management were often in sharp contrast with those of the permanent officials, and their imagination stretched beyond the oscillations of the sliding scale to questions of social problems and political action. The achievements which satisfied the generation of Alexander Macdonald did not begin to meet the expectations of Keir Hardie and other Lanarkshire miners. Increasing regulation of conditions, hours and even wages by the state before 1914 only confirmed their convictions that political success depended on determined action and independent representation in industry and government.

Much more complex in its production processes and business organisation was the railway industry which created the communications infrastructure for the regional economy in the West of Scotland. Railway firms were among the largest and most sophisticated of early joint stock companies in Britain, often combining the operation of rolling stock with the building of locomotives and carriages.[47] In charge of these giant enterprises were railway directors elected by a variety of shareholders and financial interests, remote from the everyday management of the transportation networks and great workshops which the firms built. Although they enjoyed a virtual monopoly on most routes, their powers were limited by legislative provisions and the necessity to offer competitive freight rates for comparable lines. Customer resistance to increases became a serious consideration after the booming middle decades of the century, when such great rivals as the North British, the Caledonian, and the Glasgow Railway Companies were all engaged in transferring goods and people on a competitive basis. Such damaging rivalry could be limited by gentlemen's agreements between the handful of concerns which controlled whole areas of the national railway system, but they all faced the prospect of growing American and German competition in the export of locomotives during the 1880s.[48] Even if impressive manufacturing standards were maintained, trading conditions still varied between the deep trough of 1892-95 and the bulging order books of the following five years.[49] There were also large conglomerates which specialised in locomotive engineering and repair, such as the great North British Locomotive Company formed in 1903 under the aegis of the powerful Reid dynasty.[50]

Railway employers had therefore to develop a complex but efficient framework of managerial control which could encompass the supervision of dispersed station porters, elite footplate drivers, isolated depot employees and concentrations of unionised engineering craftsmen. Like certain other large companies, railway directors introduced a highly bureaucratic organisation and almost militaristic division of responsibilities to deal with the distinct areas of work, frequently justifying the rigorous line and staff hierarchy by appeals to public safety and precise timetables. Their attempts to impose a similar style of management and discipline on the workshop tradesmen, at such great railway centres as Springburn near Glasgow, met with the determined resistance of the independent craft workers when autocratic superintendents exerted authority. The dependence of the employers on the ingenuity of their engineers circumscribed their attempts to reduce craft control, even after the energetic attack on the Amalgamated Society of Engineers during the 1896-97 troubles. In the competitive environment of the decades after 1880, railway managements were attempting to press forward with technical innovations, better organisation and a consolidation of resources, but the problems of labour intransigence became progressively more serious as pressures were applied.

Unlike the colliery owners, railway directors were completely opposed to the unionisation of their transportation and administrative grades, crushing an autonomous Scottish railway union in the bitter 1890 strike and attempting to outlaw the elite society of footplate employees.[51] These policies were fairly typical of British railway firms as a whole and help account for the widespread conflicts seen in the industry before 1914, culminating in the great 1911-12 troubles. Business repression also contributed to the sharpened political awareness of the railway employees, with similar developments at local and national levels to those seen in the coalmining industry.[52] In the last years of peace there were disturbing signs of unionisation amongst the clerical grades at the Scottish railways, threatening to bring the whole hierarchy of industrial authority into disrepute and causing some directors acute anxiety.[53] The necessity for government intervention to resolve the most dangerous of these industrial confrontations before the War again suggested the case for national ownership and control to many prominent activists.

Considerable progress had been made before 1870 in the industrial growth of the Clyde region, but it was the rise of heavy engineering and steel shipbuilding which became the mainspring of the regional economy after that date. The building and fitting of engines had been an early feature of Scottish industry, stimulated by the successive stages of manufacturing development in the area. One indicator of colonial trading had been the construction of sugar-making machinery in Glasgow, whilst the textile employers were partly dependent on looms and frames designed within the region. Firms such as Arrols benefited from the age of the locomotive in the creation of great metal bridges, whilst the steam and diesel engines needed for train haulage employed many thousands of engineering workers throughout the nineteenth century. Soon the most advanced employers were specialising in the manufacture of machine tools for other sections of engineering, such as the lathe-making firm of Langs at Johnstone, though the greatest designing achievements were to be seen in the field of marine engineering during the later nineteenth century. The advances in the capacities of engines from single to quadruple expansion chambers, and the introduction of turbines which would drive screw propellers were accomplished by an array of local employers such as John Elder of Govan, rivalling the inventions made on Tyneside by innovators such as Parsons.

In these respects engineering was more a confederation of specialised practices than one coherent trade, with overlapping skills in areas such as shipbuilding and boilermaking. Indeed, some employers had diversified out of iron and steelmaking into a range of engineering products, the prime example being the great Parkhead Forge of William Beardmore. In contrast to such giant integrated enterprises were the host of small workshops and specialist firms fulfilling the orders of customers requiring specific parts or products made to measure. Such concerns could hardly contemplate the comprehensive drive towards technical innovation and management reorganisation which larger employers undertook in the competitive environment of the 1880s-90s in areas like Clydeside. Their limited size and resources meant that specialisation in a very limited range of manufactures, frequently produced to very high standards, was the best protection against increasing rivalry in domestic and export markets. Even the leading business minds in the engineering trades were reluctant to provoke the kind of resistance over machinery and management which finally erupted during 1896-97 in engineering.[54]

The strength of workplace labour organisation emanated from the early decades of industrialisation when millwrights were called upon to adapt their pre-industrial craft skills to the requirements of mechanised technology. Their control over entry to the trade and control of the work process was largely broken in 1852, but the frontier of control was established on a fresh basis, allowing considerable autonomy to the fitters and turners of the Amalgamated Society of Engineers. Advances in the division of labour had to be practically (and often formally) negotiated with the craftsmen if only because it usually entailed an upgrading of highly skilled to 'set' or prepare the work of lesser machinists. Since the foremen were recruited from this highly accomplished elite of setters, even the employers' representatives were subject to a certain measure of craft control — despite determined moves against their union membership during the pre-War years.[55]

This last point illustrates the important changes which were taking place in the management of industry itself during these years, as the experience of competition and growth in scale, innovations and organisation suggested the need for tighter management control and improved techniques of labour direction. Professional expertise was acquired or called upon by an important section of the younger generation of Clyde engineers, such as Weirs of Cathcart and Langs of Johnstone. These progressives were influenced by the ideas and techniques, as well as the modern automatic machinery, arriving in Scotland from America during this pre-War era, and their advocacy of new payment incentives caused almost as much unrest as the related disputes over machinery and manning.[56] Similar difficulties were seen at the Clydebank works of the American Singer company, leading to the bitter 1911 troubles and the crushing of 'syndicalist' elements at the plant. Less well known are the difficulties which appeared in the handling of technical, supervisory and administrative grades at some of the largest works before the War. To a lesser extent they were also affected by the fresh division of labour and dilution of previously comprehensive tasks in the drawing office or workshop floor, usually with little consultation of the unorganised employees involved. The highly diffuse character of engineering production and the ambiguous implications of new working methods for the workforce averted any serious confrontation of the kind apparent amongst railway clerks or textile supervisors, but the fact that management was changing and that the reshaping of the workforce covered a variety of hierarchical grades was not lost upon these members of staff.[57]

Shipbuilding firms were in a much stronger market position after the 1870s, with British mercantile tonnage comprising over a third of the world total and domestic yards (led by the Clyde area) supplying virtually all of this before the War.[58] Even more so than in some engineering trades, the products were built to the particular specifications of individual customers who spent long periods consulting with company draughtsmen and engineers about their particular preferences. Certain shipyards made their reputation in a type of vessel or branch of building, from the flat-bottomed river steamers launched at Denny's to the great passenger liners of Clydebank and heavy warships constructed at Beardmore's Dalmuir slipways. This is not to suggest that the industry was without fierce competition, especially in periods of slack orders, but that specialisation and labour-intensive production imposed certain limits on the imperatives towards radical change in the organisation of the industry. There were certainly pressures for mechanisation, rationalisation and the greater integration of work processes before 1914 but the character of the market and violent oscillations in trade cycle demand tended to inhibit improvements of the form seen in engineering.[59] The early mastery of ironworking skills and the creative contribution by the shipyard workmen encouraged the persistence of 'skill intensive' methods of production under craft administration rather than tight management supervision.[60]

Objective constraints and subjective resistance from the tradesmen compelled the substantial shipbuilding employers to rely on incentive systems and loyal foremen to represent management control, and even here they were careful to win workplace consensus for changes in yard arrangements. The pattern of disputes within the shipbuilding sector reflected these different emphases in the frontier of control, with limited attempts by management to control entry to trades or training, though they were increasingly worried about the extent of demarcation exercised by the crafts and the society insistence on the physical manipulation of the heavy pneumatic and electrical equipment introduced by shipbuilders before 1914.[61] Strikes during 1909-10 did not result in the kind of defeats inflicted on the Amalgamated Society of Engineers (A.S.E.) in 1897, but there was also a new generation of managerialists amongst the Clydeside builders correspondent to that in the related engineering industry. They were convinced of the need for greater management power in the matters of payment systems, technical equipment, interchangeability of trades on jobs, and technical education. Many of these aspirations were expressed in the debates over the role of their supervisory workers, and the struggle for the allegiance of the underforemen as well as head trade foremen.[62]

The clear pressures mounting in these two heavy industries before the War led to a comparable pattern of industrial conflict, although the emphasis differed according to working conditions and the strategic position of management and labour. Their impact on the industrial relations of the sectors and the forms of organisation adopted was somewhat complex, suggesting that we should see changes in trade unionism as a series of distinct and contradictory processes rather than as modifications to a finite structure. Craft societies had grown up as a series of predominantly localised responses to production and negotiation, and only gradually did some national framework of administration and representation emerge. In the late nineteenth century the full-time officials were still trying to impose a coherent hierarchy of responsibility on their motley organisations, to gain greater credibility in the stable system of collective bargaining which they were jointly engaged in constructing. The resulting dialogue with district committees and elected local officials often divided the membership between those favouring more aggressive policies and the moderate elements, though the former frequently included conservative craftsmen opposed to compromise agreements with employers. Another important departure, briefly foreshadowed in both engineering and ship-building before the War years, was the creation of direct workplace representation to deal with matters of strict immediate concern to the members rather than an issue of district policy.[63] To characterise these groundswell initiatives as unambiguous expressions of 'syndicalism' or 'radical militancy' is to simplify the actions and exaggerate the motives of their authors. They were partly a response to deficiencies in the increasingly formal bargaining structure and partly an alternative procedure or perspective to that espoused by district or national officials.[64] Some of the bitterest disputes occurred over demarca-tion rights at shipyards where trades protected both their sectional territory *and* resisted moves to impose interchangeability at the discretion of manage-ment. Again, many employers responded to attempts to enforce a union closed shop in engineering with great hostility, whilst accepting the advantages of plant negotiations and consultation.[65] The responses of industrialists to either national centralised bargaining or local representation of grievances were no less problematic than those of their men.

Nor did these significant developments take place in isolation from broader changes in industrial relations during the decades after 1880. Employers were themselves trying to change the work practices and structure of authority in their own favour, distancing foremen from their customary links with trade societies and pressing them to implement unpopular policies against organised resistance. Growing recruitment of intermediate employees such as draughts-men, clerks and supervisors to autonomous associations was evident if still very limited before 1914, being one reaction to the division of non-manual labour and the perceived erosion of differential status in the industrial work-force. Much lower down there were the lesser skilled and unskilled, ranging from engineering handyman lathe workers to the low-paid yard labourers of the shipbuilding industry on Clydeside. These groups also showed a marked propensity to organise before the War, sometimes in retaliation at the exclusive practices or higher earnings of the tradesmen who usually directed their labour.[66] Workers such as crane drivers or common sawyers now demanded proper recognition and additional remuneration as part of the industrial workforce. The very multiplicity of groups involved in collective bargaining negotiations before 1914, and the obvious desirability of com-prehensive settlements covering sectional interests, demanded a coherent and united front from the employers — helping to explain the impressive progress in business associations before the War.

The comparison of the major industries of the West of Scotland illustrates underlying similarities of development as well as the continuing differences in the organisation and relations of these sectors. Besides dominating different stages in the growth of the regional economy, their work processes and labour force derived from the very particular physical tasks performed by the available supply of workers. Where the workforce was permitted some degree of autonomy, they could make a positive and creative contribution to the advance in the productive forces — especially when industrialists depended on some pre-mechanical expertise to establish their concerns. In shipbuilding the workers soon developed impressive ironworking skills and maintained the quality of manufacturing by restricting trade entry and training their fellow craftsmen. Colliers were deprived of the advantages of trade organisation but avoided close supervision and dictated the pace of their own efforts below ground.

Other employers operated in less favourable product markets and were impatient with the aspirations of their workforce, resorting to rigorous supervisory controls and crushing any organised resistance without hesitation. Textile concerns broke the spinners' combinations and substituted cheaper female labour wherever possible, drawing on some of the abundant supplies flooding in from outside the Clyde valley. Employers in coalmining and railway transportation were unable to dilute the labour force with women but they were almost equally successful in destroying trade unionism before the 1870s. As in textiles, this merely forced employees to resort to less obvious forms of resistance and restriction, such as refusing to work extra looms or limiting the output of coal.

After the 1870s there was a greater coherence in both the employers' initiatives and the response of labour, with deteriorating market environments and an impetus towards increased innovation in technology and management. Tighter workplace controls, heavier workloads, fresh incentive systems, mechanisation and rationalisation were seen to varying degrees in each of the major sectors, though with very ordinary results in cotton textiles and coal-mining. Partly in response to these reforms, craft societies intensified their resistance and fresh groups of employees began to organise for the first time. In most trades the business associations and individual managements achieved a negotiation of greater efforts, but the scale of conflicts — even amongst the least organised women at Leven and elsewhere — generally expanded before 1914. Where the capitalist resistance was greatest and antagonisms most prolonged, working people frequently turned to more radical solutions of state intervention as a means of resolving their grievances. Throughout the regional economy, there were contradictory forces of decomposition and resurgence within the trade union movement which were transforming the character of workplace organisation and generally increasing the active participation of industrial workers in labour disputes.

Industrial growth and working class settlements in the Clyde region

The industrial settlements which sprang up around the major forms of productive activity reflected the relations and the contradictions which were embodied in the advance of capitalist industry. Originally industrial colonies were constructed to meet the needs of a highly dispersed manufacturing process in each sector, with business units scattered throughout the region. With the coming of mass immigration and the concentration of much industry in dense urban areas, there were greater opportunities for the sharing of important social amenities in cities like Glasgow. Service occupations and middle class propertied interests blurred the sharp contrast between the industrial employers and the local workforce, though the framework for local labour markets remained a basic consideration of any industrialist intent on preserving a good supply of workers. These middle class groups were usually prominent in the organisation of local government and the membership of voluntary organisations, and it was they who contributed a cultural veneer to the spreading urban environment.

Thus it is possible to locate the evolution of industrial settlements in the broader perspective of Scottish capitalism. The dominant position of the landed interests in property relations was apparent to speculative developers in central Glasgow as well as in isolated mill colonies, remaining one of the key considerations in housing growth and the measurement of personal fortunes during the nineteenth century.[67] Professional and commercial groups were also in evidence during the expansion of larger urban centres, figuring in many of the early improvement schemes and voluntary initiatives. Industrialists were burdened with the problems of attracting and training a swelling labour force, breaking the customary resistance to rigorous discipline and instilling respect for management hierarchy as well as manufacturing property. Working people were still in the process of being fused as a distinct class during the middle decades of the century, retaining a wide variety of traditions and beliefs whilst developing fresh responses to the changing conditions all around them. Subjected to continuing divisions of labour along sexual as well as sectional lines, the industrial workers carried with them the resistance to centuries of landed oppression and the experience of severe disruptions in established relations, as well as the more articulate protests of the desperate handloom weaver and the decayed tradesman. It was with these living traditions amongst the common people, as well as the feudal relics and competitive cultural expressions within the ranks of propertied and professional Scots, that the employers were dealing during the decades of rapid industrialisation.

The marked differences in the structure of the labour force and the hierarchy of authority within each industry led to a considerable divergence in the character of areas dominated by these occupations and labour markets. Negotiations over the composition of skills and resistance to rigid supervision were conducted within the market situation prevailing, employers finding a widespread suspicion of management intervention in any area of their workers' lives. This antagonism often extended into the sphere of local housing and social amenities, since neither employees nor masters made any hard separation of their working and social attitudes. As the Scottish industrialists became less directly involved in the provision of facilities better supplied by speculative investment or local government and voluntarism, some of these distinctions between industrial direction, property relations and social authority did begin to harden and antagonisms fragment, but further changes in production were always capable of eroding these barriers and the sectional experiences they generated.

Employers' attitudes to work organisation and the role of the firm in local society were therefore shifting over time, in line with the relations they enjoyed with workpeople and other social elements. Their historical isolation from the exercise of political power and their limited influence in Scottish civil society — over such matters as education, religion and artistic standards — was in stark contrast to their responsibilities for the livelihood and control of the surging industrial workforce. They usually conceived of their role in strictly local terms and were reluctant to enter the corridors of civic government in Glasgow or Paisley. At the same time they were sensitive to the dangers of social conflicts, making conscious efforts to create and sustain stable relations as far as their social horizons allowed.

Cotton textile industrialists were among the better known of the early industrial colonists, though the planting of model villages went back to at least the rural resettlements of the eighteenth century. Attracted to the water power of hill streams, cotton manufacturers such as the Buchanans and Dales constructed the impressive factory villages of Deanston, Catrine and New Lanark in the wilds of rural Lanarkshire at the turn of the nineteenth century. Their dominant market position in the West of Scotland's cotton industry provided the substantial resources necessitated by such projects, with Deanston's transfer to the Finlay linen dynasty giving scope to the enlightened management of Alexander during the 1820s.[68] Housing and recreational facilities were provided, and a generous system of vocational training fulfilled the expectations of management until the strike waves of the 1830s swept through the township and provoked the bitter retribution of employers and local clergy alike.[69]

At Dale's New Lanark settlement, Robert Owen experienced rather different problems in his efforts to create a healthy moral climate for the workforce. As a system of industrial and social management, Owenism tended towards an authoritarian benevolence which differed only in its systematic organisation from the practices of numerous other textile manufacturers.[70] After Owen's departure in search of the fulfilment of millenarian socialism abroad, New Lanark suffered a similar fate to many other manufacturing colonies isolated from the mainstream of urban life at Glasgow. Like the cotton industry which generated its growth, New Lanark fell into a slow decline until taken over by Henry Birkmyre and the Lanark Spinning directors in the 1880s. By the turn of the century, local housing and drainage were in sore need of modernisation and the owners had to completely overhaul the organisation of production during the pre-War years. The elaborate benefits and recreational amenities were decayed, with only the stone buildings and park spaces to remind inhabitants of the earlier age of reforms.[71]

Yet New Lanark went on developing as an industrial locality, largely outside the direct supervision of its main employers. Some traces of the Owenist vision remained here as elsewhere in Britain, with the co-operative mission of 'community building' amongst the working class *not* merely degenerating into the concern with shopkeeping under competitive market conditions.[72] Alternatively, successive generations of manufacturers were intent on preserving some hold over the attitudes and beliefs of their workpeople and in the late nineteenth century continued to patronise Presbyterian ministers who adopted a latitudinarian approach to their duties, responding to the claims of missionaries who sustained a 'hold upon the religious community in the village'.[73] Whilst being principally concerned with restoring efficiency and profitability to the settlement during these decades, stripping down buildings and increasing machinery, the Birkmyres were also sensitive to modern sanitary and medical needs — funding a visiting service for the older inhabitants and improving general amenities at the colony before 1914.[74] With rather different objectives and practices than Robert Owen, these later capitalists maintained a reasonable range of benefits inside and outside their mills.

The arrival of the Birkmyres at New Lanark and its conversion to the manufacture of twine under the Gourock firm is an eloquent testimony to the decline of cotton and the prosperity of cordage production in the decades after 1880. During the middle decades of the century, the family confirmed very strong ties with the Port Glasgow area as the son of the original Henry Birkmyres supported religious and educational causes before becoming Provost of the burgh itself.[75] Although they extended their activities into Greenock, the Gourock were anxious to preserve the local identity with Port Glasgow and its public services to which they contributed both as ratepayers and as energetic voluntarists. As they argued in a Memorandum opposing the amalgamation of the Port with Greenock as a larger neighbour in 1926, they provided work for two thousand local people in good times and bad:[76]

> . . . even at a loss rather than the work people should have recourse for subsistence to the dole or to the Parish Council.

On consideration behind such benevolence must have been the escalation of the poor rate in harder times, but there was also an undeniable anxiety to sustain the morale and loyalty of workers who occupied the local labour market.

To this end the Birkmyres provided not only a limited amount of housing for their key employees and favoured pensioners, but also quite impressive medical facilities even after the passing of the National Insurance Act of 1911.[77] Just as management was becoming more sophisticated amidst the attempts to promote close personal contacts with the employers, so industrial welfare became rather more systematic despite the discretionary element in its administration. The rapidly expanding company persisted in this pursuit of a balance between economic prosperity and a personal approach to employees as late as the interwar decades.[78]

Another group of employers displaying an awareness of social responsibilities and local identity were those firms operating the works at Levenside, where the river ran red for generations with the effluence of the great dyeworks. In 1890 the largest concerns united under the aegis of the Turkey Red Company, founded with the Orr Ewing interests but managed by the Christie family. The five Vale settlements employed over six thousand workers, and were responding to changing market pressures in consolidating their interests at the end of the century. More effective and systematic management was reflected in the greater pace of technical change and the formalisation of collective bargaining procedures with the male trade unions of craftsmen and machinists. Earlier methods of labour market controls over the young women at the dye plants, ranging from the system of enquiry lines to the importation of female labour from Ireland during the third quarter of the century, were also breaking down as population stabilised and women became more resistant to male management authority.[79] When, in 1911, the National Federation of Women Workers joined with the Amalgamated Society of Dyers in recruiting the lesser grades of the Turkey Red workforce, matters came to a violent head. During the great Colour House troubles and the setting up of disputes machinery at Leven in 1911-12, the employers complained of the conflicting pressures forcing them to assert managerial prerogatives against rising resistance.[80]

The same forces which were transforming production and relations at Levenside factories were also apparent in the decomposition of stable authority relations locally. During the mid-century period of rapid growth, the Orr Ewings had erected sound terraced housing at Alexandria and elsewhere, with clear gradations of quality to complement the workplace hierarchy and continued employment being a condition of tenancy.[81] Public amenities were supported by a range of internal benefit schemes, including a Works Sick Fund and preferential treatment for supervisory staff. The handful of discretionary pensions were awarded to the highly-prized engravers and designers who created high standards and sustained the company's reputation abroad.[82] Technical education was also encouraged in the Works School and elementary classes, though with a sensible pragmatism the employers funded both a Catholic church for their Irish immigrants and provided donations for Presbyteries in a personal capacity.[83]

These institutions were insufficient to stem the currents of unrest and violence which resulted in the violent incidents of the pre-War years. Having a sharper sense of increasing workloads and unhindered by a long tradition of formal negotiations, local women resorted to spontaneous acts of harassment and ridicule which challenged the customary tranquillity of the Vale.[84] The existing arrangement of organisations and authority relations did not permit the basic expression of grievances, hence the sudden rush of protest and recruitment before 1914 and the untrammeled way in which their demands were articulated. Even had their resources permitted, older families of employers such as the Christies were hardly able to deal with such an unfamiliar and unwelcome social phenomenon as the active antagonism of local women.

Whereas many of the early textiles, ropework and dyeing firms were located in fairly remote areas, the largest carpet manufacturers managed to build their new Mile End factory in the precincts of Glasgow itself during the 1880s. Within easy reach of abundant female labour in the east end of Glasgow, the Templetons were not confronted with the daunting task of constructing housing for their workers and concentrated their energies on an array of internal benefit schemes (mostly discretionary) and public philanthropic projects.[85] Like the printing and publishing market leaders, the largest carpet manufacturers were deeply involved in the civic life of Glasgow itself, being related to other business dynasties such as the influential Dale family. Whereas the Blackies and the Collins descendants were willing to enter local government or provide important amenities for urban Glaswegians, the Templetons were prominent in such ventures as the formation of the Glasgow Workmen's Dwelling Company which constructed a number of impressive tenement blocks from the 1890s onwards.[86] Like so many other similar projects, this exercise in 'five per cent philanthropy' was more successful in bolstering the relatively affluent artisan skilled trades within the working class and catering for their housing requirements than in meeting the basic needs of the worst housed in the city. In doing so, the carpet employers were contributing to the notion of a distinct artisan culture in such cities as Glasgow, reinforcing occupational and even ideological divisions with the tangible boundaries between types of housing and amenities for a particular district.[87] It is somewhat ironical that Templetons should have amassed their fortunes on the employment of cheaper female workers and mechanised work processes, whilst indirectly fostering the image of the respectable Victorian artisan.

The settlements which sprang up around the coalmining workings of Lanarkshire in the nineteenth century displayed a greater homogeneity of production and workforce, though there were marked variations in the density of population and diversification in other trades between areas.[88] The scale of residence ranged from tiny villages such as Carmichael or Dunsmyre to large colliery centres like Bothwell, again depending on the richness of exhaustible seams and the possibility of pit closures.[89] Within the localities there was clear evidence of the predominance of male labour in the industry, frequently with dwellings graded according to workplace status and with women almost wholly confined to domestic or part-time work. Thus whilst the coalmining settlements can be contrasted in size and occupational mix, there was an even sharper sexual division of labour and more coherent hierarchy of authority than that found in the textiles districts.

Another striking feature of the colliery villages was their highly dispersed character and the high degree of company ownership of working class housing. In the decade after 1909 the employers still held between 22,000 and 25,000 dwellings in the Scottish districts, with the proportion of larger houses steadily increasing.[90] Since speculative builders were naturally reluctant to erect dwellings at the head of a coalmine with an uncertain life, owners had traditionally been involved in the construction and renting of accommodation for their shifting workforces. Even the moderate-sized enterprises were drawn into the provision of housing for immigrants who might be escaping from the desperate poverty of the Highlands and Ireland, in search of any available shelter and introducing their own pre-industrial lifestyles in the isolated townships. There was another motive in this action of the employers which illustrates the protracted character of the transition to industrial capitalism in the Scottish context. Tied housing was only one of the aspects of early serf-bondage in Scottish mining, which lasted throughout the eighteenth century. After the termination of legal obligations to labour for one master, housing continued as one less direct method of compulsion in some districts, and as late as 1917 one authoritative enquiry commented that company housing was still 'in the minds of some communities, a relic of the bondage days'.[91] In an industry notorious for its patterns of movement and migration, some settlements developed their strong network of collier families who worked within a particular area for generations. This was itself an important stabilising factor in the social life of the locale, for as the 1917 *Report* noted:[92]

> In such an industry it was to be expected that customs should become too firmly rooted to be easily changed. Where fathers, grandfathers, great-grandfathers . . . can be counted in the history of the same local industry, tradition naturally becomes a governing factor in the life of the villages.

Given the great cultural and social mix of the immigrants, this element of permanence was clearly an advantage when it could be combined with loyalty to particular employers and even a suspicion of trade unionism by many traditional miners.

Employers were partly assisted in the process of sustaining authority by the very forces of religious antagonism which afflicted the Lanarkshire coalfield during the 1860s and 1870s. Sectarian prejudice and violence were a response to the influx of Irish Catholic labour during the third quarter of the century, serving to weaken labour markets and trade union strength at quite different settlements like Coatbridge and Larkhall.[93] Having imported the Irish labourers and welcomed the weakening of unionism, it seems likely that supervisory and responsible positions were largely reserved for the Protestant colliers. Religious turmoil undermined the spread of unionism but created social problems of its own, with public outbreaks of violence and rioting leading to the injury of workmen.

The same is true of the coalmasters' intervention in the housing market during the nineteenth century, which was often carried out against the wishes of a suspicious population. Given the pressures on rapid construction and temporary provisions, reinforced by the somewhat primitive living habits of many immigrant colliers, the coalfield housing stock was in a seriously dilapidated condition by the 1890s. Miners resisted increases in rents which owners demanded as the basis for improvements, so that by the 1900s mining firms were holding one-third of total housing in the Upper and Middle Wards of the County, of which the great majority consisted of one or two apartments.[94] Even those dwellings which were not actually insanitary and which did not possess earthen floors or other unhygienic features, were described as 'dreary and featureless', with owners under pressure to modernise older housing whilst building new, larger accommodation.[95] It was usually the larger concerns with important investments in lucrative areas and with reasonably healthy general profit levels which could afford to carry out these progressive changes, though it was the older and less attractive mines which retained the worst housing.

Other features of business commitments in workers' welfare were the internal benefit schemes developed since the early part of the century, and the impressive public facilities seen during the decades after 1880. When the first great upsurge of trade unionism in coalmining occurred in the 1840s, colliery owners deployed a variety of methods to crush and destroy the workers' organisations. Perhaps the most successful were the Dixon coal and iron interests, which replaced union membership with compulsory enlistment in the Govan Colliery Friendly and Free Labour Society, with miners contributing fortnightly to a range of services which included medical treatment and coal allowances.[96] Supported by the colliery Standing Rules, this system continued past the death of the last William Dixon in 1880 under the guidance of the Trustees, as did the impressive holding of company housing at Govan.[97] Using these non-union methods of welfare provision, and pursuing a rigorous system of working in their mines and ironworks, Dixons were able to achieve remarkable levels of output and financial success before the First World War — despite the age of the colliery and other natural disadvantages.[98] The ironworkers not only mixed with the colliers in local housing but also participated in their own Funeral Fund, again long after the passing of Truck legislation prohibiting compulsory membership of such schemes.[99]

Whereas Govan was gradually swallowed up by the growth of Glasgow itself, bringing many of the facilities desired by colliers' families, there were also fresh developments in the sparsely populated Middle Ward throughout the later nineteenth century. A number of the larger employers were prominent advocates of improved recreational facilities, including workmen's institutes, parks and bowling greens as well as other means of self-improvement.[100] Owners such as those operating the large Hamilton Palace mines were energetic in encouraging such amenities, acting with other parties and groups 'interested in promoting the welfare of the community', according to one expert observer.[101] Faced with the disturbing signs of conflict and disruption amongst the colliery population of Lanarkshire in these years, many masters renewed their efforts to nurture an acceptable 'artisan' culture in the mining districts which could channel autonomous action and effort in creative directions.

Another marked trend of the pre-War period was the sharp rise in membership of regional and national employers' associations, as trade union membership spread and official leadership became more adventurous in their demands. Conflicts occurred over wages, hours and working conditions at a time when more dynamic employers were seeking for ways to increase incentives and workloads amongst the underground employees, hence the bitterness of the confrontations.[102] In the same years the issue of housing conditions became a crucial factor in both industrial relations and legislative initiatives, with serious unrest apparent from 1909 onwards. Protests from the colliery villages about their accommodation provisions continued during 1910-11, despite local government enquiries into the standard of company and private dwellings. During 1911 the central authorities responded by appointing a Royal Commission into Scottish housing for industrial workers, with particular attention given to the situation in mining areas.[103] Employers and medical officials insisted on the personal responsibility and individual effort of the miners in resolving their housing difficulties, though admitting that the problem was now a cause for serious concern.[104] Mining concerns were frequently anxious to extend their accommodation and improve social amenities in local settlements, but lacked the resources and the incentives to do so. Resistance to management initiatives at the workplace and to raising rents or levels of provision in the locality underlined the need for energetic business policies but reduced the capacity of employers to carry them out. The Royal Commission was still sitting on the eve of War, listening to the growing appeals for a more radical state intervention in the whole industry and its housing from the miners' representatives.

Rather different patterns of physical dispersal and hierarchical authority were to be found in the settlements created by the spread of the railway networks throughut the West of Scotland. The provision of railway services is itself a fairly unusual form of production, spanning large construction or maintenance depots as well as the string of stations along the tracks. This distribution of operations caused continuing problems in the supply and transportation of labour to fairly remote points in the communications system, and the accommodation for very distinct kinds of workers who experienced a different structure of management authority in their employment. As in coal-mining, the industry was overwhelmingly dominated by males, though with much greater diversity of occupations and status within the workforce grades.

Amongst the most important locomotive centres in Britain during the later nineteenth century was the great railway burgh of Springburn, transformed from its almost rural surroundings into a key industrial township during the 1860s-70s.[105] All the great railway concerns and main engineering establishments connected with construction flourished in the competitive environment of the period. Relying on the craft expertise of skilled engineers, such firms built hundreds of well-designed terraces to attract the Glasgow workmen, and by the pre-War years the rents from these dwellings were estimated in thousands of pounds.[106] With many administrative and supervisory staff employees also resident in this booming area, there were certain demarcations within the housing stock, but the high proportion of tradesmen in the labour force blurred any sharper distinctions in status.

Having made such an impressive contribution to the housing of the Springburn district, the railway directors were occasionally tempted to use their power as landlords in the pursuit of 'free labour' policies against the rise of unionism. This occurred during the 1890 troubles in Scotland, with the Caledonian Railway Company evicting striking transport employees from their homes at Motherwell — with considerable violence. After the Sheriff's Officer arrived with an eviction order, twenty thousand people resisted the court officials until troops and police forced the picketing crowds back.[107] The legacy of bitterness during these conflicts persuaded the directors against a similar course at Springburn, where many supporters of the Railway Servants lived. Equally important was the consideration that the presence of the highly organised A.S.E. members living nearby may well have provoked sympathetic support in industry or against eviction. The rival North British management had discovered a depth of popular resentment when attempting to break an earlier strike amongst engineering employees by drafting blacklegs into the district, thereby provoking direct violence.[108]

As large firms with extensive resources and highly developed management techniques, railway companies were able to design very impressive benefit schemes to encourage loyalty and identification with a particular employer. This became more important during the growing competition of the 1880s and 1890s, when railway directors such as Sir James King attempted to give a more human face to the complex organisation of shareholders and businessmen that made up a giant company. Great jamborees or annual fetes were held at Springburn to celebrate the success of individual companies, attended by all the employees and addressed by prominent directors.[109] They presented a spectacle of healthy competition between neighbouring enterprises who shared a common duty to customers and the public, in marked contrast to the scenes of industrial strife which affected transportation and construction departments in these years.[110]

Within the workplace there were benefits administered through such schemes as the Caledonian Railway Friendly Society, or the savings banks promoted and sponsored by the same company. Being regulated by private legislation, such employers could stipulate compulsory membership of societies which inevitably reduced the attraction of joining an independent trade union.[111] These services were also geared to meeting the social and cultural needs of higher grades in the workforce, with Literary and Musical

G

Societies at the North British Company as well as superannuation funds for the clerical staff at Cowlairs and elsewhere.[112] Whereas the social aspirations of skilled engineers were catered for by tangible friendly benefits and the alternative provisions of their craft societies, railway employers had much greater scope for influencing employees without a long tradition of independent organisation.

Other employers were more intimately involved with the everyday life of the settlements around their works, and also interested in progress of their manual employees. This was certainly true of the locomotive builders Neilson Reid, whose great Hyde Park interests became the major component of the North British Locomotive enterprise in the 1900s.[113] Despite the early impact made by W. N. Neilson at Springburn, it was the Reid Family who stamped their name on whole streets and parks at the railway metropolis. Employing over eight thousand men before 1914, the North British Locomotive dwarfed the rival Atlas works set up by Neilson after his departure from Hyde Park's railway shops.[114] Neilson's own contribution to local life was largely made during the genesis of the township, when the hierarchy of authority was still being negotiated in industry and the immediate society. Possessing a deep sense of moral duty and religious mission, he became one of the foremost advocates of the 'Volunteer movement' in Glasgow during the 1860s. His objections to the exclusion of working men from the regiments and insistence on moral leadership changed the character of the campaign, for as he wrote in his diaries:[115]

> the artisans must be induced to enrol themselves in the voluntary forces, and my object was to induce the masters, managers, foremen and leading men in every industry to enrol themselves as officers and encourage the workmen to come under their guidance and protection.

The nurturing of an artisan culture clearly required, in Neilson's view, the acceptance of direction rather than complete domination on the part of the respectable workmen.

Railway directors were less willing to recognise the right of autonomous initiatives amongst their transport employees, and the growing tensions overshadowed the social provisions made by companies before 1914. When North British Railway faced the difficulties of safe transport for footplate staff from Springburn to Cadder, where they worked as pilotsmen, they met bitter complaints from the men about the journey's hazards.[116] The directors heard the management argument for new housing at Cadder which could be offered at attractive rents to worthy employees, as well as allowing the residence of a local stationmaster who might 'make surprise visits at different times during the day and night and so exercise a better supervision over the staff'.[117] Thus even such a limited welfare investment as Cadder housing necessitated a deliberate review of management supervision and local unrest in the difficult years before the outbreak of War. Though there was less agitation on the housing issue itself than in coalmining, such services inevitably formed part of the broader relationship between capital and labour in the railway industry. Engineering disputes had spread to Springburn during the 1890s, and antagonisms over pay and conditions affected a variety of transport grades in later decades, including disagreements over such welfare questions as super-annuation. Like other areas of management, the welfare relationship was subjected to contradictions and tensions which employers were incapable of resolving.

Districts dominated by engineering and shipbuilding works shared the common characteristic with Springburn of having a large proportion of skilled employees in local labour markets and housing neighbourhoods. Engineering shops tended to concentrate in established urban areas where the limited resources of the smaller concerns and demand for qualified labour could be matched, whereas the shipyards required space and frontage as well as skilled trades. Labour markets and availability of key workers formed part of the calculations made by industrialists when siting their plants, though spreading urbanisation and communications also facilitated greater mobility across Clydeside. The willingness of workmen to travel distances depended on a range of factors from wage rates and travelling allowances to the availability of employment and prospects for the future. Each shop or yard usually maintained a minimum staff of foremen and apprentices to work through a depression and maintain the works, but even the most accomplished craftsmen faced periods of unemployment.[118]

Another determinant of labour supply was the size and quality of the local housing market for artisans, and the rent levels asked by landlords. Districts which made an early reputation for engineering and shipbuilding had usually been catered for in the great building booms of the later nineteenth century, though speculative activity was still going on in Govan during the 1890s.[119] The problems were more often those of space and standards in these areas, whilst isolated parts of Dalmuir, Clydebank and even Scotstoun possessed adequate space but little incentive for the builder. Shipyards with large resources sometimes preferred to construct or encourage the building of tenements themselves, as did Stephens at Linthouse and Dennys at Dumbarton in the 1860s-70s. Recent arrivals such as John Browns, Yarrows and Beard-mores were also pressed into the arrangement of building projects, given the inertia of housing speculators and the undoubted advantages of business control for employers.[120] Such shipbuilders were especially anxious to secure a skeleton staff of expert foremen, and frequently bolstered the provision of preferential housing with important welfare benefits inside the workplace.[121]

The shipbuilding industry was subject to rapid growth and considerable change in the decades after 1860, with a relocation of production downstream in some cases — leading to the creation of whole new townships. Consolidation of large-scale interests balanced the continuing specialisation in certain branches of building, and massive integrated enterprises linked foundry, engineering and shipyard operations with armaments in the pre-War years. At the same time managements were demanding a renegotiation of existing divisions of labour or methods of work, leading to serious conflicts in the 1890s and 1900s. Larger and more progressive enterprises (including those in marine engineering) were seeking a tighter regulation of work effort and more rational distribution of the workforce around the job. Tradesmen frequently expressed their resistance to such initiatives by consistently preferring other employers, though there were obvious limits to this market strategy, as similar practices pervaded management and unemployment forced concessions on the societies.

It was in this context that many of the more notable shipbuilding districts rose to fame before 1914, often retaining their strong identity with a specific locale on the riverfront. This process was assisted by the size of the yards themselves and the numbers employed — they were perhaps the largest employer for miles. The multiplicity of crafts and their sectional divisions did not prevent their common settlement within a neighbourhood, or the local identification with the production process and finished article. Alexander Stephen remarked with some surprise in 1870 that 'the shipbuilding trade has become such a public business . . . that a launch is a matter in which the community takes an interest'.[122] Whole families would attend the spectacular launchings of cruisers at Govan and battleships at Dalmuir as well as Cunard liners at Clydebank before 1914. These areas were again influenced by the sectarian heritage of Irish immigration and Protestant reaction during the later nineteenth century, often indirectly confirmed by the policies of local employers such as Harland & Wolff of Govan and Belfast. Within such districts there grew up a network of Protestant institutions, headed by Orange Lodges and Freemason Halls, They performed a valuable social function in reinforcing the friendly benefits administered by trade societies and arranged leisure activities for local artisans. This helps to account for the overlap in membership and frequent reports of Freemasonry amongst the trade foremen, leading to preferences in the labour market and the practice of arranging employment in neighbourhood pubs.[123] Descendants of Catholic immigrants, on the other hand, tended to be confined to the lesser or unskilled, for as one prominent socialist informed a Glasgow housing enquiry, 'their father had no trade union before them'.[124] Membership of craft societies and related organisations became a vital influence in the education and training·of their children, both being affected by religious connexions. Sectional divisions between trades were given a sharper common interest in the maintenance of craft status by the sectarian discrimination against Catholic labourers and their families.

This hierarchy of authority at the workplace was completed in the strict subordination of apprentices to foremen and the almost total exclusion of female employees from the work processes. The extent of adult male domination in these districts is only fully apparent in the survey of major relationships and institutions. Full-time employment, property rights, housing access, religious affiliation, friendly society membership, franchise rights, and important leisure activities were all the preserve of men. Within the male workforce there were clear occupational and status divisions which were reinforced by patterns of settlement and religious connexion, woven within the general fabric of hierarchical authority. Upon these foundations local employers could reasonably expect the commands of their foremen to be respected as the directives of a distinctive social figure, as well as the holder of management responsibility.

Besides those organisations and relationships which were linked in some way to the work processes of an area, there was a range of voluntary associations supported by industrialists among others. Certain schemes were introduced to meet the needs of the time, such as unemployment relief funds or distress committees set up during the 1900s.[125] In other cases local industrialists presided over public benevolent funds, operated workmen's institutes and assisted the work of friendly societies. With the growing awareness of unemployment in pre-War Glasgow, there arose bodies like the Partick Civic Guild which had as its stated purpose the cultivation amongst Partick citizens of[126]

a livelier sense of their duties to each other arising out of their privileges as members of the same community.

Its manifesto accepted the inadequacy of official agencies of poor relief and called on local inhabitants to support a voluntarism similar to that of the Charity Organisation Society.[127] Its activities were mainly confined to the streets around the banks of the river where dampness and relative poverty existed in this substantial shipbuilding burgh. The surrounding neighbourhoods presented to the observer almost a microcosm of Clydeside's social structure, as did the support for the Civic Guild. A Partick shipbuilding worker would emerge from the solid tenements of Dumbarton Road on a clear morning to take the ferry across the Clyde to Govan or enter yards nearby. Below his housing were the less substantial dwellings reaching down to the waterside, whilst immediately above him were the elaborate stone flats of the artisans, foremen and small shopkeeping or professional people. On the crest of Thornwood Hill and in the Partickhill area were the mansions of shipbuilding dynasties like Stephens, who could gaze across at their Linthouse yard from the billiard room or turn to walk in the security of affluent Hyndland.[128] Social contact was preserved with the respectable artisans and middle class inhabitants, but usually at a measured distance.

Beyond this terrain of workplace authority and voluntary organisations were the formal institutions of government, upholding property rights and furnishing essential services to the immediate area. It is important to emphasise the *administrative* fragmentation as much as the physical dispersal of production and the sectional divisions within the labour force on the Clyde during these decades. With the Glasgow area itself, burghs such as Maryhill, Partick and Govan were only incorporated after the 1880s and they maintained a separate political identity long after their annexation. Outside Glasgow, areas such as Scotstoun, Clydebank or Dalmuir retained their very peculiar identities whilst Greenock, Dumbarton and Paisley were regarded as separate towns with their own history and structure. The Glasgow burghs were governed by an array of authorities and commissions which had grown up in response to the uneven development of each area, administered by propertied and professional people within the locality. Employers were prominent on such bodies as Police Commissions, School Boards, Poor Law administrative agencies, Provostships of separate burghs, and so on. Their patronage extended to such institutions as schools of art, engineering departments of colleges and universities, hospitals, public parks and improvement schemes. In the absence of a powerful local authority with social services covering aspects of local life, industrialists provided a vital link between official approval and voluntary initiatives. Within the civic chambers of Glasgow proper, such employers were much less influential than the groups interested in property holding, commercial privileges, or professional and legal opportunities, and their absence may help to account for the radical shifts in municipal politics after 1890.[129]

On the other hand industrialists were increasingly aware of national politics and their slender representation in Westminster lobbies. Their traditional faith in Scottish Liberalism was badly shaken during the 1880s, when the growing influence of Lib-Labism and the disquiet over Gladstone's Irish policies crystallised in the Home Rule debate and the formation of Liberal Unionism.[130] Industrialists were deeply divided over the issue and such powerful families as the Tennants continued to uphold the Liberal cause, but growing numbers of employers joined with traditionalist academics and professionals to fight the dismemberment of empire. Among the Conservatives and Unionists who broke the Liberal domination of Scottish seats were shipbuilders such as Sir William Pearce of Govan who relied on imperial protection of overseas markets and massive naval expenditure to offset the notorious troughs of the shipbuilding cycle. Enthusiastically supported by the local network of Orange and Masonic Lodges, the Govan Conservatives were adamant in their resistance to further Gladstonian concessions.[131] They could call upon the full force of industrial authority and the private agencies of local society to reinforce this reconstitution of Scottish Conservatism, though many of these interests maintained their own perspective and some of the organisations continued to possess a democratic ethos amidst the garish beliefs and rituals of Orangeism or Loyalism.

The very pace of expansion and change also caused serious problems for industrialists in the same years that saw a resurgence of Conservatism. Within industry the scale of conflicts increased as management asserted fresh levels of control, provoking disputes over labour market entry, work processes and such questions as supervision in the engineering and shipbuilding trades.[132] There were the moves within official trade unionism to assert craft rights at district negotiations, as well as efforts at greater workplace representation within individual plants. However distinguished the shipbuilding families of Elders and Pearces were at Govan, their Fairfield yard had one of the worst reputations for management and conflict in the pre-War years. Firms with strong local connections which had previously refused to join employers' associations, such as Dennys of Dumbarton, were gradually converted to the case for collective action by the spread of union disputes throughout the Clyde area. The renewed attempts of engineering and shipbuilding managements to detach foremen from craft societies placed their supervisors under serious pressures during this period. Demarcation disputes and sectional quarrels between trades made the task of overall direction more hazardous, since employers were likely to incite serious unrest by any slight breach of customary practices.[133]

Such demarcation conflicts became increasingly bitter with the downturn of the trade cycle, as trades fought for areas of work in a diminishing order book. Even though naval and military expenditure in the era of Dreadnoughts and field guns reached unprecedented heights, Clydeside shipbuilding experienced violent changes in the numbers employed before 1914. Coupled with the successful limitation of wages by industrialists and new payment systems advocated, the skilled trades found their general living standards falling behind rising expectations. The sudden shifts in employment prospects also affected the hierarchy of authority, as newly promoted underforemen were downgraded to common workmen once conditions deteriorated.[134] Tradesmen found that the new yards and works at Clydebank or Dalmuir required considerable expense in time and money to reach every morning, and expressed dissatisfaction at the recompense offered by the management before the War. Lesser grades of employees were in a much weaker position to complain, but they also showed clear signs of unrest before 1914.

Housing itself became a major cause of contention through the Clyde area and particularly affected those shipbuilding employers seeking to attract qualified labour to their works at remoter sites. The fragmentation of property relations and character of building investment led to a situation of ineffective market demand and virtual collapse of speculative building in the decade before the War. Private builders could not afford to construct dwellings, nor investors to purchase and let them, at rentals which guaranteed a reasonable return on capital. So there existed an actual surplus of accommodation in Glasgow, whilst the size and condition of many dwellings were well below modern requirements.[135] Moreover, the stagnation of the building industry posed real difficulties of industrialists wishing to expand their works or requiring accommodation for a workforce, hence the direct intervention of shipbuilders in the housing market at this time — management frequently using the opportunity to sharpen differential privileges and enhance discipline in their works.[136] Nor did the aggregate surplus at Glasgow reflect the hard-pressed situation in populous shipbuilding districts such as Partick and Govan, where there were several protests at rising rents before War broke out. Such autonomous burghs had only accepted annexation by Glasgow on certain conditions, including freedom from rating increases for a lengthy period. When local authorities compounded Police Rates with other charges and gave responsibility for collection to the owners' factors as part of normal rent, there were serious complaints from tenants and shopkeepers alike.[137] The defence leagues and action committees formed at these local levels campaigned after investigations by official enquiries failed to resolve the question. Progressive though Glasgow Corporation was on many social issues, the presence of powerful propertied, factoring and legal interests at the City Chambers stifled any radical response to the complicated housing problems facing tenants and industrialists alike. Here the lethargy of employers told against their own need for further housing, with Alexander Stephen complaining that amongst his fellow shipbuilders 'few if any take anything to do with the Welfare of the Citizens of Glasgow or the community'.[138]

Some of the most energetic supporters of tenants' defence organisations were housewives and widows in industrial localities struggling to maintain consumption standards in uncertain employment conditions. Increases in rents and rates were hardly welcome when wages lagged behind general prices and amenities were so often lacking. Working women became aware of organisations through the growth of unionism in such trades as boot and shoe making, and the unionisation of a number of service occupations from restaurant employment to telephone operating. The wives of craftsmen were almost always housewives but could participate in such organisations as the Women's Co-operative Guilds, irrespective of their own political beliefs. Suffragist bodies such as the Women's Social and Political Union gained influence under the leadership of Helen Crawfurd among others, whilst Labour supporters joined the Women's Labour League and the Women's Freedom League in the Clyde area.[139] The propaganda disseminated by such associations reassured the large groups of women prepared to offer resistance to the factors' demands and the prices charged at local shops, limited though this market offensive was before the War.[140] Their own aspirations were usually directed towards improved standards of housing, education and consumption for themselves and their families, though the means of achieving this was clearly a matter of continuing discussion and debate.

The most important *political* expression of growing conflict in industry, housing protests and increased female participation in the Labour movement was the emergence of the Independent Labour Party (I.L.P.) in the West of Scotland. Revolutionary organisations such as the British Socialist Party (formerly the Social Democratic Federation) and Socialist Labour Party were significant ventures in the mobilisation of key workers and party cadres, but they possessed no wide platform and attracted no massive support. The I.L.P.

was able to bridge the quite distinct experiences of industry with the problems of housing and social conditions, with active individuals like Harry Hopkins at Govan or Shinwell at Glasgow pressing the claims of socialism on their respective trades councils.[141] Skilled engineers were especially evident in the early days of the Party, with John S. Taylor combining his duties as a councillor with those of an A.S.E. activist.[142]

I.L.P. leaders were only able to achieve this success by consistently campaigning on industrial and social issues at the local level. Workplace authority and cultural traditions created deep sectional, sexual and sectarian divisions within the working population at burghs like Partick, which were only painfully eradicated by a new generation of gifted socialists who included John Wheatley, Patrick Dollan, John Maclean, Andrew McBride, Helen Crawfurd and Emmanuel Shinwell. Their recruitment of important trade union activists, such as David Kirkwood of Beardmore's Parkhead works (who joined the Socialist Labour Party and then the I.L.P.), marked a crucial advance in the radical orientation of the organised workforce before 1914, and was sharply opposed by the institutions of Loyalism. Wheatley's first great achievement was as the principal architect of the Catholic alliance between the I.L.P. and the descendants of Irish immigrants committed to Home Rule, accomplished despite the preponderance of non-Catholic skilled workmen in the Party itself.[143] One of the main bodies in Glasgow public life gradually swung behind the organisation whose leadership was to include some of the Church's most brilliant followers.

By focusing on the main social questions of the day and stressing the ability of local authorities to deal with immediate problems, Labour Party activists made an important contribution to Clydeside municipal politics in the pre-War era. Campaigns on education, housing and social amenities were conducted at the parish level and within the old burgh localities. The supposedly non-political ward committees were colonised by the I.L.P. and transformed into the agencies of I.L.P. candidates during local elections, with effective trade union members like Hopkins able to bestride the responsibilities of Trades Council spokesman and School Board representative with the backing of his ward committee.[144] Although women were usually excluded from the ward elections and local government franchise, there were growing links between tenants' organisations, women's movements and the I.L.P. machinery in Glasgow, Govan, Greenock and elsewhere.

These campaigns resulted in significant organisational innovations which tapped the energy of grassroots protest and altered the character of political support. The housing question was the key to many such alliances, including the formation on the eve of War of the Glasgow Women's Housing Association — led by Agnes Dollan, Mary Laird, Mrs. Ferguson and others, under the aegis of Andrew McBride's Labour Party Housing Committee.[145] Prominent members of the Women's Labour League such as Mary Laird and Mrs. Nixon, encouraged by Ben Shaw and the Glasgow Party organisers, travelled across Glasgow to urge the creation of local housing committees and to increase support for John Wheatley's proposals of '£8 cottages' as the answer to Glasgow's overcrowding problems.[146] Councillors elected to the City Chambers continued the attack on the iniquities of landlordism and the inadequacies of speculative building in a region still expanding its industry and population. Among those sympathising with these arguments were the skilled engineers and shipbuilding workers living in hard-pressed industrial areas, frustrated at the collapse of their rising expectations.

This comparison of the kinds of settlement created during the separate stages of Scottish industrial development indicates the continuing diffusion of production over a wide geographical area. Early cotton textiles, cordage and dyeing processes were situated away from Glasgow itself and imprinted their distinctive work hierarchies on areas such as Deanston, Port Glasgow and Levenside. Coalmining villages varied considerably in their scale and occupational composition, but were also spread across a wide area of Lanarkshire throughout the nineteenth century. Railway labour was naturally divided between the large engineering and junction settlements such as Springburn, and the string of depots and stations along their tracks which grew up in the middle decades of the century. Shipbuilding and engineering firms were similarly pressed between the access to ready labour markets and the need for spacious accommodation of their work processes, hence the journey to sparsely populated Clydeside frontages. Despite the undoubted progress of urbanisation and administrative integration during the decades before 1914, such settlements maintained a strong local identity, with a range of voluntary and official institutions reinforcing this tradition.

The actual construction and maintenance of such settlements was influenced by both property relations and productive forces during the industrialisation of the region. Housing accommodation for the thousands of migrants flooding into the West of Scotland was initially in very short supply, with industrialists frequently building whole industrial colonies themselves or furnishing dwellings for key grades of workers. With the growth of the building industry and wider provision of land and investment capital, private interests took over the responsibility for working class dwellings (almost always for rental on a monthly or weekly basis). The fundamental interests in Scottish society, including the professional agencies which gave a legal framework to property and renting relations, were apparent to working class tenants by the middle of the century. The inadequacies of market forces in the provision of accommodation were also evident long before the end of the century, with colliery owners continuing their housing activities in the face of uncertain returns from low rents. Industrialists owning textile mills, railway yards, engineering shops and shipbuilding complexes also preferred to engage in extensive housing construction as late as 1914. Their determination was underlined by the problems of the Glasgow building industry and the diminishing attraction of housing investment after 1905, despite the acute shortages and overcrowding which existed in even the affluent working class districts around shipyards.

Employers were frequently anxious to provide housing as part of a broader programme of welfare benefits, distributed according to the skill and status of the recipient or on the basis of personal loyalty by a discretionary management. During the 1880s and 1890s there was a resurgence of interest in such schemes, after the earlier projects of the 1830s and 1840s had been consolidated and the urgent need for housing or public amenities slackened. Textile manufacturers and coalowners were interested in modernising older dwellings and laying out impressive institutes and parks in their townships. Railway companies provided recreational and other facilities to complement their internal schemes and encouraged literary or musical gatherings to raise the tone of the staff. Shipbuilders and engineers made a great impact through such projects as Elder Park, Pearce Institute, Denny Institute and sponsoring Masonic Halls. Again there were special provisions for supervisory and technical grades, who were expected to provide social and moral leadership for the men they commanded in local works.

Yet the development of bourgeois and artisan culture implied more complex relationships and attitudes than the simple reflection of workplace hierarchies, however much they were encouraged by business intervention in amenities. Walter N. Neilson emphasised the importance of genuine autonomy for the artisan participants in such voluntary organisations as Glasgow Volunteers, as did William Denny in his advocacy of friendly society membership for the respectable working class. The acceptance of such movements by the skilled male workers for whom they were mainly intended largely depended on their freedom from direct business patronage and the preservation of a certain democratic element in even the Orange Orders. Employers were assisted in the promotion of an acceptable urban culture by the presence of disparate propertied and professional elements in such settlements, from upper middle class philanthropists to local doctors and small shopkeepers. It was they who were also prominent in the work of religious and relief bodies, whether at New Lanark or the Glasgow burghs, which served to uphold the cause of order against the claims of Roman Catholicism or socialism. The virtual exclusion of women and working girls from membership of such institutions, or from access to the formal organs of local government only completed the hierarchy of male authority within industrial areas.

The initiatives taken by employers in this period arose partly from a growing recognition of forces threatening to disrupt existing social relations. Rising competition from England and abroad posed real difficulties for certain branches of industry, especially those which relied on a low-wage female workforce and where management found tighter supervision difficult. Resistance, taking many forms, was evident in each of the major sectors covered, and involved qualified supervisory and administrative grades as well as previously unorganised lesser skills and women. Growth in the scale of enterprise and consolidation of resources facilitated many of the changes introduced by management, though the conflict they provoked extended into even the most profitable shipbuilding concerns and weakened the whole frontier of control at the workplace. Older attitudes and divisions were also eroded by the emergence of local trade union activists and the rise of shop floor representation.

Difficulties in the housing market also tended to weaken the careful gradations between working class groups, pushing them into common resistance to landlords and collective protests at housing shortages. Employers possessed limited resources and could cater for only the most essential employees, whilst the entrenched propertied and legal interests in civic government prevented a more radical solution to complicated housing difficulties. Mounting agitation on the question involved not only the I.L.P. and its sponsored organisations, but also a growing number of women not previously active in local politics. Where employers held large stocks of working class housing, as in the coalmining industry, the spread of dissatisfaction at housing conditions became a matter of intense union campaigning and industrial action. Here the demand was heard not for state intervention in the form of local authority housing expenditure, but for the nationalisation of the industry itself.

The escalation of confrontations before 1914 suggests a much broader change in the character of relations throughout Scottish society. Economic dislocation and depression affected not only industry but also agriculture, finance and commerce during the 1870s and 1880s. After the banking and trading crises of these years, finance capital was increasingly geared to the needs of the London capital markets whilst the landed interests depended on their urban holdings and connexions with London politics. Industrialists were often severely damaged by English competition at home and abroad, but were irrevocably committed to the preservation of the imperial markets which Britain possessed as a whole. However, the growing concern over economic and social development resulted in the important fissure of propertied and professional groups during the 1880s Home Rule debate, leading to a realignment of alternative policies and a change in the attitudes of many employers. Unionist opposition to Gladstone recruited prominent academics, professionals and legal groups as well as landed elements and a number of important businessmen. Industrialists generally stayed with the Liberals, although showing a disturbing predilection for tariff reform by the 1900s. During the two decades before War, there was a clear drift of previously Liberal families such as the Dennys of Dumbarton from Radicalism to Conservatism. At the same time a significant number of professionals (including prominent barristers) left the ranks of Liberalism and joined with lower middle class and artisan voters in supporting the cause of Labour at a local level. It is this which explains the presence of such outstanding legal minds as Rosslyn Mitchell and gifted journalists like Andrew Hood on I.L.P. platforms before the War. They were joined by radical clergymen of both Catholic and Presbyterian presuasions, and by female orators of the calibre of Mary Macarthur and Agnes Dollan, who also found confidence in their educated backgrounds.

It is within these shifting class relations and alternative forms of cultural expression that we must locate such concepts as 'community', 'paternalism' and 'deference' as qualitative descriptions of the connexions between employers and workpeople in Scotland. Each of these terms formed part of contemporary literature, if not of everyday language, in these decades, and their usage gives us some insight into the meanings attached by distinct social interests to the same words. Although there were dominant ideas and principles underlying language and literature, experiences and consciousness could never be fully enclosed within a framework of fixed terms and beliefs. The very development of culture itself and the contributions from quite separate social groups precluded this restriction of words to a range of frozen images, hence the persistence of notions such as the Scots 'gentleman' and even remnants of clan loyalties long after the Jacobite disasters. Calvinism affected the culture of the artisan almost as much as that of the Scottish bourgeois, confirming his self-confidence and surviving even the indulgences of drink and debauchery.[147] Language partly reflected these inconsistencies and hypocrisies of bourgeois society, but also the straining of popular consciousness against the distortions of current ideology and received knowledge.

The contacts between industrialists and their workpeople are sometimes characterised as 'paternalistic' and the subsequent response of employees as 'deferential'. Besides the fact that such terms are deployed to convey a relationship which ranges from personal intimacy to systematic management policies, there is frequent confusion over paternalism as a welfare relationship. The connotations of the word suggest a fatherly concern for employees as indicated by provision of personal services: yet the examples from textiles, coalmining, railways and shipbuilding all show welfare decisions reached after deliberate calculation of economic costs and benefits or with an overtly strategic purpose in mind. 'Paternalism' can hardly be used to depict either the content of the services (which varied from discretionary pensions to statutory benefits), or the radically different methods by which they were administered. In fact, employers in Britain very rarely used the term and workmen bitterly resented any suggestion of paternalism or deference in their industrial relationships.[148]

Nor can the terms encompass the complex attitudes and activities which made up employer politics and working class voting behaviour in the nineteenth century. Industrialists were never fully represented by the Parliamentary system nor did they create factory constituencies of deferential artisan householders. Until the 1880s the supremacy of the Liberal Party in the Central Belt of Scotland was virtually unquestioned, as was working class support of that relatively progressive party. After that date the ranks of employers divided and relatively few were able to build a foothold for Conservative Unionism in established Liberal constituencies, with artisans usually staying Liberal or drifting towards Lib-Labism. Even when they did support Conservatism (as in

Govan), it was at least partly because they genuinely shared the opposition to Home Rule rather than from a customary respect for employers as social leaders.

What 'paternalism' *does* represent is a set of ideas concerning the hierarchical ordering of society and the authoritarian tendencies of certain practices and principles held at the time. The extremely protracted transition from feudal society and the continuing influence of landed society facilitated the resurgence of authoritarian notions during the growing unrest of these decades and the restatement of a belief in mutual responsibilities of unequal parties. One element in this conservative ideology was an emphasis on continuing *personal* contacts between master and man, which some industrialists endorsed in their opposition to trade unionism. Even as an ideology this view of modern industrial urban life had its obvious flaws, including the mounting organisation amongst employers themselves. Yet it allowed the preservation of traditional respect for established property, and justified a profoundly male-dominated society by stressing patriarchal duties. When describing any employers' activities as 'paternalist', it is crucial to keep this context of culture and ideology in view.

The language of 'community' was much more widespread and its meanings more ambiguous than unfamiliar words like 'paternalism', and its implications were quite different. Within polite society the term could stretch from being a description of very specific circumstances affecting one group, to the imagery of common interests beyond class antagonisms. These are the ways in which a voluntary body like the Partick Civic Guild would utilise the term in their appeal to local citizens to work for their common good in both the locality and society at large. Similarly, employers were contributing to this community of class co-operation in their public projects to build workmen's institutes and lay out recreational grounds. Archibald Denny publicised the work of the Dumbarton Social Union and came to be looked upon as 'the leader in things pertaining to the well being of the community'.[149] Industrialists who wished to serve the greater good of society would patronise civic Savings Banks and even stand for Parliament as the representative of all classes.

Yet this notion of 'community' was as much a part of bourgeois hegemony as the principles and practice of 'paternalism' among Scottish employers. There were still the necessary inequalities of property and rank which made up the social hierarchy, with an emphasis on discipline within the community. When Sir James King told the Springburn employees that they must all serve the 'public', it was a community made up of business needs, market efficiency and loyalty to an almost militaristic hierarchy of authority, rather than a democracy of producers or consumers. Similarly, when such shipbuilding families as the Stephens of Linthouse or Pearces of Govan served on Police Commissions, School Boards and Parish authorities, they impressed their own ideas of the stable community upon an area which relied on local yards for employment.

In contrast to these interpretations of 'community' on industrial Clydeside, there persisted an alternative vision of common interests throughout the process of industrialisation and the arrival of urban class society. Ideas of mutual assistance and common bonds in part derived from the traditions of the pre-industrial crafts and the surprising vitality of the guild corporations in the West of Scotland, flourishing as honorary societies long after the rise of trade unionism and their ethos of mutuality. The successful promotion of autonomous artisan institutions also assisted the continuation of trade communities, though the friendly societies and clubs distanced themselves from the successful journeymen who had risen to the company of employers by the later nineteenth century. More radical ideas of community were broadcast during the ascendancy of Owenism and Chartism, which were never completely subordinated to the practices of successful shopkeeping and artisan responsibility. Above all, there was the everyday experience of conflict and resistance in different industries, which placed the workpeople in direct antagonism to the interests of their employers and created a whole culture of customary restrictions as part of their working lives. It was this which management found so frustrating in their attempts to renegotiate the division of labour and reduce workers' control over their own efforts.

Deepening conflicts after 1880 tended to widen the rift between dominant ideas and the alternative imagery of a working class community in the industrial districts. Despite the anxious efforts of employers and propertied elements to bolster the respectable community with improved facilities and voluntary organisations, their resources were simply not commensurate to the problems or to the spread of dissatisfaction and resistance across industry and society. In very different sectors of production and distinct parts of the region, there was a disturbing tendency for workplace and social unrest to converge — particularly on the issue of housing conditions. It was again the I.L.P. which gave a political articulation to this physical *and* moral campaign against deprivation, combining an acute sense of ethical protest with the suggestion of a feasible alternative. Their arguments for an improved environment did not refute existing conceptions of community and the role of women, but rather *translated* these ideas in socialist terms. As Mary Laird told a Party conference on the housing question held soon after the outbreak of War: [150]

> The single apartment or room and kitchen does not permit of the growth and expansion of those domestic and social virtues upon which the welfare of the community depends . . . And when we think of the strength of character, and moral stamina of the working class as a whole, we may well be proud of the class from which we spring.

Here there is a clear statement of community welfare and moral wellbeing, but a community *of* the working class rather than one set against their particular needs and interests. The growth of the I.L.P. and its ancillary organisations involved the creation of a radically different approach to such matters as education, religion, morality and recreation as well as a tangible programme of social reforms, evoking an ideal of social relations as well as providing an analysis of current conflicts. It was precisely this which disturbed employers faced with mounting unrest on Clydeside at the outbreak of the First World War.

Clyde employers and class relations in the First World War

The conditions of wartime production had the affect of concentrating and accelerating many of the trends evident in the last years of peace, whilst decisively changing the relations of classes with each other and with the British state. These changes were much more fundamental than the unrest of engineering workers at the onset of dilution, and involved far greater numbers than those engaged in resistance during the industrial crises of 1915-16. The issues being negotiated concerned not merely radical changes in the division of labour and antagonisms over job control, but also the relations of employers to other propertied interests and to the institutions of government authority. Largely as a result of their experiences in the early years of war, industrialists recognised their internal divisions and the remarkably slender influence they exercised over the state. In consequence there occurred a realignment in their attitudes to government and in the constellation of interests which dominated the upper echelons of government. Employers became much better organised under a coherent industrial leadership at regional and national levels, just as the channels of labour representation were strengthened and refined by war-time developments. Rather than being a passive reflection of class forces, the state took a positive and creative role in this alteration of relations within and between classes. In the process its own content and character shifted from being a limited regulatory agency still marked by traditionalist attitudes to becoming an interventionist director of economic development involved in corporate industrial bargaining and eventually introducing a mass democratic franchise.

   This transition was particularly significant for the Scottish industrialists, given their historical isolation from the exercise of state power and the serious challenges which they encountered within manufacturing areas from the 1880s. Landed influence and prestige had certainly been damaged by the agricultural depression and the conflicts of the Clearances in Scotland, but industrial leaders had failed to assert themselves against the other propertied groups, and the gravitation of financial and commercial interests to the metropolis had only underlined the weakness of northern employers. Yet the major questions of 'Liberal England', namely, Irish Home Rule, the emancipation of women, and industrial unrest, were felt with greater force in the West of Scotland. General debates on the 'housing question' or the 'condition of England' acquired a deeper meaning north of the Border and were the immediate concern of Scottish local politics. The inability of Scotland's state institutions to deal with such problems, and the insensitivity of British politicians to the growing tension on Clydeside and elsewhere, caused the erosion of legitimacy before 1914 and led to a real crisis of authority during 1915-16. Employers were all the more vulnerable for being placed in a highly strategic position by wartime munitions demands, with the control of labour now a matter of the greatest political priority. They were only able to increase their standing with government by developing skills and strategies of political persuasion which they had not previously possessed or required, and to balance the advantages of official support against the dangers of increasing state direction.

The labour movement was also dramatically affected by the experience of war, with whole new groups of workers streamed into production and a number of fresh initiatives in the organisation of distinct grades of employees. Class conflicts on the different fronts of industrial conditions, housing supply, food prices, and remuneration for women were increasingly seen as part of one struggle rather than as disparate fragments of working class interests. The articulate political expression of these grievances and the consciousness of a common cause among working people was assisted by the work of socialist organisations, the most significant being the Labour Party. These fundamental advances in consciousness and organisation were most apparent in Clyde heavy industry and its surrounding districts during the early years of the War. But it signified a transition not confined to one sector of industry or any particular area, as can be seen from a survey of textiles, coalmining and railway operation as well as engineering and shipbuilding trades.

Employers in the engineering sector were preparing for another major confrontation with their skilled employees on the outbreak of war, largely due to the dissatisfaction of local workmen with the pay settlement arranged three years previously. There were further conflicts over the main issues of industrial control: apprenticeship, machinery, manning, demarcation, incentive systems and management organisation — especially at progressive enterprises like Weirs of Cathcart.[151] There were also the growing problems of trade union representation, whether in the form of official drives for a closed shop by the A.S.E. or pressures for workplace negotiations under local stewards. Some industrialists were anxious for a contest over the 'right to manage' their enterprises, whilst others were willing to settle for a compromise on future pay arrangements and more centralised bargaining procedures which would simplify negotiations and formalise communications with responsible officials.

Shipbuilding firms faced rather different problems of efficiency and control, having a much greater degree of craft administration in their works and a more complex approach to enlarging the role of technical innovation and management rationalisation. After the serious ruptures of 1908-09 and bitter disagreements over the use of Enquiry and Discharge Notes to regulate the labour force, shipbuilders enjoyed the massive prosperity of 1912-13 and were anxious that this expansion should continue. The acknowledged ability of the workforce to provide a creative alternative to any crude division of labour prevented the friction over payment systems or control of machinery deteriorating into a major conflict before 1914.[152] Even in engineering workshops the management depended on the highly qualified machine setters — who were often promoted to foremen — to overlook the work of lesser grades, thereby limiting the importation of 'handymen' unacceptable to time-served craftsmen. Within the shipyards employers again acted through trade supervisors who maintained management authority on a range of issues, including the disciplining of apprentices and dismissal of insubordinate workmen. In the pre-War period unions and trade associations fought over the loyalties of these intermediate workers, offering them an alternative range of welfare benefits in return for affiliation to their societies.

The outbreak of war threw this delicate balance of forces into disarray at the Clyde yards and workshops, with each side having greater potential power than before. Industrialists could claim to control the key sections of wartime production and were soon overwhelmed with Government supply orders, whilst the demand for skilled labour rose to unprecedented heights, thereby removing the customary sanction of summary dismissal from the foreman or manager. As thousands of key workmen came forward to join the armed services, thousands more poured into the Clyde Valley in search of ready work at high wages. The resulting dislocation threatened to place intolerable pressure on the available resources in industry and the housing market, and caused serious concern among the employers. It was in this situation that the great struggles of 1915-16 occurred in heavy industry, precipitating greater state intervention which in turn gave a sharper political edge to the disputes.

There were at least four distinct themes in the conflicts of this early period of wartime production, involving engineering and shipyard trades to different degrees and each possessing their own peculiar ambiguities. The famous strike of February 1915 was largely confined to engineering and revolved around the demand for an increase of 2d per hour in basic wage rates, reflecting the long period of restriction in increases and the disquiet at the substantial increases in prices and living costs since the outbreak of war. Whilst there were divisions amongst the trades pressing for the increase, the most noticeable impression received from the negotiations was the considerable uncertainty amongst Government officials who intervened in the dispute and also the sharp differences between employers and the state representatives.[153] After the promise of concessions and official arbitration, the restive rank and file at works like Parkhead and Springburn returned to their jobs, though with much bad feeling against ruthless employers such as William Weir. Thousands of workers had been mobilised on the issue of wages and conditions, though accepting the intercession of government as an adequate basis for a return to work before any guarantee of even 1d per hour advances.

Their experiences during the February troubles convinced employers and politicians alike of the need for a radically new approach to munitions production and industrial discipline. The results were the passing of Munitions legislation in June-July 1915 and the establishment of a joint Armaments Committee in the West of Scotland, consisting of industrialists, union officials and state appointees. Subsequent conflicts in the area revolved around the three related issues of housing supply and conditions, resistance to management coercion under the Munitions Acts, and opposition to the dilution proposals of employers and government. These disputes took place against the background of large-scale movement in the working population and widespread dissatisfaction at rising prices and rents, each of which had already become apparent by the time of the February wages claims in engineering. Unlike that strike, however, the movement against rent rises and Munitions coercion affected the shipbuilding districts as much as, or more than, localities with engine works, and the *prospect* of dilution caused almost as much concern in the shipyards as nearby engineering shops. There were significant differences in the pattern of conflicts within the overlapping trades, but the underlying issues of workplace control were basically similar. Alternatively, the residue of tradition and custom could present as great a barrier to dynamic management innovation as more overtly radical initiatives. Craft conservatism was never wholly distinct from local resistance to dilution, nor was it unchanged by the experience of conflict. Traditionalist engineers and shipbuilders were in some respects a greater threat than progressives demanding a negotiated basis for workshop dilution, and their awareness of change sometimes more influential than that of socialist shop stewards. It is inaccurate to outline policies and attitudes which were a 'correct' course for the working people of the area, implying that deviations from this caused the degeneration of a movement. We must examine the actual consciousness of different groups of the industrial population, assessing the actual effects of their struggles in the changing conditions of wartime production. Each stage of these conflicts was marked by divergent tendencies towards consolidation and fragmentation, which endows them with a basic ambiguity even when they appear most effective. It is in this context that we should view the great upheavals of 1915-16 in the Clyde district.

The first signs of housing problems in the hard-pressed engineering and shipbuilding districts came shortly after the outbreak of war, with reports of factors intimidating the dependants of those workers leaving to join the colours. Though such practices were quickly restrained by the courts under pressure from the Labour Party and ancillary organisations, tensions continued during the winter of 1914-15, and on Boxing Day Trades Councils at Glasgow and Govan joined forces to lead a group of women protestors to the Council Chambers at Glasgow.[154] In February 1915 the Clydebank Trades Council notified its Glasgow counterpart of a forthcoming demonstration on the housing and rents issue, drawing attention to the unjustified rent increases which had taken place as a consequence of wartime accommodation short-ages.[155] At this stage there were the general complaints of price increases and profiteering which figured in the engineering unrest of February-March, with Trades Councils supporting the I.L.P. campaign for the introduction of Fair Rents Courts on Clydeside.[156] The emphasis on legal resistance was further highlighted during April, when the first eviction warrants were granted by the Sheriff's Court for non-payment of rent despite protests from Labour Party lawyers and journalists.[157]

In May 1915 the housing struggles entered a new phase with the outbreak of rent strikes against wartime increases at Govan, one of the key shipbuilding and engineering localities. The Govan Labour Representation Committee joined with the burgh branch of the Glasgow Women's Housing Association to support the resistance initiated by such housewives as Mrs. Clark, Mrs. Hill, Mrs. Thom and others in the area.[158] The original centre of the rent strike appears to have been the spontaneous agitation of South Govan tenants against the proposed rent increases, although, once expressed in the form of non-payment of additional rent, the established Govan Tenants' Association under I.L.P. activist David Wardley quickly moved to support the rent strikers.[159] In the face of threats from determined factoring agents such as Neilsons, occupants refused to pay fresh increases for the substantial tenement blocks around Linthouse yard and insisted on offering the old rents to the collecting clerks. The Glasgow Labour Party organisation was not slow to promote the objectives of the nascent resistance, comparing their struggle with the recent campaign in the engineering trades and pointing out the precedents for government intercession. At a large Glasgow Green demonstration in June 1915, supported by I.L.P. and Trades Councils, civic Councillors told the massed crowds that:[160]

> the workers by means of trade unions had organised themselves to prevent their wages being reduced, and that if the Government would not interfere it would be the duty of householders to organise and refuse rents imposed since the war began.

Already there was the clear threat of direct action to restrain the power of property and the implication that there could be dangers for the War effort similar to those presented by the February unrest.

The spreading discontents fanned by Labour Party support and local leader-ship were serious enough in June and July to appear on the agenda of the West Scotland Armaments Committee which dealt with vital issues affecting munitions output.[161] Tenants in Richmond Park joined what was still a limited and fragmentary struggle, though the protests died down in Govan after increases were withdrawn and other tenants conceded increases in their rent. Conflict flared again during early August when Neilson attempted to press home his advantage by victimising strike leaders and extending increases to properties managed in the Partick district on the north side of the River.[162]

Here the agents encountered stiff opposition, again concentrated amongst a handful of inhabitants sharing one tenement 'close', and receiving early support from local I.L.P. leaders such as Andrew Hood and his *Partick Gazette*. There were disturbing reports of similar troubles in the Shettleston area which housed many of the militant Parkhead workers and where John Wheatley had laid a solid basis of Labour Party organisation.

After the setbacks of June and July, the rent strike reached its first high point during September 1915, with one newspaper noting at the end of the month that: [163]

> The revolt against the increase of house rents . . . threatens to become a very big problem . . . first in Shettleston, then in Govan, and now in Partick. These movements have widespread sympathy, and given the slightest provocation, they will assuredly spread.

Whereas Shettleston lay amongst the munitions and engineering districts at the east end of the city, Govan and Partick were key shipbuilding areas equally vital to the stretched war effort during the military crises of 1915, and their strategic significance could hardly have been exaggerated.

The concern of the authorities at the worsening housing unrest was sharpened by the escalation of industrial strife in the same areas during the summer and autumn of 1915. Having fought successfully for the exclusion of Discharge Notes from the shipyards and engineering shops during the pre-War years, industrial workers engaged in munitions discovered that the legislation of that year gave managers and foremen the right to issue or refuse 'leaving certificates' to their departing employees — without which no skilled man could hope to find alternative work. Whilst these certificates empowered industrialists with legal sanctions and were supported by a system of disciplinary Munitions Tribunals, they imposed no equivalent restriction on the right of employers to dismiss labour or any right of appeal by the sacked man against an autocratic foreman.[164] Having long experienced trouble with such insubordinate trades as coppersmiths and shipwrights at their Govan yard, the Fairfield management provoked serious unrest during August 1915 by firing tradesmen and bringing the workmen who struck in support of their mates before the Munitions Tribunal.[165] When the prosecuted men refused to pay the fines levied on them and went to prison in early September, Hopkins and the Govan Trades Council mobilised mass support across the trades for their release and against the coercive Munitions Act.[166] Lloyd George refused to interfere in the matter and bullied the shipwrights' national officials into abandoning their members' cause, leaving Hopkins and Govan activists to threaten widespread industrial strikes unless the convicted men were liberated.[167] The eventual compromise involving payment of fines by Society funds secured the objective but did little to stifle the resentment against the Government and employers. Clyde industrial leaders virtually refused to co-operate in the effective operation of the regional Armaments Committee and

were eager to insist on state repression of strikers or activists at every opportunity during 1915, though equally unwilling to be identified with such unpopular measures should they fail. The unhappy experiences of ruthless managerialists such as William Weir and Fairfields illustrated the pitfalls of taking a
hard line against recalcitrant unions when the Government was unwilling to
introduce what amounted to military conscription, on the lines suggested by
the heavy industrialists.[168]

During September 1915, specific engineering and shipbuilding districts continued to lead the unrest born of long-term grievances and immediate
pressures, though the numbers actively involved were still to be numbered in
scores of tenants rather than hundreds of protestors. The actual organisation
of the resistance combined the spontaneous forms of 'close committees' and
'washing house meetings' with the formal agencies of the Labour Party,
Tenants' Associations and Trades Councils. Whilst such Labour barristers as
Rosslyn Mitchell defended rent withholders in the Sheriff Court and Mary
Macarthur addressed large meetings in Partick, local housewives resorted to
direct action in the physical humiliation of rent collectors during their rounds
of the tenements.[169] Even the respectable Glasgow press remarked on the
effectiveness of 'the brawling women in the Glasgow rent strike', noting the
ominous signs of industrial reinforcements as workmen returned from their
overtime to discuss the question.[170] Although the articulate female activists,
frequently with connections with the Glasgow Women's Housing Association,
remained the backbone of local mobilisation, it was the danger of industrial
action in the key munitions industries which began to cause serious concern in
London.

These fears were only confirmed by the activities of Scottish socialist
groups, from the I.L.P. itself to the syndicalist Socialist Labour Party and the
Marxist British Socialist Party which included John Maclean and others.
Besides his pacifist criticisms of the War and his important contribution to the
education of progressive Clyde shop stewards, Maclean joined with Wheatley,
Hopkins, McBride and Taylor in addressing factory gate meetings during the
dinner hour at shipyards and engine shops.[171] This growing workplace support
for the rent strike was clearly demonstrated in early October, when David
Kirkwood, encouraged no doubt by his mentor John Wheatley, sent a letter to
Glasgow Corporation on behalf of the engineering workers at the Parkhead
howitzer shop, warning the Councillors that these munitions craftsmen would
regard forcible eviction of rent strikers as:[172]

> an attack on the working class, which called for the most vigorous and extreme reply, and one
> which might have the most disastrous consequences . . .

The previous day Kirkwood and his Parkhead stewards had been instrumental
in the formation of the Clyde Trades Vigilance Committee (later the Clyde
Workers' Committee), which was to become the principal forum for debate on

resistance during the dilution crisis in Clyde industry.[173] The implied threat to armaments output during this crucial stage of the War and the rents issue could no longer be ignored.

Glasgow Corporation certainly reviewed the case for housing regulation and rent restriction, but had neither the powers nor the inclination to initiate an enquiry into recent increases or present the strikers' case to the Government of the day. Labour representatives formed a sizeable minority in the City Chambers but were unable to sway the entrenched Council, bolstered by the influential owning and factoring interests and elected by the host of small houseowners and rentiers who were raising rents in an effort to deal with rising prices and climbing interest rates.[174] Industrialists most vulnerable to the spread of social unrest at their works were struggling to improve the situation by housing projects of their own, having little direct influence on civic government and being more anxious that the central state should resolve the escalating crisis. When the factors decided on the fresh strategy of summoning rent protestors to the Small Debts Court, thereby enabling owners to demand deductions from the wages of debtors at their employment, industrialists were again in danger of being drawn into a rent conflict they wished to avoid.[175] Fortunately for the unresponsive Government at Westminster, the local judiciary recognised the depth of local feeling in the overcrowded munitions districts and were unwilling to coerce workmen already resentful at their treatment by Munitions Tribunals.

Outside the courts the unrest was spreading throughout the shipbuilding and engineering areas in October, with a major demonstration from several parts of the city on 7th October. The procession, largely of women and children, numbered perhaps one thousand people, described as 'of the respectable working class' by most newspapers, and clearly the families of the better skilled workers.[176] This colourful procession — emphasising the patriotism of the working class and the disloyal profiteering of landlords — culminated in a deputation to the City Chambers headed by William Reid of the Parkhead works, who complained that the factor was exploiting what was a 'national emergency for the purpose of his private gain'.[177] Coming so quickly after the setting up of the Clyde Trades Vigilance Committee, there was again the unmistakable warning of industrial retribution should evictions take place.[178]

During the rest of October industrial and housing conflicts tended to move together, persuading a lethargic Government of the need for decisive action. On 11th October the Secretary for Scotland, McKinnon Wood, came north to interview local Councillors and report to the Cabinet on the unrest.[179] The next day there took place the prosecution of nine Partick rent strikers at the Small Debts Court, which the Sheriff settled by accepting Mitchell's defence that the increases charged on these vital munitions employees were unjustified and likely to cause disruption in industry.[180] On 13th October, Govan Trades Council took up the cause of the Fairfield shipwrights imprisoned for non-payment of Munitions Tribunal fines, telegraphing the Ministry of Munitions to demand their immediate release.[181] Against this background Andrew McBride and J. Stewart of the Labour Party Housing Committee met McKinnon Wood, giving him a clear lesson on the hazards of continued direct action:[182]

> If the Government did not deal with the situation as requested the tenants would continue the strike against the increased rent, and if any of the tenants were evicted for non-payment of the increase, then it was almost certain that industrial action would follow.

Faced with criticism in Parliament and hardening resistance to government authority, Lloyd George appointed the famous Balfour-Macassey Commission to enquire into Clyde unrest and, without waiting for this to meet McKinnon Wood, set up a similar investigation into rent increases under Lord Hunter and Professor Scott.[183] The rumours of such an initiative had reached factors earlier, and on 14th October they worsened the situation by quickly increasing rents, hoping to establish a higher level from which to compromise or deal with immediate restriction.[184]

Thereafter the lines of battle were clearly marked as increasing numbers joined the strikes and attended public demonstrations against the owners and their agents. The established authority relations which had been preserved for decades in affluent artisan areas were now breaking down as respectable tenants participated in violence against rent collectors and picketing to obstruct Sheriff's Officers. Had the wealthy occupants of Partickhill and Hyndland gazed from their ornate windows above Partick they might have seen the mass meetings of tenants and shipyard workers rather than the calm progress of battleship construction. In mid-October there took place the massive picket of two thousand people on Thornwood Hill to protect the popular Andrew Hood against eviction, and the conscientious supporters of bodies such as the Partick Civic Guild would have been dismayed to find that a police officer was one of those prominent in the Partick resistance.[185] With rent strikes spreading to such districts as Kinning Park, Maryhill, Cambuslang and even Rutherglen, the original centres of struggle remained solid.[186] The Stephens family perched in their mansion on Partickhill could see the elaborate tenements surrounding their Linthouse yard where the first serious troubles began, whilst in the next frontage space on the Clyde stood the Fairfield premises which were the focus of industrial mobilisation against the Government.

The hearings of Lord Balfour and Lyndon Macassey gave the unions a platform for airing grievances but did little to remedy the shipwrights' case, which was only settled by the officials' payment of the fines in late October.[187] Opposition to the Munitions legislation continued during the autumn, just as the first serious confrontations on the dilution question affected workshops at Glasgow, Paisley and Johnstone.[188] The statutory machinery for enforcing the intensified division of labour under dilution had been passed in the summer, but the determined resistance of workmen to the importation of unskilled male and female labour threatened to affect the qualified tradesmen who were needed to train and overlook the lesser grades at Parkhead and elsewhere. Moreover, the rise in overtime and earnings, together with the tremendous pressures on the workforce to increase output, had encouraged the continuation of output restriction, loose timekeeping and hard drinking amongst the shipyard and engineering trades. Employers were understandably anxious that the Government should resolve these problems before pressing them into a dilution programme against the clear wishes of the craft societies. They were still uncertain of the advantages brought by rapid dilution of labour, more particularly in the shipyards where the high standards of workmanship required on the intricate parts of a battle cruiser or armour-plated warship meant that craft administration of production was virtually unassailable.[189] The reticence of the large industrial concerns explains the limited character of dilution confrontation before the winter of 1915-16, and the keen attention given to the proceedings of the Balfour-Macassey findings on the workings of the Munitions measures.

Despite the efforts of these employers to distance themselves from the housing and rents protests, their works were infiltrated by the local mobilisation against factors. By early November 1915, the Labour weekly *Forward* informed its readers that:[190]

> An important development has been made by the Partick strikers this week in the form of emergency Committees in the various shipyards and workshops against the payment of increased rent . . . Trade union branches ought to interest themselves in this question.

Coming at the same time as the rise of the Clyde Trades Vigilance Committee, and the growth of local workplace representation in engineering shops and shipyards, such 'emergency committees' behind the rent strike could hardly have been welcome news for employers. On 13th November there took place a large Women's Housing Association gathering on Thornwood Hill itself, overlooking the Partick shipyards and addressed by leading Labour women such as Mary Macarthur.[191] The mood of the strikers was now jubilant, with reports of thousands of Glasgow tenants on rent strike and the leadership unwilling to accept anything short of complete rent restriction. By its inertia the Cabinet had allowed the situation to deteriorate well beyond the initial demands for the protection of servicemen's dependants and the introduction of a Fair Rents Court in Glasgow. Even before Lord Hunter started calling witnesses to his Enquiry in October, spokesmen such as Owen Coyle of the iron and steel workers had dismissed the idea that they were waiting on 'the result of any Commission of rents'. Mrs. Ferguson had also told the Partick tenants that in their entrenched position they:[192]

> would be able to refuse to accept the decision of the Commissioners appointed to conduct the Government inquiry, if they considered the terms harsh.

By the beginning of November the Labour Party and rent strikers had shifted from their long-standing demand of a Fair Rents Court, insisting on the restoration of pre-War rents without compensation to landlords.[193] Unless this was conceded by the Government and houseowners, the rent strike committees would simply enforce the old rents by direct action and meet any eviction moves with industrial strikes and total withholding of rents.

It was in this mood that the climax of the rent strike was reached with the prosecution of fifteen tenants for non-payment of increases, and an appeal for their removal by the factor. Thousands of people marched to the centre of Glasgow, with deputations from at least five main shipyards and one armaments works to represent the views of the workforce.[194] Whilst the crowds were addressed by an array of socialist orators and strike leaders, from Andrew McBride and Mary Barbour to John Maclean and James McDougall, the sympathetic Sheriff heard the testimonies of the industrial deputations in support of the defendants. Speakers from Govan, Beardmore's Dalmuir shipyard, and a spokesman from 'one of the principal Engine Shops on the Clyde' warned of the dire consequences which would follow the authorisation of eviction.[195] The leader of the Tenants' Committee and subject of the test case being heard, Reid, refused to accept any adjournment of the matter or to wait upon the Government's promised response to the Hunter Report, and eventually Sheriff Lee persuaded the owner to abandon the whole proceeding.[196] To the sound of general celebrations, socialist speakers urged the strikers to insist on a return to pre-War rents in all working class districts and to resist any other proposals.[197] Under pressure from parallel protests in vital munitions centres such as Woolwich, Birkenhead and Birmingham, the Cabinet accepted the advice of McKinnon Wood and eventually agreed to restrict the rents of all dwellings likely to be used by working class tenants. Against the propertied, financial and legal interests of Clydeside and elsewhere, the organised rent strikers had achieved an important advance.

In order to understand the complex and ambivalent reactions of Clyde engineering and shipbuilding employers to the events of 1915, it is essential that we emphasise the distinct origins of labour unrest and the changing character of state control over the munitions sector. During the February troubles the engineering workers were principally involved, but their employers included shipyards as well as engineering or foundry works. At that time the industrialists were horrified to discover that Government departments were prepared to contemplate the 2d advance, though there were important divisions between Admiralty and other elements of the bureaucracy.[198] During the drafting of the Munitions legislation under Lloyd George, the intransigence of the Engineering Federation and the disappointing record of industrialists in meeting government orders led to their virtual exclusion from discussions between trade unions and the state. Besides the granting of important concessions to labour, this became the cause of bitter recrimination between national federations and Clyde associations.[199] Throughout the spring and summer of 1915, industrialists were insisting on legal coercion of skilled workers and the virtual repression of trade union rights — with outlawing of strikes and the complete prohibition of alcohol in the munitions areas. When the Liberal Coalition was unwilling to contemplate such authoritarian policies, local industrialists engaged in a course of limited co-operation with Government officials and made only sporadic attempts to work within the framework of the Armaments Committee.[200] Apparently unable to deal with a situation which removed their threat of dismissal (given the extreme scarcity of craftsmen), many industrialists resorted to the blatant abuse of powers given under the Munitions legislation or simply ignored official advice and operated in a pragmatic way by attracting as much labour as possible.

It was clear that however unsatisfactory output performance, industrial management would do little to improve workplace relations until the state took a harder line. On the other hand, they were unwilling to introduce dilution unless guaranteed Government action to suppress such opposition as that found in Johnstone and Paisley during autumn 1915. Whilst dilution offered even the shipbuilders a golden opportunity to enforce long-awaited innovations under management control, the dangers of protracted stoppages and diehard restrictions were obvious to even bigoted enemies of unionism.[201] Employers were unrelenting in their demands for industrial conscription and legal prosecution of dissidents, but also deeply suspicious of state encroachments on the powers of management and the taxing of excessive profits on war contracts.[202]

Their reception of rent strikes and housing protests was less prejudiced, partly because they shared their employees' exasperation at the shortage of accommodation for vital munitions workers and disliked the discontents which rising prices and rents caused in local areas. As owners of housing themselves, industrialists were less interested in the small margin of profit to be gained by rent increases than in the massive returns on wartime orders. Should they be drawn into identifying with the unpopular landlords, then their own workforce could immediately demand recompense in the form of increased wages or additional bonuses beyond those already exacted. Thus when the Govan branch of the Women's Housing Association visited the managing director of Harland & Wolff at Govan, the firm responded to the case put against taking over any dwellings vacated by eviction, writing a formal letter to Mary Barbour, Mrs. Ferguson and the other Association activists.[203] This attitude was probably typical of employers who had received little assistance from the propertied interests and speculative builders when they required accommodation in the peacetime years, nor did they sympathise with the rentier profits accrued by bondholders benefiting from wartime shortages of investment capital.[204] Large employers like Beardmore, who held some housing at his steel plants and was constructing much more at the Dalmuir yard, had to tread very carefully between securing a minimum return on capital and exciting the resentment of the radical Dalmuir workers.

What was much more unsettling and disturbing was the continued success of workplace resistance and the appearance of fresh grassroots representation, often committed to a Labour or socialist programme. For the rent strikes heralded not merely an unprecedented threat to landlord authority, but also facilitated the evolution of working class organisations. These gave local working people an alternative perspective on civil society, challenging the dominant role of established institutions and authority relations. Local dynasties of employers, such as Stephens at Linthouse and Pearces at Govan, found their customary control over educational, policing and local government services now being disputed by trades councils, ward committees and elected Councillors under Labour direction. Outstanding socialists such as John Maclean were not content at spreading revolutionary propaganda at pacifist meetings or teaching shop stewards at classes in Glasgow, but attempted to introduce trade unionism to their own professions and took an active interest in local politics. In autumn 1914, Harry Hopkins had sought Glasgow Trades Council support for his efforts to democratise Govan School Board procedures and to secure the abolition of 'their Monthly Meetings in Committee', where important issues were decided behind closed doors. Seconded by local leaders such as Thom and Davidson (who were to figure in the Govan rents unrest), the Council moderates still shelved the issue despite the arguments of Hopkins.[205] The significance of this question became clear the next year, when his belligerent headmaster succeeded in arranging a Board enquiry into the conduct of the Govan schoolteacher, to be held in camera and without the right of reply from Maclean. Having the spectacle of the Munitions Tribunals, the Balfour-Macassey enquiry and the Hunter Committee before them, the Board members had no intention of allowing the Maclean case to become a forum for agitation and debate. After bitterly protesting against the victimisation of Maclean as only one participant in collective action by teachers, Hopkins went on to inform his Board colleagues:[206]

> He never heard of such a committee of enquiry in all his existence . . . they were to find out things and they refused to hear evidence. Refused to hear the side of the parties interested. M'Lean called that tyrannical and unjust, and he agreed with him.

During the final culmination of the rent strike unrest in mid-November 1915, Maclean was effectively disciplined and suspended from his post at Govan. Left all the more vulnerable as a leading theoretician of workplace resistance and uncompromising opponent of the imperialist conflict, Maclean was to be repeatedly imprisoned during the remaining years of the War along with other activists.[207]

With the triumph of the rent strikers, industrial militants were more confident than ever of negotiating a favourable introduction of workplace dilution which would guarantee trade rights and craft control of work processes. The very different conditions of engineering and shipbuilding precluded any common front on dilution, or of the united resistance which had proved so effective during the rents campaign and opposition to Munitions coercion. But the prestige of the Clyde Workers' Committee (C.W.C.), and of individual leaders such as Kirkwood, suggested that a radical alternative to enforced importation of females was likely. After the fiasco of Lloyd George's Christmas visit to Glasgow and the arrival of the Dilution Commissioners, there was widespread pessimism amongst employers about dilution prospects. Failure to agree on a practicable solution within the Clyde Workers' Committee or to persuade the Commissioners to accept the Committee as the authentic spokesman of engineering trades created the conditions for individual plant agreements in early 1916. The first important settlement was at Parkhead, where Beardmore's maverick approach to industrial management and Kirkwood's egocentric talents enabled dilution to begin. Parkhead shop stewards depended on their direct access to the dilutees, and the *organisational* links with the women's trade union, to retain some control over the dilution process. When this was prohibited by management and welfare supervisor, their whole defensive strategy was placed in jeopardy — hence the strike and crisis of March 1916 which led to the exile of Kirkwood and other C.W.C. notables.[208] This did not signify the triumph of the organised employers, particularly as plant agreements survived and became the basic model of the dilution programme, but rather provided a strong basis on which industrialists and Dilution Commissioners could negotiate the extension of engineering innovations. Any combined threat to this programme from socialist shop stewards was largely excluded, though workshop restrictions remained in the separate plants.

There were also considerable variations in the pattern of dilution achieved in engineering and shipbuilding, as well as distinct conflicts over the issue of job control during the War. Disaffection spread through the riverside and engine works over key questions of Trade Card rights, and there were similar waves of unionism amongst the technical and supervisory grades, but important differences remained in the pace of change and jurisdiction accorded to society officials. Only with the general wages campaigns of autumn 1916 and the subsequent controversies over immunity from military conscription did some semblance of common unrest return to the industrial areas. Restrained in many of their more extreme proposals for workplace repression, the Clyde employers were able to convince the government of the need for coercion in times of crisis, and during 1917-18 there was a growing rapport over problems of labour discipline. The need for such crude subordination of labour was acutely felt by industrialists who faced continuing unrest amongst the workmen and growing resistance from their key intermediate groups — unco-operative supervisors could undermine the whole hierarchy of management authority and the future of workplace dilution. Thus, in early 1918, the aggressive management of John Browns of Clydebank wrote to the Ministry of

Munitions urging the introduction of statutory penalties (including imprisonment) for anyone promoting output restrictions or strikes, adding:[209]

> In support of the foregoing suggestion I have to explain that the legitimate voice of any Trades' Union is drowned by the Socialist-Syndicalist element which constitutes about 15-20 per cent. of the Union. When a meeting is called on any subject, the fanatical minority are always present en bloc . . . only the enactment of a penal clause is likely to have a deterrent effect on industrial 'reformers'. . .

Clearly the setbacks to the C.W.C.'s attempts to achieve a common front on engineering dilution had left local resistance in both engineering *and* shipbuilding trades largely intact, with a resurgence of unrest during the later stages of the War.

One point of controversy in both labour resistance and managerial control was the status accorded to craftsmen as essential munitions workers, exempting them from military conscription. Tradesmen with memories of the per-War Discharge Note struggles and the disputes over Leaving Certificates during 1915 at Fairfields and elsewhere remained intensely suspicious of the employers' motives in administering these labour directives. Hence the opposition to the alterations in Trade Cards during 1917, and frequent complaints about the granting of Exemption Certificates to favoured employees by foremen and management.[210] It was again the Govan shipbuilders who argued for an extension of sanctions against men who restricted output or were simply bad timekeepers during the last year of the War. In 1918 Alexander Gracie of Fairfields suggested to fellow employers that the conscription of bad timekeepers would have a 'good effect upon the other workmen', whilst the Stephens were critical of the tendency for shipyard workers to stop before the final whistle was heard. The Government representative was unequivocal about official policy and suggested that:[211]

> Such ones can be dealt with by bringing workmen before the Enlistment Complaints Committee. If this has no effect the Exemption Certificate can be withdrawn.

Whilst the continuing demand for skilled labour gave these scarce employees a considerable market value, there was no question of labour controls being removed by the state. The ultimate sanction of summary dismissal was replaced by the threat of discharge and immediate conscription to the bloody scenes of the Western Front.

The fact that wartime governments were not prepared to instigate direct coercion except as a last resort, and the significant concessions made to organised labour during 1915-16, indicates the deficiency of any simple 'servile state' analysis. Rather the scope and nature of state intervention was changing as a consequence of wartime innovations, just as the forms of representation within the ranks of capital and labour were shifting from their traditional complexion. Wartime industrial relations in these heavy industries involved a continuing process of negotiation between the different levels of organisation acting for labour, as well as bargaining with their corresponding agents under capital. There were important tendencies towards more democratic and progressive shop floor representation before and during the War, but not a consistent struggle between an embattled rank and file of militant tradesmen and an incorporated trade union bureaucracy.[212] Within certain situations and under rapidly changing conditions, local or national officials might indeed accomplish a more radical or practicable policy than employees caught within craft conservatism or isolated resistance. The circumstances surrounding a specific policy or conflict and the varying estimations of future developments were crucial to the formulation and effects of that course. Therefore any appraisal of labour struggles must appraise not merely the structural constraints of unionism and dialogue between distinct levels and sections of workplace organisation, but also the political motives of the participants and the consciousness of the workforce as a whole.

Similar points may be made of the Scottish employers, who were divided among themselves, even within the heavy industries of Clydeside. The crisis of March 1916 was the consequence not only of Kirkwood's departure from C.W.C. policy to create a plant settlement at Parkhead, but also of Beardmore's refusal to stand with the engineering employers and his highly personal approach to business management. Divisions were apparent between distinct industrial interests at regional level and between local associations unhappy at the agreements made by their own federations in London. Clydeside firms were horrified to find that the Munitions legislation of 1915 was passed with the minimum of business consultation, and continued to complain that their fundamental interests were not taken into account.[213] Much of this suspicion and rancour can be explained by the historical isolation of Scottish industrialists from the exercise of political power and the weakness of organs such as the Scottish Office during the crises of 1915-16. The periodic despatch of officials north from London, including the Dilution Commissioners and Admiralty representatives, marked the process whereby Government attempted to educate the businessmen in the ways of civilised negotiation and persuade them of the virtues of conciliation above outright repression.

The hostility with which the local industrialists received the news of substantial concessions to labour during 1916-17 shows the limits of their success, but at least there was some progress beyond the abysmal failures with Armaments Committee and dilution in 1915. Above all, government officials and responsible industrial leaders were concerned to formalise and (where possible) centralise negotiations between employers and unions under the general supervision of the state. These tentative steps towards a *corporate* structure of government direction and discussion implied an advance in the role of the British state, which played a positive part in the maintenance of productive relations rather than merely reflecting them. The prospect of military defeat or social revolution was of immediate concern not only to ruling class propertied interests, but also to those groups dependent on the survival of stable government itself. There was a much greater chance of continuing stability amidst the carnage and conflict of war if the official representatives of labour played a creative role in the state regulation of private industry. Despite the acrimonious correspondence flowing between London and Clydeside, Scottish industrialists recognised the interdependence of official and private interests and never threatened to resist legislation or war effort.[214]

The imperatives for such legislation came not just from unionism or even from industry as a whole, but from the rising tide of social protests such as those which culminated in the 1915 rent strikes. With rent strikes sweeping through key munitions areas and the future of the whole war machine endangered by daily threats of industrial support, there occurred the decisive shift against the propertied and financial interests whose holdings were most affected by rents protests and who probably constituted the wealthiest groups in Edwardian Britain. Industrialists were now the most important *strategic* element of capitalism involved in the war effort and were relatively sympathetic to the introduction of rent and mortgage restriction, whilst even the landed groups were anxious at the consequence of rising interest rates and working class rents.[215] With powerful trade union, tenants' and political organisations mobilised against the landlords in numerous areas, professional politicians and the 'informed' public opinion represented in *Times* editorials advocated state regulation of property relations.[216] Government even accepted the need for monitoring the attitudes of working class consumers and had intended that such bodies as the War Emergency Workers' National Committee should act as an appendage of the civil service in offering advice to the Government on local requirements.[217] One reason for official inertia may have been the failure of the Committee to gauge the depth of feeling on the rents issue until the crisis was upon the Cabinet at Westminster.[218] Once appraised of the continuing resentment on prices and other issues, wartime administrations responded in rather similar ways to their policy on industrial unrest. Grievances were channeled into the machinery of formal consultation, with the state acting as the supposedly neutral arbitrator between conflicting parties and resolving affairs in the public interest.

There can be little doubt that the strategic significance of the engineering and shipbuilding industries in the war effort largely accounts for their tremendous impact on Government initiatives. Yet it would be a serious distortion of class relations to exclude the parallel developments which occurred in other sectors of the regional economy during these years. The manufacture of textiles, operation of railways, and production of coal were all vital to the armed services if only because they supplied and transported the servicemen using munitions of war. Although the struggles in these industries were perhaps less dramatic than those seen in Clydeside workshops and shipyards, these trades employed more people as a whole and also required government intervention in their affairs. There was the same tendency towards the convergence of industrial and social protests, whether the conflicts originated in their sector or in neighbouring districts, *and* the erosion of boundaries between previously distinct localities and occupations.

Military orders for khaki cloth and various types of cotton resulted in booming conditions for textile, twine and dyeing employers in the West of Scotland during the War. Profitability at concerns such as The Gourock Company at Greenock reached record levels during the later years of the fighting despite the relative competition from munitions works for local females.[219] Hard-pressed cotton magnates and dyeing masters who had suffered hectic competition for decades now discovered that they were unable to meet the supplies demanded by total war.

These conditions of scarcity and the growing competition for male and female labour were to have important consequences for industrial relations in areas like Leven. Before the War, management had carefully reconstructed workplace legitimacy by careful negotiations at United Turkey Red. Even the female outrages of 1911-12 had been overlaid by the machinery of disputes arbitration, although the appalling working conditions and continued reliance on low-paid workers (especially younger females) indicated a certain fragility in these agreements. The grievances of generations finally erupted during 1916, when Levenside workers could compare the soaring earnings of engineering or shipyard employees with their own handful of shillings. After prolonged unrest at the dyeworks Sir Thomas Munro arrived to arbitrate over an industrial conference at which the union representatives stated in uncompromising terms that:[220]

> The wages of the employees for whom we plead are the lowest in Scotland, and the time has now arrived when nothing short of a revolution in rates of wages is required . . .
>
> The workers are not willing that the present state of affairs shall last, and failing some more satisfactory treatment than has been given in the past, the workers must be allowed to use what weapons lie in their hands to secure the most elementary justice — the right to lead a decent life.

The very language displays a significant advance in the workforce's consciousness, combining as it does the comparison with other groups and the rhetoric of revolutionary change.

Textile employers made significant concessions at Alexandria, Greenock and elsewhere, but these neither damaged their massive war profits nor deflected the aggressive confidence of the workforces. At townships like Port Glasgow and Greenock, or in the mills of Glasgow's east end, employees could not be insulated from the opportunities open to women in heavy industry or the waves of unrest which swept workplace and rented accommodation during the war years. Females who aspired to higher earnings and independence in munitions production were understandably ambiguous in their attitudes to craftsmen who wished to exclude them from engineering, but their liberation from poorly rewarded employment frequently gave them a new confidence in autonomous trade unionism at the Clydeside plants.[221] Whilst housewives pressed for the better housing which would entail an improvement in *their* everyday working conditions, and achieved greater authority in their dealings with factors and rent collectors, working women attained unprecedented powers of consumption and self-determination in such areas.

Another industry almost inevitably affected by the events in munitions production was the railway sector, with the giant locomotive works at Springburn becoming a centre of workplace radicalism during the crises of 1915-16.[222] This railway metropolis was also an early recruit to the Glasgow rent strikes of autumn 1915, along with numerous other districts characterised as 'artisan neighbourhoods'. It seems unlikely that the large employers raised their rents at this period, at least for the dwellings of highly valuable engineering tenants, but the common stimulus to working class resistance must have cast shadows over the company boardrooms in these months. Equally serious were the antagonisms which persisted in the transportation section of the industry, occasioning numerous conferences under the Government controllers who were responsible for regulating services. These conflicts culminated in the upheavals at the end of the War, unparalleled since the national crisis of 1912 and involving widespread violence.

The Scottish railway companies were afflicted by rapid unionisation of clerical grades as well as manual workers, partly a heritage of the pre-War repression of workplace organisation. Occupants of company housing who failed to support their neighbours in collective resistance were frequently the subject of harassment and humiliation at this time. After one particularly bitter encounter between union labour and blackleg families, North British directors were compelled to find alternative accommodation for their loyal labour.[223] As one foreman remarked on the troubles at this isolated settlement surrounding a depot:[224]

> The more effective plan would have been to have cleared all the other four families altogether and their menfolk found employment at different centres. This would teach these wild venomous women that they cannot be allowed to disturb any community without having to pay the penalty . . . it is [now] more likely that quietness will only be restored until some other poor victim is singled out.

Whilst such deliberate campaigns of female violence may have remained fairly unusual during and immediately after the War, there can be less doubt about the increasing tendency for women to resort to lawless behaviour in this period. Whereas male trade unions came to support the female-led rent strikes during 1915, housewives were equally prepared to reinforce industrial solidarity whenever possible.

Like railways and shipbuilding, Scotland's collieries continued to be almost totally the preserve of a male labour force during the years of war. On the eve of hostilities there were ominous signs that managerial initiatives attempting to tighten control over work processes were causing dissatisfaction at the pits. Mineowners experienced the most progressive demands from their workers for limitation of hours, guaranteed minimum wages, improvements in working conditions and a general extension of government regulation during the years 1908-14. In fighting the Minimum Wage proposals of 1912, the owners believed they were striving not merely for 'their own existence, but also in the interests of [other] industries which are vital to the . . . country'.[225] Widespread agitation on the housing issue at this time became almost a testing ground for private ownership itself, with a strong case put by socialists and those described as 'syndicalists' for an end to capitalist control.[226]

With the War came a series of important wage advances to the Scottish miners, causing many owners to complain of squeezed profits and even losses on production.[227] Questions of work discipline assumed a fresh urgency during 1917-18 as supervisory and managerial employees at the collieries organised and demanded improvements in salaries and conditions. In spring 1918 the Scottish Mine Managers acquired permanent pay advances beyond the temporary war bonuses offered by the masters, and the supervisory undermanagers and oversmen achieved concessions beyond the minimum increases stipulated by the Coal Controller in 1918-19.[228] Even the clerical workers mobilised to improve their eroded differentials and working environment, their Colliery Clerks' Association demanding remuneration in line with rising living costs and additional burdens. After rejecting an unattractive arbitration award, the clerks were eventually given a decision by the Committee on Production.[229]

The coal employers were forced to pacify their manual and staff employees with substantial increases and to accept increasing state administration of the industry, without accumulating the massive war profits seen in the munitions trades. They were also vulnerable to the return of unrest and agitation on the housing question during the later years of war, with the 1911 Ballantyne Commission on industrial dwellings finally reporting in 1917 and including an authoritative survey of miners' accommodation in their findings.[230] The Commission's recommendations became the subject of bitter controversy during the following years, contributing to the debates on nationalisation at the time of the Sankey Commission on future development.[231] Bad housing owned by the coal concerns was held to be an indictment of private management, as radical critics like Robertson demanded government control of both industry and social provisions. Attacked on various fronts, Scottish coalowners discussed their defensive strategy, observing that:[232]

> . . . it is a case for us of washing in public the linen Robertson has been allowed to soil, or refuting Sankey's accusation of general ineptitude . . . or negativing the suggestion that because Miners do not all live in good houses the mines should be nationalised.

The convergence of industrial and social issues during this period of proposed

Reconstruction brought the miners into the forefront of the nationalisation debate, giving the owners their most serious challenge since the days of the Minimum Wage movement.

Surrounded by hostile critics, the employers sought to divide the debate into distinct parts, focusing on the housing problem as a distinct question. Firstly, they upheld the traditional conservative argument that poor housing was fundamentally a result of individual bad habits and the refusal to pay economic rents for better accommodation.[233] Secondly, the firms pointed out that significant progress had been made in the housing stock since 1900 as a result of their initiatives, and that further improvements were intended. Thirdly, the Scottish organisation noted that, contrary to being an argument for increased state ownership, inadequate housing was a serious 'indictment of public management by the State of the Housing Problem'.[234] The employers fully accepted the responsibility of the government for housing the working class, endorsing Ballantyne's suggestions of increased expenditure after the War, but they insisted that this was quite a separate matter from social ownership of the means of production or national control of industry itself. Whilst bureaucratic intervention on questions of production and pay had been necessary during the prosecution of the War, the employers pressed for rapid decontrol of mining and the restoration of legitimate managerial prerogatives.

Although the pattern of development in textiles, railways and coalmining was distinct in each sector, there were important parallels in the relations of employers and workpeople. Expansion of production and the pressures of increased output led to a resurgence of industrial organisation and aggressive demands on pay and conditions, not only from established tradesmen but also from lesser skills and the newly-recruited intermediate grades of staff employees. The influx of fresh workers and changes in the methods of production tended to erode previous barriers in the sectional and sexual division of labour, frequently threatening authority relations and workplace hierarchies. Women were much more prominent both at the place of work and in the campaigns to improve living and working conditions for housewives or families.

There was a clear tendency for industrial resistance and social protest to converge, whether at Greenock and Levenside, Springburn and Cadder, or the numerous colliery villages compaigning for state action on housing. Increased government intervention was needed to resolve many of these conflicts, with legislation to regulate railways and coalmining as well as arbitration in major textile disputes during the War. After the relative tranquillity of 1916, housing again became a major focus of working class agitation in the period 1917-19. Corporate state regulation of such sectors inevitably led to a *politicisation* of economic as well as social questions, despite the efforts of officials to distance themselves from everyday control and conflicts and to present government agencies as the neutral arbitrator of antagonistic parties. The fact that working class campaigns demanded public control of private interests in radical language also denotes a major advance in the consciousness of class, and it is this which presented perhaps the greatest threat of all to the Scottish industrialists.

Employers and the struggle for a working class political economy

The effect of these continuing struggles in different industries and distinct areas was to accentuate the confrontation between the forces of conservatism and mass revolt at this period. With the deterioration in industrial relations and social conditions went the decline in respect for management authority and property relations. The intricate web of male-orientated power which generated hierarchical, section and sexual inequalities within the workforce was damaged by the recurring unrest amongst the skilled, unskilled and supervisory employees. The very acceleration of the division of labour and the complete restructuring of labour forces in sectors such as engineering, facilitated the change in attitudes and organisation. Gradual negotiations over the form innovation might take frequently gave way under the pressures of desperate shortage and military emergency. The death and crippling injury of thousands of male workers recruited to the services and their replacement by greater numbers of women and boys led to the disruption of households, the practical emancipation of daughters, the breaching of apprenticeship indentures, and the reduction of parental controls.

Housing and rents protests challenged the customary deference of tenants to landlords and factors, whilst defying the accepted principles of market prices and contractual obligation. Legal intimidation and even prosecution were of little avail in the situation of autumn 1915, when factors were chased in the streets and Sheriffs heckled in the courtroom. The prominence of acknowledged 'artisan' tenants and 'respectable working class' districts in the rent strikes only demonstrated the extent to which more affluent groups were disaffected. Organised market resistance by consumers could be even more effective against propertied elements than strikes at the workplace against industrialists, for the tenants remained physically in possession of their dwellings even when no increases were paid and strikes occurred.

Incursions on the privileges of different capitalist groups were coupled with an invasion of the organs of local government and an assault on the institutions of civil society. Even before the War, trade union and Labour organisations had colonised such bodies as ward committees and transformed them into the springboard of Labour elections. Elected offices such as School Boards, Parish Councillors, Burgh Baillies (popular J.P.s) and Civic Councillors became the battleground of local Labour politics. Trades Councils acquired the prestige of spokesman for the local unions and expressed their opinion on such matters as sanitary provisions or recreational facilities. Labour Party organisations such as their Women's Guild, Women's Labour

League, Women's Housing Associations, and I.L.P. branches were able to increase their membership and establish a presence in even the strongholds of Orangeism such as Partick.

These facilities offered a radical alternative to the activities and ideas of the traditional voluntary agencies, such as the Partick Civic Guild or the Workmen's Institutes provided by Victorian business leaders. It was the experience of resistance which gave many of these alternative agencies their meaning and purpose in working class neighbourhoods. From these conflicts there emerged a distinctive framework of ideas which translated dominant values in terms of popular perceptions, as well as introducing fundamental contrasts to bourgeois ideology. This fluid process of translation is evident in the language of the rent strikers during the months of 1915, as well as in the campaigns of textile workers and miners' leaders. Conservative newspapers and civic leaders stressed the virtues of patriotism, sobriety and legality throughout the stormy incidents of munitions tribunals and rents protests. The workers and tenants fully agreed with these principles and were outraged at suggestions that they were violating contractual duties or harming the war effort. According to the strike banners and protest meetings, it was the landlords who assisted the Prussians by their unpatriotic persecution of servicemen's dependants, their exactions against munitions workers and their exploitation of wartime shortages. Factors were breaching every principle of legal equity by their unfair prosecution and eviction of respectable tenants. Charges of insobriety blazoned across the pages of national newspapers were seen as merely the reproduction of smears made by hated employers such as Weirs of Cathcart.

The powerful *ethical* content of the rent strikes and other actions was essential to its success as a mass movement, with radical clergymen involved in I.L.P. campaigns and speakers such as Mary Macarthur appealing to the moral fibre of local housewives.[235] This sense of morality was underlined by the cultural traditions of the socialist movement and the conscientious objection of many activists to the War itself. Speakers such as Maclean were remarkably successful in their public speeches against the imperialist conflict, however much this ran counter to widespread patriotism, just as Maclean's educational classes on working class economics attracted shop stewards disagreeing with his revolutionary politics. The Labour Party was probably the most effective organisation, partly because it combined a coherent critique of capitalism with an ethical vision deriving from very popular works such as Blatchford's. The I.L.P. also managed to bridge the divide between industrial membership and Trade Council influence, and the politics of local areas which gave working people greater control of social services and their own lives. Tangible policies on housing, education and leisure created a base of support beyond the adult males of heavy industry, providing an immediate institutional support for the work of tenants' leaders, suffragist or women's industrial agitators, and even Irish republican supporters.

Yet the construction of this political economy was beset by the same contradictions which gave rise to class conflict in the Clyde region. Although there was a persistent emphasis on the needs of 'the community' in the crusade for fair rents, and the threat of continued direct action to enforce these restrictions, there was no real objective beyond state regulation of wartime increases. Trade unions had spent weeks fighting the coercive clauses of the Munitions Acts and were to resist the directives of the Dilution Commissioners, at the very time they were demanding government intervention to restrain landlords. The speed with which the Cabinet acted during the weeks after November 17th restored much of the Government's waning legitimacy and isolated those groups who subsequently opposed official dilution policy. It is doubtful if rent increases constituted a serious burden on the vast majority of working class tenants even in most munitions districts, and it is certainly true that the rents movement gained much momentum from protests arising from quite different grievances. Leaders such as Andrew McBride frankly admitted that rent increases were concentrated upon as the focal point in consumer resistance, largely because the landlord was an easier target than the shopkeeper or food profiteer.[236]

The Labour Party also contributed their support to the rents unrest from a long-term commitment to the housing issue as a key plank in their local government platform. McBride went on to form the Scottish Housing Association with David Kirkwood, Wheatley and others, but it is arguable that the concession of rent restriction effectively shelved consideration of housing reform itself for some years. Tenants were reasonably satisfied with frozen rents amidst rising prices and earnings, whilst builders and housing investors were confirmed in their aversion to working class dwellings as a source of profit. An area of the economy had been 'captured' from private hands in certain respects, but positive action depended on future housing reform and even removed from capitalism the burdens of providing an unprofitable infrastructure for more lucrative production.

Later concessions to the trade unions and even plant shop stewards in the form of advantageous legislation and Reconstruction reforms suffered from the same ambiguities. They accorded labour leadership a role in the responsible partnership of corporate negotiations, but failed to transform the fundamental relations which placed working people in a subordinate economic position. The failure of wartime campaigns to erode the foundations of state power is partly explained by the limits of working class consciousness during the crucial months of 1915-16, before the full adjustment to total war had been made. Like the food rioters of the eighteenth century, Glasgow crowds composed a 'moral economy' of traditionalist beliefs which prescribed the fixing of commodities at the 'fair' price by authorities or popular action, together with a bitter attack on profiteering and market forces.[237] Rent strikers appear not at the dawn of liberal laissez faire, but at its demise — when classical principles were already giving way to notions of social welfare and corporate management, ill-formed though such ideas were. It would be mistaken to see the rent strikes and other movements as simply the ethical reflex of a traditionalist working class. The massed gatherings at Clydeside and elsewhere made a positive contribution to both bourgeois *and* working class political economy, extending the scope and practical limits of government intervention well beyond the boundaries of classical theory. One flaw from the perspective of working class needs was the failure to present a more thoroughgoing analysis of the political institutions which made up the state itself. The *organisational* link between the defence of imprisoned shipwrights and the mass picketing of local law courts was made, but the leap in consciousness which signified attacks on the state itself was not achieved.

The ability of Liberal administrations to make major reforms during the War indicates the degree to which the state was itself subject to considerable change at this time. Concessions to labour were often achieved by the negotiation of distinct interests *within* the state as well as between the great propertied elements and sections of the working class. Military departments such as the Admiralty were frequently model employers in their own ship-yards and anxiously conservative in their attitudes to dilution of trade skills. Politicians and bureaucrats such as Addison or Macassey were sympathetic to the claims of labour and often contemptuous of business leadership or industrial management. The events surrounding the passing of rents legislation showed how various sections of property and the professions could swing behind quite radical innovations. Scottish employers were only gradually initiated in the ways of civilised government as a consequence of the painful experiences of 1914-15 at Clydeside. During these reforms the state enlarged its responsibilities and the basis of its legitimate support, culminating in the transition to mass democracy for adult males on the termination of the War.

Yet even the most progressive of Liberal innovators recognised the dangers of state encroachments on the freedoms of civil society, including those enjoyed by employers in the management of their rightful property at industrial plants. As the distance between government and private interests narrowed during state control of production, there was a very real concern about the future stability of industrial relations — with good reason in sectors such as mining. Business leaders and enlightened officials also shared an awareness of the need to recreate the institutions and values of local life, over-shadowed by the upheavals in the organisation of industry and the spread of insubordination during workplace stoppages and housing protests. Government action to coerce the recalcitrant and incorporate the responsible was clearly essential, but positive reforms were required if Reconstruction was not to be conducted under pressure of widespread unrest and an alternative socialist programme.

One of the directions in which employers achieved some success and co-operation was that of industrial welfare provision. Before the War, internal benefits and public amenities had formed an important part of management strategy in the different sectors of the West of Scotland. The case of coalmining demonstrated the degree to which the problems had outpaced their available resources, with the result that many industrialists narrowed their energies to selective schemes and differential privileges — such as those administered by railway companies and engineering concerns. Serious phases of unemployment could only be partially relieved by the array of voluntary agencies such as the Dumbarton Benevolent Fund, in which local families of capitalists still figured. With the War came very different problems of high earnings and a relaxation of certain moral standards, including increased consumption of alcohol. Clyde trade associations reacted in typical manner by demanding the total prohibition of alcoholic sales and consumption, and were only gradually persuaded by the Liquor Traffic Control Board that subsidised canteens would present an attractive alternative to local public houses.[238]

This pattern of persuading management into enlightened policies remained the standard practice of the Welfare Section under the Ministry of Munitions, originally directed by Seebohm Rowntree. Welfarist employers were able to deduct substantial amounts from their Excess Profits Duties in the funding of such schemes, which were especially concerned with the adaptation of women to industrial life in war. These services not only insulated females against undesirable contacts with males and their trade unions by a rigorous system of welfare supervision, but were also geared to regulate the social life and extramural activities of the women workers. Official reports and investigations propagated a whole philosophy of females' normal role and moral responsibilities, which were being disrupted rather than basically changed by wartime employment. As the *Final Report* of the influential Health of Munitions Workers Committee said in 1918:[239]

> In considering the conditions of employment of women workers as compared with those of men, the Committee have recognised that account must be taken not only of physiological differences but also of those contributions which women alone can make to the welfare of the community. Upon the womanhood of the country most largely rests the privilege first of creating and maintaining a wholesome family life, and secondly, of developing the higher influences of social life — both methods of primary and vital importance to the nation.

Here the language of 'community' was being reasserted in the context of stable family relations and the return of women to their customary subordinate position as the reproducers of essential labour. Their supposed moral superiority and domestic virtue accorded women a permanent obligation in the education of children, vital for social and national efficiency. In order to safeguard the purity of younger women who would later participate in this wholesome task, there were 'women patrols' in the munitions areas who cooperated with the local constabulary in preventing 'public disorder' amongst the younger workers.[240]

The resentment and resistance with which women often responded to such assistance, and the frequent disputes with the middle-class welfare supervisors at industrial plants, indicates the limited success employers achieved in this respect. But it does illustrate the ideological implications of these initiatives and the determined efforts of officials and progressive industrialists to recreate the cultural values of a civil society heavily damaged by the ruptures of wartime production. If authority relations were to be restored at work and in local settlements, then the imagery of tranquil domesticity and the sexual division of labour was one step towards 'normalcy'. The renewal of rent strikes and violent direct action involving women after 1918 again demonstrated the deficiencies in this cultural offensive, but the mass unemployment of females pressed them back into a customary defensive position. There could be no return to the practices of pre-1914, as widespread aversion to domestic service in the twenties showed, but women undoubtedly lost much of their bargaining freedom with the declaration of peace and the resurgence of trade sectionalism in industry.

Conclusions

This survey of class relations in Scotland's major industrial region during the decades after 1880 indicates the need for important modifications to classical Marxist accounts of social development in nineteenth century Britain. The transition from feudalism to capitalism was more protracted and complex than that suggested in orthodox interpretations, being powerfully affected by political contingencies and specific historical circumstances as well as the internal contradictions of pre-capitalist modes of production. Similarly, the shift from handicraft manufacturing to mechanised factory production was incomplete even in the twentieth century, with marked regional variations in the patterns of craft organisation. Consequently there was never the scope, whatever the incentives in particular cases, for a sharp advance towards the absolute subordination of labour in new work processes and away from the formal dependence of market relations.

The disadvantages inherent in restricting the creative initiatives of the workforce frequently offset the benefits of rigorous supervision, as became clear in the case of engineering and shipbuilding. Even where industrialists did succeed in breaking organised resistance to increasing subordination, in textiles and coalmining, other forms of defence were developed at the workplace and in wider society. Cultural traditions and customary attitudes could not be breached, however energetic the management or absolute the control of working conditions. The continuing demand for fresh labour, competition from other employers or areas, and inevitable limits on working class regulation beyond the factory gates, remained important obstacles to complete domination.

Further qualifications were to be found in the character of contemporary society and culture, including the industrialists' own perceptions of their employees. Despite rapid industrialisation and the spread of urban centres, property and political relations were not overturned during the mid-nineteenth century. Other forms of property and older hierarchies and status survived the arrival of an industrial bourgeoisie, which in any case was only rarely mobilised as a coherent force in Scottish political life. These divisions within and between propertied groups helped to explain the persistence of aristocratic leadership in formal politics, and the dissemination of genteel notions amongst professionals servicing the Victorian state. They also account for the disjuncture between industrial conflict and political movements during the bitter encounters of the 1840s. The diversity of interests involved in the exercise of power and exclusion of industrialists from direction of national policies in either England or Scotland deflected a directed challenge to state authority whilst facilitating alliances across class boundaries. The Victorian state never became a standing committee of the industrial bourgeoisie, nor was it ever characterised by simple laissez faire. At the very moment that capitalist industry was being liberated from the burdens of the Corn Laws, legislation was being enacted to regulate the system of company operation and the working conditions of factory operatives.

The forces of economic change after 1880 had the effect of underlining the tendencies towards co-operation and consolidation amongst industrialists, whilst also illustrating the important divisions which remained in their specific experiences of individual trades and concerns. Perceptive employers and managers responded to the difficult conditions of the 1880s and 1890s by introducing significant technical, financial and organisational reforms in their enterprises. The scope for such change was clearly prescribed by prevailing market conditions and workplace resistance, with branches of textiles, engineering and shipbuilding able to negotiate a creative alternative to crude deskilling or increased exploitation. Other workers offered strong resistance at the labour process or local labour market, with the consequence that certain trades went into terminal decline. In many cases the struggle for an acceptable frontier of control was escalated to the level of formal associations amongst employers and labour, imposing a tighter structure on bargaining and extending the issue of control to complex negotiations between distinct areas of business or labour representation, with local industrialists and union members frequently at variance with their own official organisations.

The pace with which new groups of industrialists and workers organised to defend their income and autonomy was only one feature of the decline of local particularisms, however much it may have strengthened the formal sectionalisation of interested parties. Most of the conflicts revolving around the issue of control and prerogatives at the workplace possess this fundamental ambiguity in purpose and effect, with similar themes or objectives buried beneath the specific circumstances of individual disputes. The ways in which increasing division of labour and industrial confrontations affect non-manual (and even managerial) grades show why we need to broaden our conception of the labour process well beyond the borders of manual dexterity to include the labour of employee co-ordination and direction itself. Otherwise our under-standing of work and hierarchies collapses into a false dichotomy between capitalist management performing no labour and subordinated employees unable to participate in the direction of others. In this period *both* the boundaries of actual workplace control *and* the organisations developed to defend respective areas of control were in a state of flux. The unionisation of whole new groups of workers only emphasised the fluid character of authority throughout Scottish industry. Industrialists needed to alter the basis of pro-duction by implementing necessary improvements, whilst at the same time ensuring the stability of hierarchical authority against the forces of disruption.

Nor can the diverse labour processes of Victorian society be confined within the domain of capitalist industry, given the considerable toil required at the home and in other sections of working class life. Indeed, the fragmentation of property holding and alternate avenues of accumulation contributed to the diffusion of class conflicts during much of this period. Family networks and tenant obligations underpinned the hierarchy of male-dominated authority relationships, just as supervisors and skilled workers instigated the sub-ordination of lesser groups beneath them. Industrialists were concerned to generate a stable community which might complement the framework of managerial authority, but were themselves frequently unsympathetic to the interests of other bourgeois groups — including landlords and shopkeepers who raised the cost of living within an immediate locale. Their own desire to replace male labour with cheaper female workers, or to diminish the privileged position of higher grades, tended to unsettle the picture of a distinct artisan culture and the fabric of male superiority in industrial districts.

At the same period the rising tide of unionism amongst the lesser skills and parallel resistance amongst consumers of housing signified serious unrest before 1914. Social problems showed a disturbing tendency to overlap with workplace disputes, whilst both spheres became the subject of intense political debate before the War. The process whereby whole sections of the labour force became committed to overtly political objectives was as complex and contra-dictory as the struggle for control in the work process. It was frequently the frustration of trade union organisation that pushed such employees as textile workers and railway staff into the pursuit of parliamentary objectives. Alternatively, serious conflicts such as those in the mining industry before 1914 threatened to damage the economy by the determined direct action of the unions, thus forcing intervention upon the state. In this context it was a political elite which defined and formulated the 'national interest' as the general interest of propertied groups as a whole, and who decided to make important concessions at the immediate expense of certain industrialists. Their growing awareness of serious weaknesses vis-a-vis other capitalists and the state itself accounts for the renewed efforts of Scottish industrialists to improve access to government before the War.

It was the transformation to efficient wartime production itself which marked decisive changes in the relative importance of industrial capital and the distance between the state and British civil society. Here the central contradiction in the government's responsibilities was exposed: it had to underwrite industrial manpower policy in order to safeguard production and its own military survival, but the progress of intervention almost inevitably politicised a whole range of industrial questions — including the maintenance of workplace authority itself. Areas such as Clydeside were vital to the effective prosecution of the War, hence the unprecedented concessions in the 2d Dispute, Munitions controversy, and rent strikes. Employers locked in their own intransigence refused to move beyond the demand for industrial conscription or implement dilution, until convinced by flexible officials and their own national federations. Eventually they recognised the mixed advantages of incorporating conflicts within formal negotiations, over the dangers of allowing workplace and rent strikes to cripple industry as a whole. After the crises of 1915-16 were past, officials and a recognisable industrial leadership developed the distinct strategies of firm repression, corporate negotiation, and reconstruction reforms, in order to provide a reasonable foundation for the total war economy. Meanwhile, more peripheral interests were sacrificed in the restrictions on rents, mortgages and food, whilst certain industrial owners (including many colliery firms) failed to reap the massive profits conceded to munitions employers during the years of hostilities. Having purchased this period of stability by compromise and concession, with the promises of further rewards under peacetime governments, political and industrial leaders were able to ride out the controversies over nationalisation of the coal industry until the boom broke in 1920.

This is not to imply that all the achievements of the previous period were lost in the decades of depression at Clydeside and elsewhere. The introduction of adult male suffrage in 1918 shows how significantly the state itself had changed in character since the 1880s. Local elections in the 1920s enabled political representatives of Labour to colonise whole areas of the state during a time of industrial disillusionment and defeat. Along with constitutional organisation went direct action in the Clydebank rent strikes and the General Strike. Whatever the humiliations of the Means Test, there could be no return to the Poor Law and no sudden repeal of rent restrictions.

The changing character of both industrial and political conflict over the years after 1880 further demonstrates the deficiencies of any crude structuralist account of social institutions and the bourgeois state. At the beginning of the period there were still numerous feudal relics embodied with the government, as well as antagonistic interests represented by the agencies of judiciary, bureaucracy, legislature, military, and so on. Important reforms could be passed against the express wishes and direct interests of industrialists in Scotland and elsewhere, though always subject to moderation in their administration and legal interpretation. With the onset of war and changing industrial structure, employers found that their traditional role as regulators and controllers of labour now gave them a crucial influence in government which they used to negotiate a fresh relationship between economy and state.

Similarly, the functions of trade unions were not predetermined by their objective position in organised labour or tendencies towards bureaucratisation. Union initiatives changed in accordance with the economic conditions in which they operated and the aspirations of their membership. At certain points the most basic demand of economistic unionism, that of a wage increase, could present a far greater challenge to employers' authority than a dispute over supervisory discipline. In other situations the national leadership of craft unions might be well in advance of either local officials or workplace attitudes, depending on how the ultimate ends of policy are to be assessed. Throughout we must focus on the *relationship* between the stated objectives of different labour groups, and the context in which these are pursued. This is equally true of the political sphere. The I.L.P.'s campaign on rents and housing cannot be dismissed as simply reformist or depicted as an unqualified revolutionary movement. Such campaigns take on many of the contradictions or ambiguities of the culture in which they emerge, and their consciousness is as much affected by the responses of authority as by the presence of articulate political figures in their midst. The conjuncture of economic grievances and industrial action from distinct sections of the workforce posed an unusually serious threat to propertied income and government authority, but stopped short of a direct attack on constitutional legitimacy as such.

The decades since 1920 have not seen the untrammeled growth of industrial plant on Clydeside or elsewhere in Scotland. During the crises of the interwar years there did arise a shipbuilding leadership capable of implementing substantial rationalisation in the heavy industries, without seriously eroding craft organisation in sectors like shipbuilding. The subsequent decline of the region's staple trades has not been offset by the advance of new industries any more than its social problems have been resolved by established Labour government at local levels. The decay of its industrial dynasties and their replacement by foreign multinationals has only worsened the isolation of Scotland's business leadership. British governments are faced with a persistent crisis of hegemony in Scotland, as the political outlook of Scottish conservatism — like the religion of its industrial pioneers — has become an anachronism in its industrial heartland.

NOTES

In writing this essay I have been greatly helped by debates and discussions with others researchers, particularly Alastair Reid, Keith Burgess and Geoff Eley.

1. J. Monds, 'Workers' Control and the Historians: a new Economism', *New Left Review* XCVII (1976), pp. 81-99 for a critique of scholars such as James Hinton and David Montgomery; T. Johnston, *The History of the Working Classes in Scotland*, Forward (1929) Glasgow, Chapter XIII, for a traditionalist account in Webbian mould.

2. H. Braverman, *Labor and Monopoly Capital*, Monthly Review Press (1974) New York; S. Marglin, 'What Do Bosses Do', *Review of Radical Political Economics* VI No. 2 (1974), for example.

3. B. Elbaum, *et. al.*, 'The labour process, market structure and Marxist theory', *Cambridge Journal of Economics* III (1979), pp. 227-30; R. Samuel, 'The workshop of the world: steam power and hand technology . . .', *History Workshop* III (1977); are examples.

4. E. P. Thompson, 'Time, Work-Discipline, and Industrial Capitalism', *Past and Present* XXXVIII (1967), pp. 56-97.

5. J. Melling, '"Non-Commissioned Officers": British employers and their supervisory workers, 1880-1920', *Social History* V No. 2 (1980), for a discussion.

6. A. Briggs, 'Thomas Attwood and the Economic Background of the Birmingham Political Union', *Cambridge Historical Journal* IX No. 2 (1948), pp. 203-04, 213-16; for an example.

7. H. Perkin, 'The Development of Modern Glossop' in A. H. Birch (ed.), *Small Town Politics*, O.U.P. (1960); is one case.

8. P. Joyce, *Work, Society and Politics*, Harvester Press (1980) Brighton, particularly Chapter III.

9. A. Macfarlane, 'History, anthropology and the study of communities', *Social History* V (1977), pp. 633, 638; *cf* pp. 646, 652, for Macfarlane slipping into usage of 'community'.

10. T. Shanin, 'Peasantry as a Political Factor' in (ed.), *Peasants and Peasant Societies*, Penguin (1971) Harmondsworth, p. 244; *cf* S. Mintz, 'A note on the definition of peasantries', *Journal of Peasant Studies* No. 1 (1973), pp. 93-96.

11. K. Marx, *Pre-capitalist Economic Formations* (ed. E. Hobsbawm), Lawrence & Wishart (1974) London, pp. 68-69, 72-73 etc.; E. Hobsbawm, 'Peasants and Politics', *Journal of Peasant Studies* I (1973), pp. 5, 7-8, *passim*.

12. M. Bloch, *Feudal Society*, Routledge and Kegan Paul (1962) London, pp. 354-55.

13. C. J. Calhoun, 'Community: towards a variable conceptualization for comparative research', *Social History* V No. 1 (1980), pp. 106-07.

14. D. B. Clark, 'The Concept of Community: A Re-examination', *Sociological Review* XXI No. 3 (1973), pp. 401-04; *cf* J. Lack, 'Residence, workplace, community: local history in metropolitan Melbourne', *Historial Studies* (Melbourne) XIX No. 74 (1980), pp. 19-20.

15. T. Hobbes, *Leviathan*, Pengiun (1967) Harmondsworth, Pt. II, p. 253; *cf* H. Newby, *et. al.*, *Property, Paternalism and Power*, Hutchison (1978) London, pp. 326-27, for alternative interpretation of origins.

16. E. P. Thompson, 'The Moral Economy of the English Crowd in the Eighteenth Century', *Past and Present* LVI (1970), pp. 79, 88-90, etc.; *cf* pp. 92, 100, 131-32, for loose deployment of both 'community' and 'paternalism'.

17. J. Foster, 'Scottish Nationality and the Origins of Capitalism' in T. Dickson (ed.), *Scottish Capitalism: Class State and Nation . . .*, Lawrence & Wishart (1980) London, pp. 52-53; *cf* P. Anderson, 'Origins of the present crisis', *New Left Review* XXIII (1964), pp. 26-54 for a contrasting analysis of the English situation.

18. *Cf* W. Thompson, 'From Reformation to Union' in Dickson, *ibid.*, pp. 81-82, for a different and more emphatic account.

19. K. Burgess, 'Scotland and the First British Empire, 1707-1770s . . .' in *ibid.*, p. 102.

20. T. C. Smout, *A History of the Scottish People, 1650-1830*, Fontana (1977) London, pp. 278-88, 294-95, 300-323.

21. G. Stewart, *The Progress of Glasgow . . . During the Last Century*, Private Circ. by Chamber of Commerce (1883) Glasgow, pp. 1-3.

22. T. Dickson and T. Clarke, 'The Making of a Class Society . . .' in Dickson (ed.), *op. cit.*, p. 154.

23. N. D. Price, 'Aspects of the Scottish Liberal Party in the Central Lowland Belt, 1868-80', M. Litt. (Strathclyde, 1974), for specific evidence of Liberal supremacy.

24. W. Ferguson, *Scotland 1689 to the Present*, Oliver & Boyd (1965) Edinburgh, pp. 292-93, for immigration; J. Kellett, 'Property Speculation and the Building of Glasgow, 1780-1830',

Scottish Journal of Political Economy VIII (1961), for Glasgow building.

25. J. Melling, 'Introduction' to (ed.) *Housing, Social Policy and the State,* Croom Helm (1979) London, for some background.

26. S. D. Chapman, *The Cotton Industry in the Industrial Revolution,* Macmillan (1972) London, p. 19; A. Slaven, *The Development of the West of Scotland,* Routledge & Kegan Paul (1976) London, pp. 85-87:

27. Johnston, *op. cit.,* pp. 302-14; B. Lenman, *An Economic History of Modern Scotland,* Batsford (1977) London, p. 188.

28. W. Lazonick, 'Industrial relations and technical changes: the case of the self-acting mule', *Cambridge Journal of Economics* III (1979), pp. 231-62, for a discussion in context of Lancashire industry.

29. R. E. Tyson, 'The Cotton Industry' in D. H. Aldcroft (ed.), *British Industry and Foreign Competition, 1875-1914,* Allen & Unwin (1968) London, pp. 102-12, 120-23.

30. A. J. Robertson, 'The Decline of the Scottish Cotton Industry, 1860-1914', *Business History* XII (1970), pp. 121-24, 126, for efforts of Women's Protective and Provident League to persuade women into higher workloads.

31. H. W. Macrosty, *The Trust Movement in British Industry,* Longmans (1907) London, pp. 145-50.

32. United Turkey Red Co. (U.T.R.), Letter Books, UGD 13 3/1, 2, 3, for details on the growth of the concern after 1860s.

33. U.T.R. Private Letters (1907-08), Letter enclosing 'Census Returns for 1907' giving the structure and composition of workforce.

34. *Ibid.,* Letter 27.3.1907, for letter of Holt.

35. *Ibid.,* Letter 9.12.1907, for response of the Master Engravers' Association.

36. U.T.R. Trades Disputes Ledger (1912-16), Entry 11.12.1912, UGD 13 4/3.

37. D. Bremner, *The Industries of Scotland* (1869, 1969 reprint), David & Charles (1969) Newton Abbot, pp. 187-89.

38. The Gourock Ropework Co. Minutes, UGD 42 23/3, Minute 20.5.1899.

39. *Ibid.;* W. Tyson, *Rope — a History of the Hard Fibre Cordage Industry in the United Kingdom,* Wheatlands (1967) London, pp. 116, 124-27; Lenman, *op. cit.,* p. 188, and Slaven, *op. cit.,* p. 165, for experience of the carpet manufacturing sector.

40. C. E. V. Leser, 'Coal Mining' in A. K. Cairncross (ed.), *The Scottish Economy,* C.U.P. (1954), p. 113.

41. B. F. Duckham, 'The Emergence of the Professional Manager in the Scottish Coal Industry, 1760-1815', *Business History Review* XLIII No. 1 (1969).

42. National Coal Board, *A Short History of the Scottish Coal Mining Industry,* N.C.B. Scottish Division (1958), p. 75; Slaven, *op. cit.,* p. 168.

43. R. Challinor, *Alexander Macdonald and the Miners,* C.P.G.B. History Group No. 48 (1967-68) London, p. 29; K. Burgess, *The Origins of British Industrial Relations,* Croom Helm (1975) London, p. 212.

44. R. Walters, 'Labour Productivity in the South Wales Steam Coal Industry, 1870-1914', *Economic History Review* XXVIII (1975), p. 295, for a statement of the problem; B. R. Mitchell, 'The Economic Development of the Inland Coalfields, 1870-1914', Ph.D. (Cambridge, 1955), p. 107, for comparison.

45. Annual Reports of the Lanarkshire Coal Masters' Association, SRO CB 8/2, Annual Report 22.2.1888; Mitchell, *op. cit.,* pp. 244-45.

46. Scottish Pig Iron Traders (Scottish Iron Masters' Association), Conciliation Board Minutes, No. 2, p. 38 (1897), for example.

47. P. L. Payne, 'The Emergence of the Large-Scale Company in Britain', *Economic History Review* XX (1967), pp. 521-23.

48. S. B. Saul, 'Engineering Industries' in D. H. Aldcroft (ed.), *British Industry and Foreign Competition, 1875-1914,* Allen & Unwin (1968) London, pp. 187-88.

49. J. Thomas, *The Springburn Story,* David & Charles (1964) London, p. 16 and *passim.*

50. North British Loco., *The North British Locomotive Company* in UGD 11 12/1, pp. 10-11; Saul, *loc. cit.*

51. R. Davidson, 'The Board of Trade and Industrial Relations, 1896-1914', *Historical Journal* XXI No. 3 (1978), p. 575; H. Clegg, *et. al.*, *A History of British Trade Unions since 1889*, O.U.P. (1964), pp. 229-38.

52. *Ibid.*; H. Pelling, *A History of British Trade Unionism*, Pelican (1971) Harmondsworth, p.116.

53. Caledonian Railway Company, 'Staff Memorandum on Salaries' (1911-14), SRO BR CAL 7/2-4, for example.

54. Sir B. C. Browne, *Selected Papers on Social and Economic Questions*, C.U.P. (1918), pp. 50-51, for one prescient comment.

55. Melling, *loc. cit.* (1980).

56. W. J. Reader, *The Weir Group*, Routledge & Kegan Paul (1971) London, p. 29.

57. H. N. Casson, *Handbook for Foremen, Efficiency Magazine* (1930) London, Preface, for an insight into supervisory mentality.

58. S. Pollard, 'British and World Shipbuilding, 1890-1914; A Study in Comparative Costs', *Journal of Economic History* XVII (1957), p. 444.

59. P. L. Robertson, 'The Management of Manpower in British Shipbuilding, 1870-1914 . . .', Ph.D. Thesis (Wisconsin, 1972), pp. 38-40, 47-49; S. Pollard, 'The Economic History of British Shipbuilding', Ph.D. Thesis (L.S.E., 1951), pp. 75-85, *passim.*

60. W. S. Cormack, 'An Economic History of Shipbuilding and Marine Engineering', Ph.D. Thesis (Glasgow, 1930), pp. 150-51; Robertson, *op. cit.*, p. 130.

61. *Ibid.*, p. 120, etc.

62. Melling, *loc. cit.*, (1980).

63. See *Forward* 1.1.1916, and other issues for the continuing connections between I.L.P. leadership and such shop stewards as Kirkwood.

64. North West Engineering Trades Employers' Association (N.W.E.T.E.A.) Minutes, 15.6.1914-3.7.1914, for example.

65. See H. E. R. Highton, 'Report on the Clyde District' (August 1916) in B. Drake, *Women in the Engineering Trades*, Allen & Unwin (1917) London, p. 129, for some insight into the Beardmore management.

66. Clyde Shipbuilders' Association (C.S.A.) Minutes, 2.11.1911, for pattern of negotiations with various sections of workforce before 1914.

67. J. Melling, 'Clydeside Housing and the Evolution of State Rent Controls, 1900-1939' in (ed.), *Housing, Social Policy and the State*, Croom Helm (1979) London, for some background.

68. Finlay Papers, 'On the Origin of the Deanston Works', UGD 91/253, p. 5: 'His views were all of an enlightened and advanced kind, as he took an interest not only in mechanical improvements but also in improved conditions of the people . . .'

69. Finlay Papers, 'Historical Accounts of James Finlay & Co.', UGD 91/19; Newspaper Cuttings, UGD 91/143: Article in paper of 1910 *Kilmarnock Standard* to effect that a contemporary minister had described Alexander's attitude as that the 'riotous and idle' strikers were 'unworthy to eat the Company's bread'.

70. A. J. Robertson, 'Robert Owen, Cotton Spinner: New Lanark, 1880-1825' in S. Pollard and J. Salt (eds.), *Robert Owen: Prophet of the Poor*, Macmillan (1966) London, pp. 149-52; S. Pollard, *The Genesis of Modern Management*, Pelican (1968), Hardmondsworth, pp. 240-41.

71. Gourock Papers, B. T. Danek, 'Robert Owen of New Lanark', UGD 42 31/20, p. 9-10.

72. R. G. Garnett, 'Robert Owen and the Community Experiments' in Pollard and Salt, *op. cit.*, pp. 39-40; E. P. Thompson, *The Making of the English Working Class*, Pelican (1968) Harmondsworth, pp. 858-61; *cf* S. Pollard, 'Nineteenth-Century Co-operation: From Community Building to Shopkeeping' in A. Briggs and J. Saville (eds.), *Essays in Labour History*, Macmillan (1960) London, for a contrary statement.

73. Gourock Papers, 'Letters of Henry Birkmyre', UGD 42 105/7, Letter 25.7.1914, from Presbytery to John Nicol (Manager) 25.7.1914, stressing achievements since 1870s.

K

74. *Ibid.*, Letter 12.12.1903; *cf* UGD 42 105/7, for Letter of Duncan Glen to local authorities, and 'New Lanark Medical Report', UGD 42 2/2, for 1904 comments of H. S. Macdonald.

75. G. Blake, *'The Gourock':* a History of the Gourock Ropework Company, Gourock Company (1963) Port Glasgow, p. 53; *cf* UGD 42 148/48, 'Valuation of Works' (1908-15) and Letter 24.12.1913, for some details of company and welfare investment.

76. Gourock Papers, 'Petition of The Gourock Ropework Co. against Burgh annexation . . .' (1926), UGD 42 22/1.

77. *Ibid.;* Blake, *op. cit.*, p. 63; Gourock Ropework A.G.M. Papers and Accounts, U.G.D. 42 109/1-4, for data.

78. Gourock Papers, *The Gourock Magazine* No. 8 (1949) in UGD 42 104/1, for quote from original 1937 issue on this theme.

79. United Turkey Red (U.T.R.) Papers, Letters of Orr Ewings, UGD 1/8, Letter J. O. Ewing to Rev. Donaghue 19.9.1873; *ibid.*, Letters 25.1.1870-18.2.1872.

80. U.T.R. Trades Disputes Ledger (1912-16), UGD 13 4/3, Letter 11.12.1912.

81. U.T.R. Papers, UGD 1/8, Letter 20.2.1879, giving one dismissed tenant notice with instructions 'please therefore do not come back'; UGD 13 5/12, for loose sheafs with tenants' names.

82. U.T.R. Papers, UGD 13 1/8, Letters 24.11.1885; UGD 13 5/12, Letters 9.2.1884, 12.5.1884, 10.10.1900, etc.

83. *Ibid.*, UGD 13 1/8, Letters 10.6.1869-11.12.1878.

84. S. Macintyre, *Little Moscows: Communism and Working-Class Militancy in Inter-war Britain,* Croom Helm (1980) London, pp. 79-80 and *passim.*

85. F. H. Young, *A Century of Carpet Making: Templetons of Glasgow,* Collins (1951) Glasgow; Templeton Benevolent Trust materials in possession of firm (1976).

86. Glasgow Workmen's Dwelling Company, *Prospectus* (1890) Glasgow.

87. Melling, *op. cit.* (1979), 'Introduction' for further detail.

88. Lanark County Council, *County Medical Officer's Report for Lanark: The Housing Conditions of Miners* (1910) Glasgow, pp. 59, 100, 216, for tables covering the three districts.

89. *Ibid.*, pp. 98, 209-10, 242.

90. Coal Owners of Scotland, 'Memorandum . . .' (31.3.1919) in CB 7 5/40.

91. *Report of the Royal Commission on the Housing of the Industrial Population in Scotland,* Cd. 8731 (1918), Para. 861, p. 124.

92. *Ibid.*

93. A. Campbell, 'Honourable Men and Degraded Serfs . . . 1830-1874' in R. Harrison (ed.), *Independent Collier,* Harvester (1978) Brighton, pp. 84-86, 102.

94. County Medical Officer's Report, *op. cit.*, pp. 89, 100, 216; C.O.S. 'Memorandum . . .' CB 7 5/40.

95. County Medical Officer's Report, *op. cit.*, p. 64; *Report of the Royal Commission . . .*, Cd. 8731, Para. 28, p. 5.

96. William Dixons Ltd Papers, 'Standing Rules and Regulations . . .', UGD 1 55/5; A. Slaven, 'Coal Mining in the West of Scotland . . .', B. Litt. Thesis (Glasgow, 1966), p. 137.

97. *Ibid.*, pp. 117-18; Dixon Papers, 'The Prospectus of William Dixon & Co. 10.5.1906', UGD 1 56/7.

98. Slaven, *op. cit.* (1966), pp. 216-30; *cf* A. J. Taylor, 'Labour Productivity and Technological Innovation in the British Coal Industry, 1850-1914', *Economic History Review* XIV (1961-62).

99. Dixon Papers, 'Rent Rolls of Property (1869-80)', UGD 1 55/2; 'Standing Rules . . .', UGD 1 55/5, Rule II; Slaven, *op. cit.*, pp. 122-23.

100. Report of County Medical Officer, *op. cit.*, p. 213.

101. *Ibid.*, pp. 114-15.

102. B. Holton, *British Syndicalism, 1900-1914,* Pluto (1976) London, p. 171, for comment on pre-War situation in Scotland.

103. *Report of the Royal Commission . . .*, Cd. 8731, Para. 859-60, p. 124.

104. County Medical Officer's Report, *op. cit.*, p. 21, for orthodoxy on the personal failings of

miners.

105. Thomas, *op. cit.*, for survey of Springburn.

106. *Stock Exchange Intelligence Gazette* in UGD 14 4/21, p. 216, for details on Caledonian Railway Company finances.

107. Thomas, *op. cit.*, pp. 153-54.

108. *Ibid.*, pp. 102, 123, 154, and *passim*.

109. Caledonian Railway Papers, 'Speech of Sir James King (1896)', BR CAL 4/152.

110. *Ibid.*, where King remarked: 'Let us remember that Directors, Officers and Workmen are all servants of one great mistress, the Public, and let us try as best we can to do our best to promote the prosperity of this great Railway Company . . .'

111. Caledonian Papers, 'Salaried Staff Retirements', BR CAL 4/49; 'Directors Minute Book' No. 48, Minute 11.3.1900, BR CAL 1/54.

112. North British Railway Papers, 'Insurance Society Committee Minutes (1901-02)', BR NBR 1/226; 'North British Literary Society Minutes (1900-05)', BR NBR 1/365, Minute 10.12.1900, etc.

113. North British Locomotive Papers, *North British Locomotive Co.*, UGD 11 12/1, pp. 10-11; Saul, *loc. cit.*, pp. 187-88.

114. *Ibid.*, UGD 11 12/1, pp. 104-09, for workforce; Thomas, *op. cit.*, pp. 68, 81-82, 104, 130-31.

115. Neilson Papers, 'Autobiographical Notes of W. M. Neilson', UGD 10 5/1, pp. 89-90.

116. North British Railway Papers, 'Proposals for Workmen's Houses at Cadder', BR NBR 8/1441, Letters 10.1.1912, 9.2.1912-12.11.1913.

117. *Ibid.*, Letter 8.11.1912.

118. Cormack, *op. cit.*, pp. 192-94.

119. See Govan Dean of Guild, Plans approved for 1870: References 240-300, for example. Strathclyde Regional Archives (SRA).

120. J. L. Melling, 'British employers and the development of industrial welfare . . .', Ph.D. Thesis (Glasgow, 1980), for a more detailed discussion.

121. Cormack, *op. cit.*, p. 194.

122. John Brown Papers, 'Memorandum on the Shortage of Ironworkers', UCS 1 23/3, for a particular case.

123. J. Hamilton Muir, *Glasgow in 1901*, Hodge (1901) Edinburgh, p. 199, for portrait of archetypal Protestant workman.

124. Presbytery of Glasgow, *Report of the Commission on the Housing of the Poor in relation to the Social Condition*, Maclehose (1891) Glasgow, pp. 22-23.

125. *Reports of the Glasgow Unemployed Relief Fund . . .*, Aird & Coghill (1879-80) Glasgow, SRA L167 LK 5/521, for example.

126. Partick Civic Guild Papers, 'Objectives of the Guild' 27.12.1902, p. 2, SRA.

127. *Ibid.*; cf Glasgow Savings Bank, *Annual Report for 1907*: A.G.M. 24.12.1907, for comments of Professor G. Adam Smith on role of Bank in sustaining the moral habits of the community.

128. The Stephens mansion was still standing when taken over by property developers during the late 1970s.

129. Denny Papers, 'Papers of Peter Denny' including Scrapbook with cuttings of *Dumbarton Herald* 14.12.1904, UGD 3 28/11.

130. J. F. McCaffrey, 'Political Reactions in the Glasgow Constituencies at the General Elections of 1885 and 1886', Ph.D. Thesis (Glasgow, 1970), for a detailed dissection of political engineering.

131. Alexander Whitelaw Papers, 'Letter Books (1874-79)', UGD 79/1, for case of one local Conservative M.P. in the 1870s.

132. Melling, *loc. cit.* (1980), for fuller argument.

133. *Ibid.*; P. L. Robertson, 'Demarcation Disputes in British Shipbuilding before 1914', *International Review of Social History* XX (1975).

134. John Brown Papers, 'Memorandum on the Shortage of Ironworkers', UCS 1 23/3, for

interesting comments on this.

135. J. Butt, 'Working Class Housing in Glasgow, 1900-1939' in I. MacDougall (ed.), *Essays in Scottish Labour History*, John Donald (1978) Edinburgh; Melling, 'Clydeside housing . . .', *loc. cit.*

136. John Brown Papers, Minute Books UCS 1 1/13, Minutes 19.11.1902-23.12.1902, for one example.

137. M. A. Simpson, 'Middle Class Housing and the Growth of Suburban . . . Glasgow, 1830-1914', M. Litt. Thesis (Glasgow, 1970), for discussion.

138. Denny Papers, Diaries of William Denny No. 1, UGD 4/1, Entries 19.4.1886-16.1.1888.

139. W. M. Haddow, *Socialism in Scotland its Rise and Progress*, I.L.P. Reformers' Bookstall (c. 1920) Glasgow, p. 64; *The Word* May 1954.

140. Oral History Transcripts (August 1978), J. McFarlane, Partick.

141. Ward Committee Papers, 'Govan Ward Committee Minutes', TD 90/2, Minute 15.9.1910.

142. *Govan Press* 2.7.1915 for John S. Taylor and A.S.E.

143. *Forward* 21.8.1915; Hinton, *op. cit.*, p. 121.

144. Lord Provost Papers, 'Notes prepared by the Town Clerk for Lord Provost Stevenson, 30.3.1912, subject: Ward Committees', SRA TC D 6/606/1/43 and 6/606/12/16, pp. 3-4 and *passim* for an explanation of Glasgow ward committees; TD 90/2, 15.9.1910 for Hopkins.

145. Andrew McBride in *Forward* 4.12.1915, for Glasgow Women's Housing Committee.

146. Melling, 'Clydeside housing . . .', *loc. cit.*, for a fuller outline.

147. Muir, *op. cit.*; *cf* H. McShane and J. Smith, *Harry McShane: No Mean Fighter*, Pluto (1978) London, p. 34 and *passim.*

148. N. P. Gilman, *A Dividend to Labour*, Houghton Mifflin (1899) Boston, pp. 177, 206, for antipathy of British workers to any suggestion of 'paternalistic' treatment.

149. Denny Papers, 'Papers of Peter Denny' Scrapbook No. 5, UGD 3 28/11, for *Dumbarton Herald* 14.12.1904 account.

150. *Forward* 9.1.1915, for report of conference.

151. Official History, *History of the Ministry of Munitions* IV, pt. ii, pp. 50-54.

152. *Cf* Hinton, *op. cit.*, pp. 56-57, and *passim*, for a different emphasis; also Highton Papers, J. R. Richmond, *Some Aspects of Labour and its Claims in the Engineering Industry* (1917), UGD 102 3/10, for suggestion of impending clash in 1914.

153. N.W.E.T.E.A. (North West Engineering Trades Employers' Association) Minutes, Minute 20.2.1915, and *passim.*

154. *Glasgow Advertiser and Property Circular* 5.1.1915; *Forward* 26.12.1914; Glasgow Trades Council Papers, 'Council Minutes' 17.12.1914.

155. *Ibid.*, Minute 17.2.1915.

156. *Ibid.*, Minute 21.4.1915; *Govan Press* 8.10.1915.

157. *Forward* 29.11.1915, for Patrick Dollan's letter.

158. *Forward* 5.6.1915; *Govan Press* 28.5.1915.

159. *Govan Press* 4.6.1915; Forward 12.6.1915.

160. *Glasgow Herald* 7.6.1915.

161. *Govan Press* 9.7.1915.

162. *Forward* 28.8.1915.

163. *Glasgow Bulletin* 29.9.1915.

164. *History of the Ministry of Munitions, op. cit.*

165. *Ibid.*, pp.50-54.

166. *Forward* 4.9.1915.

167. Hinton, *op. cit.*, pp. 116-17.

168. Reader, *op. cit.*, p. 29 and *passim.*

169. *Glasgow Herald* 29.9.1915.

170. *Glasgow Bulletin* 29.9.1915; *ibid.*, 8.10.1915: '. . . women in mass have been more apt in all ages to defend the hearth by main force'.

171. *Govan Press* 10.9.1915-17.9.1915.

172. Reproduced in *Forward* 9.10.1915.

173. *Forward* 9.10.1915.

174. *Glasgow Advertiser and Property Circular* 4.5.1915, for response of local propertied interests to initial strikes.

175. W. Gallacher, *Revolt on the Clyde*, Lawrence & Wishart (1936, 1978) London, pp. 53-54.

176. *Glasgow Herald* 8.10.1915, for photographs and reports on strikers.

177. *Govan Press* 8.10.1915.

178. *Glagow Herald* 8.10.1915.

179. C. Addison, *Four and a Half Years* (1934) London, Entry 12.10.1915.

180. *Govan Press* 15.10.1915; *Glasgow Herald* 13.10. 1915.

181. *Ibid.*

182. *Forward* 16.10.1915.

183. *Govan Press* 15.10.1915; *Munitions History, op. cit.*, p. 58; *Glasgow Advertiser and Property Circular* 26.10.1915.

184. *Glasgow Advertiser and Property Circular* 12.10.1915; *Vanguard* December 1915.

185. *Glasgow Herald* 18.10.1915; *Glasgow Advertiser and Property Circular* 19.10.1915; note *Glasgow Herald* 20.10.1915 report of case apparently confuses Summary Eviction Court and Small Debts Court.

186. *Glasgow Herald* 21.10.1915, 26.10.1915.

187. *Munitions History, op. cit.*, pp. 59-60; Hinton, *op. cit.*, p. 118.

188. N.W.E.T.E.A. Minutes, 25.10.1915.

189. Clyde Shipbuilders' Association (C.S.A.) Minutes, 7.5.1918; *Munitions History*, IV, iv, p. 135.

190. *Forward* 13.11.1915.

191. *Glasgow Herald* 14.11.1915; see *ibid.*, 18.11.1915, for report of alleged letter of Lloyd George to the factor Nicholson and his solicitor in court.

192. *Glasgow Herald* 23.10.1915, 1.11.1915.

193. R. Harrison, 'The War Emergency Workers' National Committee, 1914-1920' in A. Briggs and J. Saville (eds.), *Essays in Labour History, 1886-1923*, Macmillan (1971) London, p. 233 for letter of Ben Shaw of Glasgow Labour Party to Committee 10.11.1915, explaining the advance on the demand for a Fair Rents Court to Middleton.

194. *Munitions History, op. cit.*, ii, appx. iii, p. 105, for an account of works on strike; J. Broom, *John MacLean*, Macdonald (1973) Loanhead, p. 65.

195. *Forward* 27.11.1915.

196. *Ibid.*, for an account which almost exactly reproduces that of *Glasgow Herald* 18.11.1915.

197. *Ibid.*; cf *Forward* 13.11.1915, for W. C. Anderson's comments on rent strikes.

198. C.S.A. Minutes, 29.5.1916, for views of Dilution Commissioners on this issue.

199. *Ibid.*, Minutes 19.6.1917-9.10.1917, and *passim*.

200. Melling, *loc. cit.* (1980), for the context of authority and conflict.

201. C.S.A. Minutes, 7.5.1918; *Munitions History, op. cit.*, IV, iv, p. 135.

202. C.S.A. Minutes, 19.6.1917-9.10.1917, for later examples.

203. Published in *Forward* 5.6.1915, along with other correspondence relating to the housing unrest.

204. Melling, *op. cit.*, 'Introduction . . .' for elaboration.

205. Glasgow Trades Council Minutes, 25.11.1914.

206. *Govan Press* 19.11.1915, quotes Hopkins on School Board.

207. J. D. Young, *The Rousing of the Scottish Working Class*, Croom Helm (1979) London, pp. 198-99.

208. *Forward* 21.8.1915, for Wheatley on Kirkwood at Parkhead.

209. John Brown Papers, Letter from management (unsigned) to the Ministry of Munitions February 1918 in UCS 1 58/1.

210. N.W.E.T.E.A. Minutes, 16.12.1916; cf Hinton, *op. cit.*, pp. 248-54.

211. N.W.E.T.E.A. Minutes, 24.6.1918.

212. Hinton, *op. cit.*, for this 'rank and file' approach; cf G. Roberts, 'The Strategy of Rank and

Filism', *Marxism Today* December 1976, pp. 375-83; see N.W.E.T.E.A. Minutes, 3.7.1914, for some evidence of an alternative perspective.

213. N.W.E.T.E.A. Minutes, 18.6.1915.

214. *Ibid.*, for insight into the frictions around this issue.

215. *The Times* 28.10.1915, for comments of Lord Desborough of the Land Union.

216. *The Times* 26.11.1915.

217. Harrison, *loc. cit.*, pp. 231-33.

218. *Ibid.*, p. 234 on rent strikes; A. Clinton, 'Trades Councils During the First World War', *International Review of Social History* XV No. 2 (1970), pp. 228-29, and *passim* for the role of these bodies in the mobilisation of resistance.

219. Gourock Papers, 'Balance Sheets', UGD 42 109/1-4, for some indication of the scale of profitability.

220. U.T.R. Papers, 'Trades Disputes Ledger', UGD 13 4/3, pp. 129-34, for an account of this arbitration in December 1916.

221 Highton, *loc. cit.*, in Drake, p. 129, for the Parkhead shell workers.

222. Hinton, *op. cit.*, pp. 109-10, for some discussion of this key engineering centre.

223. North British Papers, 'Correspondence on disturbances at Riccarton', BR NBR 8/1056.

224. *Ibid.*, Letter 21.10.1919.

225. Scottish Coal Owners' Papers, 'The Coal Crisis' memorandum (12.3.1912), CB 7/8, p. 14.

226. Holton, *op. cit.*, for an argument on syndicalist influence in the Scottish coalfields.

227. Lanarkshire Coal Masters' Papers, Annual Reports 14.3.1917, 15.4.1918, CB 8/2.

228. *Ibid.*, 15.4.1918, 3.3.1919.

229. *Ibid.*

230. *Report of the Royal Commission on Housing* (1917), Cd. 8731, Para. 860; cf *Minority Report*, Para. 76.

231. Coal Owners' of Scotland Papers, 'Notes and Suggestions . . . to be followed in referring to the Housing Question . . .' (1919), CB 7 5/50.

232. *Ibid.*, pp. 1-2.

233. *Ibid.*, pp. 13-14.

234. *Ibid.*, pp. 5-6.

235. *Glasgow Herald* 19.10.1915.

236. Committee appointed to Inquire into the Circumstances Connected with the alleged Rental Increases in . . . Small Dwelling-Houses in Scotland, *Minutes of Evidence*, Cd. 8154 (1916) Edinburgh, Evidence of Andrew Hood, Q 991-95.

237. Thompson, *loc. cit.* (1970), pp. 78-90 and *passim*; it is arguable that even in this period there was a rather more complex fusion of values and beliefs than Thompson implies.

238. C.S.A. Minutes, 13.6.1915.

239. Health of Munitions Workers' Committee, *Final Report*, Cd. 9065 (1918), Para. 502, p. 115.

240. *Ibid.*, Para 529, p. 119.

3

Crisis and the Division of Labour: Clydeside Shipbuilding in the Inter-War Period

Jim McGoldrick

Introduction

THIS chapter is intended to be a contribution to the study of the problem of work under capitalism, which indicates the specificity of its focus.[1] The focus of the chapter is on the labour process in the shipbuilding industry. This requires some initial qualification. The first section discusses the theoretical grounds for such an analysis and, although considerations of the scope of a discussion of this nature limit the degree to which sophisticated theoretical debate can usefully be undertaken, it nevertheless outlines the guidelines which discipline the empirical work which follows. The second section covers the development of the shipbuilding industry from the Industrial Revolution through the Imperialist phase of economic development up to 1918. The section is fairly brief and is aimed merely to outline the contours of the industry which is to be discussed. This is necessary to comprehend the industry's position in the inter-war period, which forms the third section of the chapter. The discussion of the shipbuilding industry during the inter-war period is prefaced by a short discussion of the problem of capitalist crisis which is critical for an understanding of the inter-war period generally, and shipbuilding in particular. The focus on shipbuilding moves from a general examination of the industry, but takes the Clydeside area as representative of the types of problem the industry faced and the types of solution it used to resolve them. The fourth section looks at these problems and their solutions in more depth and attention is paid in particular, through a discussion of the technical developments in the industry, to the attempts of shipbuilding firms to solve their crisis of profitability. These technical improvements, however, emerged through a complex process of negotiation, and the latter part of the fourth section examines the dynamics of this process. The final section is a short discussion of the problem of craft control which attempts to draw some conclusions from the main arguments of the chapter. The focus of the chapter is therefore more sociological than historical, in the sense that attention is directed towards themes as opposed to a relatively straightforward unravelling of events.

Labour process theory

In the Marxist theory of the labour process there is no unified position which states what exactly is meant when the labour process is being discussed. Some theorists emphasise aspects relating to the movement of capital accumulation and valorisation as the starting point, whilst others emphasise the degradation and fragmentation of labour as the characteristic feature. However, a unifying theme of such discussions is that the labour process is at the heart of the development of the capitalist mode of production (CMP). Thus the labour process allows an analysis of the general form of relations of production within the 'real' productive process, and also establishes that it is 'a particular and irreducible functional form in the circuit of capital'.[2] The process, then, is grounded in production and involves the transformation of raw materials or partial components into products with use-values; labour is set to work on these 'objects' by 'means' of simple tools or complex machinery. In capitalism the product, the commodity, has an exchange value which ties the labour process into the process of valorisation, in that it is sold for a price at which the capital involved is used profitably. Thus it is tied also to the pattern of accumulation whereby capital is reproduced and renewed. The form of production is expressed in a capitalist division of labour, which has both technical and social dimensions whereby society is divided into occupations each adequate to a branch of production. The different branches of production will then involve a more detailed division of labour which, in turn, involves specialised skills and the differentiation of types of labour, for example manual-mental, simple-complex. As Marx[3] pointed out in his discussion of manufacture, there develops a hierarchy of labour powers which establishes a pattern of differentiated social strata, as well as the cheapening of the value of labour power through its appropriation in terms of a series of 'limited functions' of labour. For Braverman[4] this latter point is the hallmark of the capitalist labour process and governs all forms of work under capitalism. Under previous productive systems the 'craftsman' engaged in a division of labour to simplify his own work; capitalism as a system appropriates the simplification and generalises it in an allocation of limited functions to individual workers. Many critics have taken up the romantic view of 'craft' Braverman uses and have argued that he misses the point that the distribution of the processes of deskilling across various branches of production was extremely uneven. Indeed, it will be argued later in this chapter that the UK shipbuilding industry represents an example where 'deskilling', as Braverman defines it, did not take place.[5] Another weakness in Braverman's analysis is the lack of a clear statement about the manner in which capital's tendency to cheapen the value of labour power and expand the value of capital, through deskilling and fragmentation of labour, was engineered into reality. Braverman puts this down to 'scientific management', but it has been argued by one critic[6] that this was more theorised upon than practised, and whilst Taylorism was important as management *ideology,* it seldom asserted itself as direct *policy.* Also, any attempt by management, especially in 'craft' sectors, to act upon their theory resulted in disputes with the workers in craft organisations. The practical issues involved in such analyses of changing labour processes will be dealt with later in the chapter. However, on another level Palloix[7] and the Brighton Group[8] have tackled the problem of precisely how it is that the tendencies of capital to continually try to cheapen labour power are expressed. They concentrate on the question of capital accumulation and the requisite *forms* of exploitation of labour to promote this: Palloix through a discussion of the change from extensive to intensive exploitation, and the Brighton Group through looking at the questions surrounding the formal and real subordination of labour.

Extensive capital accumulation in its crudest form (lengthening the working day) was limited only to the early stages of capitalist development as labour's acquiescence could not be guaranteed, and with the rise of trade unionism any attempt to lengthen hours of work was fiercely contested. Intensified exploitation was therefore achieved by altering the ratio of the length of the working day to the time necessary for the reconstitution of labour power by lowering the latter.[9] This was done by increasing the productivity of labour through the development of productive forces by mechanisation, which increases the organic composition of capital. These generalisations, however, are difficult to work out in an empirical context. The shipbuilding industry has traditionally been labour-intensive with little in the way of mechanisation until the post-World War Two period. In this case the tendency has been to force *down* the organic composition of capital rather than bear high overheads in a period of depression, and simply pay off workers. Thus the nature of accumulation is neither clearly intensive nor extensive, although development of more sophisticated handtools can imply a certain degree of mechanisation. Also the imposition of more direct supervision, overtime, and shift arrangements can imply an increase in 'abstract labour time devoted to production' which would remove some of the 'porosity' of productive labour but would not significantly extend exploitation and accumulation.[10] Despite the seeming inapplicability of these categories to this specific case there is some value in the analysis by Palloix of Marx's conception of the form of the labour process in different stages of capitalist development. Where many commentators err is in seeing these forms as fixed in relation to specific periods of capitalist development and not as existing side by side at different stages; uneven development can exist within an individual country's mode of production *as well as* across the CMP generally. The fourfold classification of the forms of the labour process

of *Simple Co-operation*, handicraft labour, *Advanced Co-operation*, a manufacturing system, *Mechanised factory system* and an *Automated factory
system* can exist in various combinations at various points in time. In terms of
this chapter only the first three of these forms are relevant; even the most technically advanced shipbuilding countries, in terms of development of the forces of
production, have not managed to go beyond an adapted factory system of
construction. The simple co-operation form relates specifically to petty commodity production and, although the general point involves the capitalist
ownership of the means of production in the case of early shipbuilding, there
were instances where workmen, especially shipwrights, owned their own
means of production. The extension of this form of the labour process into
manufacture through advanced co-operation involves the fragmentation of
'craft' skills through dilution, and the removal of responsibilities of organisation and preparation of work from the craftsman, whilst at the same time
recomposing or 'hierarchising' the workforce with responsibilities defined by a
small supervisory grade of labour. The craftsman then becomes merely a
worker, but the nature of the work stays the same: it is the division of labour
which is altered. However, the manufacture labour process is itself much more
complex than the simple determination above would suggest. The social
organisation of work involves more than the replacement of skills with
machines. Craft unions in Britain anyway have always acted as a brake on the
degree to which capital has been successful in transforming the labour process.
Indeed, when craftsmen have resisted the imposition of new technical divisions
of labour the employers' cries of 'restrictive practices' have been heard loudest.
In the mechanised factory there is a further development of aggregated labour,
where any semblance of craft autonomy is destroyed, and even skills involving
simple dexterity are appropriated through the replacement of handtools by
machinery; as Marx put it, the worker becomes merely an appendage of the
machine.[11] The development of machinery, whilst involving deskilling for the
vast majority, also produces a process of 'hyperskilling' of a minority who
organise, regulate and innovate work in the factory, which produces the new
form of the reproduction of labour power. Intensified accumulation through
mechanisation reduces the amount of time taken to reconstitute labour power,
but it also extends accumulation by increasing the abstract social labour time
devoted to production as mechanisation imposes a discipline on the rhythm of
work, creating a uniform rate of productivity and reducing the potential for its
workers' regulation of starting and stopping work, timing of breaks etc. The
commodity status of labour power becomes more apparent as the subordination of labour changes from a formal to a real situation, which receives
its ultimate expression in the automated factory labour process.[12] These
tendencies of capital, however, as we have noted, are modified in the
empirical context of specific branches of production and the pattern of
valorisation and accumulation which emerges will shape and, in turn be
shaped by, the labour process. The Brighton group argue that the labour

process is more than an abstraction from the circuits of capital in the development of the CMP. To understand these it is necessary to focus attention on the complex relationships which constitute the labour process. Many theorists have urged that attention should be directed to these relationships, but few have actually tackled an analysis of the labour process in concrete terms. Recently, however, there has been a development of research interest (of which this chapter is a part) in the labour process at a concrete level. The problem of worker resistance to 'the laws of capitalism' has recently been examined in a symposium on the labour process.[13] The starting point for the study of resistance takes the labour process as the centre of class struggle which is fought out over the question of control. The impression that capital can overwhelm any worker resistance and restructure the division of labour at will, which emerges from Braverman, and, to a lesser extent, Marx and Palloix, does not reflect the reality of work. Although there seems to be a preoccupation with the wages struggle, workers have always directed their energies towards the resistance of tendencies to homogenise labour through deskilling.

Elbaum *et al* argue that even Marx could not have 'captured all of the fundamental characteristics of nineteenth century competitive capitalist production'.[14] The method they use to overcome the problem of understanding the labour process is to make individual case-study type analyses of different industries at different periods of time. The key point of their work lies in the explicit definition of those aspects of the relations of production which are important in understanding the labour process. The basic Capital-Labour dichotomy can be studied in terms of rôles as employers and workers but they also point out the necessity to understand the contradictions within each; neither capital nor labour can be taken as homogeneous entities. This point, whilst not startling in itself, takes on significance when the type of research that it demands is actually undertaken and the complex structure of relationships which emerges goes well beyond any simple typification of formal and real subordination of labour. In one of the contributions to the symposium it is argued that in the cotton industry the formal transition from manual to mechanised production, whilst deskilling the traditional craft job, created new supervisory grades which were manned by the displaced labour. The reason for this was not the organised strength of the spinners in a craft union. Rather, the employers were internally weakened by intense competition and were unable to take full advantage of the technical changes by restructuring the division of labour to their best advantage. The introduction of the 'self-acting mule' in cotton spinning does not present 'the unfettered triumph of capital over labour through the use of the division of labour and machinery. The relations of production and the development of the forces of production interacted in a dialectical manner, primarily because there was a continual process of conflict, compromise and even co-operation between capitalists and workers over the form and content of the components of technical change, mechanisation, the division of labour and the intensification of labour'.[15] In the cotton industry, then, there was a process of *informal negotiation* of the labour process and, although this was the empirical example used by Marx of the real subordination of labour, the fact that Lazonick's study suggests the reverse points to certain problems in Marx's analysis of the industry. The point which emerges from the Lazonick study, and also that of Zeitlin,[16] is that the scope of the research extends beyond the technical processes into an examination of the relationships which surround them. In his study Zeitlin compares the positions in the engineering and printing industries around the turn of the century and demonstrates the varying degrees to which craft organisations were effective in acting as a brake on changes in the division of labour wrought by technical developments in the industries. He also examines the competitive positions of the employers: for example the engineering employers were marked by the solidarity in enforcing the 1897 lock-out, but the press 'Barons' of the newspaper industry were internally divided at the time of the 1911 strike by print workers. In the abstract sense an analysis of competitive capitalism would involve a recognition that this would represent the mechanism which produces profitable production. Therefore in the conditions in a 'perfect' market the long-term development of capitalism would display the success of those tendencies which would maximise the valorisation and accumulation of capital. However, the market and competition are not 'perfect', and in the short run, individual capitalists, or groups of capitalists, pursue very specific goals: in the shipbuilding industry the short-run goal was survival and this modified to a large extent actions taken of a more long-term nature. Thus, in terms of altering the division of labour and affecting the relations and forces of production, firms may be either unwilling or unable to affect prevailing conditions. The pattern of capital accumulation will thus inevitably be uneven, and, although not a cause in itself of crisis, it will inevitably compound the problems capital faces in such a situation. The Cambridge studies, then, redirect the attention of Marxists away from the study of the development of productive forces, and situate the labour process at the centre of the dialectical unity of the forces and relations of production. However, as has already been noted, the relations of production, whilst typically expressed in terms of the capital/labour dichotomy, also involve a complex set of relations within each category. The position of employers was discussed briefly, and will be returned to in the main part of the chapter; the position of labour also demonstrates contradictory tendencies. These are most often found in the dualism which marked the development of the British trade union movement, with a tendency towards an overall unity in the collective organisation of workers, paralleled by competitive unionism, expressed through demarcation, sectionalism and even in competitive recruitment. The erosion of craft and skilled jobs, whilst involving a degree of homogenisation of labour, does not necessarily involve the creation of a unified working class.

Thus, the development of different labour processes and the general tendency towards deskilling and the dilution of labour, and thus cheapening the value of labour power, is constantly contested, although at different levels and with varying degrees of success. The labour process is subject to negotiation but not specifically as an item on the agenda of collective bargaining. The formal aspects of the negotiation process do express themselves in terms of bargaining issues (wages, hours and demarcation etc.), but the informal aspects are not apprehended in quite such a straightforward way. However, it is hoped that in the empirical study which follows all the dimensions covered by these theoretical considerations will emerge from the scrutiny of the shipbuilding industry and the particular form of its development.

The shipbuilding industry

The early shipbuilding industry was located principally on the Thames, and areas like Clydeside and the North East of England, popularly associated with shipbuilding, were of minor importance. Up to 1830 the Clyde was launching only 5% of UK output. The scale of production of shipbuilding was small and few yards outside the Thames area employed more than 200 men or had capital assets of more than £5,000.[17] The production process, then, resembled the handicraft process of simple co-operation discussed above, and labour in the industry had its leading sections organised in craft guilds for over a century.[18]

The take-off of iron steamships did not occur until the middle of the nineteenth century, and its development brought with it a new structure for the industry with larger fixed capital and a new and more varied division of labour. The explanation for this development is not a simple matter of the proximity of resources of iron and coal; the whole technological development of the Industrial Revolution itself comes into play. The North East of England had vast resources of iron and coal but the leading development of the industry came from Clydeside. It was here that the technical innovations of the textile industries were applied to the development of marine engineering which was helped by the growing demand for bigger vessels.[19]

The Clyde domination of this new phase in the development of the shipbuilding industry has been linked by Slaven[20] to three factors: firstly, the demonstrated potential of steam power with the celebrated *Comet* of Henry Bell in 1812; secondly, the improvement in steam efficiency which came with the development of the screw propeller from 1802-1836; and, thirdly, the concomitant improvements in boiler pressures which accompanied the development of the 'compound marine engine', utilising, first of all, two cylinders and then progressing to triple and quadruple expansion. Boiler pressures improved from approximately 5 lbs in 1830, to 40 lbs in the 1840s, and up to 150 lbs by the 1890s. Despite the technical position, the initial slow development of steamships was due principally to cost in relation to sail. However, this did improve as power-weight ratios altered to give better carrying capacity, but even up to the turn of the century many steamships were enhanced by sail-power. The initial use of iron in hull construction was inhibited by a number of factors. The Admiralty and Lloyds were worried about corrosion and the problem of interference on instrumentation, which added high insurance premiums to its already high cost. However, by 1850, the price was only marginally dearer than wood and afterwards became cheaper.[21] Also important in the development of iron as the basic material were its intrinsic qualities of strength, durability and cheapness in maintenance in comparison with wood. By 1870 Clyde shipyards were producing some 70% of iron tonnage and 66% of steam tonnage, of the total UK output in each of these categories. The Clyde therefore enjoyed a leading position in the three most important areas of ship construction: steam power, screw propulsion, and iron hulls, as well as establishing the West of Scotland as the biggest employment area in the industry. The Clyde accounted for some 42% of the UK total and, with the rest of Scotland added, the position was over 50%.[22]

The period from 1870 to World War I saw the introduction of steel as the major hull construction material, although it had been in use since the early 1860s. Developments in steel manufacture made the price more economic than iron and it allowed better workmanship than iron, as steel had all the advantages of iron with added benefits of greater ductility, malleability and flexibility, making it in the end a lighter, stronger and cheaper material.[23]

During this period there were also rapid advances in propulsion; the improvement in boiler pressures have already been noted; and the transmission of power from the engines was enhanced in efficiency with the development of turbines using a geared transmission system. Also, during this period, there was the development of the diesel engine in Germany from as early as 1892, taken up under licence by some Clyde yards, and also the development of a domestic design from Barclay's in 1912. However, it is interesting to note also in that year that the *Glasgow Herald Trade Review* showed that most tonnage was powered by the reciprocating steam engine.[24] In commercial terms these developments in shipbuilding meant significant advantages for the British shipping industry, with an increased carrying capacity in a period when there was a rapid growth in world trade. This produced an interplay of mutual advantage for the shipping industry and shipbuilding when each could reap the full benefit from the other's success: the shipping industry was able to purchase at the most competitive price the most technically advanced shipping available, whilst the builders were able to enjoy 'access to a large market which provided the opportunity for mass-production, specialisation, the full use of fixed capital and external economies'.[25] Similarly, for the builders there was a relationship of mutual advantage with their suppliers who could provide cheap supplies of components and raw materials due to the large and expanding market offered by the growth of the industry;

steel makers could offer good prices for the specialised ship plates and sections, and the component suppliers in some cases could cheapen prices by moving over to some forms of mass production themselves.

In addition, during the period 1870 to 1914, the industry underwent a concentration of capital which was expressed in terms of a shrinkage of the number of firms competing in the industry. Slaven[26] estimated a contraction from 43 firms in 1870 to 38 firms in 1914 for the Clydeside industry. Pollard and Robertson[27] note that, after the early attraction of a large number of firms into the industry, there was a 'high death rate' in the 25 years up to 1914 when there were only around 50 'important firms'. During the period in question there is evidence to suggest that there was some integration of firms into others through amalgamation and takeovers.[28] However, the main responsibility for concentration lay with the operation of the trade cycle which in the age of 'perfect competition' was reflected very quickly in the demand for ships. Thus although there was an absolute expansion in the volume of world trade from 1870 to 1914, this did not take an even linear form.

Although the shipbuilding industry enjoyed an unparalleled cost-effectiveness in relation to its competitors through various forms of cheap supplies, from abroad as well as at home, and enjoyed special relationships with shipowners — even to the extent of vertical integration in both — the key point lies with the nature of the production process which was used in shipbuilding during the period. It is misleading to suggest that mass production in this period meant anything like a factory system, as there was no fundamental change in the methods of production from those which emerged with iron shipbuilding. There was certainly a degree of product specialisation which allowed significant economies of scale, but this did not involve any major development of the forces of production; indeed Pollard has pointed out that the position of British shipbuilding was to opt against such development: 'In Britain ships were built with a minimum of capital in yards that were able to contract output easily in slumps and were not inferior in efficiency in booms'.[29] The ability to contract output in this case meant simply laying off men and then recruiting them again as work picked up. This was a relatively simple process as most shipbuilding was conducted in regionally concentrated centres where the shipyards dominated the local labour market and there were only limited opportunities for alternative employment. Also of importance was the fact that the workers, whilst not enjoying the situation, did accept periodic unemployment, although the threat of it underpinned many of the demarcation issues which arose as work was beginning to slacken off. The labour process in the industry at this time had emerged with the restructuring of the division of labour with the development of iron then steel hulls. The traditional 'craft' of shipwrighting was displaced by the new skills of marine engineering and boilermaking. However, these skills were themselves the product of a division of older 'craft' skills, inasmuch as the new trades in the industry were the aggregates of different aspects of the craft division of labour used by the Steam Engine mechanics and the Boilermakers in the early stages of the industrial revolution. This did not represent any massive deskilling as such; rather, it can be seen as a revaluation of skill as the basic nature of the work was the operation of handtools, under the control of the tradesman, but almost exclusively the property of the firm who employed him. Thus ship-building in the early stages had been simple commodity production; it now became quite clearly a manufacture process. But the limits to which this could be further transformed were defined by the position which the workers took up and also, to an extent, by the nature of the product itself and the market within which it was traded. The shipwrights, whilst technically displaced (inasmuch as there was little woodworking on metal ships), were still able to secure a place in the new division of labour and retain their responsibilities for lofting and erecting, which suggests that, despite the change in materials, there was no major departure in the method of construction. When such changes eventually did take place, the shipwrights had successfully transformed them-selves into a metalworking trade. This was over a number of years and it took a very complicated course of negotiation, first of all by disputing any available woodworking with joiners, and then by frequent skirmishes with other steel-working unions who would try to extend their control. The subdivision of the Boilermakers was not a contested issue as it occurred in a period of expansion, and the traditional craft seemed pleased to spread out beyond the small boiler-shops and enhance the membership of the union organisation, as the different sections of anglesmithing, plating, caulking and riveting became trades with their own internal division of labour in the shipbuilding industry. A good indicator of the importance the Boilermakers attached to their new fields of employment was when they changed the name of their union and identified themselves with iron shipbuilding as well as boilermaking in 1852.[30] The engineering trades underwent a similar process whereby the old society of Steam Engine Makers became the Amalgamated Society of Engineers (1851) and the original 'mechanics' became the fitters and turners of the engineering and marine engineering industries.

The handicraft nature of the labour process was also reflected in the development of the productive forces in the industry in general. Despite its size, and the need for more fixed capital than most other industrial enterprises, the UK shipbuilding industry had not developed its productive forces to the extent of its only major competitors, the USA and Germany, who had invested substantially in the latest hydraulic, pneumatic and electrically powered machinery. British yards generally used 'traditional' material-handling methods with few cranes and mechanical material-handling processes: the use of blocks and tackles predominated. Nor was there extensive use of hydraulic, pneumatic or electric power (although it should be noted that some of the most advanced yards did have all of these).[31]

The reason why British yards did not invest much beyond steam-operated plant can be explained by reference to a number of factors. In terms of general yard layout there was a lack of applicability unless the whole enterprise was restructured, and this was offset against the employers' suspicion that their cost would not enhance efficiency in a profitable way. There was always the problem also of the potential conflict with labour over their introduction. However, at a more fundamental level, the craft-based system was the most successful in the world: the German and American systems had been developed through heavy investment precisely because they lacked the skilled labour that existed in areas like Clydeside and the North East of England. Any advantage that heavy capitalisation gave was a double-edged one in that the capital could only be profitable in productive use; but this was impossible given the cyclical nature of the demand for the product. Thus any advantage of profit gained from a boom was turned to loss through the burden of over-heads in a slump. Consequently, the American shipbuilding industry was only really profitable during the First World War when the major competitors were engaged in naval work. In terms of productive efficiency the relative output of tons per man per year for British shipbuilding was double that of its closest rivals; wages on the Continent were lower but production costs were not necessarily cheaper.[32]

The broad picture which has been drawn up here could convey the impression that there was no struggle over the labour process; this was certainly not the case. Marine engineering, in line with the general trend in the engineering industry, underwent a quite considerable process of deskilling as more and more semi-skilled machine operatives were employed. The 1897 lock-out, although technically a dispute over the eight-hour day, was effectively the employers taking action to assert control of 'their own shops' and to be free 'to introduce what new methods of working they chose'.[33]

In hull construction some employers also attempted to introduce pneumatic and hydraulic processes, but these were resisted by the riveters especially, who identified them as an attempt to cut wages. The introduction of these new processes was slow, and hydraulic and pneumatic riveting did not become major features of production across the whole industry until after the First World War.[34]

An account of the general pattern of industrial relations in the industry would require a separate study of its own, but, briefly, there were disputes over demarcation intimately linked to the struggle over the labour process. In accounting for this, attention must be given to the pace of technical development. Technical change in itself did not cause demarcation disputes. The varied craft structure was itself the outcome of technical change, not a survivor of previous technical systems.[35] The cyclical nature of production, as was discussed earlier, was important, and workers in any of the trades reacted to the threat of unemployment by laying exclusive claim to certain types of work, or the use of certain types of tools. The principal aim of this was to preserve the trade boundaries so that immediate unemployment would not be compounded by the encroachment of other trades when technical changes rendered the demarcation boundaries more fluid than they had been previously. The other vital element of such disputes was that they could define the pattern of future work organisation, depending upon the result. Thus the relationships within shipyard labour were delicately balanced and, whilst the question of control was ostensibly fought between competing groups of workers, it is vital that the implicit challenge to managerial authority and prerogatives be understood. This will be given more detailed scrutiny later in the chapter.

The craft division of labour in the manufacture of labour process was the cornerstone of the industry's success and, although it has been argued that there was no development of a mass-production industry, the degree of specialisation of production must also be understood, not only in its relationship to the development of economies of scale in production, but also because of its significance for the subsequent development of the industry. Specialisation took two basic forms. On the one hand, there was the identification of certain types of ship with certain yards, and on the other hand there were specialised designs developed by individual builders. A rough breakdown would show that the development of the industry had tended to concentrate *liners* principally in Belfast and on the Clyde, with individual yards subdividing into passenger liners and cargo liners. *General cargo ships*, 'tramps', were built almost exclusively in the North East of England, whilst *warships* tended to be based in the major yards in Barrow and Birkenhead, although warships were also allocated to Clyde yards and Tyne yards. *Small craft* (fishing boats, dredgers, tugs etc.) were more scattered, but the East of Scotland, from Aberdeen to Leith, and Humberside accounted for the majority of these. Thus Pollard asserts 'builders became expert in the construction of certain types of vessels and in the needs of certain types of owners; their equipment was no more elaborate than their type of vessel required, and in normal years there was no idle capacity. In view of their wide potential market some builders could even build in slack times "on-spec.", that is, before orders had been received, thus cutting one of the heaviest items of cost in a shipyard — overheads during depression'.[36] However, it should be noted that design specialisation was always subject to modifications to meet the owner's individual requirements, and to take advantage of new technical improvements in design. Nevertheless, there is evidence of some considerable advantages which accrued to certain firms who utilised a basic design model for multiple orders: for example[37] the West Hartlepool-designed 'well-deck' model had been reproduced in various forms on some 350 ships amounting to almost half a million GRT (gross registered tonnage), and the Doxford 'turret-deck' design of 1893 had produced a total tonnage of almost a million GRT on some 178 ships. However, it should be borne in mind that, despite the degree of specialisation, during a crisis most builders would take on almost any type of contract, as can be seen from the position in the inter-war period.

It has been argued so far that shipbuilding up to World War I was successful in transforming itself into a capitalist industry which, despite a fluctuating market — severe enough to cause bouts of mass unemployment and yard closures — did not experience any fundamental crisis in capital accumulation. The period between the two wars was, however, marked by an almost total collapse in the rate of profit. The nature of this phase of crisis and the attempts to resolve the problem of profitability will now be dealt with in greater depth.

The crisis in inter-war shipbuilding

In Marxist theory the concept of crisis is not taken as meaning fluctuations in the level of world trade. Rather, it is identified with the movement of the rate of profit. A crisis occurs when the rate of profit falls and capital is devalorised. Movements in world trade, however, are seen as good indicators of a crisis, and other movements in the pattern of capital accumulation. Mandel[38] has argued that there is a cyclical pattern to the development of the capitalist mode of production which underpins the operation of the classical business cycle. These 'long-waves' are closer to 50 years in length, as opposed to the 7-10 year business cycles, and he identifies them with specific phases of capitalist development. To date there have been four long-waves. The first, from the 1790s to the 1840s, was the period of the industrial revolution itself and the period of transition from handicraft to manufacturing systems of production. The second, from 1840 to 1890, was the period of the 'first technological revolution' when machine tools enhanced the manufacturing system. The third phase was from 1890 to 1940, which saw the second technological revolution and the development in all branches of production of electric and combustion engines. The fourth phase began in 1940 for the USA (1945 for Western Europe and Japan) and marks the rise of developed factory and automated systems of production, as well as the third technological revolution with the rise of nuclear power and micro-electronics. He also argues that each phase of the long-wave exhibits two patterns of capital accumulation. The first of these is characterised by a general acceleration in accumulation when the major technological advances create the 'sites' of new means of production. These surpass the existing means and the capital in use becomes devalorised. The second pattern of accumulation occurs when technological progress is transformed into productive forces and becomes the new means of production. However, this also removes the force behind accumulation, which is the development of more productive machinery, the effect of which is a slowing down in the rate of economic growth, a fall in the mass of profits and decelerated capital accumulation. Therefore, the total capital in use is greater than the amount which is necessary for production, the rate of profit begins to fall and the capital begins to lose value. The overall picture of the inter-war period shows the pattern of general deceleration within the third phase of the long-wave. The UK's average rate of growth of industrial output from 1894 to

1913 was 2.2% p.a. In the inter-war period this dropped to 2% and, although this in itself is not significant, the position of world trade in the same period shows dramatically Mandel's point: from 1894 to 1913 the average rate of growth of the volume of world trade was 3.7% p.a. In the inter-war period this collapsed to 0.4% p.a.[39] The operation of the long-waves of development is reflected in the business cycle. In a period of accelerated growth the boom periods will be longer and more intensive and slumps will be shorter and less severe. But, in the conditions of decelerated growth, the downswing of the long-wave, 'the periods of the boom will prove less feverish and more transitory, while the periods of cyclical crisis of overproduction will, by contrast, be longer and more profound'.[40] In the case of the shipbuilding industry, then, the pre-1914 fluctuations in output of 1886, 1893, 1903 and 1909 differed sharply from the inter-war period.[41]

The crisis in shipbuilding in the inter-war period provides an empirical case of Mandel's theoretical insights in that the fluctuations of the business cycle were accentuated by the evident downswing of the long-wave. In the 1920s contemporary opinions identified the slump in the industry as a manifestation, albeit an extremely harsh one, of the operation of the business cycle. The 1930s crisis, however, went even further in terms of its severity and demanded a much more fundamental approach to the problem than was seen in the 1920s, and the solutions offered were suitably radical. The slump in shipbuilding from 1921 to 1923 was precipitated to a significant extent by the false boom which followed World War I. Between 1919 and 1921 world merchant tonnage rose by 20% from 51m GRT to 62m, and orders placed by 1923 expanded this by a further 25%. The resultant glut of ships undermined any progressive demand for new tonnage for the rest of the decade.[42] The stimulus to shipbuilding production in the immediate post-war years was the need to replace wartime losses, but this was exacerbated by port congestion and slow turn-round times, which created the impression of greater shortages than actually existed. Also important was the fact that world building capacity had expanded rapidly during the war due to the fact that the predominant producer, the UK, and its main competitor, Germany, had diverted the majority of their capacity to warship building. This left a vacuum for other countries to fill in terms of fulfilling their own needs by developing a domestic industry, and also to take up the competitive space afforded by Britain's absence. Another important factor in the post-war market was the changing structure of ownership of the world's fleets. Britain's share fell from 39% in 1914 to 26% by 1938, which reduced the benefits of the close association with the shipping industry which had figured significantly in the period from 1870 to 1914. The impact of the 1923 depression, however, was uneven. In national terms the area worst affected was the North East of England because the main class of vessel which had been overproduced was the general cargo vessel, the tramp, which, as was noted earlier, represented a degree of specialisation in production for that area.[43] In the Scottish yards also the impact of the slump was uneven. In the

East of Scotland the depression was scarcely felt, indeed some yards on the Forth improved their output.[44] But on Clydeside the position was severe for some firms. However, the Clyde was less severely affected than the North East as there remained some demand for its 'specialised' class of liners and cargo liners, but it was nevertheless affected by the loss of naval contracts which had dried up altogether. The position of Clydeside shipbuilding can be seen in Table 1 below which shows that, despite an average output of just less than half a million tons per year and a relatively stable share of the UK market of 35%, the industry suffered considerably in 1923.

TABLE 1

TONNAGE LAUNCHED ON CLYDE AS % OF UK (000's GRT) 1919-1929

Year	GRT	% of UK	Year	GRT	% of UK
1919	646	33	1925	523	44
1920	672	31	1926	287	39
1921	511	32	1927	464	34
1922	388	37	1928	605	38
1923	176	26	1929	566	35
1924	538	36			

(Source: *Glasgow Herald Trade Review* 1919-1930)

The recovery from the 1923 slump was short-lived, and the market showed a down-turn again in 1926. In the North East of England the position was worse; in 1923 the output of Tyne, Wear and Tees shipyards was just 27% of the 1920 figure, a drop from 964,000 to just 263,000. The recovery there was just as short-lived as on Clydeside and in 1926 had sunk even further than the Clyde with an output of just over 200,000 GRT (only 21% of the 1920 output). The relative share of the market for the North East averaged 42% from 1919 to 1929, but in 1926 it accounted for only 28% of the overall UK output. Although the Clyde also experienced a slump in 1926, it was mild by comparison. The general context of the depression of these two areas was the decline in the UK's share of the world market. The pre-war average for the UK, which had been some 60% of world output from the turn of the century to 1914, dropped to an average share of 44% from 1919-1929.[45]

Market uncertainty made many yards pursue policy directed towards a more competitive flexibility. It has already been argued that to avoid high overheads firms preferred variable to fixed capital, but the pursuit of flexibility meant that firms tended to maintain a larger capacity, and, periodically, more men than was optimal for a return on capital. Thus, whilst there was hesitancy over investment in costly plant and machinery, there was still nevertheless a tendency during a slump towards a devalorisation of capital and a fall in both the mass and rate of profit. Throughout the 1920s firms tended to cut prices back into profit margins to meet overheads and to undercut foreign builders who enjoyed more favourable terms. Despite the fact that the position on Clydeside was not as serious as in the North East of England, some yards did suffer significantly during the 1920s slumps. John Brown's represents a good example of the sorts of problems which have been mentioned so far. After 1922 Brown's suffered severely and, despite their renown as builders of high-class liner tonnage and their special relationship with the Cunard shipping line, they could not secure a significant utilisation of available capacity. An examination of the tendering records by the firm presented by Slaven[46] shows that they were successful only on twenty-three occasions. Of these contracts only three were completed at commonly accepted levels of profitability (between 5 and 12% of price), twelve were undertaken at cutback profit margins of only 3%, and the other eight contracts were built at a substantial loss. It is not surprising therefore that the firm, and the industry as a whole, defined their problem as one of costs. In terms of raw materials and components Brown's, like other shipbuilders, sought favourable conditions from suppliers, especially steel producers, but they were not especially successful in this. Some firms did enjoy special relationships with suppliers, and Brown's may have benefited marginally from share exchange arrangements with suppliers of bolts and rivets. But other forms of vertical integration with armaments suppliers, in which the Fairfields yard were also involved, were fruitless, given the total absence of naval work in the 1920s.[47] Another feature of John Brown's position was the fact that the yard had its own engine and boiler shops which gave economies of scale when there was work available, but represented heavy overheads during depression. However, costs of raw materials and overhead charges were generally outwith the firm's control, but wages, which could amount to 25-33% of costs (depending upon the amount of outfitting work), were an item that management felt they could tackle. Wages in yards were estimated to have risen by some 225% from 1914 and 1920 due to general rises in the level of prices and cost of living, and also due to the maintenance in the post-war period of incentive payments paid during the war.[48] Wage cuts took place in the industry generally in 1921 and were welcomed by the yard management if not by the men. The problems caused by wage-cutting will be discussed shortly, but it should be noted that the employers, whilst keen to cut wages, recognised it as a source of grievance to the men, and they were themselves outspoken in their criticism of local and national government agencies whose wage levels were 'protected' and whose revenues, through taxation and local rates, meant an additional burden on overheads.[49]

From the above discussion it might be thought that the penalties on profitability from over-extended capitalisation would have acted as a disincentive to investment and the development of productive forces. But at the time the firms were caught between two conflicting impulses. On the one hand there was caution over investment and potential overheads, but on the other there was the tendency towards accumulation which emerged from competition: firms sought to take advantage of any investment which would give them the edge on their competitors. Thus, despite a general trading loss between 1922 and 1928, John Brown's did invest in new plant and machinery although the turn-over of work was only half of what was necessary to get the full value of investment. The yard's management, however, recognised that 'only those firms equipped with every type of labour-saving appliance and the most advantageous arrangements for the transport of materials can hope to hold their own'.[50] Initial investment was paid for out of profits made during World War I and in the boom period from 1919 to 1923, when the prevailing impression was of continuous growth. John Brown's spent some £356,000 in expanding their berthage capacity and improving yard layout. As the slump of 1923 set in, such investments became heavy overheads. Because of this the character of investment moved from being a planned process of expansion and modernisation and became much more contract specific and *ad hoc:* for example, in the early 1930s, the major investment was an enlargement of berthage and cranage to suit the *Queen Mary* contract. In terms of capacity expansion, early investment between 1919 and 1923 gave an additional 20% and in the same period funds were devoted to improve the capacity of the engine and boiler works. The position of investment in the engine works was interesting, as it was directed towards giving the yard capacity for the manu-facture of diesel engines for which the firm first took out a licence in 1924.[51] This investment represented a considerable risk, as in their early development stages diesel engines took longer to build, and this affected vessel construction times.[52]

It has been noted that investment in John Brown's was directed towards capacity improvement in the early 1920s. By the mid-1920s, however, there was some investment which seemed to be directed more towards production itself. It was in this period that pneumatic riveting, which had been in existence since the late nineteenth century, finally superseded hand riveting in terms of both efficiency and cost. In 1920 the yard management conducted comparative cost tests on both processes. Their initial findings indicated that pneumatic riveting was 10% cheaper, gave 7.4% greater output, and did not add to over-heads since unit power costs fell as the size of work piece was enlarged. This, however, did not signal any sudden shift to a new process, and indeed further tests were carried out in 1922. These confirmed the findings of the earlier study and showed that output per hour for the pneumatic process was 18.4 feet as opposed to 13.3 feet for hand riveting. The cost improvement was also noted, showing that hand riveting in the tests had cost 54/5, whilst pneumatic riveting cost only 35/3 and wage rates were similarly cheaper, with pneumatic riveting squads paid 6/6 per hour whilst hand squads were earning 7/3 per hour.[53] The establishment of pneumatic riveting, however, did not involve any dramatic investment in plant and machinery, and no separate items are recorded in the yard's Board minute books. It would perhaps be possible to see the gradual introduction of pneumatic riveting as a process used in tandem with hand riveting until it achieved its economic predominance. In 1927, however, the Board recommended expenditure of £5,200 on a new 'Multiple Punching machine and edge planer', which would seem to confirm the development of improved riveting processes.[54]

Other Clydeside yards did not keep as detailed records as John Brown's, and it is difficult to trace their development through the 1920s with any accuracy. There is some evidence, however, that up to 1921 the Fairfields Board of Directors were also concerned with building up yard capacity and directed expenditure on new plant, machinery and property for expanding the site of the yard. Between 1918 and 1921 £38,290 was given over to 'Extensions and improvements', of which some £11,000 was earmarked for the purchase of adjacent acreage; and in June 1919 investment in welding plant was approved.[55] After 1921 it is difficult to know whether investment stopped or whether questions of that nature were dealt with in another way, or simply recorded elsewhere. Board minutes tended to concentrate on share arrangements with other firms, dividends and profits etc. But even these are referred to rather obliquely and no clear picture of the firm's profitability emerges from the discussions minuted. Stephens of Linthouse's records show little in the way of discussions on investment policy of the firm, but from their labour records it is possible to trace the allocation and distribution of labour by contracts and from this infer when changes in the structure of the division of labour were formalised. In their records the only indication of a changeover to pneumatic riveting appears when there is a sub-classification within the riveting department's Journeymen Riveters in January 1927.[56] However, it would be dangerous to generalise from this; the whole problem of labour drift is significant due to the fairly casual nature of the work. For example, Stephens show only six riveters employed at the start of January 1927, yet at the end of the month they have 63. (Whether this was due to the holidays, the season, or the stage which construction had reached is difficult to decide on the evidence available.) However, the significance of the relationship of pneumatic riveting to the development of the forces of production can be seen from the statements of leading spokesmen for the industry at that time. These would certainly appear to indicate that, despite the development of riveting processes, the overall methods of production changed little. There is also a certain ambiguity on the part of the industry as to whether or not they really wanted any fundamental changes in methods even if they could be facilitated by improvements in riveting. On numerous occasions there were statements by British shipbuilders which condemned the idea of a standardised 'fabricated ship', which was seen as contradictory to the tendency of the industry towards contract flexibility. Also, under UK conditions, yards which produced such ships using new prefabrication techniques would prove only to be 'costly white elephants'.[57] This would seem to indicate that the industry did not develop productivity through any major step towards mechanisation in the 1920s.

The industry's uncertain attitude towards changes in methods of production was demonstrated by Sir James Lithgow, a leading Clydeside shipbuilder. In an article in 1921[58] he argued in favour of 'mass production' but defined it in terms of repeat orders from which cost-reducing economies could be gained, and not through any system of 'scientific management' and mechanisation. Improved equipment such as pneumatic riveting only represented higher charges on extra plant as, he argued, there was no appreciable cheapening in labour costs. The use of pneumatic power had 'converted many operations in which our men were specially skilled into purely unskilled jobs' and the industry could not afford to pay the 'manipulators of tools' the same rates as skilled men. But the problem for the industry was that the 'men imagine that they are entitled to the same remuneration even when half the work is done for them by mechanical means', yet the 'latent unused skill has to be paid for'.[59] Thus he argued that the resistance of the workforce to new systems of production was a significant inhibitor: 'labour clings with extraordinary tenacity to these archaic privileges which it has managed to establish in the past'. The solution to the problem of costs was to cut wages. This presents a strange paradox in that he saw that the strength of organised labour would react against changes in work practices which would cheapen the value of labour power, yet he took it for granted that labour would accept wage cuts as a normal course of events. This is true to a certain extent in that the 1921 wage cuts, whilst causing sporadic outbursts of industrial disputes and strikes, especially amongst Clydeside riveters, did not raise any articulated response across the industry as a whole. Without devoting too much attention to this point, there is some evidence that the Boilermakers were prepared to pursue wages issues on a cyclical basis in that they accepted, to a certain extent, the inevitability of cuts during a slump but pushed for high settlements during a boom.[60] Lithgow saw the ideal solution to the crisis in terms of wage cuts and an expansion of payment by results systems of piece work, which would allow for higher earnings and improved output. Thus he saw that more competitive productivity could be relatively easily achieved without recourse to heavy investment, which he argued was not feasible because of the structure of the industry itself, in that new techniques would inevitably be uneven in their impact upon employers. However, it is important not to lose sight of the context in which Lithgow was writing, when the revolutionary impact of the shop stewards' movement had represented a fundamental challenge to managerial authority and the 'Red Clyde' was prominent in employers' minds. Although we can now see the shop stewards' movement on Clydeside in more considered terms, to Lithgow it then represented a change in the character of the shipyard unions away from being trade societies to revolutionary organisations which 'espoused dangerous doctrines' which 'had obtained all too firm a hold upon the workers in the shipbuilding industry'.[61] It is perhaps significant that such 'dangerous doctrines' did not entail a serious challenge to the 1921 wage cuts. Even so, these cuts did little to improve the competitive position of the industry, which claimed that any benefits derived from these were offset by rising charges due to increased rates, taxes and power costs.

The 1923 slump in shipbuilding coincided with the first major dispute since the war involving the Shipbuilding Employers Federation (SEF) and the Boiler-makers. The SEF had concluded an agreement with the Federation of Engineering and Shipbuilding Trades (FEST) on overtime and night shift arrangements, the terms of which were objected to by the Boilermakers, who claimed that they were unnecessary because of the high unemployment rates. The Boilermakers struck against the agreement and provoked a lock-out of their members by SEF firms, which in all lasted from May to November 1923. In analysing this dispute Jones[62] has argued that it was 'The principal reason for the continued depression in the industry', which more or less echoes the employers' claims of the time. They argued that it was wasteful and un-necessary, causing a loss of 5.73m working days as well as wages, revenues and drains on union funds.[63] However, it should be noted that the industry was already in a slump and, whilst the dispute badly affected the ship-repairing industry, its effects on shipbuilding have been exaggerated. The downturn of the market was already evident in the figures quoted above in Table 1, and the recovery of 1924 was made to look more dramatic by the launching in that year of work held up by the dispute. But the real cause of the rise in orders and output for 1924 and 1925 was not any appreciable improve-ment in world trade; it was the twin effects of the Trades Facilities Acts and the low price of new tonnage which produced a rash of speculative orders. Thus the lack of any real progressive demand precipitated the slump of 1926. Another interpretation of the dispute goes beyond the view that it was the out-come of the boilermakers' bloody-mindedness in refusing to operate agree-ments which did not suit them. The reason why it did not suit them is also important. The night shift and overtime arrangements were, as has been argued already, an attempt to extend the labour time devoted to production. Although it will not be argued here that the agreement represented a conscious effort by the employers to extend the exploitation of labour, this was neverthe-less an intrinsic feature of the new arrangements. The response of the Boiler-makers in refusing to operate the scheme was characteristic of their attitude towards any attempt by employers to undermine their control or influence over the work processes. However, this is to anticipate later discussion.

During the mid-1920s there was an attempt in the industry to explain the recession in shipbuilding and the lack of competitiveness of British prices and production. The general view was that the basic cause was the growth of world capacity through an internationalisation of shipbuilding as part of a tendency towards 'industrial self-determination' fostered by World War I. The position of Britain had declined because of its position as top exporter, but this had been exacerbated by the expansion of UK capacity for construction 'beyond the requirements of trade', which created artificially high charges through over-equipment and led to uncompetitive pricing arrangements. In 1925 the industry was operating at only 34% of berth capacity.[64] An interesting feature of this analysis is the fact that it appeared to be the conclusion of the trade unions as well. There is some evidence of this over the furore which surrounded the disclosure that the Furness Withy shipping company were able to get a contract built in Germany at £60,000 lower than the British tender. The SEF and FEST formed a joint committee on costs in shipbuilding but at the end of the day came to different conclusions. The unions sought to reduce the hours of work in foreign yards through government action on an international initiative, but this was more a rhetorical than a real solution to the problem. The employers on the other hand defined the problem as lying in the organisation of labour and sought to secure agreement with FEST on issues of demarcation, interchangeability and improvement of piecework systems.[65] The unions declined to enter such discussions; indeed the Boilermakers were not represented on the joint committee in any case.

The industrial relations position in the industry, whilst certainly not the picture of harmony painted by industry spokesmen, was nevertheless relatively trouble-free in the mid to late 1920s in comparison with the immediate post-war period.[66] The number of days lost through strikes and stoppages dropped from 5.7 million in 1923 to just 4,000 in 1926 and 30,000 in 1927. However, this cannot be explained simply through the fact that there was a jointly agreed disputes procedure, although this was undoubtedly important. The agreement itself was signed at the lowest ebb in the history of the trade union movement after the defeat of the General Strike, and at a time when unemployment in the industry was at around 38% and output in some regions, especially the North East of England, was at its lowest ever level. From 1928 the position of the industry improved as world trade became more buoyant and unemployment fell to 20% of the total insured workforce; output rose to the levels achieved just after World War I. However, this recovery was also short-lived, and the caution with which the industry viewed its position at the turn of the decade was justified.

The 1930s represent, as was noted earlier, a new and more severe phase of the downswing of the long-wave. The industry, however, seemed to appreciate this and there was a general recognition that the bad times were not over, and that solutions to the chronic problems of profitability would have to be tackled. The period through the 1920s had been severe enough for the industry to see that the traditional solutions, or lack of them, had not helped the industry. It identified the problem as one of over-capacity, and for the first time there was an attempt to promote a collective approach to finding a solution. From the late 1920s there had been the creation of the Shipbuilding Conference, which was an initiative to provide a forum for discussion and communication in an industry which for the previous decade had been cutthroat in its competition.[67]

The extent of the crisis during the 1930s can best be seen in terms of output and employment. These are not definitive indicators, but for the purpose of this chapter they are sufficient to give an impression of the way in which the shipbuilding industry declined. From 1930 to 1939 the total output of the UK industry was just over 6.7 million tons, an average of 670,000 tons a year. In the same period world output was an average of 1.8 million tons a year; over 18 million tons for the decade. In comparison with the 1920s, the UK figures are almost a half of the output of 12.6 million tons for that decade, when the average annual output of the UK alone was 1.3 million tons, slightly less than the world average for the 1930s. World output in the 1920s was 28.2 million tons, an average of 2.8 million tons a year. The UK percentage share of the world market in the 1920s was an average of 46%, whilst in the 1930s this shrank to 36%. The pre-war average, from 1900 to 1914, was 60%, but even in the 1920s Britain recorded a share as big as 64% in 1924. The highest share for the 1930s was 51% for 1930, and in 1932 the share of only 26% was the lowest recorded since before 1870. The position on Clydeside can be seen from Table 2, which shows that the total output for the river for the decade from 1930 to 1939 was 2.6 million tons, an annual average of just over 260,000 tons. From 1920 to 1929 the total output of the river had been 4.7 million tons. As with the country generally, the best year on the Clyde was 1930 and the worst 1933, which at 56,000 tons was only 8.3% of the best inter-war figure of 672,000 for 1920. The position in the North East of England, again, was worse. 1930 was the best output of the decade, producing some 627,000 tons, but the effect of the 1933 slump was disastrous. The output for the whole region was just 38,000 tons that year, which was only 6% of the average from 1928-1930. The Tyne itself produced only 11,000 tons, the Wear 12,000, and the Tees-Hartlepool yards only 15,000; indeed the previous year the Wear launched only 2,000 tons.[68]

TABLE 2
TONNAGE LAUNCHED ON CLYDE AS % OF UK 1930-1939 (000's GRT)

Year	GRT	% of UK	Year	GRT	% of UK
1930	530	34	1935	172	32
1931	153	27	1936	327	33
1932	67	28	1937	361	36
1933	56	35	1938	444	39
1934	268	46	1939	239	37

(Source: *Glasgow Herald Trade Review* 1930-1939)

The employment position in the industry was at best precarious, whilst unemployment in the 1930s was chronic. Table 3 shows the rates of unemployment in the industry from 1930-1938, for mid-winter and mid-summer. The figures for the 1920s are difficult to trace in official documents, and Jones[69] could only estimate numbers before 1924. The Boilermakers Union, however, have compilations for the period, and there is little divergence in their figures from those that Jones uses. They show, as would be expected, that 1923 and

1926 were the worst years with rates of unemployment in the industry of 37% and 39% respectively. 1920 saw the best figures with only 4% unemployment; comparative rates show average unemployment for the period 1920-1929 at 29%, but for the period 1930-1938 the rate is 42%.[70] Thus the problem of un-employment was structurally more severe for the 1930s than the 1920s.

TABLE 3
% UNEMPLOYED IN SHIPBUILDING AND SHIP REPAIRING 1930-1938

Year	No. Insured	% Unemployed		Year	No. Insured	% Unemployed	
		Jan.	July			Jan.	July
1930	204,720	23	32	1935	157,230	46	43
1931	195,390	47	57	1936	161,850	37	30
1932	181,930	60	64	1937	172,810	26	22
1933	169,310	63	60	1938	175,050	21	21
1934	158,790	55	48				

(Source: L. T. Jones (1957), p. 113).

The vast fluctuations in output from the relative buoyancy of 1929/30 to the slump of 1932/33 provide a good indication of why the industry itself identified the problem as over-capacity, considering that even in the best inter-war years only 55% of capacity was in use. At the end of the 1920s it was thought that market forces would eliminate surplus capacity, with the weakest going to the wall, but this did not occur, as small firms who were not neces-sarily weak did not represent the biggest capacities. The whole programme of 'rationalisation' was conducted through a specially formed company, National Shipbuilders Security Ltd (NSSL), which acted on behalf of the industry, with the aid of the Bank of England, to buy up and put out of commission redundant yards. From its inception in 1931 to the end of the decade NSSL closed down ten yards, but still was not noticeably successful in bringing down capacity and reducing overhead costs. Slaven[71] estimated that the total capacity reduction was only around 19% and cost improvement around 5%. Jones[72] argues that the process of rationalisation could not cut costs in itself but was only 'a prelude' to real cost cutting, which could only come through 'increased specialisation and greater technical efficiency'. The problem of capacity, although primarily identified as the main problem from the point of view of collective action, was not the only strand of action the employers pursued. Despite a rigid adherence to a laissez-faire view of government, they did try to promote some 'retaliatory' measures to overcome 'unfair' foreign competition. However, it should be noted that any government aid for ship-building would have to be enacted through the shipowners, as direct inter-vention was in conflict with the industry's declared self-help schemes. The

changing attitude to government intervention was a recognition that the
operation of the market itself would not reflate the industry. In 1931 world
trade was stagnant due to the collapse of commodity prices, and three million
tons of shipping was idle. The industry and the unions both agreed that an
effective scrap and build programme should be initiated by the government.
However, whilst there was agreement on this, it did not signal a joint
approach.

The unions, especially the Boilermakers, argued for a scrap and build policy
which would be strict over the conditions for scrapping. They were
particularly hostile to the shipowners selling off ships at cheap second-hand
prices and not scrapping them, even though, they argued, ships over twenty
years old were 'floating death-traps'.[73] The employers accepted that aid could
not come to the industry other than through help to shipping, but they did
accept and welcome the Government's intervention to get the Cunard contract
(the *Queen Mary*) completed after work had been suspended in 1931.
However, the scrap and build scheme, which was enacted through the British
Shipping Assistance Act 1935, was not notably successful, and at best it
produced only some 50 contracts with a tonnage of around 200,000 GRT.
Indeed the industry was unhappy with the Act because it was contradictory in
its operation: on the one hand the tramp subsidy encouraged the owners to
hold on to existing tonnage, and on the other hand the conditions laid down in
the Act over the amount of scrap tonnage to be replaced were regarded as too
rigid by the shipping industry. Thus only 33% of the available funds were
used.[74] By 1936 the position in world trade had improved and the scheme was
regarded as a case of too little too late.

The position in Clydeside yards during the early 1930s was dire, and
although, as was noted earlier, the river was not quite as severely affected as
the North East, when the recovery began it was naval work and not merchant
shipbuilding that brought the improvement. The terms of the scrap and build
scheme favoured the 'tramp' specialist more than others. However, the Clyde
did benefit from government aid in that John Brown's were able to resume
work on the *Queen Mary* in April 1934 after the government had intervened in
the affairs of Cunard and the White Star shipping company. During the period
from the suspension to resumption of work on the *Queen Mary*, the yard had
only one other contract, and before the Cunard contract was actually won, in
December 1930, the yard was in imminent danger of closing.[75] Nevertheless,
despite John Brown's shortage of orders in this period, the position of the
company was different from that of the 1920s. In terms of tendering policy the
yard refused to take on orders at a loss price. It is difficult to say how much
this was a direct product of membership of the Shipbuilding Conference, of
which one of the basic aims was to promote a common and remunerative
tendering scheme. So, although Brown's were suspicious of the Conference at
first, they seem to reflect a limited degree of success for its aims. Up to 1938 the
yard tendered for some 63 merchant contracts and was successful in eight of

these, none of which was at an unremunerative price. The total value of the contracts Slaven estimates at £15.2m, of which £11.8m was accounted for by the two famous Cunard Queens, but all the contracts had a component for charges and a margin of profit.[76] It is difficult to assess whether or not the firm benefited to any great extent from the operation of the NSSL, which they also supported. Two neighbouring yards belonging to Beardmore's and Napier's were closed down, and certainly these firms competed for the same type of work as Brown's, although the latter did not *materially* benefit from the availability of its competitors' assets. Stephens of Linthouse were also members of the Shipbuilding Conference, but it is even more difficult to know whether they benefited from this. Their records show a certain degree of continuity of work, and they also could have benefited from the NSSL closure of some of Fairfield's berthage adjacent to theirs.[77]

The main source of benefit to Clyde yards was the resumption of work for the Admiralty, and John Brown's enjoyed double the success of their previous merchant tendering record. The firm tendered for 63 Admiralty contracts between 1929 and 1938 and were successful in seventeen. The key feature of these contracts was that all of the naval work allowed for charges and profits in excess of the merchant work levels. The position of the yard in terms of profitability changed from a loss of £69,000 in the financial year for 1934 to a small profit of £3,372 for 1935. By 1936 the profit made from the *Queen Mary* alone was £110,000. After depreciation for company housing the firm's net profits were £98,883, for 1937 they were £186,923, for 1938 £148,448 and for 1939 £221,472.[78] In terms of investment the firm directed funds towards the development of welding capacity, which will be discussed shortly.

The attention of the industry to organisational solutions to the crisis does not however provide a full explanation of the 1930s crisis. Reduction of capacity through the NSSL, and developing a marketing strategy through a common pricing system which came from the Shipbuilding Conference, were largely external to the actual process of production, although the conclusions of the Shipbuilding Conference's Price Improvement Committee, in pushing for product specialisation, did have certain ramifications for the way in which the ships were actually built.[79]

There was a parallel process which is less easily accessible than the discussion which has been followed above. The central argument of this chapter is that the solutions which capitalism will seek to the problem of crisis are to be found in production itself. However, the specific industry's definition of the problem is also enlightening. The Shipbuilding Employers Federation (SEF), which was more concerned with the industrial relations of the industry, and the management of it, believed that competitiveness could only be gained through lowering costs. The problems of cost reduction on externals have been covered, and it is the internal mechanisms to which attention must now turn. To overcome the problem of the falling rate of profit, the process of capital accumulation and valorisation has to be stimulated through a relative cheapening of the value of labour power. The shipbuilding industry sought to achieve this in two ways: firstly, to reduce wages in absolute terms through wage cuts, and, secondly, to reduce the real value of wages by implementing technological processes which would reduce wages relatively. Both of these intentions were implicit in the actions of the employers, although it is *not* argued here that they were seen by the employers as part of a conscious strategy. The cuts in absolute wages came with the introduction at the end of the 1920s of a National Uniform Plain Time Rate for wages in the industry (NUPTR). This came into effect in 1930, but was seen by the employers merely as the extension of moves to stabilise wages, albeit in a downward direction. The workforce however saw it as wage-cutting and, despite the lack of an organised response from their unions, the new system did not come in un-opposed. The official union position, of course, was seriously undermined by the massive levels of unemployment. When the NUPTR was introduced, the position in the industry was over 40% unemployed, with this figure rapidly rising by the month. But at the shopfloor level this seemed not to deter some sections of the workforce from taking action against the new wage structure. Strikes were regional in character and, interestingly, the first rash broke out in the Bristol Channel area, the East of Scotland, and on the Thames, all of which were areas with busy ship-repair yards where high earnings were not unusual.[80] The workers in dispute were all Boilermakers, although later other groups became involved, but the union did not support the strikes. Indeed the National Executive went to considerable lengths to get the men back to work. The problem of tension between the local and national union organisations was one which frequently emerged in this period. Despite this there were issues on which there was considerable unanimity. However, this point will be better covered in the discussion of welding when the larger context becomes more relevant. The wages issue, whilst given a separate weighting here in terms of the broad themes being examined, was to continually emerge throughout the 1930s, and from the shipbuilding workers' point of view it was intrinsically bound up with the other issues, even if this was not the opinion of the employers.

The introduction of welding

It has been argued in this chapter so far that welding represented the employers' attempt to reduce the real value of wages and cheapen the value of labour power generally. But welding itself was not universally accepted in shipbuilding, and its technical development was slow. The process had been used in shipbuilding since 1914[81] but never as a general substitute for a riveted structure, although there was a body of opinion in the industry which saw its potential in that direction. Ship repairing used welding more than the con-struction branch, and many of the early employer/union agreements had been made against that background. In shipbuilding welding was used as part of the craft work of plumbers and pipework fitters. Indeed John Brown's first major investment in welding plant, in 1930, was for use in the fabrication of 'steel pipes and flanges'.[82] Fairfield's also had installed welding apparatus as early as 1919, and the process had been pioneered on the Clyde by Stephens and Co.[83] Structural welding work was pioneered abroad, especially in Sweden, Germany and USA, but the objections of British Shipbuilders were not simply technical. Considering the relatively late and troubled changeover to pneumatic riveting, it is easy to understand why welding, even when proved economically and technically, was approached very cautiously by British firms. The process was cleared by Lloyds in 1932, although they did retain certain reservations with respect to standards of workmanship, and welding plant manufacturers were keen to move into the potentially lucrative market of shipbuilding.[84] The sales pitch of the manufacturers was based on the potential weight saving of the process, which they estimated as 30% of dead-weight displacement, although more considered estimates by naval architects put this figure at closer to 7%. With improvements in electrode performance, reduced porosity, deeper penetration etc. by 1933, the added advantage of stronger joints meant that, despite the crisis, or more likely because of the crisis, firms were beginning to equip themselves for wider use of the process.[85] In warshipbuilding welding became widespread by 1935, but for merchant work riveting was still considered to be cheaper. The balance was beginning to shift by 1936 as the use of welding on larger ships increased.[86] However, like many of the early developments in design which were discussed at the start of this chapter, welding did not sweep through the industry, just as iron-clad sailing ships and sail-enhanced steel steamships persisted for decades after their technological displacement. Thus welding was used in tandem with riveting until well into the 1950s. Although the introduction of welding was slow, the watershed for the process came in the early 1930s. It was then that the crisis was at its deepest and means to cheapen production were being constantly sought and, as the previous brief sketch shows, the concern with costs drove the shipbuilders towards welding. However, the employers interest in the new process was monitored by the workforce, especially the craft unions who were concerned about the security of their trades.

This process, then, points us towards an examination of the relationships and complex processes of negotiation involved in such changes in the structure of the labour process. At one level there were the negotiations between the shipbuilding employers and the workers. This relationship, however, goes beyond the formal negotiations of more general industrial relations. The official positions of each group were underpinned by diverging impulses within their ranks, so despite the seeming unanimity at the negotiating table there were complex processes of negotiation *within* each group. Similarly there were patterns of informal negotiation outside the conference room, whether through mediators appointed as arbiters, or through the actions that each took in relations to others which were not the outcome of formal decisions. The

M

most difficult part of this discussion then is to try to encapsulate the subtleties and nuances of the negotiations in a coherent form. The remainder of the chapter is given over to this task.

The re-structuring of the labour process

As welding began to develop more and more in the ship repair industry through the 1920s, and become more important in shipbuilding, the SEF set up a special committee to investigate the process and find out the extent to which welding was being overpaid. As the process developed and became simpler to operate, the employers were anxious to extract themselves from 'onerous agreements' which might be taken as a norm for future piece work and lieu rate settlements.[87] To this end the SEF circulated all federated firms employing the process to find out the distribution of welding work (i.e. what kind of jobs it was used on); the distribution of labour employed to do it (i.e. what trades, if any, used welding equipment); manning levels and wages paid, and whether they were Plain Time Rates, Lieu Rates or piecework rates.[88] The replies of the fourteen firms showed that welding work was done predominantly by members of the Boilermaking trades but that Plumbers, Sheet Iron workers and Blacksmiths also used the process. Only one firm said the work was done by labourers, and another employed what they called an 'electric welder'. All firms were paying more than the PTR for caulkers of £3 which the SEF used as a datum, and one firm was paying its welder double that sum.[89] The SEF were concerned to find such large discrepancies and took an immediate position of urging their members to standardise the rates paid, to levels close to the terms of the NUPTR wage structure. But attempts at a downward standardisation of welding prices by Cammell-Laird, the leading welding user, produced numerous disputes with the Boilermakers Society, which continued to arise up until 1935. The SEF decided that welding needed considerably more investigation, but they maintained one clear position which was that no one group of workers had any exclusive claim to the process. The SEF were concerned to make sure that the Boilermakers especially did not get any foothold with which to claim the work, and avoiding this outcome was a continuous element in their strategy. The clearest indication that the SEF saw the welding process as a stepping stone to a restructured division of labour came in 1932 when their Executive Committee ordered an enquiry into 'the question of the organisation of welding operations on the most economical basis possible without regard to existing ideas as to the rights of the members of certain unions to carry out the work, and also (of) introducing sectional methods in welding'.[90] This statement represents also a change in direction for the industry's consideration of cost improvements through welding, which hitherto had been seen simply in technical terms of weight saving. The position now was to see the process as *changing* the pattern of work, not simply being adapted to the existing pattern.

However, a more factual report later revealed that on existing arrangements of work, welding was beginning to prove itself with a cost saving of 20-33% for work which needed just one run, that is, on plates up to 3/16th thick; but on heavier plate riveting was still unsurpassed in terms of cost. The method of working using the welding process changed only marginally from the riveting system; there was no extensive use of prefabrication. Another point which emerged from the report was the information that the Boilermakers Society were enforcing an output restriction of 6 ft per hour when the SEF reckoned that 12 ft was easily possible. This situation was more likely to be a case of each trying to set norms for piece rates, but it is interesting to keep in mind as a datum for later use of piece rates.

The development of a 'Welding Plan' for the industry was hurried by the pace of the use of the process in some districts, which, despite the crisis, were busy and were planning to increase their welding capacity. Vickers of Barrow in Furness intimated to the SEF that they intended employing those trades which welding had displaced in the process, and also to employ a separate category of apprentice 'welders'. The firm sought Federation advice on piece rates lists it should offer. The SEF, which had no experience of large volumes of welding work, and which was still trying to promote the NUPTR where possible, urged against piecework prices and instead argued for a PTR to be paid. They allowed the firm to make its own decision on the manning levels but warned against the use of platers because their PTR was 2/6 higher than the rest. The firm decided to pay a Standard Rate for welding irrespective of who was doing it. This meant a cut in wages for some trades and was in breach of agreements signed in 1924 and 1931 with the Boilermakers Society. It also meant that the firm was subject to numerous disputes with the Society until 1934.[91] There seem therefore to have been two separate strands to the SEF's activities. The first was to develop an immediate policy on welding which could cover the minutiae of individual yard arrangements. The second was to attempt to incorporate into this the necessary changes in the structure of the division of labour, and possible changes in the system of work, which would accommodate the forthcoming transition from riveting to welding and which would ensure the highest return on investment in welding plant. The practices of the SEF committees of the time interwove these strands but did not produce a clearly defined policy. It was obvious that the introduction of welding would wholly displace Riveting, Drilling and Caulking and that there would be fundamental alterations to the work of Platers, who were responsible for shearing, punching, joggling and flanging in preparation for riveting. The report of the SEF executive committee on the future of shipyard working practices then was striking in one major area; it defined the new processes principally in terms of the effects on tasks undertaken by Platers. The position which the report urged was a concentration of the highly skilled elements of the trade into a smaller group of tradesmen, allowing the relatively simple machine operative tasks to be undertaken by semi-skilled and even unskilled labour. They estimated a cutback in Platers' numbers of some 50%. However, a vital point of this report was that prefabrication and sub-assembling were seen as of lesser importance to production than the saving to be gained from reducing the number of highly paid — in relative terms at least — Platers. The system of work overall would change in terms of the distribution of labour employed on it, but the overall method of construction, especially in erection, would be broadly similar to that in use with a riveted structure.[92]

Thus, in terms of the evolution of a more sophisticated labour process described earlier in this chapter, the industry ignored the significance of the importance of prefabrication and large-scale sub-assembly, which welding rendered possible in the development of a basic 'factory' system. An explanation for this perhaps can be found in the basic conservatism of the employers. In their approach to ship construction they laid great emphasis on the 'craft' nature of the process, albeit from a different perspective than that of the craft workers. An important factor was the past success of these methods which on the one hand made British shipbuilding firms cautious and hesitant over heavy investment, and in some cases openly scornful of the 'white elephants' of those rival American and Continental yards who were much more capital intensive. On the other hand their past success had created a certain traditional pattern of management which at the level of immediate and middle supervision was the product of an informal promotion structure from the ranks of the craftsmen. This is also a reason why 'scientific management' did no more than raise the occasional interest of shipbuilders.

The SEF report on the changes possible in the division of labour did not become an immediate matter of policy, but it did represent the type of considerations which occupied the Federation when welding was being introduced. The other issue involved which prevented their views on the division of labour being implemented lies in the terms of reference of the report itself, which were to consider the issue without reference to existing arrangements and organisation of labour and existing trade union practices. This was an unrealistic position, as the SEF were well aware. To say that they viewed conflict with the unions, especially the Boilermakers Society, with trepidation is not an overstatement. The 'industrial relations' in the industry at the time of the introduction of welding were, as has been noted, relatively peaceful but the resentment of members of the Boilermakers Society at reductions in their wages through the NUPTR was ongoing, and the major issues were not resolved until 1934/35. Anxiety over the Boilermakers gaining control of welding was uppermost in the SEF's thinking when the scheme was being drawn up. As early as May 1931 the SEF were concerned that a 'dangerous precedent' had been set by some firms who had all their welding work done by a special department; 'where this has already taken place a number of firms have unfortunately allowed the Boilermakers Society to enforce claims for the exclusive use of the plant to be given to their members'. This had meant that employers had been 'forced to pay extremely high lieu rates to the specialists' instead of the work being done by various tradesmen at the PTR.[93]. Thus there were two basic positions which shaped the SEF's attitude to welding in general in the period from 1930 to 1933, and were incorporated into the final scheme presented to the workforce in 1933. Firstly, they held that no group of workers had any exclusive claim to welding (manning was purely a managerial prerogative), and, secondly, that where welding was in use there would be no piecework price paid until the full extent of the problems surrounding welding could be properly gauged.

However, despite the emergence of these two positions within the 1933 Welding Scheme the SEF had undertaken considerable discussion and their position in the period of forming the policy was by no means unanimous. There were various points of disagreement, the most fundamental of which was over the question of skill. One position argued that welding required mere dexterity and did not require extensive training — suggestions of length of time varied from a few weeks to a few months at most — and that there were no justifiable grounds for giving the operation of the process the status of a trade. The job, they argued, could be done by labourers and should be paid accordingly. The other main point of view was that the specific application of welding to hull structures made some kind of extensive training programme necessary. The particularity of ship construction required a wider knowledge of the problems involved than the limited considerations of workshop techniques. Thus welding should be done by tradesmen and should be paid a tradesman's rate. In a certain sense both these positions represent a specific point of view on the question of 'control' of the work process — the formal and the real subordination of labour. The first group, the radical 'deskillers', saw the introduction of welding as a chance to break the strength of the Boilermakers Society, who were, and remain, the biggest single union in the industry and the majority union in hull fabrication (the Shipwrights were principally involved in marking and erecting). They thought that welding could be a wedge to drive through the Boilermakers organisation whilst at the same time maximising the cheapened value of the labour power engaged on welding. The other employers' group also saw welding as a chance to diminish the power of the Boilermakers but not by driving a wedge of unskilled labour through their ranks; rather, by denying them exclusive access to the organisation of the process, the competition with other unions would divert their energies. This point of view prevailed but it contained serious implications for demarcation by encouraging inter-union competition. The question of cheapening the value of labour power was more sophisticated in the second employer group's point of view. The naked aspect of the exploitation was clothed in the retention of trade *status* but at cheaper wage rates. Thus, whilst the absolute cheapening of labour power demanded by the first group was rejected, there was a recognition that wage cuts could be achieved without any major resistance from the displaced trades. It should be pointed out here that the employers were not arguing their cases in the abstract; at the time of their deliberations the Boilermakers were fighting a vigorous campaign to control welding. The 'moderate' tendency within the SEF was the winner of the internal debate but the final vote for the eventual scheme was very close.[94] Unfortunately the details of the debate were not presented in terms of which firms were actually for which point of view. This would have been interesting, as the whole discussion took place when the 1930s crisis was at its deepest and morale within the workforce was low, and when the trade unions were ravaged by the recession. The SEF were convinced that the unions would accept the scheme precisely because they were in a difficult period and also had been relatively quiescent over the wages question. However, as has been noted already, the unions saw the SEF welding scheme as an attempt to cut wages, and the Boilermakers specifically saw it as an attempt to erode their craft status.

The formal debates between the SEF and the shipbuilding unions[95] took place in May 1933 when the employers' welding plan was presented, with the expectation of implementation by October that year. The basic points of the scheme were as follows. There would be a new trade created called a 'Shipwelder' which would be paid at the basic PTR of £3.00 per week. Entry qualification to the trade would be a five-year apprenticeship for new boy recruits; other trades displaced by welding could take up the trade after a two-year training period; other shipyard workers, labourers, and apprentices could enter the trade after minimum training of two years (in apprentices' cases they had to complete a full five-year apprenticeship); trainees' remuneration would be a proportion of the full PTR.[96] The statement was taken back for discussion by the FEST and the other individual unions, on condition that the October deadline was withdrawn. The reply was given in July 1933 and the unions' position was a united one which rejected the scheme unilaterally on the grounds that it was wage-cutting, damaging to existing demarcation arrangements, an attempt at dilution, and also that it was unnecessary as there were adequate numbers of welders for the work involved within the existing structure of organisation and collective agreements. The Boilermakers contested the employers' statement that it was a new process requiring new arrangements and suggested that, even if the employers were correct, they were morally bound by custom and practice to allocate the work only to displaced tradesmen.[97] The employers saw the unions' opposition as a challenge to the principles of the scheme but tried to continue discussions through the existing negotiating machinery. The problem went to a General Conference with an independent chairman on 1 November 1933 and, whilst the SEF were prepared to make modifications to the arrangements in the pay of trainees not in the level of pay for welders, they were not prepared to drop the scheme. The unions were themselves still unanimous in their opposition to it. The General Conference failed to produce agreement and the employers decided to introduce the scheme despite being unable to secure agreement on it. The SEF instructed all federated firms to give notice of termination of existing arrangements, which signalled the end of the formal negotiations.[98] This of course did not end the matter and the process of negotiation became more informal and localised.

The union position, of opposition to the scheme, was the outcome of a complicated process of negotiation itself. The employers, as has been shown, arrived at their scheme after much internal wrangling but the union debates had more participants. All of the major unions involved had a point of view of their own and several claimed an exclusive right to operate welding processes. Out of all these groups it was the Boilermakers who carried out the most intensive campaign to secure the work of welding for their members, and in the overall struggle, both with the SEF and the other unions, they were successful, although this was not really conceded until after World War II. Their success was based on two principal points. Firstly the Boilermakers saw as clearly as the employers the future trends in ship construction and were determined not only to minimise any restrictions which would be imposed on their control over their own work, but to try and extend that control over the new process itself. Secondly, they were best organised to do so in terms of numerical strength and the concentration of their membership in the shipbuilding industry. The early welding work done in shipbuilding in the 1920s was traditionally done by caulkers who were a trade section of the Boilermakers. The work mostly involved sealing runs on bulkheads, the internal 'walls' of ship compartments, making them watertight. Thus the process used in this way did not displace riveting or caulking but operated side by side with it. The Boilermakers then were in a good position to claim shopfloor custom and practice when welding was extended, and most firms recognised welding on hull construction as a caulker's job, unaware at the time of the precedent being set. However, this did not mean that other trades accepted the Boilermakers' early claims. The plumbers claimed exclusively welding work on pipes and flanges and the Boilermakers conceded this, but did not allow the plumbers to use this as a basis for extending the scope of their claim to structural welding. Indeed, the SEF also recognised plumbers', and other trades', rights to carry on welding work which was a natural part of their everyday craft work. In letters to the SEF the Shipwrights and the Blacksmiths claimed the right to welding work and accused the Boilermakers of 'poaching' and 'intimidating' their members who were using welding equipment.[99] The Shipwrights' drillers section claimed the work as a displaced trade, whilst the basis of the Blacksmith's claim was that they were the originators of the process through forge-welding. The SEF was sympathetic to both groups and the grievance they felt they had with the Boilermakers. The Federation's early aggressiveness towards the Boilermakers was sustained by the knowledge that the 'blacksquad' crafts were set against each other over the welding issue. However, the Shipwrights eventually relinquished their claim in 1944[100] and the Blacksmiths' claim was never taken that seriously; their members who were doing electric welding mostly joined the Boilermakers Society. It became apparent that the Boilermakers were the real leaders of the opposition to the employers' welding scheme, although the resentment of the other unions lay beneath the surface of their later collective opposition.

The approach of the Boilermakers Society was a good deal more sophisticated than the above discussion would suggest, and there is some evidence that besides poaching and aggressive recruitment (not necessarily intimidation) they were also more attractive to 'welders' than other unions. By March 1932 the Society was issuing membership cards to a welders' section,[101] something the employers did not like. They informed member firms that these cards were not acceptable as proof of apprenticeship, even though this was standard practice for other trades.[102] The SEF was suspicious that the Boilermakers were relaxing their rigid entry qualification rules to expand the membership of their new section. However, it was another aspect of the Boilermakers' strategy which showed both their commitment to organising welding and a clear statement of craft values. In the Glasgow area the Society's District Committee began talks with the local education authority in April 1932 about the prospect of setting up evening classes in the theory and practice of welding for members of the society and invited the Clyde Shipbuilders Association (CSA) to attend. The local employers were concerned and sought SEF advice. The employers maintained their previous insistence on management's prerogatives on manning and recruitment, and dissociated themselves from the talks, arguing that workshop and on-the-job training was better. Nonetheless they were clearly caught out by the Society's initiative and, realising their lack of foresight, wrote privately to the Glasgow City Council's Education Department to arrange separate discussions.

The Boilermakers persisted in their attempts to get the evening classes going, despite the SEF's warning to the Education authorities that the Society did not represent the whole industry, and maintained discussions up to May 1933. In that same month the Society was able to report the success of the Manchester District Committee in setting up evening classes with the aid of their local authority. The West of Scotland District began to hold discussions with Renfrew County Council for similar classes to be held in Greenock in August 1933. Later in 1933 space was given over to technical discussions of welding in the Society's monthly reports.[103] These developments ran in tandem with more traditional trade union methods of pursuing policy objectives, and there was a spread of industrial action over welding wages issues before and after the SEF scheme was introduced in 1934. The other effect of these disputes was to push forward the Boilermakers' claim to have employers recognise the Society as the sole representatives of welders' interests. The initial impetus for the Boilermakers' actions over welding came from the District organisations and was not the product of central executive policy. Indeed one of the features of the Society's history had been the continuous dispute between the national leadership and the local organisation over strikes and other industrial actions — the opposition by local branches and shops to the NUPTR in 1930/31 was not backed by the Executive. Nevertheless, when the SEF began to draw up their welding plan the Society began to develop an 'official position'. It has already been noted that they considered existing practices met the industry's needs adequately but they surveyed their membership in order to find out the precise numbers of their welders who were 'capable and available for work'. By August 1933 they declared themselves ready 'for anything in the way of gradual or sudden developments in electric welding'.[104] They recognised that despite the slow growth of the process a rapid acceleration in the use of welding was imminent. The position was clarified by the leadership as follows: 'The official attitude of the Society is that, in conformity with all past practices, the work formerly done by our members must remain in their hands, no matter what the form of application or the machine used may be. This position will be maintained throughout all negotiations with employers and our fellow trade unions.' This position was also the outcome of a number of different, but not necessarily conflicting, views of welding. In some local areas it was seen as a good issue around which to articulate wage issues, the process itself in this case being something of a secondary concern. Other districts had a technical interest in the process in that they did recognise its potential to do away with riveting, and were concerned not to allow any threat to trade security. Thus, despite certain differences, all seemed to recognise the need for a national policy on welding in order that the employers could not use it to 'set district against district'. Consequently, when the SEF finally introduced their scheme in April 1934, the Boilermakers were able to respond with a clearly defined national policy which was well supported amongst the rank and file of its membership on the shop floor.

The collective position of the shipbulding unions generally reflected the militant position of the Boilermakers. But it should be noted that the militant stance of the FEST was more rhetorical than practical. When it came to the crunch of actually taking industrial action, it was principally the Boilermakers who led the way. However the Society never took 'official' action on the scheme despite widespread strikes against it. This of course was not an unfamiliar position for the Boilermakers, who throughout the history of their union exhibited a tension between local and workshop militancy and national protection of funds. Even so, the shipyard unions did agree: 'where any union was in conflict with the SEF in regard to the welding scheme such union should receive support in refusing to do work under dispute'.[105]

The first stage of the scheme, when it was put into operation, was to cut down by stages piece and lieu rates to the £3.00 PTR level. This produced a rash of strikes on the Clyde and the Tyne. The welding position on Clydeside was shown in the CSA's returns for February 1934. These showed that only seven major yards were employing welders at this time.[106] Of these seven, three firms, Scotts, Lithgows and Stephens, were paying the SEF recommended rate of £3.00 per week, and in terms of the number of welders involved they employed 27, 5, and 5 respectively. Stephens' records show that they began to employ 'welders'[107] as a separate category from September 1933, when they had six men and four apprentices, which gives some support to the Boilermakers' claim that some SEF firms had 'jumped the gun' on welding and were implementing the scheme before negotiations were exhausted. The other four firms in the CSA returns were all paying more than the SEF rate. Denny's of Dumbarton employed six welders and were paying £3.5s per week; John Brown's, who also had six welders, were paying £3.5.4d; Yarrow's had only four welders and were paying £3.10.8½d. The last firm, Fairfield's, were operating a piecework system despite the SEF policy against it. However, in Fairfield's case, it is not clear whether or not there was extensive use of welding, although they employed ten welders. In all cases anyway the rates of pay were negotiated by the union and the individual firm. Thus the Boiler-makers' strategy to dispute the welding scheme locally was the obvious course of action. In addition, there were some firms in the SEF returns who were paying considerably higher than the highest Clyde yards; Harland and Wolff in Belfast were paying £4.10s and one firm was paying as much as £5.3.5d per week. What this amounted to was a position of average earnings for welding of around £3.10s per week, which meant that the SEF scheme did involve sub-stantial wage-cutting.

As noted earlier, the first strikes over the scheme occurred while negotiations were still taking place, since many firms were anticipating the success of the SEF in securing union agreement and began to implement the terms in 1933. On Clydeside there were welders' strikes in April 1933 in Denny's, Yarrow's and Stephen's, where the dispute lasted until June. In Lithgow's there was a strike in November, which was settled pending the out-come of the General Conference which had just been convened. These were coupled with a threatened strike against unemployment by all the Boiler-makers on Clydeside. In the English yards there were numerous strikes as well, with the biggest occurring in the Swan Hunter yard in the North East where 38 welders were on strike; and in Camell-Laird on Merseyside where welders were on strike over wages and manning levels.[108] There were two particularly important features of these strikes. Firstly, all were Boilermakers; secondly, none were official, although some of them lasted up to two months. This of course was where the line was drawn for the official support of action in opposition to the SEF scheme. The leadership were still hesitant about diverting funds to localised disputes, despite the fact that they were the architects of the strategy to fight the SEF scheme at that level. However, a vital point to be noted is the fact that the strategy of the Boilermakers Society was largely successful, despite the lack of official backing for it.

The employers' resolve in pushing through the scheme in opposition to union views did not last. Despite a formal united front there was internal pressure from individual area associations, dominated by certain large firms, to modify the welding scheme. Those firms most advanced in terms of using the welding processes argued that they now had sufficient experience of its productive use to operate effective piecework systems. This broke one of the vital threads of the scheme, that piecework was not to be used as a system of payment for welding; and with the pressure on the industry being exerted by the Boilermakers breaking into the other, that no single group had exclusive claims to the process, the whole scheme began to crumble. A third factor which was of great importance was the improvement of the industry's position in 1934/35. Those firms that were improving wished to consolidate their position by taking what advantage there was in welding by tying it to a PBR wages system and recognising the claims of the Boilermakers to operate it, thus removing the twin sources of the local disputes which stood in the way of their competitive advantage. The leading firm argument which is suggested here is validated by the fact that, under pressure, the SEF did allow for the limited re-introduction of piecework.[109] The SEF, which lacked any constitutional power, could not do otherwise but bow to the wishes of the 'better informed' individual firms, even though members of these firms had been involved in drawing up the scheme which they now sought to drop. In April 1934 the firm of Swan Hunter and Whigham Richardson drew up and agreed piecework price lists for their Wallsend Yard with representatives of the men who were members of the Boilermakers Society. On 25 April 1934, just a few weeks after the scheme had been implemented nationally, the Barrow Shipbuilders Association concluded an agreement on piecework prices with representatives of the Boilermakers Society: the largest shipyard in Barrow was that of Vickers who were busy in 1934 with naval contracts. On 1 December 1935 Cammell-Laird on Merseyside were able to end the continuous disputes over welding which had arisen in the period from 1930, when they signed an agreement with the Boilermakers Society on piecework price lists. And in December 1937 John Brown's on Clydeside followed the norm set by the others and signed an agreement with the Boilermakers on piecework prices.[110] A common feature of all these agreements was the amount to be paid for the basic welding operation of downhand, or flat, welding for either 'butt' or 'fillet' joints, which was 2¼d per foot. Other types of run with greater complexity and accessibility, using different thicknesses of steel etc., were paid different prices according to criteria set by the conditions prevailing in each of the different yards. If the basic 2¼d per foot is taken as a datum, some estimates of possible earnings can be deduced. It was noted earlier in the chapter that both the Boilermakers and the employers had set out different levels of output per foot for welding work, and it was argued that each was seeking to maximise piecework price advantages. If the estimates of each are taken, a comparative earnings estimate can be made. The Boilermakers held output at a maximum level of output of 6 feet per hour which under the 1934/35 price lists would give an average hourly rate of pay of 1.1½d. This was less than the corresponding rate being paid under the PTR of the SEF's scheme, which gave 1.3d per hour. The employers' estimate of an output of 12 feet per hour would correspond to an hourly rate of 2.3d, which was much higher than the PTR, and higher also than the best earnings achieved in 1931 before the SEF cut the piece rates. It seems obvious that the Boilermakers and the SEF in turn understated and overstated the output position, but it can be seen that, under the technically improved conditions prevailing in 1934/35, earnings from piecework would be based more realistically on an output of 9 or 10 feet per hour. Thus hourly rates would be quite significantly higher than those imposed by PTR and the SEF's whole position on the new welding scheme was fundamentally weakened. The SEF welding scheme at the end of the day was unsuccessful in re-structuring production in the industry on a more profitable basis. The recovery of shipbuilding was largely stimulated by the upswing of the classical business cycle which was accentuated by re-armament. The Second World War, which was followed by a long-wave with an undertow of expansion, in terms of economic growth, was able to create a degree of profitability in the industry up to the period of the mid-1960s, but this goes beyond the scope of this chapter. However, the experience of the industry in the 1930s marked the beginning of a new approach to the problem of crisis for the shipbuilding industry. The fact that the solution attempted did not work does not detract from the overall tendency which was argued at the beginning of this chapter.

Conclusion: Craft control and the labour process

One of the most striking features of the whole question of the introduction of welding in the early 1930s, besides its complex processes of negotiation, was its degree of intensity. In February 1934, when the SEF surveyed all its constituent associations, it reported that there were only some 204 welders, 212 apprentices and 78 trainees: just short of 500 workers out of a workforce of some 159,000.[111] Obviously it was not the number of men involved which was the issue. The Boilermakers' annual growth rate after the worst of the depression exceeded that number quite easily. The essence of the struggle over welding lay in the whole question of control. Hinton[112] has argued that the whole notion of craft control embodies a view of the labour process in which there is a unity of conception and execution of work which eschews the very idea of a detailed division of labour. The craft worker, he argues, builds up a series of controls which serve to both defend the worker's material interests and act 'as a means of resistance to the reduction of craft labour to commodity status'.[113] In the case of the shipbuilding industry in the 1930s the Boilermakers regarded the integrity of their craft as paramount, and the strength of their organisation, despite the depression, was designed to protect it. However, it has been pointed out in the foregoing discussion that the SEF survey of the most highly skilled section of the Society, the platers, revealed that much of their work had lost its 'skill' content. Indeed, despite the conferring of the status of a skilled trade upon welding work, the 'deskilling' group of employers were to a certain degree correct in arguing that, whilst physically quite demanding and occasionally extremely difficult and complex, welding could be learned in a relatively short period of time. During the Second World War women workers who had never been in a shipyard, and dilutee labour, proved quite capable welders. Also, in other major shipbuilding countries, there was no such trade as 'welder', or indeed Boilermaker, but competitive shipbuilding was still successfully undertaken. The key point here is to understand the context of the negotiation of the labour process. The Boilermakers were able to maintain a *craft organisation* despite the erosion of the intrinsic skill content of the original craft work. The apprenticeship system therefore, whilst acting as a regulator of labour supply by imposing restrictions on the market operations, was also an agency of socialisation into the values and norms of the craft organisation. The centrality of the apprenticeship system to the trade cannot be dealt with here at any length, but another dimension of the Boilermakers' opposition to the welding scheme was that employers were using it to dilute the trades by employing apprentices in larger ratios than the Society felt were tolerable during a period of mass unemployment. However, the apprentice-ship question did not become a major issue until 1937 when the Boilermakers tried to enforce a ratio of 1:7. The position of the Society throughout the early 1930s, in preserving an organisation which could resist capital's attempt to alter the structure of the division of labour, did not extend beyond this into a wider form of class struggle. For the most part their orientations were instru-mental and directed towards specific interests, both materially and ideologic-ally. The struggle over welding was a struggle over the definition of the boun-daries of the Society's organisational influence. There was nevertheless a movement within the Society which did try to reconcile craft interests with class interests in much the same way that the leaders of the Clyde workers' committees did over the question of dilution. The shipyard unions generally defined the welding scheme of the SEF as an attempt at dilution, with its con-ditions allowing labourers to become tradesmen after only two years' training, and the excessive use of apprentice labour was seen as another part of this process. The National Minority Movement was active in the Boilermakers Society after the crushing defeat of the General Strike, even though its influence elsewhere was waning.[114] In 1931 it was able to produce a rank and file broadsheet within the Society in opposition to the official leadership which had placed bans on Communists representing the Society at the TUC and in the Labour Party.[115] The editor of the bulletin, Harry Pollitt, was the leading industrial organiser of the Communist Party and a major figure within the Boilermakers Society.[116] Despite this, the left group within the Society did not succeed in pushing the militancy of the rank and file in a revolutionary direction; as has been noted, this militancy was as much directed against the other unions as it was the SEF.

Thus, to return to the issues raised earlier in the discussion of the value of an analysis of the labour process, it can be argued that on the basis of the fore-going study the tendency towards a capitalist re-structuring of the division of labour facilitated by technical change may be resisted by the workers, with varying degrees of success. The Boilermakers in shipbuilding were able to exert considerable control over their work because of their organised strength and also because of the divisions within the ranks of the employers. In the end the conclusions of this chapter serve to point out the complexity of the problems involved in an analysis of the labour process. The relationships of negotiation represent the real terrain of industrial relations, and this is a process which goes beyond the formal institutional analysis which tends to occupy a leading place in sociology generally. The other general point which emerges reinforces the conclusions of Elbaum *et al,*[117] which suggest that the general tendencies of the labour process are themselves mediated by the complexity of what really constitutes the relations of production.

NOTES

1. This chapter is drawn from research being undertaken towards the degree of Ph.D. with the support of the SSRC. Acknowledgements are due to Professor J. E. T. Eldridge, H. F. Moorhouse, A. G. Hyslop and A. Pollock who all read and commented on an earlier version of this chapter.

2. Brighton Labour Process Group (1977) — "The Capitalist Labour Process', *Capital and Class,* No. 1, Spring 1977.

3. Marx, K. (1977) — *Capital,* Vol. 1. Lawrence & Wishart (p. 339).

4. Braverman, H. (1974) — *Labour and Monopoly Capital.* Monthly Review Press. See especially Chapter 3 on the division of labour.

5. There are numerous critical articles on Braverman's work; those consulted here are: Coombs, R. (1978) — 'Labour and Monopoly Capital: review article', *New Left Review,* 107, Jan./Feb. 1978. Cutler, T. (1978) — 'The Romance of Labour', *Economy and Society,* Vol. 7, No. 1, Feb. 1978.

6. Elger, T. (1979) — 'Valorisation and Deskilling', *Capital and Class,* No. 7, Spring 1979 (p. 78).

7. Palloix, C. (1976) — 'The Labour Process from Fordism to Neo-Fordism', CSE Pamphlet Stage 1, *Labour Process and Class Strategies,* CSE Publications.

8. Brighton Group — *loc. cit.* (pp. 6-13).

9. Palloix — *loc. cit.* (pp. 50-52).

10. *Ibid.*

11. Marx — *op. cit.* (pp. 298-340).

12. Palloix — *loc. cit.* (pp. 51-58).

13. Elbaum, B., Wilkinson, F., Lazonick, W. & Zeitlin, J. (1979) — 'Symposium on the Labour Process', *Cambridge Journal of Economics,* Vol. 3, No. 3 (pp. 227-230).

14. *Ibid.* (p. 227).

15. Lazonick, W. (1979) — 'Industrial Relations and Technical Change: the case of the self-acting mule', *Cambridge Journal of Economics,* Vol. 3, No. 3 (p. 257).

16. Zeitlin, J. — 'Craft Control and the Division of Labour: Engineers and Compositors in Britain 1890-1930', *Cambridge Journal of Economics,* Vol. 3, No. 3 (pp. 263-272).

17. Pollard, S. & Robertson, P. L. (1979) — *The British Shipbuilding Industry 1870-1914.* Harvard Univ. Press (p. 71).

18. See Webb, S. (1950) — *History of Trade Unionism.* Longman (p. 45). Dougan, D. (1975) — *The Shipwrights.* F. Graham Ltd. (pp. 1-17).

19. Cormack, W. S. (1930) — An Economic History of Shipbuilding and Marine Engineering on Clydeside. Unpublished Ph.D. thesis, University of Glasgow (p. 339).

20. Slaven, A. (1975) — *The Development of the West of Scotland: 1750-1960*. RKP (p. 175).

21. Lenman, B. (1977) — *An Economic History of Modern Scotland*, Batsford (pp. 177-180) quotes the 'Strang Estimates' on comparative costs which show that in 1852 iron hulls cost approximately £12.00 per ton whilst wooden hulls were £14.00 per ton. See also Slaven, *op. cit.* (p. 131).

22. Slaven — *op. cit.* (p. 132).

23. The major technical improvements in the production of steel came with the development of the Bessemer Conversion process (1856), which was subsequently improved by the Gilchrist Thomas process (1880). Steel prices started to improve in relation to iron in the 1880s. Average prices per ton for steel in 1881 were £9.12.6d., and iron was around £6.0s. per ton. By 1886 steel had fallen to £6.2.6d., whilst iron stayed constant. Slaven — *op. cit.* (p. 179).

24. *Glasgow Herald Trade Review*, Dec. 1912 (GHTR).

25. Pollard & Robertson — *op. cit.* (pp. 23, 24, 48). See also Pollard, S. (1957) — 'British and World Shipbuilding 1890-1914: A Study in Comparative Costs'. *Journal of Economic History*, No. 17 (p. 444).

26. Slaven — *op. cit.* (p. 182).

27. Pollard & Robertson — *op. cit.* (p. 75).

28. *Ibid.* (pp. 96-102).

29. Pollard — *loc. cit.* (p. 437).

30. Mortimer, J. E. (1973) — *History of the Boilermakers Society*. Vol. 1, Allen & Unwin (p. 51).

31. Pollard & Robertson — *op. cit.* (pp. 121-123).

32. Pollard — *loc. cit.* (p. 438).

33. Webb — *op. cit.* (pp. 484-486).

34. Pollard & Robertson — *op. cit.* (pp. 120-123).

35. Robertson, P. L. (1975) — 'Demarcation Disputes in British Shipbuilding before 1914'. *International Review of Social History*, No. 20.

36. Pollard — *loc. cit.* (p. 433).

37. Pollard & Robertson — *op. cit.* (pp. 84-86). See also Tyne and Wear County Council (1975) — 'A Study of the Shipbuilding Industry in Tyne and Wear'. Planning Report for Tyne and Wear County Council (pp. 4, 5).

38. Mandel, E. (1975) — *Late Capitalism*. New Left Books.

39. *Ibid.* (pp. 120-121, 141-142).

40. *Ibid.*

41. Lloyd's Register of Shipping — 'Annual Summary of Merchant Ships Completed in the World'. Various reports from 1892-1977.

42. Slaven — *op. cit.* (p. 187).

43. Jones, L. T. (1957) — *Shipbuilding in Britain*. University of Wales Press (p. 98).

44. Lenman — *op. cit.* (p. 216).

45. The figures in this discussion are drawn from Lloyd's Register of Shipping (see note 41) and *GHTR*, 1919-1939.

46. Slaven, A. (1977) — 'A Shipyard in Depression: John Brown's of Clydebank 1919-1938'. *Business History*, Vol. 19, No. 2, July (pp. 197-198).

47. Minutes of Board of Directors' meeting, Fairfield Shipbuilders Ltd: Papers held in Strathclyde Regional Archive as part of UCS collection. References to these papers are as follows: UCS1 John Brown's; UCS2 Fairfields; UCS3 Stephens. Board minutes for Fairfields show discussion of firm's stake in Coventry Ordnance Works: UCS2 1/5 and 1/6.

48. Slaven — *loc. cit.* (p. 205).

49. *GHTR* contains an article by leading members of SEF every year: discussion of external charges in article by Ropner, L., *GHTR*, 1922.

50. Slaven — *loc. cit.* (p. 208).

51. Minute 31/3/24: John Brown's Board shows allowance of £19,126 allocated for diesel capacity. UCS1 1/2.

52. Slaven — *loc. cit.* (p. 211) gives detailed breakdown on general investments summarised for the period 1919-25. Total investment £409,145. Depreciation £293,777.

53. Details of tests. UCS1 58/9.

54. John Brown's Board Minutes 28/10/27. UCS1 1/2.

55. Fairfield's Board Minutes 26/6/19. UCS2 1/5 and 1/6.

56. Stephens' Contract Labour books. UCS3 24/1.

57. *GHTR* 1919-1921.

58. *GHTR* 1921 (p. 36).

59. *Ibid.*

60. Mortimer — *op. cit.* (pp. 62-69). See also McGoldrick, J. (1980) — 'A Profile of the Boiler-makers Union', paper for SSRC Shipbuilding Seminar: 'Scottish and Scandinavian Shipbuilding: Development Problems in Historical Perspective', Sept. 21-23 1980 (pp. 5-11).

61. *GHTR* 1921 (p. 36).

62. Jones — *op. cit.* (pp. 96, 97).

63. *GHTR* 1924.

64. *Ibid.* 1925.

65. Jones — *op. cit.* (p. 88 and p. 174).

66. *Ibid.* (pp. 166-169). See also *GHTR* 1926 (p. 29) and 1927 (p. 42).

67. Shipbuilding Conference set up in 1928. John Brown's were among its first affiliates on Clydeside. UCS1 9/35.

68. *GHTR.* Annual summaries of output 1930-1939.

69. Jones — *op. cit.* (p. 113).

70. Boilermakers *Monthly Report (MR),* Feb, 1931.

71. Slaven — *op. cit.* (p. 189).

72. Jones — *op, cit.* (p. 140).

73. Boilermakers *MR,* April 1934.

74. Jones — *op. cit.* (pp. 141-157). See also *GHTR* 1935.

75. Minute Books. UCS1 1/2 (1/12/30).

76. Slaven — *loc. cit* (p. 202).

77. Brown's minute books 1/10/31 show approval of the purchase of 'cheap machinery' of the value of £214.0s. from Beardmore's and purchases from Napier's of £49.7s. UCS1 1/2. See also Jones — *op. cit.* (pp. 133-140).

78. Minutes of Board meetings 1935-1939. UCS1 1/2.

79. Shipbuilding Conference — 'Price Improvement Committee', papers held in Stephens' collection November 1934-May 1936. UCS3 1/236, 237, 238, 239.

80. SEF Circulars 229/31 and 281/31. Held as part of Shipbuilders and Repairers National Association collection (SRNA) in the National Maritime Museum, Greenwich, London. For discussion of nature of collection see Ritchie. L. A. (1980) — 'Modern British Shipbuilding: a Guide to Historical Records'. *Maritime Monographs and Reports,* No. 48.

81. The first all welded ship, the *Fullagere,* was built by Cammell-Laird in Birkenhead in 1919.

82. Board minutes show approval of expenditure of £2,025.0s. on welding plant. UCS1 1/2.

83. Slaven — *op. cit.* (p. 213).

84. *GHTR* 1932 (p. 65).

85. *GHTR* 1933 (p. 39).

86. *GHTR* 1935 (p. 26).

87. Piece rates were generally paid to those workers who were engaged on work which could be carried out continuously; thus in shipbuilding most hull construction trades were paid this way, whilst most outfitting trades were paid a basic time rate. The lieu rate was generally higher than time but lower than a piecework average and was paid to certain specific operations which would normally be given a piecework price.

88. SEF Circular 73/31.

89. SEF Circular 191/31.

90. SEF Circular 115/32.

91. SEF Circular 199/32.

92. SEF Circular 49/33.

93. SEF Circular 133/31.

94. SEF Circulars 214/32, 226/32, 59/33, 99/33.

95. The major unions federated to the Federation of Engineering and Shipbuilding Trades were the National Union of General and Municipal Workers, The Shipwrights Association, Blacksmiths, Sheet Metal Workers, Furniture Trade Association, Brass and Metal Mechanics, Patternmakers. The unions not federated were the major craft unions including the Boilermakers, the Engineers, Plumbers, Painters, Woodworkers and Sheet Iron Workers.

96. SEF Circular 110/32.

97. SEF Circular 153/33. See also Boilermakers *MR*, April 1934.

98. SEF Circulars 211/33, 225/33, 8/34, 11/34.

99. SEF Circulars 69/32 and 86/33.

100. Lorenz, E. (1980) — 'The Labour Process and Industrial Relations in British and French Shipbuilding: the inter-war years'. Paper at SSRC Shipbuilding Seminar: 'Scottish and Scandinavian Shipbuilding: Development Problems in Historical Perspective', 21-23 September 1980 (p. 9).

101. Boilermakers *MR*, March 1932.

102. SEF Circular 44/32.

103. Boilermakers *MR*, May, Nov., Dec. 1933. See also SEF Circular 168/33.

104. Boilermakers *MR*, April, August 1933.

105. Press statement by shipyard unions; see 'Lloyds List', 29 March 1934.

106. SEF Circular 40/34.

107. UCS3 24/1.

108. SEF Circulars 73/34, 82/34, 93/34, 183/34.

109. SEF Circular 82/34.

110. Piecework price list agreements from private papers of Finlay Hart, who was Chairman of Clyde Welders Advisory Committee of Boilermakers Society. (a) 'Welders Price List', agreement between Swan Hunter and Whigham Richardson Ltd and the Welders at the Wallsend yard. (b) 'Electric Welding Piecework Price List', agreement between Barrow Shipbuilders Association and Boilermakers Society. (c) 'Electric Welding Prices', agreement between Cammell-Laird and the Boilermakers Society. (d) 'Welders' Piecework Rates', agreement between John Brown's & Co. and the Boilermakers Society; figures for this agreement are taken from the settlers' measurement book which was used in calculating welders' earnings.

111. SEF Circular 40/34.

112 Hinton, J. (1973) — *The First Shop Stewards' Movement.* Allen & Unwin.

113. *Ibid.* (pp. 93-94).

114. Lane, T. (1974) — *The Union Makes Us Strong.* Arrow (pp. 150-154).

115. 'The Boilermaker', *Minority Movement Bulletin*, No. 1, 24/7/31).

116. See Mortimer — *op. cit.* (p. 7). See also Pollitt, H. (1950) — *Serving My Time: An Apprenticeship to Politics*, and Mahon, J. (1976) — *Harry Pollitt: a Biography.* Lawrence and Wishart.

117. Elbaum *et al.* — *loc. cit.* (pp. 227-228).

4

The Vale of Leven 1914-1975: Changes in Working Class Organisation and Action

Roddy Gallacher

Introduction

The Vale of Leven in Dunbartonshire, which developed with the bleaching, dyeing and printing industry, is one of the older industrial areas in Scotland and as such has shared some of the experiences of the Scottish working class.[1] During the 1920s and 1930s it gained a reputation as a centre of radical political activity, with the Labour Party, the Communist Party and Independent Labour Party uniting to challenge, and then gain control of, the various branches of local government in the area. This alliance, whilst gaining some limited successes, was also fragile and periodically collapsed, finally ending after the Second World War, when the militancy of the interwar years became routinised into the instrumentalism of Labour Party politics. This chapter will attempt to describe the economic, social and political processes at work in the community, and to suggest some reasons for the discontinuity between working class action and consciousness in the 1920s and 1930s and that of the post-1945 period.

In particular it will be suggested that the distinctive features of the locality are crucial to an understanding of the shifting nature of working class consciousness and action in the Vale of Leven. Thus it is the impact of wider economic and political forces on the 'community' and the perceptions of the inhabitants of the community as a significant focus for action, which require explanation.[2] In this context it will be argued that the different forms that working class consciousness and action have taken in the Vale since 1914 have depended critically on variations in the level of unemployment, the locus of control of that unemployment, and the capacity of local working class leaders to focus on the community as a base for working class action.

Paternalism and working class sectionalism before 1914

The Vale of Leven, lying approximately 20 miles north-west of Glasgow and straddling the River Leven, consists of five settlements: Renton, Alexandria, Balloch, Jamestown and Bonhill, all originally separate but now more or less continuous.[3] The Vale grew with the local textile industry, which first started in the locality in 1715 with open field bleaching at Dalquhurn in Renton.[4] The River Leven flows from the south end of Loch Lomond and enters the Clyde at Dumbarton, a distance of some five miles. This supply of soft water, coupled with a comparatively cheap supply of labour, attracted the attention of Glasgow merchants, and by 1719 there were three printfields and four bleach-fields in the Vale, providing fluctuating employment for about 1,000 people. Approximately half of those employed were women, and about 70 were children under 10 years of age.[5] The growth of these local enterprises under-lined the historical importance of the textile industry in Scotland. Between 1727 and 1772 the state, recognising investment problems in lengthy bleaching processes, subsidised the creation of new bleachfields at the rate of up to £50 per acre. Both the Dalquhurn and Cameron fields in the Vale were assisted under this scheme.[6] The population of the area grew steadily from roughly 1,200 in the mid-eighteenth century to over 16,000 by the early 1900s.[7]

The working class of the Vale of Leven during the nineteenth century has been portrayed as displaying docility, encouraged in a community dominated by a handful of paternalistic employers. Thus Willie Stewart could write in 1912: 'They were an example of frugality and respectability and docility to the entire world. On 18/- a week for the men and less than half of that for the women they managed to keep themselves alive and work for ten hours a day. They went to the kirk on Sundays and won football matches on Saturdays. Scottish thrift found its apotheosis in the Vale of Leven.'[8] Tom Johnston also claimed that: '. . . the Vale of Leven . . . (has) a semi-serf tradition which paralyses to this day any local effort towards class freedom and human dignity'.[9] While these comments, as Young argues, may reveal more about the attitudes and political sensibilities of Stewart and Johnston than those of the working class of the Vale of Leven, the involvement of the textile manu-facturers in many aspects of political and social life in the area, highlights a division in the working class which presented barriers to collective action of the type later to be witnessed in the 1920s and 1930s.[10]

There were four principal firms in the Vale during the latter half of the nine-teenth century, and all were involved in printing, dyeing and bleaching: James Black & Co, John Orr Ewing & Co, William Stirling & Sons, and Archibald Orr Ewing & Co. Between them they provided work for over 6,000 people.[11] The owners and managers of these firms lived close to their factories and were intimately involved in the locality, influencing political, cultural and social life. Sir Archibald Orr Ewing was the local Conservative Member of Parlia-ment from 1862 to 1892, and Alex Wylie, a partner in William Stirling & Sons, was Member between 1895 and 1906 as a Liberal Unionist.[12] They were elders in the kirk, patrons of the many societies which proliferated in the area, providers of educational facilities and donors of public halls, reading rooms and a public park. The dominant recreational and cultural activities in the locality consisted of Educational Societies, Mechanics' Institutes, Masonic Lodges, music societies and bands, sporting clubs, a Burns club, a Co-operative Society and a Unionist and a Liberal Association. There had been a Trades Council in the area from the late 1860s but union membership was generally confined to skilled male workers.[13] Those workers also tended to be Protestant. The local Catholic population provided part of the unskilled labour force of the local textile industry as well as labourers for the Clydeside shipyards. This section of the working class emigrated from Ireland between 1850 and 1900, helping to double the population of the Vale during that period. Discrimination by employers and hostility from the indigenous labour force placed Catholic workers in unskilled jobs and inferior housing.[14] The picture that emerges of class and culture in the Vale during the nineteenth century is partly one of docility and incorporation, and partly one of the frag-mentation of the working class in terms of religion, gender and occupation. Alongside this picture, however, some history of working class action must be traced. Class conflict periodically crystallised into working class resistance in the Vale of Leven. During the last decade of the eighteenth century the employers changed their method of payment from day wages to piecework, and the ensuing conflict was described by the Reverend Gordon Stewart. In 1791, he pointed to the previous two years of violent disputes over wage rates, control of the work process and the number of apprentices, and stated that '. . . it will be easily foreseen, that one of the parties must be in complete sub-jection to the other, before trade can be upon a proper or sure footing'.[15] Violent industrial disputes arose during the nineteenth century, as, for example, in 1834 when the Master Calico Printers of the West of Scotland dis-missed their workers and replaced them with '. . . starving handloom weavers at a wage of seven or eight shillings'.[16] The reaction of the workers in the Vale of Leven to this was of such ferocity that troops were sent to the area and hundreds of arrests were made. There was also considerable support in the Vale for Chartism, and it had one of the most active and militant branches in Scotland.[17]

The incidence of industrial disputes increased towards the end of the nine-teenth century as the paternalism of the factory was eroded by a series of take-overs and mergers in the local companies which left the bulk of local enter-prises amalgamated under the United Turkey Red Co Ltd (UTR). A remaining firm, James Black & Co, was absorbed into the Calico Printers' Association (CPA) in 1899. These two new firms were run from Glasgow and began to experience difficulty due to the general decline of the textile industry at the turn of the century.[18] The processes of rationalisation of work in the local industry heightened conflict, and in 1911 a major strike was called by two unions which had recently recruited the majority of the unskilled and female workforce. The Amalgamated Society of Dyers, Bleachers, Finishers and Kindred Trades, and the National Federation of Women Workers, put forward a long list of claims including a 10% pay increase, a 55-hour week and proper overtime rates. The subsequent strike lasted about three weeks and resulted in a victory for the workforce.[19] The influences of the local employers were further reduced by the opening, in 1906, of Argyll Motors Ltd which, for a while, enjoyed the highest production of vehicles in Europe and employed some 1,500 people, paying rather more than local wage rates. Production ceased in 1914 with the firm going into liquidation.[20]

Thus it can be argued that the Vale of Leven before 1914, although occasionally exhibiting open signs of conflict between capital and labour, was primarily characterised by the absence of significant collective working class organisation and action. The major reasons for this were, on the one hand, the control of work by local employers with a clearly identifiable involvement in the cultural and social life of the community, and on the other, by the sectionalism within the workforce on the lines of religion, occupation and gender. However, by 1914, the control of work in the Vale by local employers was already slackening. Also, increasingly after 1914, a number of forces began to encourage a greater need for, and consciousness of the possibilities for, wider working class solidarity.

The inter-war period: working class solidarity and resistance

The First World War was, for many people in the Vale, a radicalising experience. Over 500 soldiers recruited locally lost their lives — this was out of a population of just under 20,000. The development of disenchantment with the war was typified in a scrapbook collection of poems cut from local and national newspapers by a woman who was subsequently active in the interwar labour movement. Poems at the beginning of the scrapbook resound with militarism and jingoism often dealing with local soldiers. By 1917 the book increasingly emphasises pacifist poetry.[21] This growing discontent with the war was further demonstrated by the reception given to parliamentary candidates in the General Election of 1918. The Liberal candidate was asked if he supported the release of John McLean. The Coalition candidate was heckled loudly at Renton and the chairman's comment about Renton's great war record was greeted with anger. Elsewhere in the Vale some discharged soldiers disrupted an election meeting and then marched through the area singing the Red Flag.[22]

In the Vale of Leven at the end of the First World War the *potential* for political radicalism was influenced by four factors. Firstly, the amalgamation of the local firms and the resulting displacement of employers with community ties from the locality. This left a gap in political, social and cultural life in the Vale. Secondly, the dissatisfaction over the war and the expectation that improvements in working class life would follow. Thirdly, the growing unionisation of the local workforce and the existence, for a while, of the

Argyll Works which provided much better conditions and wages than the UTR or CPA. Finally, the impact of widespread unemployment for the entire inter-war period. As Young points out, if the traditional view of the nineteenth century Scottish working class people as 'inarticulate, docile and malleable' is correct, then it should be emphasised that the corollary of this is an apparent volatility and unpredictability which, in certain circumstances, can provide the basis for radical class consciousness and action.[23]

At the end of the First World War the local economy of the Vale of Leven collapsed. The Ministry of Munitions, which had been producing armaments in the Argyll Works, closed in 1918, throwing 2,000 people out of work. (The factory remained unused until 1935, when the Admiralty recommenced munitions work.) The United Turkey Red Co closed the Levenbank Works in 1918, and subsequent years saw the closure of their factories at Milton, Cordale and Dillichip. Only three of their fields — Milton, Dalquhurn and Croftengea — continued production throughout the 1920s and 1930s. The Calico Printers' Association continued with only one plant, closing this in 1922.[24] It is difficult to estimate accurately the numbers of unemployed during the interwar period, since Renton lay in the parish of Cardross, while the rest of the locality fell within the administration of Bonhill parish. These parish areas were, until 1930, the units of administration for payment of relief to the able-bodied unemployed and the poor. Parish councils enjoyed a degree of autonomy which enabled councils to pursue individual policies towards poverty and unemployment. This was changed in 1930 when Scottish local government was re-organised and responsibility for relief passed to the county council. However, approximate unemployment rates for the Vale of Leven and Renton between 1922 and 1939 have been calculated and show that, in 1922, 58% of insured workers in the area were unemployed. This rate fell until 1927 when it stood at 13%. By 1931 it had risen to 60% and did not drop below 25% again until 1939.[25]

Social conditions in the locality were often abominable, as illustrated by a member of the ILP in this period. When, in 1915, his family moved from Lennoxtown to Govan Drive into a 4-storey tenement, 'There were seven of us, including my parents. That was, one girl, four sons and my father and mother. We were in a room and kitchen where we had a toilet on the stair-heid.'[26] It should be noted that this single toilet served at least four flats. These conditions were by no means unusual in the Vale.

In Bonhill we find Milton Terrace with 96 houses, 433 inhabitants and only 17 privies — a total of 27 people to each toilet! Linnbrane Terrace had 106 people in 24 houses sharing 4 toilets, and two other streets with 70 inhabitants between them provided only 3 WC's. Housing conditions were so bad that, even by 1939, two-thirds of the Vale's residences were deemed to be unsatisfactory.[27] Bonhill Burn was used as an open sewer and was not covered until 1929. Despite the 'deplorable conditions of the streets in Alexandria', the Streets and Footpaths Committee of the County Council never met for the 15 years between 1910 and 1925. Disease and infection were rife; for six months in 1927 there were 187 cases of infectious disease in western Dunbartonshire — 166 of them in the Vale.[28] It was this combination of extremely high levels of unemployment and deplorable living conditions which gave local working class activists both the impetus and ability to organise a collective response.

At the end of the First World War those who represented the organised working class can be typified by a brief description of the Board of the Vale of Leven Co-operative Society. They were male and office holders in an inter-locking mesh of organisations such as the Friendly Societies, the Order of Foresters, Rechabites, the Humane Society, local councils and the Trades Council. There were mainly skilled or supervising workers employed in the locality. The reaction of such working class representatives to rising un-employment after 1919 was to form a Distress Committee which contacted various bodies requesting help.[29] This organisation was quickly outpaced in 1920 by the newly formed 'Vale of Leven Unemployed' which soon affiliated to the National Unemployed Workers Movement (NUWM). This formed in tandem with the local branch of the Communist Party and was strongly influenced by CP members. The Vale of Leven's UWM developed and utilised the militant tactics of street politics. They campaigned on a platform of improved parish relief and would often assemble and march on the council rooms, electing delegates to enter and make their demands. A flute band was set up and was often present at demonstrations. The band was also used to intimidate certain local opponents. The clerk to the Parish Council was frequently met in the morning by the band, which accompanied him to his work, collecting him in the evening for the return journey.[30] This form of intimidation was common. One hapless schoolteacher who made a derogatory comment about Lenin and Trotsky to a class of children signed a written retraction under threat of similar treatment from the band![31] However, the UWM and the band were not solely organised and supported by the CP and fellow travellers. The treasurer of the flute band was, in fact, a member of the Labour Party, and the band reflected the same general mix of left wing political opinion that was beginning to emerge in most working class organisa-tions in the Vale, as younger and more militant workers sought and gained election to them. By 1922 the Trades and Labour Council had been sufficiently radicalised to put forward a combined platform of CP, ILP and LP candidates for the Bonhill Parish and Dunbartonshire County Council elections. The main protagonists in cementing this alliance were members of the ILP who managed to mediate between the other two parties despite their suspicion of each other.[32] The alliance was immediately successful, gaining 9 of the 15 seats on the Parish Council. The new councillors immediately implemented the policies they had been demanding: rates of Parish Relief were increased; children of the unemployed received boots and clothing; maternity bundles were made available to pregnant women; waiting time for Parish Relief was abolished; and an appeals tribunal, with delegates from the unemployed, was constituted.[33] The Council immediately found itself in conflict with the Scottish Board of Health which threatened to surcharge councillors for the payments in excess of permissable rates. Some Labour members, intimidated by suggestions of a surcharge of over £400, and concerned about the illegality of their actions, withdrew their support for the package of reforms, although some changes in relief were retained.[34] The Board of Health retaliated by refusing permission for a bank loan to the Council at the beginning of May 1923. The Council continued its increased rates of relief, with the Vale of Leven Co-operative Society cashing vouchers issued in person by councillors when the Council's clerical staff refused to 'break the law'. By the middle of May the Co-op could no longer meet the needs of the Council, and the Board's conditions and scales of relief were reluctantly re-adopted. This brief skirmish demonstrated, to the local working class, the immediate benefits of combined militant action (as well as the strains of such a left-wing alliance). The implications of such collective action were remembered with pride and humour in the community: 'Everyone in the Vale had new boots and jackets,' recollected one activist, 'it was "Happy Days are Here Again".' Renton, however, was part of Cardross parish, a rural area, and did not benefit immediately from the election of left-wing candidates, who were unable to make much impact on a predominantly right-wing council. After 1930, however, the Vale of Leven and Renton fell under the Vale of Leven District Council, and combined action on a range of issues became possible.

Nevertheless, despite these victories, the strains of an alliance between the three major working class parties were considerable and, by 1925, the alliance had begun to crumble as each party's activists sought a dominant role in working class leadership. The LP, ILP and CP contested each other's seats in the local elections of that year. The 'moderates', being mostly Conservatives, were thereby returned in control of the parish and county councils, and it took a full decade before the electoral alliance could be re-cemented. In this sense it seems that the militancy of the working class of the Vale of Leven in the 1920s was at its peak in 1922 and 1923. These two years saw an acceleration in the decline of the local industry. In 1922, having been unable to pay dividends to shareholders for two years, John Christie, head of the UTR, wrote to his remaining workforce reminding them of shared joys and sorrows in the past and claiming that 'The last eight years have been unprecedented in my lifetime. Following the horrors and wreckage of the war, want of business and unemployment has laid a heavy hand on all of us. But I feel sure, in the light of past experiences that by united effort and cheerful co-operation we shall win through yet again. Let us endeavour to understand one another better, let us appreciate each other's difficulties and let us be determined by putting our shoulders to the wheel to keep our industry going.'[35]

John Christie and his fellow employers did not, in fact, make serious attempts to understand and co-operate with their employees. Socialists and (especially) Communists were victimised and dismissed from their jobs, as unemployment rose. This policy was so effective that by the mid-1920s most of the local Communists were unemployed and some had become self-employed. Labour Party and ILP members also suffered a degree of victimisation.[36] Despite poor electoral success from 1925 to 1935, working class organisations continued to increase their membership and support. Street committees were formed to assist in the gathering and dissemination of information, and to prevent evictions by packing the house and stairs, thus preventing the serving of eviction notices.[37] The growth of such solidarity and organisation presaged the General Strike, which had widespread popular support in the Vale. The local Council of Action was one of the best organised and best supported in Scotland.[38]

In addition, there were two important industrial disputes in the Vale during the 1925-1935 period. The first was the Dyeworkers' strike in 1931. About half of the UTR's 3,000 workers ceased work in April 1931 in response to a demand by their employers for wage cuts. They had already accepted nationally a small wage cut but Scottish employers wanted to make further reductions. The dispute lasted until the end of May when the work-force were forced to accept the reductions. The strike did, however, permit the cementing of closer relations between the Dyeworkers' Union and the UWM which co-operated fully during the dispute. The second major strike was at the newly-opened British Silk Dyeing Company. The factory was not unionised although one or two Communists and members of the Labour Party and ILP were employed there. Some of the more militant workers had discussed organising the factory but they were taken by surprise when a walkout stopped production at the beginning of August 1934 with a strike committee quickly being elected. The firm was an unpopular one, with strong anti-union attitudes, and the UWM Band, along with a large crowd of supporters, assisted the strikers on picket duty. There were some scuffles on the picket line and several arrests were made, including some of the strike leaders. Five other people were arrested for assaulting and intimidating a Mr and Mrs Brown out-side their home. This couple had been crossing the picket line at the BSD factory.[39] A Workers' Defence Committee was set up at the end of August to arrange for legal advice, defence and financial support for the people charged during the dispute. This Committee provides an excellent example of the new structure of the Vale's working class organisations. As well as representatives from the three parties of the left and a large number of Socialists and Trade Unionists, there were delegates from 16 local working class bodies. These included Trade Unions, the Trades Council, Friends of the Soviet Union, Young Communist League, Co-operative Comrades' Circle, NUWM, Co-operative Party, Women's Co-operative Guild and a number of Tenants' Associations.[40] They managed to raise sufficient money to pay fines, repay bail and cover legal expenses. These organisations enjoyed considerable support. The local branch of the NUWM was claiming 1,300 paid-up members by 1931, and the Friends of the Soviet Union branch had over 300 members —

one of the largest in Britain.[41]

The co-operation of the parties of the left in industrial disputes during the early 1930s helped to forge the alliance for the local elections of 1935, again through the initiative and mediation of the ILP. This united front, as in 1922, gained control of the Vale of Leven District Council by securing 14 seats (6 Communist, 5 Labour and 3 ILP), with 1 ILP, 4 Communists and 3 Labour councillors representing the locality on the County Council in Dumbarton. This resounding success did not have such immediate, radical effects on the local people as in 1922. The County Council was now responsible for many services including relief and it was more conservative, drawing representatives from rural areas. This shifted working class demands for improved rates of relief, sanitation and housing away from the Vale towards the County Council. Co-operation in local elections continued until after the Second World War when, as will be seen below, the Labour Party and the Communist Party began to nominate rival candidates. However, 1935 marked a turning point for working class control of local government, and the Vale of Leven District Council was retained by parties of the left, except for 1955-1958, until it was absorbed into Dumbarton District Council by local government re-organisation of the mid-1970s.

In addition, however, the events of 1935 also drove home to local working class activists the point that, not only were employment prospects increasingly determined outside the locality, but also the control of local government could no longer give them a lever on the crucial decisions relating to such matters as poor relief. In this sense 1935 marked a double watershed as it inevitably began to point the attention and actions of the working class of the Vale to events at a national and international level.

An immediate illustration of this was that, since working class councillors on the Vale District Council did not have control over scales of relief, their attack on these consisted of marches to Dumbarton to demonstrate support for the demands of their councillors on the County Council. In addition some councillors had acquired considerable knowledge of the rules and procedures governing payment of relief and were able to successfully represent claimants on tribunals.[42] A renewed onslaught on social conditions which could be directly affected was undertaken and a new sewage disposal scheme was implemented. The Vale proclaimed its radical identity, despite strong opposition from the County Council, by naming streets in a new council housing scheme: Burns Street, Engels Street, Muir Street, Hardie Street and Lansbury Street.[43] In 1937 the Council also refused to participate in the Coronation celebrations. As an alternative it organised 'workers' celebrations', and the Communist Party issued a 'Vale of Leven Workers' Coronation Souvenir' bearing the words of the 'Red Flag' on its cover.[44] Increasingly, however, these moves at a specifically local level were primarily gestures of defiance as the main focus of working class moved to a wider plane, with the growth of the Labour Party nationally, the fight against fascism, and the revival of employment in the locality as rearmament occurred.

This has been a necessarily brief account of the 1920s and 1930s in the Vale. A fuller account of the role of the Communist Party in the Vale can be found in Stuart Macintyre's book on *Little Moscows*, where he examines three communities where the Communist Party exerted significant influence: Mardy in South Wales, Lumphinnans in Fife (both mining villages) and the Vale of Leven.[45]

Macintyre explains the success of the CP in the Vale in terms of the potential which existed after the decline (or partial decline) of four dimensions of fragmentation within the working class. These were, according to Macintyre, the existence of a labour aristocracy in the local textile industry, the subordinate position of female workers, a 'dominant ethic of respectability' and the importance of religious differentiation.[46]

The concept of a labour aristocracy is problematic in itself when applied to this period, and has given rise to much debate. It is not my intention in this chapter to enter this argument.[47] However, it should be noted that, although the 'relatively small number of craftsmen (required) to supervise the dyeing operations, engrave the patterns for printing, mix the colours and print the cloth . . .' did provide an articulate grouping which was disproportionately represented in local organisation, this was counterbalanced by an interlocking mesh of social and kinship networks which tended to undermine common interests among the Vale's working class.[49] The marriage register for Bonhill parish in 1910 records 96 marriages.[50] Out of 96 weddings, 28 of the brides were registered as printfield hands, with a further 6 being yarnworkers. Their husbands included skilled and unskilled workers; 15 of them were involved in the bleaching, dyeing and printing industry: 5 labourers, 4 printfield hands, 2 yarnworkers, 1 dyeworker, 1 colour mixer, 1 machineman and 1 printer. Others were skilled workers in the shipyards or engineering works. This certainly presents a picture of a diverse occupational structure but with 'evidence to suggest that the daughters of skilled, as well as unskilled, workers would work in the dyeworks; and also that there was considerable intermarriage of skilled and unskilled'.[51] The distinction between skilled and unskilled in the locality was further eroded by the solidarity of workers at the Argyll Motor Works, drawing on their trade union experiences as car workers, outwith the Vale.[52] The point being made here is that the existence of occupational stratification does not necessarily result in a fragmentation of the working class, and some evidence suggests greater cohesion between skilled and unskilled than might have been expected.

The position of women in the Vale is accurately described by Macintyre, and he correctly concludes that the interwar radicalism did not offer a serious challenge to dominant sexual and family stereotypes. In fact they were often strengthened in the desire, by working class activists, to present a 'respectable' image. Male leaders in the labour movement found themselves vulnerable to actions by their wives. During a rent strike, between the wars, the landlord, in an attempt to weaken the resolve of his tenants, published the names of those who had been paying rent. One leading left wing activist was greatly embarrassed to find his wife had kept the rent fully paid! The wife of another militant recounts how she was ordered to join the Co-operative Women's Guild and the UWM shortly after her marriage. Women, then, were expected to provide political support to their menfolk, but through less strident organisations like the Friends of the Soviet Union and the Co-operative movement. There was, in fact, only one woman councillor from the Vale during the interwar years — Rosina Kirkpatrick, a member of the Co-operative and Labour Parties and a tireless worker for the labour movement. Politically she was to the right of the parties. She found herself limited in her ability to challenge dominant views of women and the family, firstly by her political beliefs, and, secondly, by the fact that she relied on a significant Catholic vote for her seat on the Council. As late as 1955 she was warning the County Council about the dangers of allowing the Family Planning Association use of council clinics.[53] Religion, as Macintyre points out, provided a further barrier to working class solidarity. As previously mentioned, there was a large Catholic population in the area. This group was isolated in a series of ways. The men were generally unable to secure employment in the local dyeworks and travelled to Dumbarton and up the Clyde to work as labourers in the shipyards. The interwar years saw the Catholic Church express hostility to the Labour Movement and its left wing in particular. It was common for local ILPers and Communists to withdraw from the Catholic Church or embrace atheism with their socialism. Some local activists even transferred their children from Catholic schools.[54] Nevertheless, Catholics by the early 1920s were demonstrating support, in Scotland, for the Labour Party and must also have been voting for the ILP and CP, especially during the elections where there was a united front of working class candidates.[55]

Perhaps the most interesting part of Macintyre's work on the Vale is his account of the traditional concept of 'respectability' and its attempted redefinition by the local militants. It has already been argued that the demise of the family firms and the creation of large companies caused the withdrawal of employers with community ties from the locality. This had two results. Firstly, the local *petite bourgeoisie* were left to defend the local apparatuses of social control against working class attack. Secondly, since the amalgamating of the bleaching, dyeing and printing industries was an indication of the coming decline of that industry, widespread unemployment in the Vale was inevitable. The experience of unemployment itself was a radicalising one. Not only did it highlight the limitations of reliance on paternalistic employers, it also provided an opportunity for the development of a range of working class organisations which were not 'work-orientated'. This situation, as Macintyre points out, enabled the left wing to challenge the dominant social and moral order. In fact the Communist Party had two main strategies. The first obviously was the organisation of the unemployed and the attempted radicalisation of the local movement as a whole. The second was a deliberate attack on the existing social order by a frontal assault on the defenders of the political and economic system. While the first strategy was more successful in providing lasting benefits for the working class, the boldness of the latter is often better remembered. On one occasion the right to use a local cinema for afternoon meetings of unemployed workers, free of charge, was achieved after a picket reduced cinema audiences to a handful. It is still recounted with pride how the owner of the picture house, a staunch Tory, was obliged to call at the NUWM rooms and ask for the picket to be removed.[56] Occasionally the challenge to the existing social order was one of violence or threat of violence. In the early 1920s a bus carrying 'moderate' members of Cardross Parish Council, returning to Renton after a meeting, was ambushed, stoned, and overturned by unemployed workers.[57] This incident was related with great hilarity by a member of the Labour Party who participated in the attack. Direct physical violence, however, was uncommon. The usual tactic was public rebuke, often using the flute band. This placed the working class activists in an awkward situation. They had recognised a political necessity for tactics of open confrontation but also wished to demonstrate ability and respectability as representatives of the labour movement. This ambiguity towards respectability and a radical challenge to dominant values was never successfully resolved by the activists and in turn reflected their dependence on support which was fragmented by religion, gender and occupation. For these reasons the growth of working class solidarity and organisation between the wars in the Vale was inherently fragile, both in terms of the tenuous nature of the political alliance it generated, and also in terms of the cohesiveness of the base from which it drew its support. These problems were to be well illustrated by developments after the Second World War.

The Vale after 1945: reformism, economic growth and disillusion

During the Second World War the political conflict of the previous two decades was reduced. Many local activists volunteered or were conscripted into the armed forces and local organisations suffered. The Co-operative Society's Hall was destroyed by fire in 1940, leaving no regular venue for members' meetings, and attendances declined.[58] The CP and LP fought a Parliamentary by-election in February 1941. The Conservatives did not contest the seat and pledged support for the Labour candidate. After some consideration the ILP and SNP decided not to fight the election. The CP selected M. McEwan, who campaigned on 'a people's programme and a people's Government, which will seek a people's way out of the war — a way which involves neither surrender to Hitler nor a prolonged and exhausting war'.[59] The Labour Party selected A. McKinlay, former MP for Partick, who welcomed the opportunity to attack 'the Communist type of propaganda', regarding the election 'as a straight issue between support for the national war effort and capitulation to Hitler'.[60] Just before polling, the Conservatives and Unionists issued a further statement in support of the Labour Party, who gained 21,900 votes to the Communist's 3,862.[61] Despite this acrimonious contest, the parties continued their co-operation in local politics. The 1945 local elections saw the continuation of the left wing 'slate', and the working class councillors retained control of the Vale of Leven District Council.

The local councils during the war found themselves performing administrative tasks within Britain's tightly controlled wartime economy. What agitation emerged was confined to the early years of the war and was mainly organised by the Communist Party, who were active in calling for the provision of air-raid shelters and setting up a committee to assist conscientious objectors in representing their case. When Germany invaded the Soviet Union, the Communist Party reversed its opposition to the war and turned to support for the national war effort.

Working class activists, in addition, found themselves operating in a situation where there was full employment. Indeed, even those blacklisted during the 1920s and 1930s were able to find work.[62] The ILP had begun to dissolve during the early 1940s and many members had moved into the Labour Party. This removed them from their more radical political base and placed them within the milieu of the Labour Party's more reformist approach.[63] These trends, assisted by the Labour Party's continuing unease at co-operating with the Communist Party, led to further stress in the inter-party alliance, and in 1948 the parties contested each other's seats. The explanation for these changes in working class action and organisation in the Vale must, however, be sought in terms of wider changes. Since 1945, the Scottish economy has had, as a central feature, an increasing proportion of its productive activity externally owned and controlled. In particular, American-owned companies have multiplied through take-overs, expansion and the opening of new factories. This process has been described and analysed elsewhere, showing the number of American-owned firms in Scotland rising from 5 in 1939 to 169 by 1975.[64] In the Vale of Leven, American investment mirrored the national pattern. Westclox, Wisemans and Burroughs commenced operations in the late 1940s, producing clocks and watches, industrial lenses and adding machines respectively. Their impact on the local workforce was crucial. Firstly, unemployment in the Vale dropped from about 16% in 1946 to 3% by 1950 and maintained comparatively low levels until the late 1950s.[65] Secondly, these factories, concentrating on light engineering and the production of consumer durables, had an approach to industrial relations much different from that of the Vale's traditional industry. Thirdly, as branch factories, they were more vulnerable to depressions in trade and movements in capital investment. By 1952, out of a local working population of about 12,000, some 2,000 people were employed on Strathleven Industrial Estate, over 1,500 of them in Burrough's and Westclox.[66] At the same time there were only 1,672 people —

fewer than 600 of them men — employed in the local textile industry. This means that, taking account of the 350 employees at the French-owned British Silk Dyeing Works in Balloch, about 23% of the Vale's working population, employed in the locality, were in foreign (mainly American) firms. In addition almost half the economically active female population in the area was to be found in these firms.[67] These American firms were sited on a new industrial estate near Renton which had been planned during the war. As early as December 1942 the Vale of Leven District Council established a Post-War Reconstruction Committee. Potential radical implications of this were thwarted when H. McCulloch, generally considered to be on the right of the Labour Party, successfully persuaded his colleagues to defeat a motion from an ex-ILP-er calling for economic reconstruction through the control of industry rather than the mere attraction of new investment.[68]

Working class radicalism during the late 1940s and 1950s was thus limited. The Vale of Leven District Council organised a successful demonstration to protest about the County Council's proposed rent increases in 1948, but the major period of demonstrations and street meetings had passed.[69] The councils became increasingly involved in planning for social and economic reconstruction. As previously mentioned, housing conditions in the Vale were less than satisfactory, and in January 1952 planning permission was granted for a public housing development at Haldane in Balloch: 122 acres were to be used for 1,100 houses. This housing was certainly needed. The density of housing even at that time was causing concern, with areas like Govan Drive — a street of 4-storey tenements — having a density of 123 houses per acre.[70] The new approach of the local authorities can be seen by examining their development plans. They estimated that 4,113 new houses were needed for the future population. This was seen not merely in terms of rehousing slum tenants but as a necessary condition for the future economic development of the Vale: '. . . the introduction of new industries has helped to balance the economic structure of the area and it is essential that this trend should be encouraged by the allocation of sufficient land to meet the needs of modern industrial development. Residential accommodation will also require to be provided for the skilled workers who will be employed in the new industries . . .'[71] This statement is to be compared to one made by the Labour Party in the mid-1930s: 'What the nation and the world needs is not scarcity-creating, but co-operation for prosperity. The Labour candidates stand for the Socialisation of Production and Distribution, which would mean that there would be work for all with the fruits of their labour as their reward. Under Capitalist production and distribution — Unemployment, Wage Reductions, Economy Cuts, the Means Test and Poverty.[72]

The extract, taken from a Labour Party election leaflet for the 1935 local elections, was endorsed by some of the people who approved and implemented the Survey Report almost twenty years later. The policy of trying to attract new industry after 1952 did not entirely succeed during that decade.

Certainly, existing firms such as Westclox expanded their operations, but this could not fully balance the effects of the collapse of other enterprises.[73] The Vale of Leven Trades Council was sufficiently concerned about unemployment to issue a report at the beginning of 1958. It showed that several small businesses had recently closed in the Vale: two bakeries, a laundry — Customs and Kemp — who occupied a new factory on the industrial estate, and a Coats factory in Bonhill. Coupled with this, employment in the Scottish textile industry peaked in 1951, in marine engineering in 1955 and in shipbuilding and ship repairing in 1956.[74] All these industries provided work for the local people who travelled out of the area, and expansion on the new industrial estate had made little impact on an unemployment rate which was almost 6% in the Vale in 1958.[75] The potential threat that rising unemployment presented to the local community helped secure Labour's victory at the local elections in May 1958. From 1945 the Vale District Council had remained under the control of the Labour Party, but in 1955 the 'moderates' gained a majority of seats on the council. This was the first time for 20 years that the local left wing had lost control of the District Council, reflecting a general shift to the right in national politics as well as a change in the political awareness of the Vale's working class. Industrially this was mirrored in the fact that the local workforce had been rather slow in seeking unionisation in new firms. Burroughs, with 1,000 employees, a notoriously anti-union firm, remained unorganised until 1960.

The dominance of this strategy of seeking economic growth above all can be seen also in the reaction of employers. In the mid-1950s employers initiated 'Productivity Committees' to encourage increased production. Edward Denny, head of his family's firm of shipbuilders, played a leading role in the setting up of the Dunbartonshire Productivity Committee. It was formed in March 1955 at a meeting in the offices of Denny's Shipbuilders in Dumbarton. A committee consisted of managers and owners from Denny's, Burroughs, Esso, UTR, Dewrance and Co and the Scottish Gas Board. Places on the committee were set aside for trade unionists who, along with the local authority, gave it support for a number of years.[76] The first public meeting of the council was held in Dumbarton where Sir Walter Puckey, immediate past president of the Institute of Production Engineers, denounced, before an audience of 600, company pension schemes and full employment as causing reduced labour mobility and 'lack of incentive'.[77]

The immediate post-war period, therefore, saw the predominance of activity aimed at promoting industrial growth. The potential for working class radicalism was subsumed by low levels of unemployment, the dominance of foreign-based firms, the slow growth of unionisation in local factories, and the high proportion of female labour in new enterprises. However, as a number of the factors began to change after 1960, there were also signs of alterations in working class action and organisation. The start of the 1960s saw two distinct trends. Firstly, a rationalisation in the economic base of the locality and, secondly, an increasing militancy among workers in the firms on the industrial estate. In March, workers at Burroughs went on strike for union recognition and an increase in their wages. The AEU and TGWU obtained their demands, and the first of a series of disputes was ended.[78] The United Turkey Red Company, which had continued production in one factory, became the subject of a take-over bid by its main British rival, the Calico Printers' Association. The local UTR workforce of 1,350 were concerned that, if the CPA were successful in their attempt, they would close the factory in the Vale.[79] As the CPA gained a majority shareholding, the labour movement set up a committee to fight the threat of closure. The three delegates from the Vale of Leven district Council to the committee included its only two Communist councillors on this delegation.[80] However, the bid by the CPA was successful and the UTR factory was closed in January 1961. The other remaining textile factory in the Vale, the British Silk Dyeing Works, was also taken over in 1960, becoming a subsidiary of the American firm, United Merchants and Manufacturers Incorporated.[81] The Royal Naval Torpedo Factory, housed in the old Argyll Motor Works, had continued with production after the war. In 1960 the factory was threatened with closure, but this was postponed after the agreement of new working practices. By June 1962 unemployment was 6% (twice the Scottish figure), and future prospects had been damaged by Burroughs' decision to delay expansion because it was 'dependent on peaceful labour relations'.[82] Denny's Shipbuilders in Dumbarton, an important source of local employment, went into voluntary liquidation in mid-1963 and unemployment in the Vale rose to $7\frac{1}{2}$%.[83]

The problems which were beginning to emerge in the Vale in the late 1950s were being generally recognised as national problems by the early 1960s, with industry and government attempting to restructure both the economic base and working class consciousness. The Labour Party, under Wilson, won the 1964 election and the Party's manifesto demonstrated a commitment to technology and science as the paths to social justice, rather than the more traditional concerns with inequalities of power and wealth. This was demonstrated when they claimed that '. . . social ownership (has its) part to play in meeting the dangers of monopoly, in achieving a fair distribution of the national dividend — and, most important of all, in helping to fulfil our national plan for economic growth'.[84] And also: 'The fundamental inspiration of "Signpost for the Sixties" and the statement which followed is the need to make Britain up-to-date, dynamic, vigorous and capable of playing her full part in world affairs. . . . We begin from the need to strengthen Britain's economy, to secure a steady and purposive expansion in industrial production.'[85]

By formulating these ideas, the Labour Party had clearly nailed its flag to the mast of economic growth above all. In fact, it was not alone in its response. The Conservatives established the National Economic Development Office and Council, and in July 1961 Selwyn Lloyd explained: 'I envisage a joint examination of the economic prospects of the country, stretching five or

P

more years into the future. It would cover the growth of national production and distribution of our resources between the main users, consumption, Government expenditure, investment and so on. Above all, it would try to establish what are the essential conditions for realising potential growth . . .[86]

The effects of these policies in the Vale were seen by the mid-1960s. Burroughs and the Royal Naval Torpedo Factory had forced new working practices on to their employees despite initial resistance. New factories were opened by local entrepreneurs, and Polaroid commenced production at Strathleven Industrial Estate. An increasing dissatisfaction with pay and conditions began to be expressed by the workers during this period, and most local factories experienced several disputes over heating, overtime rates and closed shop agreements.[87] Although this represented an increasing union membership and a growing militancy, this was not immediately transferred to more collective and community-orientated action. By April 1968 the Vale of Leven Trades Council had foundered and the STUC were obliged to contact Dumbarton District Trades Council to suggest they form a new body to include the Vale of Leven. Some delegates from Dumbarton voiced concern over the participation of members from a Trades Council which had demonstrated financial and organisational inefficiency, although the STUC's request was eventually granted.[88] The lack of collective identity was also mirrored in the setting up of a system of councillors' surgeries in the early 1960s. This is to be compared with the public debate of common problems seen in the Vale during the 1920s and 1930s.[89]

The implications of post-war planning and a controlled economy were highlighted in the Vale at the beginning of the 1970s by the closure of the Royal Naval Torpedo Factory and its subsequent purchase by Plessey (UK) Ltd. There has, as yet, been no full account of the occupation of the Plessey factory, so a brief summary of events is necessary, as they indicate the start of possible changes in working class consciousness and certainly a dissatisfaction with post-war consensus politics. After the Second World War, reduction in the workforce at the RNTF was expected by local people but the factory remained in operation. Some torpedo production from RNTF, Greenock was transferred to the Vale in the early 1950s, and it was not until 1969 that a decision was taken by the Admiralty to close the factory. Despite strenuous protest by the unions, the Ministry of Technology and Scottish Industrial Estates Ltd began to seek a purchaser for the factory and machinery.[90]

As part of a take-over of Ferranti's operations in Dalkeith, encouraged and supervised by the Industrial Re-organisation Corporation (IRC), Plessey had given a moral undertaking that Scotland's numerical control industry would remain north of the Border. Plessey, with its close contacts with the Ministry of Defence and its commitment to place numerical control work in Scotland, emerged as the only serious purchaser of the Argyll Works.[91] In May 1970 Plessey moved into the factory, taking on a workforce of 420, with the stated intention of opening a machine shop and starting numerical control operations, which they 'saw as the fastest growing business at that time.[92] By late 1970 there were 520 employees in the factory and Plessey had described plans for further expansion which would provide for 1,000 jobs initially and a further 1,000 within two years.[93] Despite this company optimism, some of the workers were becoming concerned. No proper toolroom programme had been set, and the management, all but three of whom had come from the Ferranti factory in Dalkeith, were seen as being rather ineffective and having no clear picture about the future development of the factory.[94] In May 1971 Plessey announced the intended closure of the factory, and during the following months the workers discovered, firstly, that Plessey had found prospective purchasers for the machinery and, secondly, that they had only paid £650,000 for the factory, which contained not only a large amount of valuable plant and machinery but also a dust-free workshop which the Admiralty had installed in 1969 at a cost of over £1.5 million.[95]

On 3 September 1971, the day of the closure of the factory, the convener of shop stewards, Eddie McLafferty, and about 20 other union representatives brought down the company flag, peacefully expelled security personnel and took possession of the factory. The occupation lasted 22½ weeks, ending with an agreement that Plessey set up an industrial estate and retain the remaining 70 people who were still in occupation.[96] During the occupation the local labour movement and the community in general provided considerable support and the Vale once again witnessed mass agitation with street demonstrations and public meetings.

An unemployment rate of over 12% in 1972,[97] coupled with the experience of a collective confrontation with a multi-national company, heralded a change in working class attitudes and action in the Vale. Opposition to the Tory Housing Finance Act in 1972 was initially strong, although fears of being surcharged finally encouraged implementation by the County Council. The Vale District Council continued to oppose rent increases and attempted to organise local tenants in a rent strike. This was finally abandoned, although they had the support of 600 council house tenants.[98] Support for the Scottish National Party, which regularly ran candidates from 1964 onwards, also illustrated a growing discontent with post-war political processes. The Vale of Leven had been represented in Parliament by the Labour Party since a by-election in 1936, and the Party regularly obtained over 50% of the vote until February 1974. The SNP, in the three elections up to 1970, failed to poll over 15% of the vote. In Febraury 1974, however, it gained 27.2% of the vote and by October of the same year had increased that to 33.7%, forcing the Conservatives into third place.[99] The Nationalists were quick to realise that, following re-organisation of local government, a 'gap could be filled in communities like the Vale', as one local Nationalist put it. They joined or set up tenants' associations and, by highlighting problems with housing in the area, were able to convince the electorate that the Labour Party could not deliver the services demanded by them.[100] This was a deliberate onslaught on the

Labour Party and its success was demonstrated in May 1977 when the SNP took four of the five Vale seats on the new Dumbarton District Council. The remaining seat went to an Independent. These local elections took place while the unemployment rate was rising above 14%.

The local economy was also beginning to experience difficulty, with Burroughs and Wisemans closing their factories in 1977 and 1978. Burroughs produced mechanical adding machines and were unable to compete with the range and complexity of electronic calculators.[102] Wisemans followed in 1978 as they contracted their lens production. More closures and contractions have occurred since then: British Silk Dyeing Works was closed in May 1980 and Polaroid are presently moving part of their operations from the Vale to Eire.

Conclusion

The preceding pages have described the development of a working class community from its initial identification as a 'left-wing stronghold' in the 1920s to the post-war era of a less radical class identity, presenting a striking disjunction in working class consciousness and action between the two periods. Macintyre argued that a comparable disruption in the Vale's social and economic life occurred during the period of the First World War, and his explanation of the interwar militancy can be summarised and paraphrased as follows.[103] The Vale of Leven at the turn of the century presented a picture which typified what Young describes as 'canny Scotland'.[104] The town was dominated by a series of owners and managers from the local bleaching and dyeing industry. They ran the industry, provided political leadership, were church elders, patronised the social and cultural activities of the area, and financed much of the education system. Through these mechanisms they encouraged and supported a dominant ethic of 'respectability'. This acted to further fragment a working class already segmented by occupational stratification, the inferior position of women, and religious prejudice. The labour movement which emerged was mainly organised by skilled Protestant workers who re-affirmed the dominant definitions of respectability. This 'old order' came under attack as the second decade of the twentieth century began. The loss of family firms though mergers and take-overs weakened the influence of local employers, who by now had begun to sever their ties with the community. A series of disputes in local factories, and the subsequent unionisation of women and unskilled workers, began to challenge a social order which now could only be defended by local traders, shopkeepers and foremen. The collapse of the economy after 1919 was the final chapter in the story. Young militants, led by the Communist Party, challenged, then defeated, more cautious members of the labour movement and then achieved partial success in overcoming the local *petite bourgeoisie*. The alliance of left wing activists, drawn from three political parties, came under increasing strain and from time to time was broken, resulting in the loss of many of the gains already made.

This summary is swift and superficial but captures the main elements in the argument. Some qualifications are, however, necessary. Firstly, it has already been suggested that the pre-1914 labour movement was not quite as submissive or inexperienced as Macintyre suggests. In fact a continuing tradition of militancy can be traced at least to the Chartist period when 'Bonhill . . . (had) hardly a Tory in it' and some Chartists 'actually went the length of purchasing muskets'.[105] It should also be noted that of the many people active in the inter-war labour movement, the overwhelming majority came from families with a history of participation in the labour movement. One ILP veteran described how his father had been a 'Blatchford Socialist' and his mother an active member of both the ILP and the Co-operative movement. Another recounted how his father had been a member of the ILP, and many local Communists were members of Communist families.

Secondly, while Macintyre does not ignore economic factors in encouraging or inhibiting militancy, he does underestimate the impact of mass unemployment as an absence of normal structural constraints. There are two strands to this argument. Firstly, the Communist Party, which is correctly identified by Macintyre as being one of the main radical forces within local political alliances, failed to develop a coherent industrial strategy because of its concern with local political processes and the problems CP members had in obtaining employment. Secondly, the raw experience of unemployment can be seen as having a more direct effect on support for the left wing than Macintyre seems to allow. He concentrates on analysing how the fragmentation of interests among the unemployed was, from time to time, inhibited by common struggles or exaggerated by the retention or adoption of the 'old order's' notion of respectability. The point being made here is that success for the parties of the left at local elections depended on their co-operation. The urgency of their desire to do so follows the rise and fall of unemployment during the 1920s and 1930s. So, when the rate of unemployment of almost 60% in 1922 'declined' to 23% in 1924, the united front collapsed. With the rise of unemployment in the early 1930s, pressure to defend the living standards of the local working class mounted and the ILP, Labour Party and Communist Party put forward their common slate of candidates. It should be noted here that the ILP and Labour Party were the ones to spurn national party policy by making alliances with the CP. The latter almost always fell in with national party policy and was seen by other local activists as being the party which made united action difficult. In February 1928 the Communist Party articulated its policy towards the ILP and the Labour Party when Stalin stated that Lansbury, Maxton and Brockway were 'worse than enemies'.[106] This policy was reflected in the CP 'Election Special' for the 1928 local elections in the Vale. The Labour Party were dismissed as class collaborators and the document made it clear that they 'are not soliciting votes for a Labour Programme dictated by the Labour Bureaucracy'.[107] Furthermore the Labour Party and the ILP did not share the

Communists' longstanding view of the limitations of local councils which were said to be 'part and parcel of the capitalist state machinery, and as such, are not designed to be sympathetic or speedily responsive to the needs and aspirations of the working class, for whom the problem of poverty and insecurity can only be solved by the overthrow of the capitalist system and the establishment of socialism by means of the Soviet form of Government so successfully organised by the workers of the Soviet Union'.[108]

This view of local government corresponded closely with that of the 5th Party Congress of 1922. Their policy towards local government was described in a few blunt lines: 'The Communist Party does not enter on local government to help in their work but to expose and destroy them as part of the bourgeois machinery of administration. For this purpose the work on them must always be subordinate to the objects and tactics of the mass struggle outside.'[109] The suspicion of the Labour Party of this type of understanding of local government was difficult to overcome, and it is easier to understand their final ending of the local electoral understanding in 1949 as Britain moved into a period of cold war hostility to the Soviet Union and the Communist Party of Great Britain.

The existence of mass unemployment in the Vale of Leven meant that, for a large number of people, the normal constraining and regulating structures of the factory were not part of everyday experience, and this encouraged an approach to militant working class politics which had its focus away from employment and the workplace and towards the community. The proliferation of working class organisations in the 1920s and 1930s followed this tendency. The Friends of the Soviet Union, Co-operative Men's and Women's Guilds, the setting up of the Co-operative Woodcraft Folk (a youth organisation which had members from both sexes and with no religious affiliations), and the organisation of concerts and variety shows for the unemployed, all created a rich social, political and cultural milieu where working class ideas and activities were encouraged. This network of organisations provided not only a method of dissemination of information but also offered legitimacy to a culture which was not only defensive but innovative.

The social and cultural elements in working class life were crucial to the cohesion of the locality. The printworks and bleachfields, even at the peak of their production, were unable to provide employment for more than half the local workforce. In 1906, one employer claimed that 'five or six thousand men had to travel daily to Dumbarton, Clydebank and other parts to secure employment'.[110]

The immediate impact of the outbreak of war in 1939 was the revival of employment as war production began, and the subsequent decline in attendance of meetings and socials throughout the area. These were never seriously revived, and entertainment became more of an individual or family experience through television. The post-war boom with its low unemployment rates assisted in the isolation of the Communist Party which, along with the now almost defunct ILP, had provided the radical edge of working class politics. As previously stated, the CP suffered from having no clear industrial strategy for the locality. The ILP had one or two trade unionists in their ranks but, like the CP, they stood in envy of the Labour Party with its longstanding links with the Bleachers' and Dyers' Union as well as most other local unions.[111] A further vital factor in the decline of support for the Communist Party was the belief that the 1945 Labour Government was going to transform British society. As one left winger said, 'I remember going through the Vale after the election results were known, everyone was pleased and we were shouting and waving to each other. We thought we had made it.'

The new firms which entered the Vale after the Second World War presented problems for the local labour movement. Firstly, as already stated, the trade unions tended to be dominated by those on the right of the labour movement. Secondly, these firms were based on new technological processes which were dependent on the skills of control of the workforce. The success of personnel management and 'industrial relations' can be seen in Polaroid's factory in the Strathleven Industrial Estate. Jobs in this plant are highly sought after. Workers negotiate through an Employee Representation Committee set up by the company. There has never been a strike at this factory and, although there are a few union members working there, the majority of employees are represented through the Works Committee which 'provides a forum at which free exchange of views on all matters of factory-wide interest and the operating efficiency of the total enterprise are discussed'.[112] The technical control of the workforce on the production line and on the negotiating committee was extended into physical structure of the locality and the social structure of the community. In the early 1950s Dumbarton District Council demonstrated the increasing professionalisation of local government with its implied decrease in working class involvement. Its survey plan, dealing with very real problems in housing, transport, health services and welfare services, mirrored the structures found in industry by attempting to define social groupings and legitimate communities within the Vale of Leven. We find therefore that 'it is appropriate that the area should be developed to provide the convenience and amenity of access which its topographical position demands' and that 'demands of the future population and the deficiencies will require to be remedied . . . by regrouping the principal commercial centres and providing subsidiary shops in the residential areas (and) by providing additional accommodation for social activities'.[113] Community now has become defined not by the local working class, but by professional planners acting within a framework of the restructuring of the economic base. By the early 1970s 'community' had become an area of concern. The 'Quality of Life Experiment' in Dunbartonshire was developed to select four areas 'remote from the influences of traditional "metropolitan" art' and ascertain how 'existing activities could be developed and extended by a concerted drive at local level'.[114]

We have seen, therefore, that the Vale of Leven is a particular industrial area with its own set of experiences within the wider context of the development of Scottish capitalism. Conclusions about the distinct processes in operation in this locality are difficult to reach and generalisations must be made with great care. However, the Vale can be seen as passing through three phases since 1919. Firstly, the interwar years saw a working class radicalism emerge which was based on the absence of structural constraints forging a deep sense of community. The second period was post-1945 to the late 1960s when a belief in the Labour Party, a restructuring of the economic base and consensus politics gradually gave way to the final period — a growing militancy and a declining economic base. The fractures in the political co-operation of sections of the labour movement do not deny its effectiveness and impact. What emerges from the Vale is a picture of militant united action being undertaken in the face of adverse social and economic processes and the development of an uneven but continuous experience of common interest and community identity which provides both a buffer against the stark realities of a deprived area and a framework for further changes in consciousness and action. These relationships are a vital component in the understanding of the growth and development of working class communities, their collective consciousness and action, and as such must be given due attention by sociologists, historians and socialists.

NOTES

1. I would like to thank all the people who have helped me in this work by providing information, documents and hospitality during my research. A special thanks to Joyce Gallacher for her tolerance, Peter and Barbara Macnaughton for their hospitality and Tony Dickson for his advice, encouragement and indulgence over deadlines.

2. The literature on working class communities is large. A good introduction to the topic is M. Bulmer (ed.), *Working Class Images of Society*, London, 1975.

3. It is important to note that local usage sometimes distinguishes Renton from the four other settlements which then fall under the collective heading 'Vale of Leven'. However, when the 'Vale' or the 'Vale of Leven' is used in this chapter, it can be assumed that, for the sake of simplicity, it refers to the whole area, including Renton. If specific settlements are to be identified, this will be done in the text.

4. A. F. Jones, unpublished Research Paper on Bleaching and Dyeing — held in Dumbarton Public Library.

5. P. Abercrombie & R. H. Mathew, *The Clyde Valley Regional Plan, 1946*, Edinburgh, HMSO, 1949; *Statistical Account of Scotland 1791-1799*, Vol. IX, 1978.

6. A. Slaven, *The Development of the West of Scotland 1750-1960*, London, 1975. For a fuller account of this, see A. J. Durie, *The Scottish Linen Industry in the Eighteenth Century*, Edinburgh, 1979.

7. This is an estimate from the relevant census reports and Statistical Accounts for Scotland.

8. *Clarion*, 5 January 1912, quoted in J. D. Young, *The Rousing of the Scottish Working Class*, London, 1979, p. 181; and S. Macintyre, 'Forms of Authority in the Vale of Leven 1900-1939', unpublished paper given at CSE conference in Stirling, 1978.

9. T. Johnston, *A History of the Working Classes in Scotland*, Glasgow, 1929.

10. J. D. Young, *op. cit.*

11. R. A. Peel, 'Turkey Red Dyeing in Scotland — Its Heyday and Decline', *Journal of the Society of Dyers and Colorists*, Vol. 68, December 1952.

12. John Neill, *Records and Reminiscences of Bonhill Parish*, first published 1912, reprinted 1979.

13. *Ibid.*

14. See J. A. Jackson, *The Irish in Britain*, London, 1963; B. Lenman, *An Economic History of Modern Scotland: 1660-1976*, London, 1977.

15. *Statistical Account for 1791, op. cit.*

16. T. Johnston, *op. cit.*, p. 306.

17. See A. Wilson, *The Chartist Movement in Scotland*, Manchester, 1970.

18. See R. H. Campbell, *The Rise and Fall of Scottish Industry 1707-1939*, Edinburgh, 1980; J. Neill, *op. cit*; A. Slaven, *op. cit.*

19. Copies of some strike documents in my possession.

20. A. C. McDonald & A. S. E. Browning, 'History of the Motor Industry in Scotland', *Proceedings of the Automobile Division of the Association of Mechanical Engineers*, 1960-61, No. 9.

21. Scrapbook in my possession.

22. *Lennox Herald*, 14 December 1918.

23. J. Young, *op. cit.*, Ch. 6.

24. J. Agnew, *The Story of the Vale of Leven*, Gartocharn, 1975.

25. S. Macintyre, *Little Moscows*, London, 1980, p. 117.

26. Interview with Colin Britton, 31.1.80.

27. Communist Party local election literature, 1928; P. Abercrombie & R. H. Mathew, *op. cit.*, p. 276.

28. J. Agnew, *op. cit*; Communist Party local election literature, 1928; *Lennox Herald*, 21 April 1928; J. Neill, *op. cit.*

29. *Lennox Herald*, 2 July 1921.

30. Numerous local informants.

31. Interview with C. Britton.

32. Interviews with W. Skinner, 25.1.80, J. Gallacher, 20.4.80.

33. Bonhill Parish Council Minutes (BPCM), 14 January 1923.

34. BPCM, 26 January 1923, 23 February 1923. The surcharge was withdrawn by the incoming Labour Government.

35. Reproduced in J. Ferguson & J. G. Temple, 'The old Vale and its memories', limited circulation, 1927.

36. Interviews with C. Britton, R. Brookes, 10.8.79.

37. This tactic was widespread in Scotland at the time; see L. Flynn, *We Shall be All*, Glasgow, 1978.

38. J. Skelley (ed.), *The General Strike 1926*, London, 1976, p. 118.

39. Interviews with B. Brookes, T. Abrahams, 24. 8. 79; *Lennox Herald*, 11 August 1930; strike leaflets in my possession.

40. Minutes of the Workers' Defence Committee — copy in my possession.

41. Interviews with G. McDonald, 7.3.80; R. Brookes, 10.8.79; S. Macintyre, *op. cit.*, 1980, p. 100.

42. Interviews with G. McDonald and E. O'Hare, 6.3.80.

43. Vale of Leven District Council Minutes (VLDCM), 7 February, 3 April, 8 May, 3 July and 7 August 1936.

44. Vale of Leven Workers' Coronation Souvenir 1937 — copy in my possession.

45. S. Macintyre, *op. cit.*, 1980.

46. *Ibid.*, pp. 85-88, quote taken from p. 88.

47. See, for example, H. F. Moorhouse, 'The Marxist Theory of the Labour Aristocracy', *Social History*, Vol. 3, No. 1, January 1978 and the subsequent debate with A. Reid in Vol. 3, No. 3, October 1978.

48. S. Macintyre, *op. cit.*, 1980, p. 85.

49. S. Macintyre, *op. cit.*, 1978.

50. *Ibid.*

51. *Ibid.*, p. 90.

52. *Ibid.*, esp. Ch. 6.

53. *Lennox Herald*, 24 December 1955.

54. Interviews with several local activists.

55. J. G. Kellas & P. Fotheringham, 'The Political Behaviour of the Working Class', in A. A. MacLaren (ed.), *Social Class in Scotland*, Edinburgh, 1976; J. F. McCaffrey, 'Politics and the Catholic Community since 1878', in D. McRoberts (ed.), *Modern Scottish Catholicism: 1878-1978*, Glasgow, 1979.

56. Interviews with E. O'Hare and G. McDonald.

57. *Lennox Herald*, 10 March 1923.

58. Co-operative minutes have been destroyed — I have been forced to rely on several interviews.

59. *Lennox Herald*, 25 January 1941.

60. *Ibid.*, 1 February 1941.

61. *Ibid.*, 22 February 1941 and 8 March 1941.

62. Interviews with G. McDonald and E. O'Hare.

63. Interview with C. Britton and J. Gallacher.

64. See, for example, J. Firn, 'External Control and Regional Policy', in G. Brown (ed.), *Red Paper on Scotland*, Edinburgh, 1975; D. O. C. Forsythe et al., *US Investment in Scotland*, USA, 1972; N. Hood & S. Young, *European Development Strategies of US Owned Manufacturing Companies Located in Scotland*, HMSO, Edinburgh, 1980.

65. Unpublished Department of Employment figures (DEP).

66. *Lennox Herald*, 23 February 1952.

67. County of Dumbarton Survey Report, 1952.

68. Vale of Leven District Council Minutes (VLDCM), 24 December 1942.

69. *Lennox Herald*, 28 February 1948.

70. County of Dumbarton Survey Report, 1952.

71. *Ibid.*

72. Vale of Leven Labour Party Manifesto for 1935 local elections — in my possession.

73. *Lennox Herald*, 4 January 1958.

74. Toothill Report, cited in T. Dickson (ed.), *Scottish Capitalism*, London, 1980, p. 293.

75. Unpublished DEP figures.

76. *Lennox Herald*, 12 March 1955.

77. *Ibid.*, 1 October 1955.

78. *Ibid.*, 12 March 1960.

79. *Ibid.*, 11 June 1960.

80. VLDCM, 6 July 1960.

81. *Lennox Herald*, 3 September 1960 and correspondence with BSD Ltd.

82. Unpublished DEP figures; *Lennox Herald*, 30 September 1961.

83. Unpublished DEP figures.

84. 'Signpost for the Sixties', Labour Party Manifesto for 1964, quoted in P. Foot, *The Politics of Harold Wilson*, London, 1968, p. 131.

85. H. Wilson in the *New York Times*, September 1963, quoted in P. Foot, *op. cit.*, p. 148.

86. Selwyn Lloyd, Hansard H C Debates 645, Col. 439 (25 July 1961), quoted in A. Budd, *The Politics of Economic Planning*, London, 1978, p. 92.

87. This is drawn from interviews and correspondence with local employers and trade unionists.

88. West Dunbartonshire Trades Council Minutes, 11 April 1963.

89. Interviews with M. Haran, 1.8.80; J. Todd, 5.9.80.

90. *Lennox Herald*, 17 December 1969; 16 January 1970.

91. Interview with Plessey spokesman, 20 November 1979.

92. Plessey (UK) Annual Report, 1970-71.

93. *Lennox Herald,* 2 October 1970.

94. Interview with convener of shop stewards — E. McLafferty, 26.1.80.

95. Interview with E. McLafferty; *Lennox Herald,* 4 June 1971; 13 August 1971.

96. Interviews with E. McLafferty, I. McKee and Plessey spokesman.

97. Unpublished DEP figures.

98. Interviews with M. Haran and J. Todd.

99. These and all other election figures are drawn from the *Lennox Herald* and the *County Reporter.*

100. Interviews with members of the SNP.

101. Local Plan No. 1, Dumbarton District Council, 1980.

102. Interview with J. Stevenson.

103. S. Macintyre, *op. cit.,* 1980.

104. J. Young, *op. cit.,* Ch. 6.

105. J. Neill, *op. cit.,* pp. 127 & 128. See also A. Wilson, *The Chartist Movement in Scotland,* Manchester, 1970.

106. J. Degras (ed.), *Soviet Documents in Foreign Policy,* Vol. 2, London, 1952, quoted in H. Dewar, *Communist Politics in Britain,* London, 1976.

107. Communist Election Special, 1928 — copy in my possession.

108. Vale of Leven and Renton election special — issued by the Communist Party — copy in my possession.

109. Quoted in Dewar, *op. cit.,* p. 33.

110. W. A. Smith, 'Argyll Companies New Motor Works Inaugural Address', cited by S. Macintyre, *op. cit.,* 1978, p. 13, fn. 15.

111. Interviews with C. Britton, J. Gallacher and W. Skinner.

112. Information from visit to Polaroid factory.

113. 1952 Council Development plan, *op. cit.*

114. HMSO, *Leisure and the Quality of Life,* London, 1977.

5

Occupational Stratification and the Sexual Division of Labour: Scotland since 1945

Ian Watt

Introduction

THIS chapter is concerned with the changing employment patterns and prospects for women workers in Scotland in recent decades. In particular, we shall be concerned with the effects of several interrelated themes which bear directly on the conditions under which female labour is increasingly employed, and located in the labour market. Thus it will be argued that women form a growing sector of the labour force because of the change in the industrial base of Scotland, characterised by a need for greater flexibility in production and for an equally flexible labour force.

Section 1 provides emperical data which illustrates the changing fortunes of women at work, the increase in married women working and for greater periods, whilst skilled 'male' jobs have steadily dropped. This can be seen as part of a broader process of decline in traditional areas of employment and a movement towards service industries and new forms of 'deskilled' production. Section 2 takes up this issue, suggesting that the emergence of large monopoly and multinational investment is a key factor in this process since the new areas of expansion have been dominated by 'branch' or assembly-type systems of production relying heavily on women. This is part of a larger 'centre-periphery' argument which claims that fluctuations in production can be more easily exported to the 'branch' level and thus necessitate the pursuit of a labour force which is most easy to dispense with — women.

The problems and possibilites this situation poses for women are discussed in Section 3. Dual labour market theory is utilised to illustrate the structural difficulties faced by women at work as opposed to those ahistorical theories which generalise about the perceptions and orientations women have about and towards paid employment. This also permits a clearer grasp of how investment and production patterns of monopoly firms exacerbate sectionalism in the labour force.

Section 4 attempts to work through some of these processes. The accelerating trend towards deskilled jobs is highlighted along with the potential for change and organisation. However, the inertia of the trade union movement is also illustrated. In particular, the failure to adequately evolve a strategy towards the novel work settings many women find themselves in and the precise problems women face are discussed. Attention is drawn also to the world of work as a labour process which affects the employment prospects of men as a direct result of the terms on which female 'substitute' labour is available. Finally, some speculative and tentative suggestions are made about the possible outcomes of the above processes on particular sectors of the female labour force in the coming period.

1. Patterns of employment for women

In any review of employment patterns, attention is quickly drawn to the dramatic increase in the incidence of paid employment amongst women, especially married women, since the Second World War. Of equal signifi-

TABLE 1. Population and Labour Force G.B. 1911-68, 1973-4

| | | Labour Force | | Percentage of total labour force per thousand | |
	Population	Male	Female	Male	Female
1911	40,831	12,927	5,424	70	30
1921	42,769	13,656	5,701	71	29
1931	44,795	14,700	6,265	70	30
1951	48,918	16,007	7,419	68	32
1968	53,781	16,322	8,936	65	35
1973	55,900	16,200	9,400	63	37
1974	56,000	15,700	9,400	60	40

Source: H. Wainwright, 'Women and the Division of Labour', in P. Abrams (ed.), *Work Urbanism and Inequality,* p. 165.

TABLE 2. Employees in Employment: Scotland, England and Wales (000s)

Scotland	Total	Males	Females	Females/Males
March 1978	2,058	1,190	868	0.73
June 1978	2,079	1,202	877	0.73
September 1978	2,088	1,203	885	0.74
December 1978	2,081	1,199	882	0.74
England & Wales				
March 1978	19,998	11,822	8,176	0.69
June 1978	20,142	11,887	8,272	0.70
September 1978	20,223	11,923	8,300	0.70
December 1978	20,319	11,907	8,412	0.71

Source: Fraser of Allander Institute, *Quarterly Economic Review,* Vol. 5, No. 1, July 1979

TABLE 3. Employees in Employment by Industry

1968 SIC Order Numbers	Thousands											
	1965	1966	1967	1968	1969	1970	1971	1972	1973	1974	1975	1976
Males and Females, Total Employment	2,116	2,120	2,080	2,068	2,075	2,058	2,003	1,989	2,050	2,084	2,076	2,071
Males, Total Employment (Analysis by sector)	1,352	1,342	1,312	1,290	1,286	1,267	1,216	1,194	1,221	1,227	1,219	1,210
I Agriculture, forestry, fishing	67	62	56	55	52	50	47	47	45	43	42	41
II Mining and quarrying	60	54	51	44	40	38	38	36	34	33	33	34
III-XIX Manufacturing industries	502	499	486	480	491	488	460	439	447	457	438	420
XX Construction	172	177	177	178	172	164	149	148	163	160	162	159
XXI Gas, electricity and water	30	31	29	29	28	26	26	24	24	23	20	24
II-XXI Index of production industries	763	761	743	731	731	715	673	647	667	672	655	636
XXII-XXVII Services	522	519	513	504	502	502	496	500	510	511	522	532
Females, Total Employment (Analysis by sector)	764	777	768	778	789	794	787	795	828	857	858	861
I Agriculture, forestry, fishing	11	10	9	9	9	9	8	7	7	7	7	7
II Mining and quarrying	2	2	2	1	1	1	1	1	1	1	1	1
III-XIX Manufacturing industries	223	236	216	219	224	221	209	203	210	219	199	188
XX Construction	9	10	9	9	9	9	9	9	10	11	11	12
XXI Gas, electricity and water	4	4	4	5	5	5	5	5	5	5	5	6
II-XXI Index of production industries	237	242	231	234	238	235	225	219	227	236	217	207
XXII-XXVII Services	516	525	527	535	542	547	554	569	594	614	633	647

Source: Scottish Abstract of Statistics, No. 8, 1978.

cance, however, are the continuing inequalities of pay, opportunity and security associated with female employment, and its effective 'balkanisation' in the labour market. This section attempts to assess the interconnectedness of this structured inequality and to discuss its implications for the employment prospects of working women. It is abundantly clear that women form a growing section of the labour force, particularly in Scotland where the female/male ratio is consistently higher, as Table 2 illustrates. From 1970 to 1977 female employment has risen by over 10%, with women now forming around 42% of the total employed in Scotland.[1] It remains true also, unfortunately, that this growth has been allied to the consigning of women to specific sectors of employment, those associated with services, and with the caring for other people's needs as an extension of the tasks related to the domestic 'role' of women. Table 3 highlights this trend, with women's entry into the service sector in Scotland in general increasing from 516,000 in 1956 to 647,000 by 1976.[2] By comparison the increase for men was a mere 10,000. Similarly, the segregation of occupations by sex is evident in the 'Index of Production Industries' where men dominate — 636,000 in 1976 and only 207,000 women. The distinct separation of the sexes in employment is mirrored also in the relative skill and responsibility characteristics of the two labour forces. In Scotland nearly three quarters of all women are employed in the service sector. The remaining 25% are almost all employed in the manufacturing sector, primarily in four industries: food and tobacco; textiles; paper and printing; and clothing and footwear.[3] This process culminates as expected in marked

TABLE 4. Predominantly Female Occupations G.B.

90% or over female occupations	*All persons*	*Women (thousands)*
Hand and machine sewers, embroiderers	238	230
Nurses	432	394
Maids, valets, etc.	443	428
Canteen assistants	304	293
Typists, secretaries, etc.	770	759
75% and under 90% female occupations		
Shop assistants	969	786
Charwomen, cleaners and	522	456
Kitchen hands	122	100
Office machine operators	177	153
Hairdressers, etc.	159	124
Telephone operators	107	89
60% and under 75% female occupations		
Clerks and cashiers	2,475	1,546
Waiters and waitresses	113	82
Primary and secondary teachers	496	318
Packers and labellers, etc.	183	121
Bartenders	103	73

Source: H. Wainwright, 'Women and the Division of Labour', p. 169.

TABLE 5. Average Weekly Earnings by Industry Group, April 1978 New Earnings Survey.
Manual and Non-Manual Male (21 and over) and Female (18 and over) Employees

	Scotland Manual Weekly Earnings £	Scotland Non Manual Weekly Earnings £
Full-time Men		
All industries and services, I-XXVII	81.4	99.8
All index of production industries, II-XXI	86.3	107.1
All manufacturing industries, III-XIX	86.2	106.4
All non manufacturing industries, I, II, XX-XXVII	77.8	97.8
Full-time Women		
All industries and services, I-XXVII	50.2	56.6
All index of production industries, II-XXI	53.3	52.3
All manufacturing industries, III-XIX	52.8	52.8
All non manufacturing industries, I, II, XX-XXVII	47.2	57.1

Source: *Scottish Abstract of Statistics*, No. 9, 1980.

differences in earnings between the sexes. The connection between the rapid increase in the utilisation of female labour and its relatively low cost provides important returns to capital in Scotland. This is revealed when we come to examine changes in the industrial and productive base in Scotland, dominated as it has been by traditional heavy manufacturing and primary industries — shipbuilding, engineering, mining, etc. In recent years this important source of employment (especially for men) has declined, as Table 6 illustrates.

TABLE 6. Employment Changes (000s)

	Scotland	
	1965	1977
Agriculture, Forestry, Fishing	78	49
Mining and Quarrying	61	35
Manufacturing Industries	725	608
Construction	180	171
Gas, Electricity, Water	34	29
Services	1,037	1,179
Total	2,115	2,071

Source: Scottish Development Agency: 'The Scottish Economy: A Concise Analysis', p. 10.

Today service sector employment accounts for approximately 58% of total employment; by comparison manufacturing industries have dropped to around 29% of total employment in Scotland.[4] It is clear that change in the sex structure of employment is derived from increases in demand from the service sector and that this trend will continue in the foreseeable future.

TABLE 7. Projected Employment 1979-1984 (000s)

| | Males | | Females | |
Total	Manufacturing	Services	Manufacturing	Services
1979	405	524	204	681
1980	401	517	203	683
1981	396	511	201	682
1982	389	505	199	686
1983	380	500	197	689
1984	372	494	195	692

Source: Fraser of Allander: *Quarterly Economic Review*, Vol. 5, No. 1, July 1979.

The massive increase in married working women, now approximately 55%, indicates the integration of paid employment with domestic activity and contributes to the 'attractiveness' of hiring women in Scotland.[5] The generalised assumptions made about the attitudes of women to paid work etc (see Section 3), and the movement towards service industries, and the sex of the incumbents, emerge in the projections of Table 8.

TABLE 8. Activity Rates Scotland 1978-1993 (000s)

| | Males | | Females | |
Age	1978	1993	1978	1993
16-19	.627	.606	.584	.572
20-24	.869	.834	.670	.678
25-29	.954	.921	.576	.599
30-34	.967	.934	.536	.556
35-39	.970	.937	.721	.762
40-44	.969	.936	.721	.762
45-49	.965	.931	.721	.776
50-54	.955	.922	.721	.776
55-59	.937	.904	.567	.567
60-64	.840	.810	.299	.313
65-69	.257	.248	.088	.093
70+	.093	.090	.021	.021

Source: Fraser of Allander Institute, *Quarterly Economic Review*, Vol. 5, July 1979, No. 1.

Clearly, the comparisons between men and women in the age range 35-55 show the possibilities for the employment of women. In effect, women's working lives now exhibit a 'two-phase' or 'bi-model' pattern, with women working before their children are born and returning to work in ever increasing numbers as children grow up:

In 1901 only one ever-married woman in ten was economically active, by 1971 one in two was active in the labour force. This represents a proportional increase in labour force participation of almost 400% for wives.[6]

It is also true that the overriding majority of part-time workers, around 307,000 in 1976,[7] contributes to the adverse situation many women (and men) find themselves in, especially concerning trade union representation, equal pay, etc. The drawing in of women to the labour market has also been assisted by the high levels of migration from Scotland since the war. Between 1951 and 1975 the net loss of population through migration from Scotland was 667,800.[8] In the decade 1970-80 approximately 10,000 jobs a year have been lost in indigenous manufacturing industry. By drawing all our data together, it would appear that in Scotland dependency on traditional industry remains higher than in the rest of the country but is, nevertheless, experiencing rapid decline. This has led to a steady loss in the 'prime age' skilled males, an increase in structural unemployment amongst males and a movement towards new light engineering, electronics industries, with the expansion of the service sector and an influx of female labour. Table 9 illustrates this by locating the stratification of unemployment by sex and identifying the contours of the labour market by employment sector.

TABLE 9. Scottish Unemployment by Occupation: March 1979

| | | Unemployment | | Unemployment/ Vacancies by |
Occupation	Male	Female	Total	Occupation
Managerial & Professional	5,609	4,221	1,485	4.7
Clerical & Related	5,642	15,464	21,106	6.8
Other Non-Manual	2,714	8,211	10,925	6.8
Craft & Similar	18,643	2,103	20,746	4.8
General Labourers	56,636	12,473	69,109	58.0
Other Manual	26,710	11,499	38,209	5.2
Total	115,609	53,971	169,580	8.6

Source: *Department of Employment Gazette.*

Thus the majority of the unemployed are general labourers, with 72% of unemployed males manual workers, compared to 44% of the female unemployed. Most unemployed females are found in clerical and related occupations. By far the most striking statistic is the excessively high unemployment/vacancy ratio for general labourers, a category dominated by males.

The future appears bleak for many sections of the labour force in Scotland, both male and female. The decline in heavy industry and the emergence of new industry in the service sector have to be seen as part of the same process — the movement towards new forms of exploitation through the generation of assembly or branch-type production and the attendant forms of labour this mode of production necessitates.[9] It is to the first of these issues we now turn.

2. Multinational investment in Scotland

The most important dimension of the new industries in Scotland has been the emergence of multinational, particularly American multinational, investment. Currently, around 200 American companies and 60 from elsewhere are manufacturing in Scotland. Together they employ over 100,000 people, with the EEC market of 260 million a key consideration when making investment decisions. One in six of total manufacturing jobs are now provided for by these foreign firms: over 90% by North American firms, with 50% of U.S. production destined for export. The range of product is initially impressive, and has mainly been in science-related sectors — electronics, plastics and pharmaceuticals. From the 1970s, companies associated with oil and gas developments have also arrived; they have provided inputs in the areas of commercial vehicles, engineering, food processing, packaging, rubber textiles and so on. Thus around 26% of mechanical engineering employment, 39% of electrical engineering employment and 60% of instrument engineering (with its associated domination by female labour) is attributable to American companies.[10] Overall, 42% of employment created by foreign investment in Britain has come to Scotland. By comparison the second most popular region, South-East England, attracted only 16% of the jobs.[11] Most importantly of all, U.S. companies employ on average workforces of around 500 with a male/female ratio of 2 to 1. Other overseas companies employ men and women in a ratio approaching 1 to 1.[12] Foreign firms have also been concerned to establish independent manufacturing subsidiaries, or to set up licensing agreements with Scottish firms enabling them to manufacture their goods in Scotland (exchange controls on royalties are minimal). Thus a high degree of production/investment flexibility is wedded to secure established production and marketing facilities and a high availability of cheap labour — women (see Table 8). Similarly, the financial inducements provided highlight this process.[13] From at least the 1960s external control of the Scottish economy has emerged with the destruction of traditional industries and a re-gearing of capitalist production and investment. According to Firn:

> One of the most important findings that has emerged so far is the relationship between the size of plants and external control . . . with nearly 46% of total employment in manufacturing falling within the 110 enterprises that employ over 1000. This would suggest that the Scottish economy is effectively dependent upon the decisions made by a relatively small number of companies and thus attempts to stimulate the Scottish economy might be more successful if concentrated initially on these particular large companies . . . basically the larger the enterprise the more likely it is to be controlled by a North American company . . . for of the 106,000 employees in the 110 largest enterprises, nearly 40% are in externally-controlled branch plants, where past experience would suggest a relatively low level of autonomy in decision-making. This again would seem to have very important implications for our understanding of long-term economic growth at the regional level, with the leading plants in a region like Scotland being firmly tied in to the national and international economic systems of the multinational enterprises.[14]

Firn goes on to list six major conclusions:

1. Only 41% of manufacturing employment in Scotland is controlled internally.
2. The larger the enterprise, the more likely it is to be controlled externally.
3. Over one quarter of total manufacturing employment is in non-local branch plants.
4. 110 enterprises account for 46% of total manufacturing employment.
5. The faster growing the sector, the lower is the amount of Scottish participation.
6. The five fastest growing sectors have less than 14% indigenous control.[15]

Linking the above to the outward movement of young skilled males brings out more clearly the 'mismatch in terms of the male-female ratio between the jobs that have been lost to the region, and those that have replaced them in the new enterprises'.[16] Firn goes on:

> The nature of new jobs provided by external plants has been principally orientated towards female, semi-skilled assembly operations in such as electronic plants, whereas the jobs lost have been mainly of male, highly-paid craftsmen. Almost certainly, therefore, there has been a net wage-reduction per new job provided, as well as an element of de-skilling.[17]

Two broad categories of employment emerge for women — the 'traditional' service jobs indicated in Table 4, and the light engineering/instrumentation assembly-type jobs imported by the multinationals with their attendant service sectors. The reasons for the former will emerge in the 'sociological' section, the latter can be more fully appreciated by addressing in more detail the implications for women of branch-type production. This entails a discussion of various theories associated with the concept of 'centre/periphery' in regional and economic policy and capitalist planning.[18]

Attention has been drawn to changes in the employment distribution as a result of alterations in the industrial structure. It has been shown, for example, that

> developments in employment and industry are, in fact, closely linked and that, in essence, the industrial structure determines stratification and segmentation in the labour market, with corporate strategy determining the loci for particular strata and segments.[19]

This appears particularly true in Scotland for several reasons, not least the influence of multinational corporations. The domination of the economy by these firms, with massive research and development back-up and suitable economies of scale, leaves them in a not unfavourable position. It is this imbalance in trading arrangements that provides the basis of 'core' and 'periphery' operations. The generation of high capital investment issuing in high monopolist profits erects barriers that other firms cannot breach. Similarly, the expenditure of large sums on capital investment necessitates mass production and continuous flow processes, along with a high incidence of deskilling and low manual exertion in many cases. This, of course, brings many jobs within the orbit of the female labour force. By comparison, firms at the periphery lack these resources. They can be characterised as small and in competitive markets, unusually labour intensive, returning low profits and paying low wages with suitably low levels of investment. On a national level these firms do not have the same relationship to governmental policies, or to the country's economy. They are also, generally, in a subordinate position either in relation to the market or to the core firm sector.[20] As we have seen in Scotland, a common trait is the importing of technology, sometimes under licence from the 'core' firms — usually for assembly work or partial production before export. The activity is essentially a sub-contracting one. Thus 'satellite' firms are some way between being peripheral competitors and wholly owned subsidiaries. In this context they provide flexibility for the centre firm — capital saving, risk transference in times of economic recession, and excess capacity. They permit the minimal disruption of the core with its expensive plant investment so dependent on long-term stability. Fluctuations in demand will, whenever possible, be 'exported' to the periphery. (In Scotland between 1977 and 1980 Honeywell, Hoover, Monsanto, Singer, B.S.R., etc.) The logic of this dichotomy in the labour market is in the instability of employment between the two sectors: unlike core firms, those at the periphery are in a poor market position. Prices and investment and demand are decided upon elsewhere. This culminates in high turnover at the periphery with the requisite hardship and uncertainty for the low-skill workforce.[21] This process is highlighted by the variation in levels of employment. Peripheral firms show marked increases in employees in times of high employment and rapid decreases in recession, as the core firm's level of sub-contracting is reduced to stabilise its own capital utilisation over time. This results in job uncertainty for peripheral workers due to their minor position in the market and low product range. The links are clearly established between primary firms' investment trends and their own desire for stability in employment. High capital investment is inextricably linked to high investment in 'human capital'. Workers at the centre are expensive to train and their retention is of crucial importance. The opposite is the case with periphery or secondary workers.[22] The firm's market situation limits wage levels much more drastically than the monopoly sector with the expected low trade union presence, etc. As a consequence of these factors, at the periphery labour-intensive processes and product instability instigate a low level of skill, wages, and high turnover:

> Unable to restrict entry to the labour market of their firm and at the mercy of high firm turnover, the environment of the labour force in the periphery firm contrasts starkly with that in the centre firm.[23]

This situation, as already indicated, also obtains for those workers at the lower levels of centre firms, those sectors whose skill levels remain markedly lower than the bulk of the labour force — especially women in routinised repetitive jobs. Thus the various barriers erected in the labour market grow naturally out of underlying technological differences between the centre and periphery firm. These are also related to the ideological and social system present in society (expectations about the role of women, the entitlement of men to paid employment, the subjective beliefs of women themselves, and so forth). It is this combination of factors which has led a recent study by Massey and Meegan to suggest at the urban level:

> in absolute terms, the bulk of the losses in cities was of relatively skilled jobs . . . the reorganisation of production in Group 1 industries was bound to have a particularly signifi-cant impact on male, skilled labour.[24]

And similarly at the regional level Payne claims:

> Clearly, Scotland has become more working class and its population is less skilled vis-a-vis England, than at any time since the First World War.[25]

This is also highlighted by emigration from the industrial central belt. Scotland's population is 5.2 million, with three-quarters being in Central Scotland. Between 1961 and 1968 the population of Strathclyde region fell by 5.5% and Lothian region by 4.6%.[26] Jobs have been lost by skilled males, the inner cities and manufacturing industries, and gained by semi-skilled females, the outer cities and service industries. Developing alongside this is part-time female employment in the outer areas (New Towns, etc) greatly favoured by foreign firms, with virtual stagnation in male rates. Danson draws the decisive conclusions where he comments:

> female part-time service workers are less likely to unionise . . . less likely to have on-the-job training, specific skills, monopoly rights over jobs etc., i.e. the Internal Labour Markets in which many of the new post-war jobs have been created will be weak. This will be true both absolutely and relative to the Internal Labour Markets of the declining industries. Thus Clydeside, based on coal, steel, engineering and shipbuilding, has seen the breaking down of its old, strong Internal Labour Markets in plants in Glasgow, Motherwell, Clydebank, etc., and their replacements with new, weaker versions in the State sector and services in the New Towns and suburbs. The latter are founded on skilled craftsmen and labour intensive pro-duction in contemporary terms. The actual job losses in the declining industries have been to the fastest growing developing countries — Korea, Brazil, Taiwan and, earlier, Japan; all of these, whilst investing heavily, have weak labour organisations . . . By contrast, the key industry-core economy plants of chemicals, steel, vehicles etc., have migrated for a variety of reasons to the outer areas and greenfield sites.[27]

We are now in a position to assess the implications for the pattern of industry in Scotland and the relative split between centre/periphery with its effects on the labour force — both male and female. The trends, as we have seen, indicate a 'flight' to suburbia and new centres of population. However, it is also true that for many women in the inner cities traditional sources of employment remain for them (unlike men): clothing, footwear, furniture, food, drink, tobacco and government services, the latter attracting high levels of commuting. The trenchant attacks on the public sector by successive governments mean also, of course, that the brunt of job losses has been borne by the lower levels, especially those occupied by women:

> The cheap sites and cheap labour of the city centre . . . and the competitive nature of the industries remaining make for cycles of cumulative causation: with the secondary worker increasingly trapped by limited skill opportunities . . . the move to an outer city location, for a capital-intensive producer, therefore facilitates the segmentation of the labour force,

replacing an old, established Internal Labour Market in Glasgow with one predominantly female, suburban and less militant.[28]

Female employees find themselves in a double bind, exploited in the inner cities for the reasons already mentioned, yet, at the same time, found at the lower levels of monopoly firms and their subsidiaries through deliberate hiring policies on the part of the centre firm: in effect peripheral workers in centre firms.[29] Employers become 'prepared' to accept secondary traits for flexibility in hiring practices; for example, competition for labour is less intense in outer areas, so strengthening the monopsony power of the centre firm and diminishing wage rates. Indeed these centre firms themselves appear so only by comparison with the declining traditional industries, since they are themselves branch plants subservient to the international strategy of the firm. The

TABLE 10. Hours worked by Part-Time Female Labour Force

	Manual	Non-Manual
Less than 6 hours a week	6.3%	5.7%
8-16 hours a week	21.6%	16.7%
More than 16 hours a week	71.1%	77.6%

Source: *New Earnings Survey* 1978.

TABLE 11. The Number of Women and Young People covered by Special Exemption Orders allowing them to work more than the legislated Maximum hours.

Great Britain, as of 31st July, 1978

Type of Exemption	Females (18 & over)	Young People aged 16 & 17		Total
		Males	Females	
Extended Hours (1)	21,620	1,264	1,668	24,552
Double Day Shifts (2)	36,755	3,283	2,755	42,793
Long Spells	11,254	395	1,454	13,103
Night Shifts	68,163	2,123	346	70,632
Part-Time Work (3)	14,876	121	214	15,211
Saturday Afternoon Work	4,155	309	203	4,667
Sunday Work	54,955	1,394	1,966	58,315
Miscellaneous	6,659	360	171	7,190
Total	218,437	9,249	8,777	236,463

The numbers shown are those stated by employers in their applications. The actual number of workers employed on conditions permitted by the Orders may, however, vary during the period of validity of the Orders.

Notes: (1) 'Extended hours' are those worked in excess of the limitations imposed by the Factories Act for daily hours of overtime.

(2) Includes 18,491 employed on shift systems involving work on Sundays, or on Saturday afternoons but not included under those headings.

(3) Part-time work outside the hours of employment allowed by the Factories Act.

Source: *Scottish Trade Union Review*, No. 3, Autumn 1978 (see also Note 31).

willingness to hire women for what appear to be primary jobs emerges if this component of the economic system is grasped. Light engineering, instrumentation, service production etc., incorporate a high female labour force which is exposed to employment instability as a key input and requirement of the 'core' sector of the particular firm. It is this relationship which is at the heart of international investment and the specific employment strategies of these firms. The extent to which women must accommodate themselves to fluctuations in production emerges in the range of hours worked by part-time women,[30] and the various exemptions vis-a-vis the legislation on maximum hours.

The immediate prospects for the labour force show no signs of change. Foreign firms appear set to increase their domination of the economy whilst atrophy increases in indigenous production. These two factors, it should be recalled, are interlinked. The ascendancy of multinational corporate planning in Scotland replaces and subverts national planning. (Indeed the activities of government agencies bear witness to the collusion already institutionalised in the political system.) The branch form of production once set in motion effectively draws in other resources and denies similar resource utilisation to indigenous firms. With the implanting of multinational production, peripheral dependence in the form of ancillary and component production increases, as does dependency, skill loss, reduction in local control over production and factor sales.[31] More importantly, dramatic increases result in firm and export concentration. The branch firm also leads to trading between the firm and its subsidiaries abroad (around half of the bigger companies' trade is now with their own subsidiaries). The results of this for international trade and job and skill dispersion are equally disadvantageous. Scotland loses out on the benefits of product and national trading, and, paralleling this, increases its shortfall between primary and secondary employment. (See labour force projections in Tables 7 and 8.) The 1980s and '90s may well show an acceleration in the process, given its internal logic and the evidence of the trends so far. Several symbiotic themes emerge; taking Scotland as a region, key positions in the multinational corporate hierarchy are lost. The growing strength of the peripheral supply sector leads to increased demand (and supply) of secondary jobs as the power of the centre also increases. The emergence of duality in the economy delimits the entry of new indigenous enterprise. As this process unfolds, the incidence of serious research and development/design innovation also declines (branch production has no need of it): centre firms always ensure rigid central control of this, one of their greatest assets, and one of great significance in political bargaining with national governments. The results and implications of this for the division of labour are clear — both in terms of skill levels and sex of occupants. Geographical redistribution of production is inextricably bound up with occupational segmentation:

> The strong internal labour markets of the centre firms in the North and inner cities have been threatened and replaced with employment structure biased towards secondary jobs whilst the

previously poorly organised South and suburbia have captured both more centre firm employment and more State sector and corporate sector upper primary jobs.[32]

What conclusions, if any, are to be drawn from these depressing scenarios? If these processes continue to develop unchecked, the effect on the Scottish economy and working population will be catastrophic. At the risk of labouring the point, it is important to grasp the linkages in the process — the reliance of core firms on periphery firms, subsidiaries, and the deskilling of the labour force with increased employment of 'disorganised' female labour as a key trait of the labour market as it develops.

All of which, taken together, suggests that it is essential to examine the social situation of Scottish working women — the position they find them-selves in, in the world of work, the way they are treated by employers, by the male labour force, by trade unions, by the state and so on. By considering some of these issues we may be more able to assess the ways in which 'quiescence' is built up amongst women workers and to point out the areas of working life that facilitate both occupational and ideological division.

3. Women in paid employment: the experiences of work

The experiences of work for any individual are the result of a vast array of interacting factors, ranging from the 'orientations' brought to the job, the 'technical implications' of the work, its associated supervisory patterns, the forms and nature of group activity to the influence of trade unions and so on.[33] The failure of academic research and the labour movement in general to grasp the interconnectedness of this activity for all workers is reflected in the marked divisions that now exist in the labour force. This has increased the degree and extent of occupational segregation with dire results for the work-force overall.

Much of the problem has been created as a direct result of the confusing of sex (a biological category) with gender (a psychological and cultural category).[34] Thus it has been too uncritically assumed that women as a sector of the labour force have a low commitment to work. This belief is based upon an ill-defined (if defined at all) notion about the 'natural inclinations' of women — that by and large they are drawn towards domestic activity/work, the looking after of husbands and children, the provision of emotional support etc. This becomes both explanation and, unfortunately, justification for the employment profiles of women. They do the sorts of jobs they do because they are not really interested in working. They are not as committed to organisa-tion, to trade unionism as men are, and so forth. Essentially what results is perpetuation of inequality as a direct result of these sentiments. The high visibility of women in poorly paid unstable jobs is explicable not in terms of their psychological make-up but in terms of the characteristics of the occupations they find themselves in, the employment strategies of firms and the apathetic, if not openly hostile, attitudes of male workers and trade unions.

A useful way of prising open the discussion is to make the seemingly simple yet immensely important point that traits and characteristics of jobs should not be confused with the 'predilections', traits and characteristics of several thousand workers.[35] If this qualification is held in mind, then a host of issues emerge which beg for theoretical and empirical examination. It seems not unreasonable to suggest, therefore, that men, if placed in similar work settings, would react in a comparable way. The implication of this is that if women experienced the same 'advantages' as men, their orientations would begin to approximate those of men.[36] It is this concern with the structural constraints women face at work that provides a point of departure rather than a battery of unsupportable stereotypes.

As indicated above, it remains true that women's employment displays a high degree of segregation from male work and is also concentrated in specific sectors. The continuance of this situation has significant consequences for the perceptions of the labour force — both male and female. These divisions set in motion a series of links which result in distinctive ideological and social structures being erected. Barron and Norris draw attention to this by indicating in a schematic way the several elements which coalesce to provide an ideological and material basis to labour market segmentation, or more precisely — to the components of a dual labour market. They preface their discussion by indicating the sexual norms which 'define the place of men and women in the household and outside it' but, more importantly, go on to show the reinforcement of this in the labour market, and the benefits to capital which accrue.[37] Thus, it is claimed, 'the household sexual division of labour — is relegated to the status of an explanatory factor which contributes to but does not of itself determine the differentiation between the sexes in their work roles'.[38] This proposition is supplemented by a discussion of the primary and secondary labour market, its forms of work and the types of skills each sector requires (see Section 2). Significantly they draw attention to the historical forces that determine the sorts of labour employed in the secondary sector. Thus in the United States black people are a plentiful source of cheap labour. In Scotland the same is true of women. Women are assumed to be an ideal base on which to build a dual labour market, for several reasons:

> There seem to be five main attributes that may make a particular social group or category a likely source of secondary workers: dispensability, clearly visible social difference, little interest in acquiring training, low economism and lack of solidarity.[39]

Dispensability incorporates several propositions, and is related to the ease with which an employee can be removed from a redundant job (bearing in mind the exclusions from the Redundancy Payment Act etc), whether that removal be voluntary or involuntary. For example, it is well known women change jobs more frequently than men. It is also true, however, that childbirth and the raising of children are a 'brake' on the work profile of women regardless of commitment and are a factor that is too easily overlooked in assessing the possibility of recruitment to trade unions or in the provision of training facilities/promotion. For example, in 1949 there were 903 nurseries in Britain. By 1970 the figure was down to 435.[40] Recent research has shown the high levels of continuity that adhere to work profiles in stable, well-paid jobs for women once the effects of childbearing have been taken in to account.[41] This suggests that empirical evidence must be provided before it is possible to attach any credence to the suggestion that women willingly collude in their exploitation. One question that emerges is the time-scale between the birth of children and the return to work by mothers:

> This, of course, raises the problem of State provision of nurseries, lengths of permitted absence etc to facilitate this, and, in practice, bisects the desire to return to work and having the resources to do so.[42]

Flowing from this problem is high turnover on the basis of low pay/poor working conditions and prospects. The non-provision of childcare facilities limits the range of jobs available, which encourages turnover. Given the requirements of the secondary sector, this is a gain for employers. It also helps to justify the presence of women in this type of work. Essentially what emerges is a circular process where factors feed in and reinforce one another. In a less obvious way it also conditions the expectations of women workers. Thus the way in which this influences work commitment is revealed as much more contingent, much more dependent on structural factors than attributes of individual workers or collections of workers, an issue we shall return to.[43] A further aspect of dispensability is the relative ease with which women can be involuntarily removed from employment. If it is generally felt by women workers that men are more entitled to paid work than they are, then it facilitates the removal of women from jobs to protect the interests of 'male breadwinners'. If women do not subscribe to this belief, they nevertheless lack the 'cultural space' from which to argue their entitlement to employment. The implicit beliefs about the alternative sources of income available to women are most starkly revealed in the provisions for unemployed women. Married women receive lower benefit rates when unemployed, they are unable to claim social security benefit, they do not have to register as unemployed, etc.[44] Yet in Scotland approximately 10% of the population live in one-parent families, and it is not unreasonable to assume these families will normally be headed by women since they are usually given custody of children. This has important repercussions for the employment prospects of these women and the female labour force in general. The extent to which the former group can compete in the labour market is drastically reduced — the domestic responsibilities they face, allied to lack of training, compel them to seek employment in the high turnover secondary sector. These sectors, of course, are low-paid with poor prospects and almost non-existent trade union organisation. Given this situation, the capacity to resist and organise is reduced. The genuine poverty experienced by the labour force also erodes the desire to resist unfair treatment.[45] This enhances the stereotyped image held about women in the labour market, perpetuating structures of inequality and segregation. The historical antecedents for this are missed competely or, at best, downgraded. This is crucial if we consider the main vehicle for the expression of working class solidarity — trade unions (see Section 4).

A further obvious characteristic of women as a secondary labour source is social differences:

> It is likely that an employer will prefer as a candidate for a secondary sector job a worker who can be sharply differentiated from primary sector employees by some conventional *social difference*, preferably one which emphasises the relative inferiority of the secondary group.[46]

This draws attention to the active behaviour of employers in exploiting prior divisions in the labour force as much as deriving production stability and competitive wage rates. Sexual divisions more than any other are implanted in the social consciousness at every level; thus this 'master status trait' has enormous influence if linked with structural constraints at work legitimising the 'natural' division (and inequalities) of the sexes:

> . . . the existence of a primary-secondary jobs division can be both obscured and justified by the fact that it coincides with this social division.[47]

The all-pervading influences of sexual differences mean that segmentation of the workforce can take place in a completely unconscious way. Timeless assumptions about women come 'naturally' into play, in many cases substantiated by reference to generalised data and resulting in the building in of 'Statistical Discrimination' — the colouring of treatment/hiring practices on the basis of empirical information about a sector of the workforce rather than the merits of individual workers. As indicated above, this variation in the treatment of particular workers is made more easy if women also share the assumptions to some degree: if they feel they do not have the same rights as men. The underlying assumptions about low commitment or 'pin money' easily follow once this basic idea takes hold. Hence, women are not too worried about training or wages because they do not wish to invest time or effort in training, apart from whether it is right for a woman to earn as much as a man! Most women are also confined to the lowest skilled/lowest paid jobs, generating an unquestioned mental image of the sorts of jobs and rates of pay they have. Against this backcloth it is too easy to link low pay with employment instability, to suggest that women are somehow suited to repetitive tasks and low income:

> the sexual categorisation of jobs into men and women's work enables the question to be avoided: women are lower paid as a group because their sort of work is low paid . . . it works in precisely this sort of circular way: because women are confined to these tasks they must have a special aptitude for them . . . The separate nature of men's and women's social lives outside the workplace facilitates the maintenance of similar divisions within it.[48]

The way in which this constellation of beliefs hinders the future prospects of women is, as we might expect, in the general area of training. Repetitive work is also associated with low levels of investment in human capital — training of the workforce in specific and valued skills. Once forms of work have been de-skilled and their tenure rendered problematic (for the variety of reasons discussed in Section 2), conditions of work and work commitment develop accordingly. This is especially true of job expectation. It is reasonable to suggest that workers who find themselves in this type of employment will evidence a low interest on the basis of hard experience irrespective of their sex. These attitudes will spill over into valuations of the usefulness or point of trade unions, reinforcing the process. It is here that strategic intervention could be, but is not, made by trade unions. The concentration of women in precise areas of the economy (see Table 4) illustrates their presence in large numbers, but in many cases in positions in the occupation structure which do not have a high male presence. Consequently, they are largely ignored by trade unions, or are only addressed on questions defined within areas thought important by male-dominated unions (see Section 4). On a more general level centuries of inequality have obviously left their mark upon the consciousness of women; socialisation processes have been perpetually concerned with highlighting the differences between the sexes (invariably to the detriment of women), imbuing women with a sense of their inferiority to men and hence lowering their expectations and achievements.[49] Similarly in practical terms the 'dual load' associated with domestic duties and career aspirations conflates problems of organisation with problems of entitlement to a career.

Finally for this discussion of the profile of women as secondary workers we can note in passing (as it will be more fully developed in the next section) the question of 'solidarity' — concern with attitudes towards trade unions. It is obvious that the myriad issues broached in this section indicate a host of intervening variables that exert a powerful influence on attitudes to this question. At the purely practical level, the astronomical number of small firms women work in present qualitatively different problems from those unions confront in the case of men.[50] This leads to problems of contact, of organisation, and of the maintaining of links. The instability of tenure also produces a novel situation. In these forms of work it is hardly surprising that paternalism may overlay work relations (or open coercion — as at Grunwick where a largely immigrant labour force in London was excessively abused and finally removed by management in 1977 for trying to form a trade union). The sorts of problems and issues which women face are not necessarily those that are normally tackled by unions (dominated as they are by men); thus they may feel a lack of sympathy in work attitudes and in the attitudes of fellow male workers (for example, the open hostility of male workers at the onset of the Trico pay dispute in London in 1977). Much of the above leads unions to adopt pessimistic attitudes towards the point of, or possibility of, recruiting women (if we add in part-time workers the problem is further compounded).[51]

The working model of a dual labour market sketched out so far highlights the implicit and overt assumptions abounding around the issue of women and work. The arguments presented are intended to illustrate the manner in which ideological and employment constraints enmesh with one another to render women's employment prospects less than attractive. In the last section we assess the merits of these arguments and suggest ways of rethinking the orientations of women workers and the possibilities for change.

4. Occupational stratification and the sexual division of labour

The most basic point to be made is that workers sell their labour to capital as individuals, and it is the way that bargain is struck, defined and developed historically that should provide the entry point for assessing the work settings of individuals and their reactions to that setting.[52] It is too easily assumed that stratification in the labour market is to be divorced from segregation between sexes, from a sexual division of labour.[53] It is suggested, therefore, that this prior dichotomy in the population directly influences the way in which women as individuals enter the labour market and mediates between the individual and the structures faced when labour is sold. This approach highlights the extent to which differences in the occupational distribution of the male and female labour force can be addressed in terms also of sexual division. At the most basic level traditional stratification theory has taken the occupational framework as a basis for locating individuals and for tracing the connections between skills and rewards. Be that as it may, however, it is true that the occupational structure as the dispenser of rewards is also inhabited by women, and yet the order of rewards appears decidedly different from those enjoyed by men:

> It is difficult to synchronise the ranking of 'positions and persons' in such a way as to describe the condition of both men and women . . . and yet the occupational positions which they fill cannot be isolated from each other; the occupational framework of society is common to both.[54]

The thrust of bourgeois sociology is towards a perception of the labour market as structured by factors external to ideological and social construction and understandable in the main in terms of technological and economic efficiency. If the former is admitted to the analysis, then it suggests:

> . . . analysis can be extended beyond the task of mapping inequalities of position and person to the investigation of the formation and reproduction of the positions to which unequal advantage accrue.[55]

The range of characteristics developed by Barron and Norris essentially highlights the traits which secondary workers bring to the labour market and tries to show how this leads to the accruing of 'unequal advantage'. However, it is also a static ahistorical model which fails to draw sufficient attention to the concrete situations women find themselves in and to the possibilities of change. Such factors as the forms of production, its relation to the terms on which labour is available, trade union activity, all contribute to the understanding of the limits within which secondary workers can be maintained as secondary workers.[56] The possibility of subordination and of change are thus open to empirical investigation:

> Any analysis . . . must therefore ground itself in an adequate theory of the relation between labour and capital at the point of production: the workplace . . . we think Marxists have failed to present a convincing analysis of the relationship between labour and capital at this level, or the relationship between class struggle at the level of the factory and class struggle at the level of society as a whole.[57]

The availability of women workers affects the ways in which labour processes are transformed and is thus among the determinants of change in the occupational structure. The change taking place in the division of labour between the sexes reflects and engenders this inequality and in fact is at the heart of this imbalance since it is both cause and effect of stratification in the labour market. It is unrealistic then to ignore sex as an input when discussing the nature of stratification; thus it is equally important to address the question of class at various levels, one of which is sex. Inequalities emanating from this level are important because they are reproduced in the social structure overall. This does not mean women form a separate class, but it does mean that we are drawn to perceive the concentration of women in the lower sections of every occupational category; to ignore this when discussing class is to ignore a 'primary definer' of the terms on which class relations are mediated and the terms on which labour is sold. The importance of the relationship has been clearly demonstrated in Scotland — the emergence of new forms of production — in many cases predicated upon the attraction of female labour and repulsion of male labour. Participation of women in the labour market dramatically affects the complexion of that market for both sexes, since changes in the occupational structure, the terms on which capital makes its bargain with labour, the manner in which technologies evolve and industries develop hiring patterns for male and female labour, are complementary and interdependent. It is this relationship Braverman discusses (though, as we shall see, he fails to distinguish historically the range of factors faced specifically by women at work). He draws attention to the importance of women for capital accumulation. Most particularly he integrates changes in the labour process with changes in the demand for labour, particularly labour processes which are characterised by large numbers of low-paid workers doing unskilled repetitive jobs and utilising the 'reservoir of female labour'. Changes in women's employment are thus inextricably bound up with the processes through which the occupational division of labour is transformed. Braverman thus moves from looking at capitalism as a system of distribution to providing a critique of capitalism as a system of production. Dramatic though this increase in women's work has been, we should still recall changes in the division of labour in the home have not developed apace — with all the implications of this for women workers. Thus this brings us back to the need to discuss the particular problems faced by women workers before we can assess their prospects in the labour market and their perceptions of work in the broadest sense.

Looking at dual labour market theory, a range of problems emerge which require more examination before much of what is entailed in the theories can be usefully employed. The high visibility of women in the secondary sector with all the variations in this sector, for example women in traditional service jobs, women as secondary workers in primary sectors etc, means that it becomes a conceptually difficult and as yet empirically undiscovered exercise to ascertain the generality of congruence between secondary occupations and the extent to which women fill these places:

> they (Barron and Norris) describe the characteristics of secondary occupations and then examine the 'fit' between common 'female' characteristics and these occupations, yet never actually demonstrate that in concrete situations women are employed in particular secondary occupations for these reasons.[58]

More work is needed to study the range of options and hence rejection of secondary status that different groups of workers will demonstrate. The extent to which this simple point is never fully considered indicates the theoretical and empirical 'sexism' displayed when industrial sociologists and labour economists address themselves to the work experiences of women: '. . . the major concentrations of female employment exist in different sectors of the economy, women being distributed horizontally — employed in particular industries and occupations — and vertically — employed mainly as unskilled and semi-skilled workers. In the conflation of the multifarious forms of employment into a heterogeneous category of secondary sector workers, the important differences between these predominantly female occupations becomes submerged'.[59] Different employers will use different strategies to 'mould' labour forces. Gordon suggests that, as well as the need to retain skilled primary workers, there is the need to engender sectionalism in the workforce, along the lines of skill/training etc and sex. Consequently the interventions made by trade unions are immediately placed on the agenda if we want to understand the response of the labour force — both male and female. Similarly the question of dispensability, social differentiation, low inclination towards training, towards organisation, etc, should not be abstracted from the equation — are they present in every case, what factors promote or erode these attributes? How, in fact, are we to understand the links between the strategies of employers, changes in forms of production and the response of labour? A proper understanding can only be reached by simultaneously demonstrating the direct tie-up between the effects of domestic work for women and the effects of the labour process as it unfolds. Women are not allocated to the secondary sector (whatever form that may take) solely on the 'value-system' they bring to employment, but are at the same time allocated by the situation they are confronted with in definite forms of work organisation:

> the dual labour market approach relegates the sexual division of labour to the status of an exogenous variable, while the dynamics of the labour market are assumed to be the determinant factor in explaining the position of female labour. Barron & Norris's conceptual framework is essentially Weberian in this respect.[60]

It may prove useful at this point to summarise the main argument in terms of how concrete forms of work and organisation directly influence the stability over time of women as secondary workers. In particular in the case of women it is important to consider the non-intervention of trade unions 'on their behalf'. Historically it is the case that the active intervention of male-dominated trade unions ensured the exclusion of women from large areas of industry, preparing much of the organisational economic and social ground for the present-day status of female labour.[61] (This is also true unfortunately of their record in supporting post-war legislation dealing with sex discrimination):

> First, workers and worker organisations must be assigned an active role in the development of labour market structure. Second, changes in the employment structure under monopoly capitalism must be taken into account, and their effects on labour market segmentation examined.[62]

Gordon has suggested that this can be demonstrated by the extent to which employers may forego maximum efficiency in the interests of long-term control and maintenance of differentiation in the workforce. Hence this points up the strategies employers may evolve to counter organised labour.[63] This also suggests the importance of counter organisation by trade unions. Given the new distribution of employees and employment in Scotland, the lack of interest shown by unions in female labour is indeed remarkable; not just in recruitment but in representation and involvement. For example, it was not until 1933 that a woman was elected to the General Council of the S.T.U.C. Since then only one more woman has 'made it', and that was in 1974. Similarly there are an estimated 300,000 women members of the S.T.U.C., more than 30% of the total membership, but only one woman on the General Council of 21 members (nationally only two women are on the General Council of the T.U.C. — from places 'reserved' for women). Representation of women at Congress is equally depressing. In 1978 39 delegates were women, 510 men:[64]

> . . . since 1897 there have only been nine women serving on the (Scottish) Council. Together they gave a total of 34 years service in a period covering 80 years. In other words, for half the lifetime of the General Council there has been no woman's voice heard . . . But it has to be left to affiliated unions to take up these resolutions for themselves and move them at Congress. And the kind of resolutions which concern women — women's health, welfare, working conditions and child care — are rarely seen on Congress agenda.[65]

The relative levels of organisation amongst the workforce have strategic importance for the prospects of workers in Scotland, particularly in the light

TABLE 12. Women in Trade Unions

Union	Total membership		% age of women members		NEC		Full-time officials		TUC delegates	
	m	f	'76	'75	m	f	m	f	m	f
1. APEX	62,438	75,278	55%	54%	11	4	5	1	10	3
2. ASTMS	351,000	62,000	18%	15%	23	1	65	5	19	1
3. ATWU	23,122	19,027	45%	41%	16	6	19	5	7	2
4. AUEW Eng. Sec.	1,036,720	166,000	14%	13%	9	—	186	1	35	—
5. BAKERS	30,122	20,325	40%	42%	14	4	25	1	10	—
6. CATU	20,768	23,636	53%	53%	16	2	6	—	7	2
7. COHSE	42,420	101,059	70%	67%	27	1	35	5	8	—
8. CPSA	69,451	145,693	68%	68%	18	8	24	4	22	8
9. CSU	29,108	17,676	38%	36%	21	2	10	1	8	2
10. EETPU	361,193	52,996	13%	13%	14	—	150	—	13	1
11. FTAT	73,857	10,243	12%	11%	24	—	40	—	11	1
12. CMWU	592,073	290,283	33%	32%	30	—	272	10	64	4
13. LRSF	23,093	31,827	58%	57%	25	3	6	1	9	—
14. NALGO	357,942	267,221	43%	40%	61	5	174	17	69	5
15. NAS/UWT	70,000	15,000	18%	—**	35	3	8	—	6	2
16. NUBE	58,118	48,957	46%	44%	21	3	28	3	13	—
17. NUDBTW	35,186	20,138	36%	39%	14	1	25	1	6	5
18. NUFLAT	32,187	30,268	48%	49%	15	1	46	2	13	—
19. NUHKW	19,887	52,836	73%	73%	23	2	29	2	11	1
20. NUPE	201,847	382,638	65%	64%	20	6	120	2	29	4
21. NUT	66,896	197,453	75%	74%	41	7	24	2	30	1
22. NUTGW	13,359	96,070	88%	87%	10	5	34	6	11	5
23. SCS	85,000	17,000	17%	16%	22	4	17	3	17	—
24. SOGAT	123,876	69,928	36%	36%	30	2	67	3	31	5
25. TASS	126,895	15,571	11%	9%	26	1	36	2	14	4
26. TGWU	1,511,000	289,000	16%	15%	39	—	480	3	76	2
27. TSSA	55,600	15,705	22%	22%	28	2	50	10	13	2
28. TWU	7,318	13,381	65%	66%	18	1	6	3	4	1
29. UPW	147,679	42,321	22%	25%	14	5	11	1	12	2
30. USDAW	153,653	223,649	59%	58%	16	1	129	4	21	5

** No women members prior to amalgamation with Union of Women Teachers.

    Source: T.U.C. *Annual Reports* 1976, 1977, 1978.

of the forms of work Scotland is developing. True though it may be that capital has a class interest which binds different sectors of capital together, it is also reasonable to suggest that individual firms are exposed to industrial action by workers, the activities of rival firms, the unexpected consequences of new technology, etc, and therefore the intervention of the workforce — if properly organised. The deskilling tendencies analysed by Braverman indicate just how variable the segmentation of the labour market is; deskilling can generate a homogeneity in the labour force which poses problems of control, whereas skill and industry-specific training can increase costs (and introduce a level ·of work autonomy as a result of individual control and application of craft skills). This poses all sorts of questions about the effects on the consciousness of women at the point of production, indicating as it does the areas of weakness and contradiction in employment strategy. These 'weaknesses' are of course, by and large, left undisturbed by the labour movement. The substitution of female for male labour proceeds with destructive results for both, particularly in an expanding sector:

> More often substitution takes place in the context of capital restructuring, of bringing in new machinery which transforms a skilled job into a semi-skilled or unskilled one, or of moving jobs around the country. In either case the substitution of female for male labour, while bringing in long-term savings in wage costs, requires capital investment. Such investments are unlikely to be made where output is stagnant and wage rises are restricted.[66]

The problem is compounded if we take the employment of women overall — by combining both traditional and emergent areas of employment for women. The lack of interest shown by unions is then seen to be a function also of the increasing segregation of the labour market and the levels which women cluster around in the occupational hierarchies of particular sectors.[67] (This, as we shall see, has major implications for equal opportunities — a fact which both employers and male-dominated trade unions are not ignorant of.) The effects of this provide a further deadweight on the levels of 'radicalism' which may adhere to particular female labour forces, with a consequent lowering of 'terms' for both sexes in negotiations with employers.[68] Because of this, crucial opportunities for unions are being missed; the effect of a slump in any given industry is different for women than for men. Women's employment has risen at a far greater rate than men's in recent decades, but recently so also has unemployment, especially amongst single women.[69] The rapid influx of women into paid employment has concealed the extent to which those seeking work find it. The influx has also reduced the impact of unemployment on women in many sectors. The particular pattern of women's employment, its concentration in a limited range of the expanding service sector, has limited the impact of the recession on women's opportunities as a whole. Nevertheless, public sector cuts have had a tremendous influence on employment levels, affecting vast numbers of 'traditional' secondary employment sectors; similarly the downturn in the economy has increased unemployment in manufacturing sectors — generating high levels of unemployment in these sectors for women. It is this variety in the work experiences of women that has been neglected. Thus married women may be retaining their jobs as compared to single women — what consequences does this have for women's employment overall? How, for instance, might it be linked to continuous flow, highly capitalised multinational production emerging in Scotland? (How the current slump affects part-time workers suggests a further series of questions.) Married workers may be in a relatively 'protected' position solely because of the cheapness and flexibility of their labour, a factor identified by Braverman as influencing the exchange between male and female on the labour market. A further area of concern is the possible effects rationalisation may have on the traditional service sector. This area of work with low-level, repetitive and boring work has long been dominated by women for a variety of reasons. The work has been low-paid, excluding men due to the labour intensive nature of the work. It has provided a stable source of employment for women, expanding even when 'men's jobs' were being cut back. With the emergence of microprocessors a further novel set of questions emerge.[70] Clearly then, the characteristics and importance of secondary sector employment generally have been inadequately analysed, and the relationship between the development of the employment structure and the formation and evolution of structured labour markets has yet to be fully explored. The development of labour processes, of forms of organisation, whatever the relative levels of skill, and splitting of the labour market into sectors is as much dependent on the accretions of 'solidarity' based upon experience as it is upon organisational forms based upon craft skill or control:

> What may therefore be crucial for the mass of workers in their relations with their employers is not whether mechanisation and scientific management techniques decrease their opportunities to use judgement and knowledge, but how they affect their bargaining opportunities . . . where workers were in direct contact with machines and thus exercised some control over a greater output than their own unassisted labour could produce, created improved bargaining opportunities for the mass of workers.[71]

Rubery goes on to suggest that where organisational forms have evolved through control residing in particular groups in many cases, this is now linked to deliberate practices on the part of 'skilled' labour to maintain these stratified forms. Thus she suggests it is the experiences of labour and its skill in bargaining that also perpetuate sectionalism and exclusion in the labour market. The levels of deskilling present in modern industry draw attention to organised resistance on the part of previously skilled workers which is historically derived independently of current skill levels and distorts the labour market. In terms of the sexual divide it is institutionalised in work practices of organised male labour and trade unions. This influences the organisational forms of female labour and its reaction to trade unionism. This is a recurring tension in union organisation and practice, and in seriously approaching the particular obstacles female labour is faced with:

> . . . all workers are threatened by the obsolescence of skills or by replacement by other equally skilled workers who are in plentiful supply. This threat may induce defensive actions on the part of the workers to stratify the labour force, control entry to occupations and maintain skill status long after these skill divisions have become irrelevant.[72]

In particular female wage labour has suffered from the historical emergence of bargaining between organised labour and employer: many jobs retain notions of 'skill' on the basis of control of entry as much as on the type of occupation itself. Paradoxically, amalgamation of unions — in particular the drawing in of previously unskilled or semi-skilled labour as a response to de-skilling and possible job loss — has brought many women workers into the orbit of organised labour. This indicates the importance for the future of adequately addressing the problems faced by the female labour force and the vital need to more fully integrate this rapidly growing source of labour with male-dominated unions. Several areas of 'contact' emerge which might provide a basis for integration, though it is inescapable that both academic research and the labour movement overall can only establish these criteria by careful empirical investigation. An immediate task is to move away from the myopic 'women workers as problem' type of research, concerned as it is with all manner of things which conflict with women's paid employment and their 'real' concerns. Brown summarises this school thus:

> The largest category of studies of women qua women as employees is that which regards the employment of women as in some way giving rise to problems — for the women themselves in combining their two roles; for the employer in coping with higher rates of absence and labour turnover, and demands for part-time work; for the social services in providing for the care of children of working mothers, or in coping with the supposed results of maternal neglect; for husbands and other kin in taking over part of the roles of wife and mother; and even for the sociologist in attempting to discern the 'motivation' of women in paid employment.[73]

Equally unsatisfactory is research which may look at women at work but makes no meaningful distinction between the experiences of the sexes in employment, treating all workers as 'unisex'; or may deem those indicators of class consciousness etc associated with men to be the only criteria which workers in general would employ, regardless of the appropriateness of these criteria for the work settings women inhabit. More importantly, what little research has been carried out fails to theorise and examine the particular issues which are conducive to radicalising women workers in concrete situations. Studies focus on groups of workers chosen because they represent traditional, prototypical or technologically advanced work situations. The industries studied therefore have been predominantly male fields of employment:

> In the literature of industrial sociology there are a large number of studies which make no mention of women as employees for the very obvious reason that virtually no women work in the industry in question. This includes many of the industries which have attracted a lot of attention from social scientists for one reason or another; their propensity to strikes; the role of technical, organisational and/or market change; unusual conditions of work; the existence of large (and perhaps more accessible to research) plants and firms; or some other circumstances making employment in them more problematic than elsewhere.[74]

The various forms of inequality experienced by women in the labour market (see Section 3 above) — in many cases similar to men — should also be comprehensible in terms of their specific needs and problems. The particular exploitative nature of the relationship between mothers and employers provides an obvious example, the lack of childcare facilities, related as it is to shiftwork and turnover, effectively cutting down on training prospects and expectations, etc. The influence of stages in the 'life cycle' is equally important, for example the range of pressures on mothers both financially and emotionally at different stages in their working lives. These factors reduce wage levels, deriving legitimacy also from the assumptions made about alternative sources of income available to women. However, given the long-term trends, we know women are here to stay in the labour market; we also know the vital importance of paid work for almost all working women but know relatively little of its effects:

> . . . there are significant distinctions within the 'married women' category; that, for example, there are important differences in 'orientations to work' between women with young or school age children, older married women without such responsibilities, and older single, widowed and separated women . . . There were significant differences in labour stability and turnover, absence and output as between young single, young married with children, older married and widowed or divorced women, from which — given that tasks and conditions were similar for all — one could infer differences in expectations and priorities . . . the studies . . . have demonstrated the relevance and importance of considering stages in the life cycle.[75]

This suggests also that the conflation of domestic burden, forms of work, level of organisation, male attitudes etc, all colour the perceptions of women workers along with stages in the life cycle in quite different ways from men. Thus issues such as trade union membership, solidarity, are being comprehended and appraised from inside markedly different life experiences. Similarly, large numbers of women workers are dependent solely or mainly on their own earnings to support themselves and dependents. Issues such as bad working conditions, concern with sympathetic treatment of family problems, may be of greater significance for women workers. Family structures of support in certain circumstances may encourage militancy, for example the support derived from husbands in the Trico dispute. The value placed upon the role of mother may be a source of militancy, for example management reluctance to grant time off when children are ill. The list could obviously be added to, but what we are trying to draw attention to is the distinctiveness of the female labour force, not only in terms of the institutionalised and structured forms of inequality highlighted throughout this chapter, but also how the effects of inequality in the labour market influence the social consciousness of women workers, imbued as it is with a wider sexual division. While discrimination may be derived from family structures to some degree, it cannot simply be reduced to them without consideration of structures of work and trade union organisation and how these areas of working women's lives interact with one another.

Finally, it may be a useful exercise to review speculatively the degree to which the situation of women might be changing in one area given great publicity in recent years — equal pay/opportunities etc. This may indicate the extent to which trade unions are responding in at least one area to the legitimate demands of women workers and equally importantly the extent to which this recognition might alter the balance between employers and women in the workplace.[76] The Equal Pay and Sex Discrimination Acts eventually both became operative in December 1975. Both were intended to eliminate discrimination against women in wages and in work. It is also the case, however, that for a variety of reasons the mere setting down of legislation in no way whatsoever guarantees the realisation of equality for women. In particular, the nature of family organisation — the dual load — is completely ignored:

> The presence of deeper inequalities, rooted in the nature of the family and in the sexual division underpinning the family's relation to production was scarcely perceived . . . these Acts extend the principle — although not the full reality — of equal rights, from the political institutions which concerned the early campaigners to economic institutions. Their *intentions* stop at this. They do not directly challenge or provide the conditions for reorganising sex-based domestic labour.[77]

Similarly, both Acts rely heavily on enforcement through individual complaints to industrial tribunals, with all the attendant difficulties this situation generates and the lack of success that results:

TABLE 13. Equal Pay Cases at Scottish Tribunals

Year	Cases Registered	Cases Heard
1976	199	60
1977	80	60
1978	19	35

Source: C. Aldred, 'Women Workers in Scotland and the Equal Pay Act', *Scottish Trade Union Review*, No. 4, Winter 1979.

Overall in Britain, of 2,493 equal pay cases taken to tribunal in 1976 and 1977, 1,421 were withdrawn, 768 lost and only 304 won. Of 472 sex discrimination cases, 276 were withdrawn, 155 lost and 41 won.[78]

It is clear this dramatic decrease in registration is due to several factors (there never has been a 'dramatic' success). Department of Employment figures indicate that in Scotland the average gross pay of all women full-time workers actually fell as a percentage of men's pay in the year April 1977-78, and this situation is also true for Britain as a whole. The gains made between 1970 and 1976 are now being steadily eroded with marked decreases in the last two years.[79] Employers (with the active assistance of male employees) are also finding ways of evading what already was inadequate and loose leglislation:

> A halt in progress towards Equal Pay before the level of women's gross average weekly earnings even reaches two-thirds of men's average weekly earnings must indicate either that the Equal Pay Act is being evaded, that it is not being used or enforced or that it is too narrow in scope.[80]

Basically the Equal Pay Act contains two approaches to equal pay: one individual and one collective. Equal pay (and other contractual terms) can be claimed by a woman doing comparable work with a man at the same (or an associated) workplace, or doing work which though different has been given an equal value under a job evaluation scheme. The segregation of women at work means in many cases that there are no comparisons to be made, and low wages thus prevail:

> Data on the occupational structure of the labour force that are used to study occupational segregation are based on broad national classifications of occupation; whereas implementation of the Equal Pay Act is with reference to more detailed classifications and comparisons of jobs within particular plants and companies.[81]

A further way of avoiding the requirements of the Act is with regard to 'material differences' in work. The five years between publishing the Act and its coming into force provided a period, not for implementing equal pay but for devising ways of introducing 'material differences' in most cases — increasing segregation of work, job evaluaton schemes which concealed discriminatory grading behind unisex labels — length of training or service, etc.[82] The extremes to which employers may go is revealed by the following:

> Training might on occasion constitute a material difference, but was dismissed when St. Cuthbert's Co-operative Association attempted to claim a Mr. Dewar was paid more than Ms. Thomson, the applicant, because he had attended a one-day training course on the use of a tape measure![83]

Much more worrying is the movement towards excluding part-time workers from the provisions of the Act, given the large numbers of women working these hours and the 'buoyancy' of the industries they work in; this illustrates again the attractiveness of hiring female labour in growth industries.

The second dimension of Equal Pay policy relates to collective agreements — wages council orders, pay structures etc, particularly male only or female only wage scales. Where these scales operate they can only be amended by referral to the Central Arbitration Committee, with women being brought up to the minimum male wage rate at least (the discriminatory grading mentioned above meant, in many cases, that the minimum rate was the norm). One unresolved problem, however, is the groups of women not entitled to equal pay under any of the provisions of the Act because they are not doing like work and are not covered by job evaluation, an agreement or order or an employer's pay structure. This would incorporate significant numbers of service workers, part-time cleaners and canteen workers, who fall outside agreements covering manual workers in the same organisation.[84]

It is clear that the impetus provided by the Equal Pay Act has now peaked and is decreasing. Difficulties in taking grievances to tribunals are compounded by the vagueness of interpretation and by the strategies employers have evolved. The placing of the burden of proof on the applicant is directly affected by this:

> A survey of cases in Scotland up to February 1977 reported that of the 39 published decisions 14 had been successful.[85]

Generally the concentration of women in low-paid segregated industries perpetuates evasion and inequality, as does the lack of access to promotion and education/training as a way out.[86]

The second piece of legislation concerned with ending inequality between the sexes is also invested with a range of loopholes and shortcomings. Essentially it is a 'negative and passive piece' of legislation which is intended to deal with non-contractual areas of discrimination — recruitment, education/training, facilities, etc. Thus it fails to encourage positive undertakings on the part of employers and unions to break down segregation and to create genuine equal opportunities in employment, for example in ignoring those sections of the Act which allow positive discrimination:

> With few changes to practices, procedures, attitudes, and an economic situation where turnover and recruitment were in any case low, the effects of the Act on the employment of women in the organisations have been minimal . . . Legislation doesn't mean a company will act differently. We won't change our personnel decisions, just how we go about them . . . Just as we keep a 'good' mix on race by finding reasons to reject most Asians, so we will find reasons to reject women for some jobs.[87]

For many of the reasons discussed above, it is clear the effects of Equal Pay legislation have peaked and that the addition of the Sex Discrimination Act in 1975 has not broken down the barriers of rigid sex-segregation that underpin low pay and opportunity.

Conclusions and prospects

This review of women workers in Scotland has tried to demonstrate the movement towards female labour in key sectors of the economy and has tried to show in general the integration of women into the paid labour force. In particular the linkages between primary-secondary firms and labour forces have been stressed:

> If Braverman's hypothesis is correct, the future development of monopoly capitalism will lead to a relative increase in secondary sector employment. In that case, the interesting question is, of course, how far these currently low paid occupations could be transformed into primary-type occupations; this transformation, we shall argue, must depend on the potential for, and effect of, trade union development.[88]

The capacity of trade unions to respond to changes in the labour process in the widest sense is intimately dependent on their awareness of and willingness to respond to these trends. It is this commitment to the emergent female labour force that will facilitate the extending of organisation and bargaining power in general. In particular the specific problems faced by women at work have to be systematically addressed (see Section 4). Paralleling this are the expressions of sexual inequality external to 'the factory' — the segregation of education and training from the earliest years, the exclusion from legislation of taxation policy, and many areas of National Insurance and benefit systems. Similarly the questions of childcare and abortion are, for all practical purposes, excluded from union activity, etc (in spite of recent action over the Corrie Bill). In general, then, the expansive nature of women's inequality is not on the agenda for trade unions as yet (the decision of the S.T.U.C. in 1978 not to positively discriminate in favour of women on the executive councils or other key posts highlights this). The breakthroughs made on Equal Pay have to be linked to a wider policy which confronts the sexual divisions of society. The implications of the legislation are that it can provide a basis for raising the expectations and consciousness of women workers. The nature of the labour market today suggests this is an important and immediate task; increasingly women's employment covers larger areas with the attendant effects on their perceptions (and with the experience of unemployment being more widely dispersed also). The extent to which this process places male workers in jeopardy is related to the flexibility of the female labour force and the capacity of the trade union movement to reduce this. By so doing, both sectors will become more secure:

> The long term shift towards women in the workforce cushioned women's employment against the shorter term (cyclical recessions). The signs are that this particular phase of capital restructuring may be over; that one of the bases of the long-term expansion of female employment — the cheapness of female employment — may be declining in relative significance, given new technological developments . . . The implications of this analysis are not that the solution lies in attempting to equalise the incidence of increasing unemployment between men and women. Rather, it is that the fight for jobs will increasingly be a fight for women's jobs. Thus if the labour movement is to be able effectively to resist unemployment, now more than ever before, it urgently needs to devise more effective strategies of defending women's jobs and the right of women to work.[89]

In particular the dramatic increase in service sector employment (scientific, professional, insurance, banking and public administration) draws attention to the importance of white-collar work as the major growth area for women workers, representing an increase of 150,000 over the last 15 years in Scotland, and still accounting for almost 75% of all female workers.[90] This also illustrates that though the economic importance of British monopoly and multinational investment is a crucial input in the Scottish economy, it is still a trend, not yet the dominant one, for women employees. Allied to this, significant losses have been experienced in the textile industry, indicating a movement towards new service sectors as much as towards new areas of manufacturing. Thus within the manufacturing sector overall some distinctions may be drawn: approximately two-thirds of Scotland's manufacturing industry is now controlled outside Scotland. In the major sectors around nine-tenths of the workforce are employed in these industries, with 40% employed in Scottish-owned companies, 40% in enterprises headquartered elsewhere in the U.K. and 20% in foreign — mainly American — owned concerns. Some key questions for the future emerge. Looking at American investment, as we have already seen this is notable for its high concentration, with around two-thirds of female employees in approximately ten firms. Thus areas, such as Dundee, which traditionally have had high levels of female employment, now provide increasing sources of female labour as older industries decline. Hence it may be that higher levels of conflict may emerge due to the greater experience of the labour force. By comparison, New Towns — Cumbernauld, Glenrothes, East Kilbride etc — may provide markedly different industrial relations. This is particularly true given the confidence with which American firms in these newer areas have resisted attempts at unionisation, and provides a distinctly different set of conditions for the labour movement to deal with since British-based monopolies have a more 'flexible' response to trade unions. Similarly, the increasing prominence of incoming firms also conflicts with indigenous capital in terms of labour market requirements, conditions, provisions, etc, and may well be expressed in differing priorities for trade union legislation etc, as advanced by the Scottish C.B.I., E.E.F. etc. Particular trade unions (e.g. A.U.E.W./T.A.S.S.) may thus be faced with a series of differing labour market strategies, reflecting the logical tensions between different capitals with different requirements. British monopoly investment in Scotland also poses questions about the extent to which the trend to corporate planning is the decisive movement — that corporate planning has superseded national planning, since British monopolies have always operated as far as they could at British state level as well as local level. Taking all of the above together indicates the potential and actual conflict that may emerge between British and U.S. monopoly capital in terms of strategic planning, given that they have radically different relationships with the state. Differential success in achieving monopoly interests thus emerges because of these constraints and provides a lever by which the labour movement may discern the particular areas of conflict in the coming period (for example the nature of incoming firms and reasons for withdrawing — do these have specific labour market problems or characteristics compared with others?). It is linkages between the demands of differing firms and their relation to national planning that may well provide the basis on which the labour movement organises key sections of the female workforce and also directly intervenes in strategic planning in 'collusion' with key firms at crucial periods.

By comparison, the growing service sector mentioned above is less easy to speculate about since greater diversity exists and less obvious economic conflict between competing capitals is present. However, the importance of this sector with its attendant 'feminisation' should not be ignored.[91] The significant movement into white-collar areas outwith traditional trade unionism — either non-unionised or within weak and non-political unions (for example the Educational Institute of Scotland) — indicates the importance of adequately addressing this phenomenon if any comprehensive inroads are to be made into the female labour force.[92] In particular the 'deskilling' processes identified by Braverman show this to be a long-term trend predicated upon the utilisation of female labour. At the same time, increases in white-collar unionism conceal worrying gaps, as high growth rates may represent absolute numbers as part of a growth in the number of white-collar occupations rather than an increasing 'density' of membership. Similarly, unions may conflate memberships which include both manual and non-manual workers as a single category. It is beyond the bounds of this chapter to speculate on the 'orientations' of white-collar workers, but it seems clear that increasing mechanisation and rationalisation have been linked in some areas to increasing unionisation as 'professionalism' as a source of identity has waned. The relative decrease in the gap between manual and non-manual labour's wages and conditions has also contributed to this process. However, at the same time these developments have not been systematically linked to the female labour force — the sector of the labour force most affected. This is partially explained by the belief that women are 'less union-minded' and therefore have not been seriously considered by the trade unions (see Section 3). However, the strong presence of women in small establishments draws attention to the decreasing levels of unionisation if the labour force is small and vice-versa. Thus the idea that women in white-collar work are less union-minded than their male counterparts is also undermined by the fact that there is a higher proportion of unionisation among women than among men in the public sector, and, in fact, the greater the degree of employment concentration, the greater the density of white-collar unionism.[93]

Taking the above points and the suggestions made about 'orientations' for service workers might indicate that increasingly, as public sector workers are directly linked to political programmes (as the latter half of the 'seventies has demonstrated) vis-a-vis government economic policy, then women workers (again as the recent period has shown) may more rapidly evidence an increasing radicalism. For the trade union movement it should also provide a basis for the better organisation of the service sector generally and for a change in the complexion of what has traditionally been thought of as a conservative force in the labour market.

NOTES

1. *Scottish Trade Union Review*, No. 3, Autumn 1978, 'Statistical Section'. In the U.K., expansion of workers betweeen 1951 and 1971 was 2.5 million, of which 2.2 million were women.

2. 'The service sector encompasses transport amd communications, distributive trades, insurance, banking and business services, professional and scientific services and a variety of miscellaneous services. These are Orders XXII-XXVI on the 1968 Standard Industrial Classification', Fraser of Allander Institute, Vol. 5, No. 4, April 1980, p. 31.

3. Census of Employment, 1975.

4. Fraser of Allander, *ibid.*, p. 31.

5. Family Expenditure Survey 1978, 'Regional Characteristics', p. 117.

6. C. Hakim, *Occupational Segregation Research Paper No. 9*, Department of Employment, 1979.

7. *Scottish Abstract of Statistics*, No. 8, 1978.

8. G. Norris, 'Poverty: The Facts in Scotland', *Poverty Pamphlet 30*, Child Poverty Action Group, October 1977, p. 4.

9. See, amongst others, N. Hood and S. Young, 'U.S. Investment in Scotland—Aspects of the Branch Factory Syndrome', *Scottish Journal of Political Economy*, Vol. 23, No. 3, 1976. J. Firn, 'External Control and Regional Policy', in G. Brown (ed.), *The Red Paper on Scotland*, Edinburgh, 1975. D. Hunt, 'The Sociology of Development', *Scottish Journal of Sociology*, April 1977. A. Friedman, *Industry and Labour: Class Struggle at Work and Monopoly Capitalism*, London, 1977.

10. Scottish Development Agency, *Scotland — A Market Base in Europe*, pp. 7-8.

11. Fraser of Allander Institute, Quarterly Economic Commentary, Vol. 5, No. 1, July 1979, p. 31.

12. Scottish Development Agency, *op. cit.*, p. 9.

13. This includes S.D.A. loans building programmes, the designation of Scotland as an Area of Expansion with Special Development Area, Development Area, or Intermediate Area Status, thus attracting a whole battery of financial inducements: Regional Development Grants (though these are currently being reappraised), Interest Relief Grants, Service Industry Grants, Contracts Preference Schemes, Training Assistance, Taxation Allowance on buildings and plant, as well as H.I.D.B. assistance and the assistance of the EEC through the European Investment Bank, etc.

14. J. Firn, *op. cit.*, p. 159.

15. *Ibid.*, pp. 162-163.

16. *Ibid.*, p. 163.

17. *Ibid.*, p. 163. Similarly the female/male unemployment relative currently stands at 46 women for every 100 men, indicating the importance of women in the labour market and, more importantly, the instability of female employment in spite of the increase in demand. This is in keeping with the expectations we would hold about 'branch' economies.

18. There are several varieties and models, but I shall rely heavily on a recent paper by M. Danson, 'The Industrial Structure and Labour Market Segmentation: Urban & Regional Implications', Discussion Paper No. 32, *Urban and Regional Discussion Papers*, Glasgow, 1980. See also A. Friedman, *op. cit.*, N. Hood and S. Young, *op. cit.*

19. M. Danson, *op. cit.*, p. 2.

20. *Ibid.*, p. 3.

21. It is equally true that market fluctuation can render once 'core' firms 'peripheral' as technology changes. In this context see Friedman, *op. cit.* Thus it remains true that in many cases women can be employed at the 'core' and periphery also, as is obviously the case in Scotland.

22. Much of the discussion of the primary/secondary worker dichotomy can be subsumed under the general heading of 'dual labour market' theory. See D. Gordon (ed.), 'Problems in Political Economy: An Urban Perspective', Lexington, 1971; R. D. Barron and G. M. Norris, 'Sexual Divisions and the Dual Labour Market', in D. Barker and S. Allen (eds.), *Dependence and Exploitation in Work and Marriage*, London, 1976. It remains true that much dual labour market theory overstates the 'passivity' of the secondary work force. For a concise appraisal see J. Rubery, 'Structured Labour Markets, Worker Organisation and Low Pay', *Cambridge Journal of Economics*, Vol. 2, No. 2, 1978. Rubery draws attention to the structure of the organisations secondary workers find themselves in as an important component of 'passivity' rather than *individual* traits of the workforce. See also M. Blaxall and B. Reagan, *Women and the Work Place*, Chicago, 1976; R. C. Edwards et al, *Labour Market Segmentation*, Lexington, 1975.

23. M. Danson, *op. cit.*, p. 8.

24. D. Massey & R. Meegan, 'Industrial Restructuring versus the Cities', *Urban Studies*, Vol. 15, 1978, p. 282.

25. G. Payne, 'Occupational Transition in Advanced Industrial Societies', *The Sociological Review*, Vol. 25, 1977, p. 33. See also M. Danson, 'Male and Female Employment Change for Inner Cities Clydeside', Mimeo, Glasgow University.

26. *Scottish Abstract of Statistics*, No. 9, 1980, p. 3. This is starkly highlighted in the

electronics industry. Around 36,000 jobs have been created with 50% in Strathclyde and 24% in Lothian Region. The industry is dominated by American firms, female labour and export-directed production. Thus the U.K. as a whole is a *net importer* of computer equipment, given the level of production (assembly only, etc). The attendant problems of research and development so important in competing are particularly acute for indigenous firms, J. Cooper, 'The Electronics Industry in Scotland', *Scottish Trade Union Review*, No. 5, 1979.

27. M. Danson, *op. cit.*, p. 14. In a similar context see H. Beynon, *Working for Ford*, London, 1973, who outlines the attractiveness of hiring a 'green' labour force when the Ford Motor Company were engaged in decision-making about factory location. This is also true in a later study by H. Beynon and T. Nicholls, *Living with Capitalism*, London, 1977, 'Study of chemical production in Northern England'.

28. M. Danson, *op. cit.*, p. 16.

29. In this context, see J. Rubery, *op. cit.* Rubery highlights the attitudes of management and trade unions towards women in many centre industries, highlighting their special exploited status.

30. Part-time workers are, of course, exempt from many of the provisions of the Equal Pay, Sex Discrimination and Redundancy Payment Acts and, given the 'flexibility' required by many firms, are an ideal source of labour. See M. Snell, 'The Equal Pay and Sex Discrimination Acts: Their Impact in the Workplace', *Feminist Review*, No. 1, 1979; I. Breugel, 'Women as a reserve army of labour: a note on recent British experience', *Feminist Review*, No. 3, 1979.

31. See also E. Hunter, 'Restrictions on Hours of Work' *Scottish Trade Union Review*, No. 8, 1980.

32. M. Danson, *op. cit.*, p. 19. Similarly the fall in population has depressed demand for some services, further reducing living standards and placing greater numbers in the secondary employment sector.

33. These 'celebrated' issues are, of course, at the heart of industrial sociology. See, amidst a plethora of work, J. Goldthorpe *et al*, *The Affluent Worker*, 3 Vols; J. Woodward, *Industrial Organisation: Behaviour and Control*; G. K. Ingham, *Size of Industrial Organisation and Worker Behaviour*. What is most striking is the truly remarkable hair-splitting that has taken place. How many sociologists have made their reputations on 'critiques' or 'reworkings' of Goldthorpe? By comparison the research on women workers has incorporated their work experiences in a catch-all category — if they have been studied at all! For a lucid review of this neglect in the realm of industrial sociology see R. Brown, 'Women as employees: some comments on research in Industrial Sociology' in Barker and Allen (eds.), *op. cit.* See also E. Garnsey, 'Women's Work and Theories of Class Stratification', *Sociology*, Vol. 12, No. 2, 1978; V. Beechey, 'Women and production; a critical analysis of some sociological theories of women's work', in A. Kuhn and A. M. Wlope (eds.), *Feminism and Materialism*, London, 1978.

34. For a discussion of this confusion see A. Oakley, *Sex Gender and Society*, London, 1972.

35. It is this sort of preliminary theme that provides many of the important entry points for those researchers concerned with examining the bases to secondary labour markets: see Barron and Norris, *op. cit*; J. Rubery, *op. cit*; D. I. Mackay *et al*, *Labour Markets under Different Employment Conditions*, London, 1971; R. Rumberger and M. Carnoy, 'Segmentation in the U.S. Labour Market: Its Effects on the Mobility and earnings of Whites and Blacks', *Cambridge Journal of Economics*, Vol. 4, No. 2, 1980; D. Gordon, *op. cit.* See also F. McNally, *Women for Hire*, London, 1979.

36. Some empirical investigation of this suggestion and confirmation is provided in my recent paper, 'Linkages Between Industrial Radicalism and the Domestic Role Among Working Women', *Sociological Review*, Vol. 29, No. 1, 1980. See also S. Taylor, 'Parkin's Theory of Working Class Conservatism: Two Hypotheses Investigated', *Sociological Review*, Vol. 29, No. 9, 1978; J. Evans, 'Women in Politics: A Reappraisal', *Political Studies*, Vol. 28, No. 2, 1980.

37. The question of roles within the family based on sex is, of course, an extremely important point since it influences the way in which the sexes confront each other in paid employment. However, a detailed discussion of this topic goes beyond the bounds of this chapter. Rather it is unfortunately 'noted in passing'.

38. This contention is itself not unproblematic, being concerned as it is with a larger debate over the nature of domestic labour, whether it is productive or non-productive, the exact way in which capital utilises it in the process of accumulation. See amongst others, M. Molyneux, 'Beyond the Domestic Labour Debate', *New Left Review*, 116; P. Smith, 'Domestic Labour and Marx's Theory of Value', in Kuhn and Wolpe (eds.), *op. cit;* S. Himmelwelt & S. Mohun, 'Domestic Labour and Capital', *Cambridge Journal of Economics*, Vol. 1, No. 1, 1977.

39. Barron and Norris, *op. cit.*, p. 53.

40. H. Wainwright, *op. cit.*, p. 176.

41. I. Watt, *op. cit.* Turnover rates between men and women in a Glasgow factory revealed 'For men the figure is 7%, for women 14%, but of the actual female figure, 239, 207 left in the 18-19 age range, the range where most women will leave for one reason — to have children', p. 59.

42. *Ibid.*, footnote 12, p. 72.

43. It should also be stressed here that I am primarily addressing those women found in the most 'traditional' jobs. I would further suggest that the findings reported at 36 above would be true of the growth areas in the Scottish economy.

44. This issue is comprehensively discussed in several areas by K. O'Donovan in 'The Male Appendage: Legal Definitions of Women'; S. Burman (ed.), *Fit Work for Women*, London 1979. See also H. Land, 'Who Cares for the Family?', *Journal of Social Policy*, Vol. 7, No. 3, 1978; H. Land, 'The Family Wage', *Feminist Review*, No. 6, 1980. J. Pahl, 'Patterns of Money Management Within Marriage', *Journal of Social Policy*, Vol. 9, No. 3, 1980. Pahl, for instance, makes the important point that cash income to household does not reflect poverty since it assumes equal distribution between individual members, p. 314. L. Hamil, 'Wives as Sole and Joint Breadwinners', D.H.S.S., *Government Economic Service Working Paper*, No. 13, 1978.

45. For example, W. W. Daniel suggests women may be less willing to resist job loss because they find it easier than men to gain alternative work. 'Whatever Happened to the Workers at Woolwich?', *P.E.P. Broadsheet*, 1972. It is just as plausible to suggest that this is a realistic reaction to the inability to do otherwise! The point is that it requires research to tell us anything about this. Similarly Martin and Fryer in their study of redundant workers write: 'Seven hundred and thirty-four (619 males) hourly paid employees, manual workers and three hundred and twenty-two (183 males) monthly paid employees, non-manual workers, left Casterton Mills between the beginning of February 1967 and the end of November 1968: we interviewed a one in three sample of male manual leavers (voluntary and involuntary) and a two in three sample of male non-manual leavers', pp. 9-10. No reason is given by the authors for the exclusion of women from the sample. What were their assumptions? R. Martin and R. H. Fryer, *Redundancy and Paternalist Capitalism*, London, 1973.

46. Barron and Norris, *op. cit.*, p. 57. The reader should recall that in the new industries of Scotland many of the jobs have primary traits and that not all aspects of the secondary sector prevail in women's employment. Thus in this context it is the ease of severance as much as wage rates that attracts employers to women.

47. *Ibid.*, p. 57.

48. *Ibid.*, pp. 58-59. See also Bruegel, *op. cit.*

49. Sufficient evidence is available from psychological and educational research, e.g. the marked deterioration in the educational achievement of girls on reaching puberty. This is because it is considered unfeminine to be more intelligent than boys, or more importantly that it questions a key ideological construct — the domination of women by men. For an interesting empirical study of this see A. McRobbie, 'Working Class Girls and the Culture of Femininity', in Women's Studies Group, *Women Take Issue*, London, 1978. See also R. Deem, *Women and Schooling*, London, 1978.

50. It is part of the received wisdom of sociology that undeniable correlations can be made between size of plant and trade union membership. The reasons for this are beyond the scope of this chapter, but it is evident that should a sector of the workforce not be in this type of employ, then that is a feature of the culture of the workplace rather than the incumbent. My own research verifies this on a series of issues ranging from attitudes towards supervision to support for trade

unions etc. In this case, the women workers were in a factory setting more usually associated with men and evidenced similar sentiments to those usually connected with men. See also G. K. Ingham, *op. cit.*

51. For a study of the difference in attitude of part-time women workers towards work and trade unions, see H. Beynon and R. M. Blackburn, *Perceptions of Work*, Cambridge, 1972. However, we should be wary of isolating the attitudes of part-time workers to paid employment from their domestic situation. Given the remarkable expansion of this sector of the labour force, it is a glaring gap in our knowledge. Evidence is urgently required on the constraints placed on these workers by the interplay of domestic and employment factors.

52. For a discussion of how this is neglected in terms of women's relationship to the class structure, see J. Acker, 'Women and Social Stratification', *American Journal of Sociology*, Vol. 78, No. 4, 1973. See also C. Middleton, 'Sexual Inequality and Stratification Theory', in F. Parkin (ed.), *The Social Analysis of Class Structure*, London, 1974.

53. See J. Lipman-Blumen, 'Towards a Homosocial Theory of Sex Roles: An Explanation of the Segregation of Social Institutions', in Blaxall and Reagan, *op. cit.*

54. E. Garnsey, *op. cit.*, p. 225.

55. *Ibid.*, p. 225.

56. Much of this is, of course, discussed by Braverman, who attempts historically to discuss the relationship between the strategies adopted by capital for organising the labour force and appropriate technologies for the accumulation of capital. H. Braverman, *Labour and Monopoly Capital*, Monthly Review Press, 1974. See also T. Elgar, 'Valorisation and De-skilling: A Critique of Braverman', *Capital and Class*, No. 7, 1979.

57. P. Cressey and J. MacInnes, 'Voting for Ford: Industrial Democracy and the Control of Labour', *Capital and Class*, No. 11, 1980.

58. V. Beechey, *op. cit.*, p. 175.

59. *Ibid.*, p. 179.

60. *Ibid.*, p. 179.

61. This important structured aspect of oppression is only now being seriously addressed historically. See, for example, H. Hartmann, 'Capitalism, Patriarchy and Job Segregation by Sex', in Blaxall and Reagan (eds.), *op. cit*; E. Boserup, *Women's Role in Economic Development*, London, 1970; L. Mackie and P. Patullo, *Women at Work*, London, 1977; S. Lewenhak, *Women and Trade Unions*, London, 1977, who mentions how the T.U.C. enforced provisions forcing unemployed women into domestic service before the war, preventing them from competing for 'men's jobs'; R. Davies, *Women and Work*, London, 1975; B. A. Carrol (ed.), *Liberating Women's History*; J. Scott and L. Tilly, 'Women's Work and the Family in Nineteenth Century Europe', *Comparative Studies in Society and History*, Vol. 17, 1975; E. Hunter, 'Restrictions on Hours of Work', *Scottish Trade Union Review*, No. 8, 1980; S. Rowbotham, *Hidden from History*, London, 1973; R. Milkman, 'Women's Work and Economic Crisis', in *Review of Radical Political Economy*, 1976.

62. J. Rubery, *op. cit.*, p. 19.

63. D. Gordon, 'Capitalist efficiency and socialist efficiency', *Monthly Review*, July/August 1976. See also A. Gorz, 'Technical Intelligence and the Capitalist Division of Labour', and S. Marglin, 'What Do Bosses Do?', both in A. Gorz (ed.), *The Division of Labour*, Harvester, 1976. This approach, concerned as it is with the 'frontier of control', has a long tradition in industrial sociology. That that is so reflects on the lack of research on the possibilities women have of 'pushing back' these frontiers and of the 'active' nature of work for the labour force regardless of sex.

64. *Scottish Trade Union Review*, No. 4, Winter, 1979, p. 15.

65. *Ibid.*, p. 15. See also J. Collins, Women Workers and the Trade Union Movement 1945-1975, University of Strathclyde, B.A. Dissertation, Department of Politics, 1976.

66. Breugel, *op. cit.*, p. 21, footnote 9.

67. See R. Milkman, *op. cit.* See also Breugel, *op. cit.*, particularly her discussion of 'unemployment amongst women', pp. 14-16; C. Hakim, *op. cit.*, Chapter 3, 'Occupational Segregation in

Britain 1901-1971'.

68. This point is taken up by several authors in D. Gordon (ed.), *Problems in Political Economy: An Urban Perspective*, Lexington, 1971; and D. Gordon, *Theories of Poverty and Underdevelopment*, Lexington, where attention is drawn in particular to the lowering of wage rates and conditions for all workers in particular areas of America due to racist divisions between blacks and whites in the labour force.

69. 'Between 1974 and 1978 in Britain the official rate of unemployment amongst women increased more than three times as fast as that of men'. Breugel, *op. cit.*, p. 15: 'Calculating from the General Household Survey data 1974 and 1976:

	1974-76
Change in total male unemployment (registered and unregistered)	+10%
Change in total female unemployment (registered and unregistered)	+28%
Change in total single female unemployment (registered and unregistered)	+42%'

Footnote 14, p. 21

70. *Counter Information Services*, The New Technology, 1979, London; H. Downing and J. Barker, 'Word Processing and the Transformation of Patriarchal Relations of Control in the Office', *Capital and Class*, No. 10, 1980.

71. J. Rubery, *op. cit.*, p. 27.

72. *Ibid.*, p. 27; Friedman, *op. cit.* See also J. Hinton, *The First Shop Stewards' Movement*, London, 1973.

73. R. Brown, *op. cit.*, p. 27. See also V. Beechey, *op. cit.*, Section II; Beynon and Blackburn, *op. cit.* Indeed to date almost all research has been in this mould: see, amongst others, A. Myrdal and V. Klein, *Women's Two Roles*, London, 1970; V. Klein, *Britain's Married Women Workers*, London, 1965; R. & R. Rapoport, *Dual Career Families*, Harmondsworth, 1971.

74. R, Brown, *op. cit.*, p. 23. Brown goes on to list examples of this process, pp. 23-24.

75. *Ibid.*, pp. 45-46, note 6. See also Beynon and Blackburn, *op. cit.*, where their sample is stratified in terms of similar categories.

76. For a concise history of the various positions adopted by government and unions towards the implementation of equal rights (especially in Scotland), see J. Collins, *op. cit.*, Chapter 3. See also J. Coussins, 'Equality for Women', *Marxism Today*, January 1980; J. Coussins, *The Equality Report*, London, 1976; W. B. Creighton, *Working Women and the Law*. M. Snell, *op. cit.*, is an invaluable article in general for the problems associated with the legislation and for providing data.

77. H. Wainwright, *op. cit.*, p. 162.

78. M. Snell, *op. cit.*, p. 57, footnote no. 8.

79. D.O.E., 'New Earnings Survey', *Scottish Economic Bulletin*, 1980.

80. C. Aldred, *op. cit.*, p. 8.

81. C. Hakim, *op. cit.*, p. 48; see also Table 4. Nearly 70% of women, as mentioned earlier, are in service industries; in manufacturing most women are concentrated in a few industries — food, drink, tobacco, clothing, electrical engineering. Thus the low degree of overlap between the sexes evades the basic principles of the Act.

82. For a detailed discussion of the plethora of strategies evolved to avoid equal pay, from altering job evaluation schemes or job content to introducing 'material differences', see M. Snell, *op. cit.*

83. C. Aldred, *op. cit.*, p. 10.

84. For a discussion of this, see M. Snell, *op. cit.*, pp. 38-39.

85. C. Aldred, *op. cit.*, p. 9.

86. See H. Wainwright, *op. cit.*

87. M. Snell, *op. cit.*, pp. 48-49 (Snell is citing evidence here from a sample of organisations surveyed. She also provides data on the inertia/hostility of unions). See also pp. 50-53, 'Barriers Women face in the Workplace'.

88. J. Rubery, *op. cit.*, p. 25.

89. I. Breugel, *op. cit.*, pp. 19-20.

90. *Scottish Abstract of Statistics*, No. 9, 1980.
91. See, amongst others, F. McNally, *op. cit.*, Chapter 2, 'The World of White Collar Work'.
92. *Ibid.*, Chapter 2.
93. For figures on white-collar union rates for women, see *ibid.*, Chapter 3.

6

The Scottish Labour Movement and the Offshore Oil Industry

Peter Wybrow

OIL has become the single most important resource necessary for the continued productivity and growth of modern capitalist societies. It is also the base on which the world's greatest multinational corporations have been built. Access to *uninterrupted* supplies of crude oil has become of paramount importance for the continued economic power of advanced western nations. Nowhere has this been more so than in Britain. Access to its own reliable source of crude oil has been seen by successive governments since the mid-60s as a panacea for Britain's balance of payments problem.

Conventional accounts of the development of North Sea oil usually start with the 'discovery' of oil in the late 1960s. This chapter attempts to show that a number of multinational oil corporations suspected that oil and gas might be present in the North Sea some twenty years earlier. During this time these corporations were able to build up close links with the civil servants advising governments over policy decisions concerning the exploration and exploitation of the North Sea. Knowledge concerning a resource, which remains the property of the state until it is extracted from the ground, was a private commodity traded by the companies.

It was not until 1972 that North Sea oil became of real interest to the Scottish labour movement.[1] In England even less concern was shown — Aberdeen was so far away — despite the fact that a large proportion of offshore workers had been recruited from England. Figures for 1979 show that approximately 52.5% of the offshore workforce on installations gave their usual place of residence as Scotland, 40.4% as England.[2]

Throughout the 1970s the Scottish labour movement pressed primarily for the maximum exploitation of oil resources in the North Sea to the advantage of British industry. It also pressed for the use of oil revenues for the express purpose of aiding depressed areas of Britain in general and Scotland in particular. By the mid-1970s the movement was particularly concerned at the lack of adequate trades union recognition within the industry and the way in which health and safety legislation for the offshore workforce lagged seriously behind that afforded to the workforce in industry generally onshore.

This chapter looks at the fears and anxieties of the Scottish labour movement concerning developments offshore as expressed in particular through the Scottish Trades Union Congress (STUC), and the methods used to try to bring influence to bear on governments and companies. The latter part of the chapter will attempt to demonstrate the extent to which their efforts have been a success or failure, with reference to the Burgoyne Report on *Offshore Safety*, 1980. In particular it will be argued that the primary concern of the oil companies, and of successive British governments, has been to emphasise the rate of oil extraction. A major consequence of this has been that the conditions of work, safety, and industrial organisation of labour involved in the offshore oil industry have been neglected. One result has been the startlingly high accident and mortality rates of workers in the industry. The Scottish labour movement, having started from a position which tended (like British governments) to stress the necessity of deriving the maximum economic benefit from oil extraction, rapidly came to realise the appalling conditions prevailing in the industry for its workforce. Increasingly, therefore, representatives of the labour movement began to organise themselves to press the government and the oil companies for reforms in the areas of work conditions, union representation, and health and safety legislation. The rest of this essay traces these attempts to bring about change in these areas, and shows how successive governments, civil servants, and the oil companies, resisted such pressure in the belief that the economic interests of the government and the relevant owners of capital were of primary importance.

The ownership and control of oil resources

A brief historical introduction to the legal background of developments in the North Sea will provide a 'back-drop' against which to view the problems experienced by the labour movement in later years.

Since the 1934 Petroleum (Production) Act the British government has owned, exclusively, the property rights over all natural gas and oil found both onshore and within UK territorial waters. In terms of international law, states exercised sovereignty only over those areas of the seabed beneath their territorial waters, in most cases limited to three miles from their coastlines.

In 1945, in what became known as the Truman Proclamation, this situation began to change. The United States government announced that it regarded 'the natural resources of the seabed of the continental shelf beneath the high seas, but contiguous to the coast of the United States, as appertaining to the United States, subject to its jurisdiction and control'. Forty-six other states had made similar declarations by 1951. These states did not include any of the North Sea Littoral States, who were waiting for some form of international agreement to evolve. These North Sea Littoral States subsequently supported the request for the United Nations to convene the first United Nations Conference on the Law of the Sea (UNCLOS I) in 1950, and for the International Law Commission to prepare a treaty on the Continental Shelf.¹ UNCLOS I was convened in Geneva in 1958, and the Continental Shelf Convention was adopted.³

The Convention extended the jurisdiction of the littoral states to that area of 'the sea bed and subsoil of the marine areas adjacent to the coast' outwith the territorial sea. This area was extended to the point at which the sea reached a depth of 200 metres, or 'to where the depth of the superjacent waters admits of the *exploitation* of natural resources'. Shelf rights were exclusive but the waters above retained their status as high seas.

The extent of each state's rights with regard to other bordering countries could be determined by any set of principles. If, however, agreement could not be reached by other means, Article 6 of the Convention established the equidistance principle: 'In the absence of agreement, and unless another boundary is justified by special circumstances, the boundary shall be determined by application of the principle of equidistance from the nearest points of the baselines from which the breadth of the territorial sea of each state is measured.'

Even before the UN conference, as many as twenty companies were carrying out seismic surveys of the North Sea. These activities were not subject to the jurisdiction of the coastal states, and the information gained by these surveys was not available to those states. Likewise, until such times as the coastal states of the North Sea ratified the convention and enacted legislation to extend their authority over the regulation of the Continental Shelf, protection was not afforded to oil companies in relation to property rights in the event of their carrying out exploratory drilling demonstrating the presence of oil and/or gas. Thus, the 'division of the Continental Shelf originated in pressure from the oil companies for the establishment of secure legal regimes under which the North Sea could be explored and exploited'.⁴

The authority to regulate the exploration of the UK Continental Shelf was granted under the Continental Shelf Act of 1964. This Act made certain sections of the Petroleum (Production) Act (1934) applicable to licences issued for exploration and production on the Continental Shelf and 'added a number of new provisions directed at the particular problems raised by production at sea'.⁵ Under the Act the Ministry of Power could grant licences for the exploration for and extraction of oil and gas in particularly designated areas of the UK Continental Shelf. These designated areas were produced by dividing the UK sector of the North Sea into equal blocks each of approximately 100 square miles.

The passing of the Continental Shelf Act on 15 April 1964 enabled the British government to ratify the UN Convention on 11 May 1964. There still remained, however, the problem of the Norwegian Trough. This was important because the delimitation of the British and Norwegian sectors entailed British acquisition of three-quarters of the North Sea continental shelf area south of 62°N. The Trough, which passes quite close to the Norwegian coastline, extends to a depth of some 800 metres and technically constituted the outward extension of the Norwegian Continental Shelf. The dispute was settled in 1965 when Britain decided to ignore the Trough in determining the median line between Britain and Norway. Had the British government known at the time of the mineral resources available between the agreed median line and the Norwegian Trough, it is questionable whether Britain would have been so quick to reach agreement. As it was, the British government was being pressed by economic problems, and by the oil companies, to proceed with exploration as quickly as possible. Fear of a lengthy battle at the International Court at the Hague persuaded the British government to take a somewhat hasty decision. According to most legal authorities, Britain would almost certainly have obtained a much higher proportion of the North Sea if it had pursued its case in the International Court.

This decision highlights clearly the British government's most consistent error, that of allowing its own, and the oil companies', financial needs for quick revenues to force it into speedy and ill-considered decisions. These decisions were eventually to lead to legislation which to a very large extent failed to adequately protect the 'life and limbs' of the men who were to provide the labour for the exploitation of the North Sea.

From the very beginning of the history of North Sea oil governments were unable to provide direct management of these resources. Governments have, to date, been dependent on a symbiotic relationship with oil companies: 'Whatever their capacity to govern, governments (had) no capacity to drill oil wells, build pipelines, or perform any of the other highly technical tasks required to exploit petroleum resources.'[6] Governments were restricted, therefore, to making regulations to bring about given economic criteria, determined by that same government, which compel oil companies to make commercial decisions to achieve those ends. Governments cannot make these regulations completely independently. A number of these regulations were the result of agreements between governments and companies. As Mason points out: 'It is not very difficult to observe that governments do not have a free hand to make whatever regulations please them, whether they are working through the process of national, transnational or international politics. One of the constraints on the effectiveness of regimes as instruments of management is that their content is limited by what can be agreed between those whose consent is necessary to their formulation, implementation and enforcement.'[7]

The British government lacked the knowledge and expertise to deal with the oil companies effectively. In the 1950s and '60s this lack of knowledge, coupled with the relationship of certain senior civil servants and the oil industry, ensured that successive British governments acted in the long-term interests of the oil companies rather than in the interests of the nation in general or of the workforce to be employed in the North Sea in particular. Evidence of this relationship is, of course, by its very nature, elusive, but some evidence will be demonstrated in a later section dealing with the Dissenting Note to the Burgoyne Committee Report.

The labour movement: response to North Sea oil

There was a significant time-lag between the discovery of North Sea oil and the formulation of systematic policy by the Scottish labour movement towards the rapidly growing oil industry in Britain. But, by 1972, the STUC had begun seriously to examine the implications of the discovery of oil off the coast of North-East Scotland. The General Secretary and Chairman of the Congress sought a meeting with Sir Philip Southwell, Managing Director of Brown and Root, in order to establish the scale of oil-rig production plans at Nigg Bay.[8]

At the time of the 1972 Congress, the Economic Committee were considering the possible consequences of North Sea oil for the Scottish economy. It was felt at that time that little value would be gained for Scotland unless the 'necessary refining and associated petro-chemical plant (came) to Scotland'.[9]

The main concern of delegates at this Congress about North Sea oil was the long-term impact on the UK in general and on Scotland in particular. In moving a motion on 'Oil Development, Scotland',[10] Mr R. R. Webster (Aberdeen Trades Council) asked that the government 'ensure that the public authorities concerned have the necessary financial resources available to provide (the) full economic exploitation' of these resources and for the creation of a National Fuel Policy. He went on to demand: 'Further, so that Scotland derive benefit in the shape of new industrial development arising', that '(i) the Government ensure that there be oil refinery and associated hydrocarbon chemical development in Scotland; and (ii) that a share of the royalties and other revenues accruing from the oil industry be available for the financing of substantial new Government investment in Scottish industry'.

The main thrust of his subsequent argument was that central government should ensure 'backing in the form of hard cash' in order that local authorities could help towards the proper exploitation of the North Sea. An adequate infrastructure in the North-East had to be planned and developed. The future prosperity of the area must be protected. Aberdeen should not, Mr Webster said, become another Yukon.

In seconding the motion, Mr A. M. Donnet (General and Municipal Workers Union) stressed the need for the securing of 'substantial additional Government investment in Scotland and in Scottish industry within the framework of an effective regional policy'.[11] The motion was carried unanimously.

At the Annual Conference of the Labour Party, later in 1972, Bob Middleton (Aberdeen South CLP) moved resolution 141 regretting 'that in the past exploitation of North Sea oil has been marked by hesitant planning, hasty resort to expedients and undue deference to commercial interests alone, with little regard for the social and wider economic consequences . . .'[12] In the discussions that took place in private following the debate on this resolution a number of trades unionists got together. These men, mostly shop stewards, were particularly concerned at the lack of orders going to east-coast shipyards for supply vessels needed for North Sea oil developments.[13] As a result of the discussions these trades unionists decided to instigate a North Sea Oil Action Committee (NSOAC). The NSOAC was set up at a meeting of the Confederation of Shipbuilding and Engineering Unions: Aberdeen No. 41 District on 19 October 1972.[14] The main concern of the Shop Stewards' Committee of the Confederation was that most of the work related to offshore developments was going abroad. Few orders for oil supply vessels were on the order books of Scottish east-coast shipbuilders, and many of the new orders were finding their way on to the American yards.

At their meeting on 19 October 1972 the shop stewards passed a resolution which, as Bob Middleton pointed out, 'was not formulated for purely instrumental motives', indeed it 'went well beyond that insular attitude and is worth recording since it embodied a principle that in my opinion is more typical of the average British trade unionist than they are generally given credit for. That is a concern, not only for themselves, but a real concern for the conditions of workers in other industries and a desire to see the nation prosper'.[15]

The resolution was as follows:

'The Confederation of Shipbuilding and Engineering Unions District Committee welcomes the development of Britain's North Sea oil resources and requests the Government to press the oil companies to make greater use of British industry and the available manpower in the exploitation of North Sea oil.

'The Government must ensure that the British people will enjoy the maximum benefits from the exploitation of North Sea oil.

'That exploitation is not prejudiced against any particular region or people.

'Therefore co-ordination of planning and control is required in the regions, so that present and future priorities may be established. Meanwhile, every encouragement and incentive should be given to existing industry to meet the challenge of North Sea Oil Exploration.'[16]

By November 1972 it was felt that the NSOAC should attempt to establish itself as a non-partisan body. A number of public figures from across the political spectrum were approached to become honorary members of the Committee.[17] The were:

Michael Barratt	—a BBC interviewer and Rector of Aberdeen University
Lord Boothby	—a member of the Conservative Party
Andrew Cruickshank	—a television personality well known for his Scottish interests
James Jack	—Secretary of the STUC
Viscount Thurso	—a Liberal peer

The NSOAC were not only interested in the problems of bringing orders and hence jobs to Scotland. They were becoming very concerned about the problems of working and living conditions on board drilling rigs. Their Action Committee quickly grasped the nettle and turned to the media as a tool with which to make progress in raising support for their campaign. Information was filtering through to the unions from the rigs that there was room for a great deal of improvement, not only of the living and working conditions of those working in the North Sea, but also in the level of trade union organisation offshore.

The Action Committee held weekly press conferences which received local and national coverage. As a result of stories of bad conditions existing in the North Sea, the matter was raised by Mr Dick Douglas MP with the Secretary of State for Employment, the Rt. Hon. Maurice Macmillan. In reply, on behalf of the Secretary of State, Mr Peter Emery replied:

'The Mineral Workings (Offshore Installations) Act 1971 contains powers enabling the Secretary of State to make regulations concerning the safety, health and welfare of men employed in offshore drilling and production. Regulations are now in course of preparation and in fact the question of standards of accommodation is currently receiving attention amongst the subjects that are of importance to health and welfare. I have asked the Department's Inspectors to bear in mind your remarks during their detailed consideration of the proposals for regulations.

'It is intended that the regulations should provide for an adequate standard to be maintained for all installations used in areas under this country's jurisdiction and it is proposed to set appropriate minimum requirements on the subject to which you have drawn attention, as part of a comprehensive statutory code for offshore mineral workings.'[18]

Thus Government Ministers were seen to have to react to the public pressures brought to bear on them by the early publicity campaign by the Action Committee.

The Economic Committee of the STUC met with the NSOAC on 17 January 1973 to discuss the subject of the North Sea. As a result both sides resolved to keep the subject under continuous review and to gather together as much information as was possible to stimulate research into the impact of North Sea oil and gas.

For their part, the Action Committee decided that every effort should be made to pursue the publicly stated aims as detailed in their five-point plan which had been circulated to government departments, industries which the Action Committee felt should be involving themselves in the North Sea, individual trade unions, the STUC, local authorities and political parties.[19] The Committee members were very busy during 1973. Children in schools in the North-East were encouraged to take part in a Slogan Competition, and the winning entry was used as a motif for stationery and car stickers. Press conferences were held every Saturday morning to report on the events of the previous week. Journalists from national newspapers were talked to and ministers and civil servants were lobbied. Men working offshore, particularly those working for charter rig companies operating in the North Sea, were interviewed about their experiences.

Dossiers on most of the companies operating in the North Sea were built up. It was believed at the time that most of the charter rig companies 'employed management techniques and imposed working conditions the likes of which had not been seen in Britain since the Industrial Revolution'.[20] The companies refused to employ trade unionists, and opposed any kind of organisation by either trades unions or *ad hoc* committees from within the workforce. The Action Committee did however come to believe that the companies themselves were organised in some informal manner. The Action Committee collected together a number of Contracts of Employment which showed 'a remarkable similarity in the conditions they imposed'. There was a common approach throughout the companies to the employment and use of labour. Thus, as Middleton writes: 'The North Sea was unionised but, of course, it was a bosses' union . . . The Association of Chartered Rig Operators (British Chapter) . . .'[21] A largely unorganised sector of Scottish labour was once again pitted against organised employers.

The Action Committee went about collecting facts on living and working conditions, sackings, accidents (fatal, serious and minor), violence, and some cases of racial discrimination. Information was not always easy to come by. Men were frightened of losing their jobs. Very often reports would come into the Action Committee by anonymous telephone calls.[22]

In 1973 a man working on the rigs could expect to work 12 hours a day for 14 days. Accommodation was cramped, to say the least. Often bunks were so cramped together that, once in a bunk, there was no room for a man to turn over. Ventilation was often very poor. On the worst rigs the 'hot bunk' system operated where there was only half as many bunks as there were workers and alternate shifts used the same bunks. For working these long hours in appalling conditions the average wage was £98. Two weeks' work was followed by one week onshore, without pay. Training on the rigs was inadequate, and opportunities for advancement to better jobs were negligible. Instant dismissal could follow sickness or injury and for minor infringements of rules. As the Action Committee soon learned, complaints to government departments and ministers were met with the same reply: 'nothing could be done because these men were employed outside British Territorial Waters'. This situation did not begin to be remedied until 1974, and even then improvements were made only piecemeal. Unfortunately changes came about, not because of the direct efforts of the Action Committee, but because it was becoming more difficult to recruit men willing to work in the existing conditions.

When competition for labour between companies started to occur in 1974, conditions began to improve. Some companies began a seven-day, twelve-hour shift followed by seven days off. Pay and bonuses increased. Attempts were made at simple training schemes for roustabouts, and the numbers of sackings grew less. Some companies at this time were complaining of turnover of rig personnel of 40% per two-week shift.

The new Labour government of 1974 brought some comfort to men working offshore. As a result of lobbying by the NSOAC and others, the new Minister of Employment, Michael Foot, included in the Employment Protection Act a three-line clause extending it to those areas of the North Sea ceded to the British government outwith its territorial waters.

During 1974 members of the NSOAC met with every new minister involved, no matter how remotely, with the offshore oil industry. These ministers were given details of every incident and accident of which the Action Committee had been notified, together with the Committee's view on why these events had taken place. Demands were constantly made for more stringent safety measures to be operative in the North Sea. However, new safety measures in themselves were not sufficient without adequate means of enforcing them. The NSOAC thus pressed government ministers hard, with the result that in 1977, on 3 August, an Order-in-Council extended the powers of the Health and Safety at Work Act to cover the North Sea offshore industry.

There were other successes for the NSOAC. One particular example was the helicopter landing pad at Forresterhill Hospital Complex, Aberdeen. In the early years of North Sea developments it had been the practice for urgent medical cases to be flown direct to hospital from rigs and vessels in the North Sea. As the hospital complex increased in size, the Hospital Board felt that this facility could no longer be offered. The number of people employed offshore was approaching its peak, and the number of accidents, particularly to divers, was increasing. One did not need to be a doctor to realise that often seconds counted in saving men's lives. The Action Committee thought the attitude of the Hospital Board was 'outrageous and that to remove such a facility at this time bordered on the criminal'. A vigorous press campaign was conducted by the Action Committee. Letters of protest were sent to the Hospital Board and to government ministers. Thanks to the Action Committee, common sense prevailed and the landing pad has remained to this day.[23]

However, the NSOAC did fail in its consistently fought campaign for a situation in the British sector of the North Sea where all the vessels operating in the oil industry should operate under the British flag. The Action Committee felt that the existing conditions under which companies operate under foreign flags, the British flag or flags of convenience, working out of ports in the North-East of Scotland, could only lead to a major accident at some time in the future.

It must be underlined however that, without the intervention of the NSOAC regarding the conditions offshore highlighted by them, things 'may well have got worse, and most certainly would have continued longer, had it not been for the work of that Committee'.[24]

The finance for the Action Committee came principally from the workforces of the engineering shops and shipyards of the North-East. 'Bob-a-nob' collections were made on pay day, given willingly by men who knew that it was being used to fight a cause which was not directly theirs.

Throughout the life of the NSOAC it was dependent on the efforts of the formal trade union movement, and in 1974, at the instigation of the Action Committee, a committee of full-time officers from eight trades unions was formed. It became known as the Inter-Union Off-Shore Committee, and subsequently took over responsibility for continuing the work of the NSOAC.

On 11 May 1973 members of the Economic Committee of the STUC met with representatives of the Scottish Parliamentary Labour Group. Basically the agenda for the meeting was the International Management and Engineering Group (IMEG) report published in the winter of 1972. This meeting and the two that followed between these two groups were to set the scene for a very important change in the emphasis on the issues brought to the fore by the exploration for and exploitation of North Sea oil. The Scottish labour movement and the trade union movement in general were to move from an emphasis on the economic benefits that must accrue to the nation to a greater interest in the effect on workers in the industry in terms of their relatively poor living and working conditions and in the health and safety hazards of such work.

The Assistant General Secretary, outlining the development of attitudes of Congress, said that the attitude had changed in recent years from pessimism to optimism in terms of the benefits that were possible from the North Sea. Congress, he said, cautiously welcomed the IMEG report but would have preferred more government intervention. One important area had been overlooked, however, in the report and that was 'the conditions under which people had to work and the legislative problems associated with such employment. The trade unions were seriously handicapped in that the firms involved were notoriously anti-trade union'.[25]

Members of Parliament, the meeting agreed, must be kept informed of these aspects of North Sea oil exploration and exploitation. It was doubted, for instance, if the National Insurance Acts were relevant to the North Sea, and whether these Acts applied to people working for non-British firms. It was known that the Redundancy Payments Act and the Conditions of Employment Act did not apply to people working on rigs. Another problem was that if a rig was self-propelled, then whilst it was moving the workers on board were treated as merchant seamen but, if stationary and drilling, then they were governed by the Mineral Workings (Offshore Installations) Act.

Mr W. Dougan, the STUC representative on the Standing Conference on Oil, expressed concern at the general attitude to working people. He felt that from that time on 'increasing emphasis should be put on the effect of oil exploration and exploitation on workers and the general public'.[26] Mr Dougan went on to express serious concern at working conditions offshore and pointed out the North Sea Oil Action Committee was considering a test case on conditions of work. It was agreed by both sides at the meeting that not only should further collaboration take place between them but that collaboration must be seen to be taking place.

A second meeting between the two groups occurred on 6 July 1973, at which a paper was presented by the Scottish Parliamentary Labour Group on the rate of exploitation of the UK sector of the North Sea. The paper pointed out that the continually changing nature of developments in the North Sea meant that information had to be continuously updated.

Concern was expressed at the declared intention to continue to endeavour to integrate each new development of oil and gas producing capacity into the pre-existing European refining pattern. It was realised that the companies intended to refine the bulk of North Sea oil on the continent. When new refineries had been built in the '50s and '60s, those in Britain were designed to refine the heavier type of crude oil imported from the Middle East. North Sea oil is a lighter (sweeter) kind of crude requiring different sorts of plant.

The participants of the meeting were told that developments in the North-East of Scotland were progressing very quickly in terms of various shore-based activities. The necessary infrastructural provisions were failing to keep pace, however. Inadequate roads were being used to transport materials, whilst there were not enough houses for the workers attracted to the area.

Concern was expressed about the lack of ability of Scottish firms to seize an adequate slice of the £300-£350m per annum the IMEG Report calculated to be the market for supplies and materials on the British Continental Shelf.

On 22 June 1973 the General Council convened in Glasgow a conference of all the unions involved in the oil industry. For the General Council it was stated that North Sea oil had at first been seen as the answer to all of Scotland's economic problems. Indeed it was part of the STUC's stated policy that oil revenues should be used to help depressed areas of Britain.

Above all the General Council believed that Britain in general and Scotland in particular should use every conceivable means of taking advantage of developments in the North Sea. The fiscal régime and licensing regulations should be tightened up, whilst the government should stimulate the development of a British oil technology capability, thus ensuring that British industry could 'break into the world market as offshore industry developers'. Britain, the Council declared, should learn from the experience of Norway. At the same time the STUC were anxious to see the development of a significant proportion of refining and processing being carried out in Scotland. They were aware that such processes were capital rather than labour intensive but it was thought that the by-products could be used as a means of generating further industrial development and thus employment opportunities.

Whilst discussions concerning the economic problems occupied a considerable proportion of the debates, a lengthy discussion developed over the subject of the organisation and safety and the legal position of employees working offshore. The unions were experiencing great problems in coming to terms with the companies involved in the oil industry. It was felt that to a large extent this difficulty was made worse by the fact that every contract was arranged on an individual basis. Wage rates were poor (£90 for fourteen 12-hour shifts). The unions experienced difficulties in approaching men working offshore. Usually the only access was to single men who were living in hotels when they came ashore.

Drilling companies made it clear that any man found distributing trade union leaflets would be sacked. The Transport and General Workers Union made an abortive attempt to lean on the oil companies nationally, and so it was felt that the STUC should attempt to intervene with the government on behalf of all the trade unions involved in the North Sea.

At the STUC Conference in 1973 Mr W. McLean moved a composite motion which started out by demanding the nationalisation of North Sea oil and gas. It was appreciated within the motion that the government of the day was unlikely to support such a policy and so the motion went on to demand more government intervention in the North Sea in order that the benefit of these energy resources should accrue to the people of Britain. The motion demanded stricter licensing arrangements bringing in more revenue to the exchequer and ensuring state participation, full implementation of the recently published IMEG report and better forward planning in order to obtain the maximum benefit to Britain in general and Scotland in particular. Mr McLean went on to say that there had been nine motions on the agenda all covering this issue, '. . . and in recent months no topic had been more discussed than the future development of North Sea oil. Naturally being a new industry, they had very deep concern in the future development, planning and exploitation of oil'.[27] The unions, he went on to say, were concerned about land speculation and, in the future, problems for the mining industry that might arise as a result of North Sea oil. He welcomed the fact that the Labour Party included in their election programme a promise to nationalise North Sea oil and gas (a commitment that was to be reneged on by the new Labour Cabinet as soon as it came to power during the next year). Mr McLean concluded by urging that the General Council should 'convene a meeting of all unions involved in the industry to draw up a common policy for North Sea oil and gas which must be immediately nationalised by the next Labour Government'.[28]

A copy of the resolution was sent to the Rt. Hon. Peter Walker MP, then Secretary of State for Industry in the Conservative Government, who replied in some detail.[29] Basically the Secretary of State said that the Conservative Government were undertaking a major review of their North Sea oil policy and then went on to cover all the points raised by the STUC resolution.

The reason for the government's review of its position was the publication of the Report of the Public Accounts Committee in 1973 entitled *North Sea Oil and Gas*. After the close questioning of senior advisers to both Labour and Conservative Ministers of Energy, it was obvious that these Ministers had not been fully informed of the implications of the finds in the North Sea, nor of the policies devised by the oil companies. The following points were of vital importance to the national interest and were either misunderstood or mis-interpreted.[30]

i   The importance of the finds and the associated decrease in risks as knowledge of the geological structures increased.

ii   The inadequacy of the conditions laid down in the licences for safeguarding the interests of the nation.

iii The likely rate of profit arising from these inadequacies.

iv   The loopholes in the tax system that could be used to avoid British taxation.

v   Even in the case of gas, where there had been adequate powers to secure the nation's interests, these powers were deliberately unused and must now be considered to have lapsed.

Whilst the Public Accounts Committee did not mention matters concerning health and safety regulations or unionisation in general, the point must be underscored that the evidence and advice presented to governments throughout the '50s, '60s and early '70s was primarily in the interests of the multinationals — exploiting the North Sea as quickly and as profitably as possible.

The winter of 1973-74 saw the advent in Britain of the miners' strike, which eventually led to the fall of the Heath administration, and the 'oil crisis', leading to the quadrupling of oil prices and the temporary shortage of crude oil in Europe and elsewhere. The incoming Labour government blamed oil price increases for the inflationary spiral gripping Britain's economy. Most popular accounts of inflation in Britain in the 1970s characterise it as being led by OPEC oil price rises.

In fact the world was in the grip of a recession long before the Yom Kippur war. In 1971-72 real earnings rose by 7.4% whilst money earnings rose by 15.4%. By 1972-73 money earnings had risen 13.9% whilst real earnings rose 1.1%. Inflation had reached 20% on an upward curve, and by 1974 only wage increases of around 30-40% could bring any real improvement. Unemployment had risen sharply to one million and profit margins were declining in industry generally. The balance of payments deficit in 1974 was £4,000 million in a year in which public expenditure had risen by 40%. It is against this background and Labour's inherited balance of payments deficit that the government's attitude to the North Sea must be understood.

By 1974 North Sea oil was taking an increasing proportion of the time and concern of the STUC. The Scottish labour movement generally was involved in both the collection of more information about working conditions and in pressing its demands on the new Labour Government. The General Council was by now spending a considerable amount of time discussing the subject.

At the 1974 Annual Conference of the STUC Mr R. R. Webster of the Aberdeen Trades Council moved the following motion: 'That this Conference is extremely concerned about the lack of safety, health and welfare regulations covering UK Continental Shelf development. Congress therefore demands that Government use the powers vested in it within the Mineral Workings (Offshore Installations) Act, 1971, to introduce and impose stringent regulations covering such developments. Action is required

i   to ensure legislation covering safety, health and welfare provisions;

ii   to ensure that all rigs, platforms, supply and safety vessels have a certificate of sea-worthiness before being allowed to operate on the UK Continental Shelf;

iii   that legislation is enforced to cover the period when a rig is being towed to its site.'[31]

Mr Webster went on to remind members of some of the events of the previous *mild* winter. The *Ocean Venture* was blown off its station and was later towed to Stavanger. The *Sea Quest* had to be towed to the Firth of Forth for repairs. Later it had to be towed back to Stavanger for repairs and it lost its anchors due to waves over 35 feet in height. The *Ocean Voyager* also lost its anchors in the storms, whilst the *Trans Ocean III* capsized. God help their members on the rigs, he went on to say, when they were out in the North Sea in a bad winter!

A statement had been made by the previous Tory administration that new regulations were to be introduced providing for a Certificate of Fitness covering the design and construction of offshore rigs. The certificate did not come into operation until 31 August 1975 and thus there was another year and another winter of unnecessary hazards to be faced by workers in the North Sea.

The accident rate amongst those working on rigs was, Mr Webster claimed, estimated at fifty times that of industrial workers. His organisation felt therefore that it was imperative that there should be established a specially trained inspectorate whose responsibilities would be to maintain a close surveillance over the operation of rigs, platforms and other offshore activities. Such an inspectorate should have the power to stop operations and evacuate personnel when necessary. It was felt that the existing inspectorate was inadequate for carrying out its present responsibilities because it was weak in members and in training.

Mr A. Clark of the Merchant Navy and Air Line Officers' Association, seconding the motion, said his organisation was concerned not only with the safety generally in the North Sea but in particular with the safety of British seafarers serving on British flag vessels. Such officers were, he claimed, often working in excess of 100 hours per week for periods of not less than six weeks at a time. 'While making anchor in ships in adverse weather conditions some of his members were on their feet for 70 hours at a stretch, and they had to take the ship back to port.'[32] Mr Clark left it to the imagination of congress to visualise how fit these officers were after working such hours in the winter time in the North Sea. The Association, Mr Clark continued, was concerned that one day there would be a major accident in the North Sea due to the exhaustion of officers in charge of the watch. They had drawn to the attention of the Department of Trade and Industry the conditions on supply vessels. The Department had expressed its concern but that was as far as it had gone. In summing up, Mr Clark said 'they had heard plenty about exploration in the North Sea, but very little about the exploitation that was going on in these waters'.[33]

By the mid-70s reports of accidents, and cases in which men sought compensation for unfair dismissal only to find that their cases fell outside the jurisdiction of industrial tribunals, were becoming almost daily occurrences in the Scottish press. The rapid pace of exploration and development was still more important than men's health or even lives.

At the 78th Annual Conference of the STUC in 1975, held that year in what was becoming known as the 'oil capital of Europe' (Aberdeen), Aberdeen Trades Council again pressed home their concern at the increasing numbers of deaths and casualties involved in North Sea exploration and demanded 'immediate action to eliminate these casualties'.[34] It also expressed concern at the long hours of duty still performed by officers on supply boats and the low rates of pay applying to the supply industry generally. Speaking in support of the motion, Mr A. Clark of the Merchant Navy and Airline Officers' Association told congress that his union had been endeavouring to find out exactly how many lives had been lost and how many accidents had occurred in the offshore oil industry. The Depart of Trade and Industry had told them that this information was not available!

Working in the North Sea on a supply boat was one of the most dangerous jobs at sea, he told Congress: 'In the winter, crews had to unload machinery and supplies from decks that were often awash and rising and falling anything up to 20 feet. Heavy anchors had to be lifted and relocated; this could be a dangerous job requiring a great degree of seamanship and skill. Supply boats were the life line of the rigs. Without them the whole North Sea operation would grind to a halt. In the rush to get North Sea oil ashore it appeared that little concern was given by the Department of Trade to the safety of crews.'[35]

One wonders what price the companies placed on employees' lives. The previous autumn, Mr Clark reported, the unions had asked owners to supply survival suits at a cost of £55 each. The unions were informed by the companies that at that price the suits were a 'high cost item' and that before supplying them a company would have to be 'absolutely sure that the price, durability and performance was right'.[36] Robert Hughes, Labour MP for North Aberdeen, made a demand for the 'utmost vigilance' in reducing risk of accident in the North Sea.[37] Commenting on a letter he had received from Mr John Smith, Junior Energy Minister, Mr Hughes said he was glad the department agreed 'that operations conducted in connection with the quest for North Sea oil continue to be unacceptably hazardous'.

By 1975 a general pattern had begun to emerge. Most accidents, perhaps not

T

surprisingly, occurred on and around the drilling floor, followed in number by accidents involving cranes, diving accidents and accidents on attendant vessels.[38] January 1975, however, did see the introduction of safety regulations governing diving operations on the UK Continental Shelf, but it was to be the end of the decade before companies agreed to share technical information gained as a result of diving accidents. Divers' lives continued to be placed in greater danger than necessary because companies put the private acquisition of such knowledge above the lives of men working for other companies.

Despite new regulations, six divers died during 1975 during operations on the UK Continental Shelf, bringing the total number between 1971 and 1975 to 17.

In January 1976 the then Labour Government was still *talking* about extending employment legislation to cover workers on offshore oil installations. A Department of Employment consultative document had been sent to all industry and trades union leaders involved in offshore activities, outlining the extension of existing and new employment legislation covering rigs, supply vessels and other offshore activities.

By this time the law covering employers' liability for compulsory insurance had been extended to offshore installations, and the Government expressed a desire to extend the relevant employment legislation as soon as possible. The areas which at this time remained uncovered in the offshore industry were security of employment, industrial training, redundancy payments, contracts of employment and the Trade Union and Labour Relations Act. It was also hoped to extend the jurisdiction of industrial tribunals to cover offshore activities. The trade unions hoped that such changes in legislation would enable them to place statutory safety representatives on rigs and to use the Employment Protection Act to secure general recognition of trade unions in the UK offshore industry, a hope still being expressed by the unions in 1981.

The Annual Report of Congress for 1976 carried a report of a submission from the Amalgamated Union of Engineering Workers engineering section. The submission referred to a report by an *ad hoc* committee of the Scottish Council of the British Medical Association published on 4 September 1975. The report highlighted a number of problems faced by the workforce offshore: 'Firstly the accident rate amongst all workers on rigs is very high. From January to September 1975 there were eight fatalities and twelve serious injuries. The risk of death was found to be some 10 times greater for an oil rig worker than for a coal miner and 50 times greater than that faced by a factory worker. Deaths from accidents to riggers numbered 2-3 per thousand, compared to 1 per thousand for deep sea trawlermen. Divers on oil rigs, however, face a much higher risk of death at work, the fatality rate being 10 per 1,000 workers — that is, 8 times the risk to which trawlermen are exposed and 33 times the risk faced by miners, 220 times that faced by factory workers.'[39] The BMA committee also stated that a 'large and unmeasured' incidence of psychological disorders occurred amongst men working offshore, often exacerbated by violence and alcoholism. The AUEW submission also reported on the proposals put forward by the Inter-Union Off-Shore Oil Committee recommending that a single Code of Practice should be applied under the Health and Safety at Work Act, 1974, to offshore oil installations on the UK Continental Shelf outwith British territorial waters.

The official statistics show that a further 20 men died working offshore in 1976, and in addition there were another 57 serious accidents as compared with 50 in 1975.[40] The fatalities in 1976 included seven diving deaths, and during that year new regulations were made, under the Petroleum and Submarine Pipe-lines Act, to try to reduce this number.

Officially 1977 saw a further 17 men die offshore working on or around installations. A footnote to the report in the 'Brown Book' for 1977, however, underlines the inadequacy of this figure. It states that this figure only includes accidents on or around rigs or platforms covered by the Mineral Workings (Offshore Installations) Act 1971. It goes on to say: 'Regulations are in preparation on the reporting of accidents in the course of work on pipelines; at present there is no requirement to report. In addition there are foreign registered vessels such as crane barges on which reliable information would be impossible to collect, and in connection with which there is no obligation to report accidents. Finally deaths on British registered supply vessels must be reported to the Department of Trade, although again reliable information on all supply vessels, including accidents associated with them, is not available.'[41]

The facts are plain. The true number of deaths and serious injuries experienced by men working in the British Sector of the North Sea simply is not known. All we can know is that the figures shown in the official government statistics are the minimum that have been suffered.

The Burgoyne Committee and safety legislation

The code of regulations planned under the enabling legislation in the Mineral Workings (Offshore Installations) Act 1971 was finally completed in 1978. This year also saw the Secretary of State for Energy, Tony Benn, set up an independent committee, chaired by Dr J. H. Burgoyne, to review the offshore safety regulations and procedures for which the Department was responsible. The formation of what was to become known as the Burgoyne Committee was announced on 7 September 1978. The committee was to investigate offshore safety with the following terms of reference: 'To consider so far as they are concerned with safety, the nature, coverage and effectiveness of the Department of Energy's regulations governing the exploration, development and production of oil and gas offshore and their administration and enforcement. To consider and assess the role of the Certifying Authorities. To present its report, conclusions and any recommendations as soon as possible.'[42]

The committee, consisting of eight members including representatives from the trades unions, industry and the academic field first met on 11 January 1979. They were addressed briefly by Tony Benn, who confirmed the urgency with which the report was required. The committee resolved to meet at weekly intervals until the report was completed. The committee saw its job to be:

i   'To obtain as full an acquaintance as reasonably possible with the present situation through invited presentations to the Committee by appropriate Government departments, operating companies, certifying authorities, and others; and by visits to offshore installations and related establishments (and)

ii   To invite and consider written submissions of evidence from all interested bodies and persons'.[43]

A memorandum was sent to 124 potentially interested 'bodies and persons inviting written submissions of evidence' and an advertisement was placed in twelve newspapers and journals inviting anyone interested to submit evidence.

Sixty-five formal submissions were received by the committee, and in the following meetings thirteen organisations were invited to make presentations to the committee on general and specific matters. Visits were made by members of the committee to fourteen establishments including seven platforms and a drilling rig.[44]

The position in relation to safety was found, by the committee, to involve a number of different legislative provisions. As was shown earlier, the Continental Shelf Act, 1964, extended the provisions of the Petroleum Production Act of 1934 to cover the United Kingdom Continental Shelf (UKCS). When the first round of licences were issued under these regulations they contained the following model clauses in relation to safety matters:

i   to obtain the consent of the Minister to the drilling or abandonment of a well;

ii   execute all operations in accordance with good oilfield practice; and

iii   comply with instructions given by the Minister relating to (ii) on the safety, health and welfare of persons in the licensed area.

Essentially these provisions were designed to minimise the risks of a blow-out and to promote 'good operating practices' aboard offshore installations.

Experience in the early years of operations in the North Sea demonstrated that the risks of operating in such a hostile environment had not been adequately envisaged, and a new Act — the Mineral Workings (Offshore Installations) Act — was passed in 1971. This Act applied to 'drillships, jackups, semi-submersibles and fixed steel or concrete platforms' operating in the area of the UKCS. This Act enabled regulations to be made for the safety, health and welfare of workers aboard offshore installations. In particular it laid down the duties of concession and installation owners and required the appointment of an installations manager who would be responsible for safety, health and welfare and for the maintenance of 'discipline and order'. It also enabled the Secretary of State to appoint inspectors and provided the police with the 'powers, protection and privileges that they have on land'.

The Act also identified the following areas which were in need of regulatory control:

i   Registration of offshore installations;

ii   Design, construction and operation of offshore installations;

iii   Appointment of managers;

iv   Appointment of inspectors and reporting accidents;

v   Diving operations;

vi   Emergency procedures and equipment.[45]

The most important Regulations as far as the Burgoyne Committee were concerned were:

a   Inspectors and Casualties Regulations 1973, which provided for the enforcement of regulations on all offshore installations on the UKCS by inspectors of the Department of Energy and requires the reporting of accidents and casualties.

b   Construction and Survey Regulations 1974, laying down the regulations for the certification of all fixed or mobile installations used for exploration or production.

c   Diving Operations 1974, laying down the duties of all those involved in the employment of divers. They require the appointment of diving supervisors, the medical certification of divers and the maintenance of equipment.

d   Operational Safety, Health and Welfare Regulations 1976, in which all those concerned with offshore installations, both employer and employee, are required to ensure compliance with these regulations. Competent persons must be appointed to 'take charge of various potentially hazardous operations, and all operational personnel must be either fully experienced themselves or work under close supervision of someone who is'.

e   Emergency Procedures Regulations 1976, which require that each manned installation has an Emergency Procedures Manual. These manuals have to list procedures to be taken in the event of such incidents as blow-out, fire, collision and structural failure. Everyone on board should know these regulations, and 'regular practice drills must be held'. These regulations also require a 'standby vessel' to be within five miles of every installation which should be capable of taking on board everyone in the event of the evacuation of the installation.

f   Life-Saving Appliances Regulations 1977. These require the provision of survival craft, life-saving equipment, public address and alarm equipment on installations.

g   Fire-Fighting Equipment Regulations 1978. These regulations require the provision of many varieties of fire-fighting, gas detection and alarm systems in installations.

In both (f) and (g) examinations are required to be carried out by Surveyors of the Marine Division of the Department of Trade, acting on behalf of the Secretary of State for Energy.

None of these regulations made under the Mineral Workings Act 1971 could be applied to submarine pipelines on the UKCS. As a result provision was sought in the Petroleum and Submarine Pipe-Lines Act 1975 for the safe construction of submarine pipelines. The Act required all pipeline constructions to be authorised by the Secretary of State and that these authorisations 'include requirements concerning safety matters'. Two sets of further provisions have been made under the Act to bring the regulations into line with those of offshore installations:

i   Submarine Pipelines (Diving Operations) Regulations 1976;

ii   Submarine Pipelines (Inspectors etc) Regulations 1977.

On 30 July 1976, in a written answer in the House of Commons,[46] the Prime Minister announced that the Health and Safety at Work Act 1974 should be extended offshore. At the same time the Health and Safety Commission (HSC) would take on the 'policy responsibility' for occupational safety offshore. The Secretary of State for Energy was to retain responsibility for structural safety and 'blow-out' risks and the Secretary of State for Trade was to retain responsibility for structural safety of laybarges. The Petroleum Engineering Division (PED) of the Department of Energy was to act as agent for the HSC on occupational safety matters, and the co-ordination of Government responsibilities offshore was to be undertaken by an Interdepartmental Committee on Marine Safety.

The Order-in-Council extending the Health and Safety at Work Act 1974 was made on 26 July 1977 and came into operation on 1 September 1977. From that date the HSC assumed policy responsibility for offshore occupational safety.

An Agency Agreement,[47] effective from 1 November 1978, made provisions for the Secretary of State to act on behalf of the HSC. The Secretary was to appoint inspectors under Section 19 (1) of the Health and Safety at Work Act, and the cost of these inspectors was to be met in full by the HSC.

The PED of the Department of Energy currently have the responsibility of enforcing the Mineral Workings (Offshore Installations) Act 1971, the Health and Safety at Work Act 1974, as applied offshore, and the Petroleum and Submarine Pipelines Act 1975. To undertake these functions the PED has three inspectorates, the Petroleum Inspectorate, the Diving Inspectorate and the Pipelines Inspectorate.

After reviewing the current legislative position the Burgoyne Committee went on to examine the accident statistics for the North Sea.

Annual figures for accidents occurring in the oil industry offshore in the

North Sea are given in the Annual Report to Parliament known as the *Development of the Oil and Gas Resources of the United Kingdom*, more commonly known as the 'Brown Book', and published by the Department of Energy. In these annual statistics accidents are sorted into nine categories.[48] Most accidents are accounted for in five of these nine categories, construction, drilling, diving, cranes and boats. Using the tables provided, the successive 'Brown Books' show that between 1965 and 1979 there were 102 'fatal accidents' and 405 'serious accidents'. Figures for 'minor accidents' are not usually published; however, the Burgoyne Report shows that there were 3,706 accidents characterised as 'minor' between 1974 and 1978.

The statutory compulsory reporting of accidents occurring offshore dates only from the Offshore Installations (Inspectors and Casualties) Regulations (SI No. 1842, 1973). Before the foregoing instrument came into force, accidents 'in the licensed area' were reported to the Department in accordance with formal arrangements in the licences. From 1974 the figures account only for accidents occurring on 'Offshore Installations' and they therefore exclude occurrences such as diving accidents from vessels outwith the 500-metre zone, and on such vessels as pipelay barges and support vessels. Despite the Department of Energy's desire to do so, there seems little point in trying to draw even tentative conclusions from these figures. According to the Burgoyne Report, 'an offshore worker is about twice as likely to have an accident as a worker in general manufacturing and about half as likely as a miner'.[49] However, as the Report itself shows, doubts must be cast particularly on the figures for minor accidents and 'dangerous occurrences'[50] because of under-reporting and 'because of doubt about the definition of a reportable occurrence and the difficulty of educating all concerned to make such reports'.[51]

Even where accidents have been reported, their exact nature and cause have not always been clearly understood because 'the accident reports received by the Department (of Energy) are sometimes so brief — no more than 10 words or even less'.[52]

After studying offshore safety regulations and their enforcement, together with details of accidents and dangerous occurrences, and after taking cognisance of the submissions presented to it, the committee observed that safety will not be assured by regulatory controls alone: 'Safety operations depend on the wholehearted commitment of owners, employers and employed who must fully accept their individual responsibility for the provision and operation of safe structures, plant, systems and procedures.'[53] The basic finding of the Burgoyne Committee was that the government should discharge its responsibility for offshore safety through a single government agency. The report claimed that the Department of Energy is capable of discharging that responsibility effectively. The report goes on to make 58 recommendations for extending legislation, tightening up of controls over policing and enforcing existing legislation, on reporting of accidents, management responsibilities, safety training and research.[54] In a dissenting note, the two trades union representatives, Mr Ron Lyons of ASTMS and Mr John Miller of the TGWU, state that, whilst they are prepared to accept the recommendation for a single government agency, 'this must be based firmly on the principle that a Government Department substantially responsible for the direction and control of an industry should not in any way be responsible for the standards and enforcement of occupational health and safety in that industry'.[55]

As Tony Benn pointed out in an interview following the publication of the Burgoyne Report, 'inevitably the Department of Energy . . . has a prime responsibility of getting the oil out of the North Sea as quickly as possible. They have a very close relationship with the industry, and it is not right that a department which has that prime responsibility should also be responsible for checking production in circumstances where safety may be a factor'.[56]

Parallels are that the Factories Inspectorate is not under the Department of Industry, but under the Department of Employment in the HSE; the Mining Inspectorate which used to be under the Ministry of Power is now under the HSE; the Nuclear Inspectorate which was under the Ministry of Technology is now under the HSE. Clearly it is impossible for a regulatory body to pursue its objectives of, in the case of the Department of Energy, being responsible for standards and enforcement of occupational health and safety independently from the interests of the industry concerned or the wider demands of the economy as a whole. As the dissenting note points out, 'from its inception, the Department has been directly involved in implementing a policy designed to encourage rapid exploration and development of the North Sea with a view to early self-sufficiency of oil supplies'.[57] Thus members of the Petroleum Engineering Division of the Department of Energy may experience conflict of interest between the desire to cope with the 'exigences of production' on the one hand and the requirement to oversee safety on the other.

Evidence was given to the committee on the subject of the conflicts of interest within the Department of Energy in the areas of production and safety and the interchange of personnel between the oil companies and the Department of Energy. Hard evidence is difficult to come by for obvious reasons. In 1978, in a debate on the Bingham Report on Rhodesian sanctions busting, Dr Jeremy Bray MP, a junior minister at the Ministry of Power from April 1966 to January 1967, had this to say about a 'potentially incestuous' relationship between an Under Secretary in the Department of Energy and the oil industry:
'The Under Secretary of the Petroleum Division was Mr Angus Beckett, . . . (who) had been in and out of oil matters in Government since the 1940's. He had a knowledge of the jargon, gossip and personalities of the oil industry unequalled in Whitehall. He was largely responsible for the first four rounds of North Sea oil and gas licensing, and had been publicly quoted by Sir Laurence Helsby as an example of how versatile and expert an administrative civil servant could be.

'In fact I found that whenever I pressed Mr Beckett on any business, financial or economic question, he quickly took refuge in generalities. His view was that whatever was good for the oil companies was good for Britain. He passed on to Ministers the views of the oil companies regarding their own supra-national status and the folly of any Government intervention, adding pepper and salt of his own. He was so obviously in the pocket of the oil companies that I do not think they had any great respect for him. Certainly when he retired and sought the reward that, alas, seems now to be the expectation of many civil servants who have had responsibility for industry, he did not get a job in any of the oil majors but obtained one with William Press, the North Sea oil contractors . . .[58]

'In my experience, Mr Beckett deliberately blocked information going to Ministers. We were a small Department with only two Ministers, Richard Marsh and myself; Dick Marsh gave me free reign in the Department. When I asked for some information on refinery capacity and throughputs, the Petroleum Division was unable to supply it. I asked the statistics division and it produced some data. When Mr Beckett found out, he blocked any further such information coming to me, not only from his own division, but from the statistics division.'[59]

As Lyons and Miller point out, the implication must be that top civil servants failed to pass on vital information to ministers.

Another important aspect of the use of Department of Energy inspectors for monitoring safety standards is the possibility of 'shared values and membership of closed groups'. PED inspectors are normally recruited with oil industry backgrounds and are specialists in particular areas rather than health and safety generally. As far as Lyons and Miller could determine, none of the inspectors had special training in occupational health and safety (other than in connection with diving). Furthermore, reports prepared after visits offshore by PED inspectors have not made specific reference to health and safety matters unless there had been a particular matter of concern.[60]

The Health and Safety Executive (HSE) has on numerous occasions asked the PED inspectors for detailed reports on fatal and serious accidents. The PED does not appear to have provided this information on a regular basis. Where such reports have been handed on they have very often omitted important factual evidence and have shown 'insufficient consideration of legal aspects necessary to identify contraventions of laws or regulations'.[61] There appears to be an inadequate consideration given to enforcement procedures generally or legal proceedings in particular. Until the publication of the Burgoyne Report the actions of the PED had not included the service of any prohibition or improvement notice whatsoever. Furthermore, no offshore safety committee visited by Lyons and Miller had ever seen a PED inspector, and the TUC representatives had been told by PED that 'they have never needed to meet safety committees or safety representatives offshore, or advise them of their visits offshore'.[62]

In their evidence to Burgoyne the PED in fact confirmed that there are 'virtually no Safety Committees offshore'.[63] This is underlined in the Dissenting Note when it is explained that on one offshore platform visited, which started up production in 1976, there was no safety committee and no safety representatives whatsoever. The same company operating in the Norwegian sector of the North Sea has a very comprehensive system of safety committees and safety representatives on its platforms.

The committee found that major differences occur concerning employees' rights in the UK and Norwegian sectors. On Norwegian platforms the trade unions are recognised and their rights taken for granted. In addition to safety committees there are 'safety delegates' for each sub-group of workers on each shift of each platform. Every platform has a senior trade union official seconded, full time, to health and safety matters. The 'safety delegate' has the right under law to stop the job at any time, a fact fully accepted and implemented by the operating companies in the Norwegian sector.[64]

The position in the UK sector is 'really quite scandalous'. Over the years the Inter Union Offshore Oil Committee (IUOOC) has come to a number of agreements with UKOOA, dating back to 1976, over trades union rights, access, and recognition offshore. Despite this fact 'a battery of devices are used to minimise the trade union presence amongst permanent platform employees involved in production. To date there is only one collective bargaining agreement offshore, covering gas platform staff in the southern sector, and that was only secured after several years of resistance. Elsewhere, pressure, intimidation, temporary bribes, and other means are used to hold back the development of bona fide trade union organisation and recognition'.[65]

Conclusion

In the introduction to his book, *Politics in Industrial Society*, Keith Middlemas characterises the development of industrial politics of Britain in the twentieth century as exhibiting 'corporate bias'. That is to say, there is a 'triangular pattern of co-operation' between government, industry and the trades union movement. Trades unions and employers' associations, according to this theory, are elevated to a new status, that of becoming a 'governing institution'.

The developments in the North Sea in terms of the trades union fight for recognition, better working and living conditions and better health and safety standards points to the failure of the attempt to incorporate the trades union movement. The STUC has not seen its role as taking a similar stance to the English TUC and absorbing the English-dominated political culture of incorporation.

The Scottish labour movement have fought 'tooth and nail' for every small step forward in their demands. They started 10-15 years behind in information and access to government departments. Early research concerning North Sea oil by trades unionists was conducted in an amateur and piecemeal fashion, often at the personal expense of individuals. The separation of powers, wherein bodies responsible for the implementation of policy, in this case the Department of Energy, are separate from the bodies responsible for formulating those policies, coupled with a close relationship between oil company personnel and civil servants, with their shared ideology and technological skills, has ensured the domination of the long-term interests of oil companies at the expense of the offshore workforce.

It has been shown how conditions of employment in the British sector of the North Sea more closely resemble those of the onshore industry in the nineteenth century than those of the late twentieth century. The use of 'enabling legislation' in formulating policy with regard to the health and safety regulations ensures that policy to be of an *ad hoc* nature, new legislation being enacted only when it becomes absolutely necessary because of public pressure, in this case mainly from the Scottish labour movement.

The failure to implement leglislation enforcing trades union recognition offshore means that even in 1981 there is continued pressure on men working offshore to ignore safety regulations. Of course the very nature of the oil industry attracts individualists, but there is plenty of evidence to show that employers, especially drilling companies, recruit people who are specifically anti-trade unions. The 'macho' image of the oil industry is all too often invoked to pressure men to work in unsafe conditions: 'if you're not man enough to do the job — stand down'.[66]

Although, as was shown earlier, considerable legislation has been enacted by various governments, they have never shown a desire to provide adequate policing of offshore installations or an adequate enforcement procedure. It has been shown that such policing and enforcement *is* possible; it occurs in the Norwegian sector with the full co-operation of the oil companies. The question must be asked, why does the British sector lag so far behind the Norwegian sector in these matter? To use Miliband's terms, 'politics' sanctions what is 'permitted',[67] thus politics 'permits' the relations between members of conflicting classes.

The failure to bring the trades union movement adequately into the decision-making processes of government policy-making has ensured a continuing conflict in which the offshore workers continue to be the losers. In no other industry in the world does a workforce 'operate such advanced technology for communications and mobility; few industries are so dependent on a constant flow from production to consumption, and therefore so vulnerable to strike action'.[68] This fact makes it imperative that multinationals keep unionisation in the North Sea to a minimum and is an explanation, given their desire to expedite production as rapidly as possible, of why successive governments have connived at such blatant disregard for 'life and limb'.

NOTES

1. I am indebted to Councillor Bob Middleton, of Grampian Regional Council, for stimulating my interest in writing this chapter.

2. *Development of the Oil and Gas Resources of the United Kingdom, 1980*, p. 44.

3. For a fuller account of these issues see Bernie & Mason, 'Oil and Gas; The International Regime' in *The Effective Management of Resources*. Ed. C. M. Mason, Francis Pinter, London, 1979, pp. 26-27.

4. Bernie & Mason, *ibid.*, p. 25.

5. Dam, K. W., *Oil Resources*. Chicago Press, 1976, p. 23.

6. Dam, K. W., *ibid.*, p. 3.

7. Mason, C. M., 'Resource Management and International Politics' in *The Effective Management of Resources*, p. 7.

8. *75th Annual Report*, STUC, 1972, p. 15.

9. *75th Annual Report*, STUC, 1972, p. 16.

10. *75th Annual Report*, STUC, 1972, p. 306.

11. *75th Annual Report*, STUC, 1972, pp. 308-309.

12. *Report of the 71st Annual Conference of the Labour Party*, 1972, p. 184.

13. Author's interview with Bob Middleton, 5.3.80.

14. For a fuller account of the NSOAC see Bob Middleton, *The North Sea Oil Action Committee: A Successful Pressure Group*, a paper given to the Department of Business Studies, Robert Gordon's College of Technology, September 1977.

15. Bob Middleton, *ibid.*, p. 1.

16. An expanded version of this resolution was widely circulated in order to win support for the campaign to ensure Scottish industry played a major part in providing equipment and services in the North Sea. This expanded version appears in the *76th Annual Report*, STUC, 1973, pp. 69-70.

17. Bob Middleton, *ibid.*, p. 3.

18. *76th Annual Report*, STUC, 1973, p. 70.

19. Bob Middleton, *ibid.*, p. 4.

20. Bob Middleton, *ibid.*, p. 6.

21. Bob Middleton, *ibid.*, p. 7.

22. Bob Middleton, *ibid.*, p. 6.

23. Bob Middleton, *ibid.*, p. 10.

24. Bob Middleton, *ibid.*, p. 11.

25. *77th Annual Report*, STUC, 1974, p. 102.

26. *77th Annual Report*, STUC, 1974, p. 103.

27. *76th Annual Report*, STUC, 1973, p. 287.

28. *76th Annual Report*, STUC, 1973, p. 288.

29. The full text of the reply is to be found in *77th Annual Report*, STUC, 1974, pp. 99-101.

30. See Lord Balogh, 'The North Sea Oil Blunder, in *The Banker*, March 1974, p. 282.

31. *77th Annual Report*, STUC, 1974, p. 499.

32. *77th Annual Report*, STUC, 1974, p. 500.

33. *77th Annual Report*, STUC, 1974, p. 500.

34. *78th Annual Report*, STUC, 1975, p. 622.

35. *78th Annual Report*, STUC, 1975, p. 623.

36. *78th Annual Report*, STUC, 1975, p. 623.

37. Report in the *Press and Journal*, 17.10.75.

38. *Development of the Oil and Gas Resources of the United Kingdom, 1975*, p. 6.

39. *79th Annual Report*, STUC, 1976, p. 144.

40. *Development of the Oil and Gas Resources of the United Kingdom, 1977*, p. 15.

41. *Ibid.*, p. 15.

42. *Offshore Safety*, Burgoyne Committee Report, Cmnd 7366, March 1980, p. 1, HMSO.

43. *Ibid.*, p. 1.

44. Details of Memorandum, Recipients of Memorandum, Press Advertisements and Formal Submissions received and listed in Appendices 2:1, 2:2, 2:3 and Appendix 3 of the *Offshore Safety, ibid.*, pp. 69-75.

For lists of organisations invited to give presentations, establishments visited and organisations invited to clarify or amplify their written evidence see the Report, *ibid.*, pp. 1-3.

45. For details of the Regulations made under the Act see Appendix 5, *Offshore Safety* Report, pp. 80-81.

46. For full text of the Prime Minister's statement see Appendix 10, *Offshore Safety* Report, p. 96.

47. For full text of Agreement see Appendix 11, *Offshore Safety* Report, p. 97.

48. See Appendix 10, *Development of the Oil and Gas Resources of the United Kingdom, 1980*, p. 45.

49. *Offshore Safety* Report, *ibid.*, Appendix 14, p. 104.

50. 'Dangerous Occurrences' are those events which, whilst not causing death or injury to persons, might have done so.

51. *Offshore Safety* Report, *ibid.*, p. 104.

52. *Offshore Safety* Report, *ibid.*, p. 111.

53. *Offshore Safety* Report, *ibid.*, p. 51.

54. *Offshore Safety* Report, *ibid.*, pp. 52-57.

55. *Offshore Safety* Report, *ibid.*, p. 58.

56. Interview on the 'World this Weekend', BBC Radio, 30.3.80.

57. *Offshore Safety* Report, *ibid.*, p. 59.

58. Two reliable sources have suggested to the author that this may not have been, as Dr Bray suggests, because they were not offered but because such offers may have been blocked under the rules concerning the employment of civil servants of the rank of Under-Secretary and above. These regulations are enforceable within two years of resignation or retirement from Government service. See *Royal Commission on the Standards of Conduct in Government*, HMSO, 1976, Annexe 73.

59. *Hansard*, 7 November 1978, Cols. 797-799, quoted in Kellner, P. & Lord Crowther-Hunt, *The Civil Servants*, Macdonald, London, 1980, pp. 169-170.

60. *Offshore Safety* Report, *ibid.*, p. 59.

61. *Offshore Safety* Report, *ibid.*, p. 60.

62. *Offshore Safety* Report, *ibid.*, p. 60.

63. *Offshore Safety* Report, *ibid.*, p. 60.

64. *Offshore Safety* Report, *ibid.*, p. 62.

65. *Offshore Safety* Report, *ibid.*, p. 62.

66. Author's interview with a 'roustabout', 4.7.80.

67. Miliband, R., *Marxism and Politics*, OUP, London, 1977, p. 19.

68. Nore, P. & Turner, T., *Oil and Class Struggle*, Zed Press, London, 1980, p. 1.

Bibliography

Chapter 1   Class and Class Consciousness in Early Industrial Capitalism: Paisley 1770-1850
Tony Clarke and Tony Dickson

R. Brown, *The History of Paisley*, 2 Vols. (Paisley 1885).
T. Dickson (ed.), *Scottish Capitalism* (London 1980).
J. Foster, *Class Struggle and the Industrial Revolution* (London 1974).
M. McCarthy, *A Social Geography of Paisley* (Paisley 1969).
W. M. Metcalfe, *The History of Paisley* (Paisley 1909).
N. Murray, *The Scottish Handloom Weavers* (Edinburgh 1978).
Paisley Pamphlets (held in Paisley Public Library).
J. Parkhill, *The History of Paisley* (Paisley 1857).
Report of the Select Committee on Distress (Paisley) 1843.
Report of the Select Committee on Handloom Weavers' Petitions (1835).
T. C. Smout, *A History of the Scottish People* (Glasgow 1969).
E. P. Thompson, *The Making of the English Working Class* (London 1968).

Chapter 2   Scottish Industrialists and the Changing Character of Class Relations in the Clyde
Region c. 1880-1918   Joseph Melling

Derek H. Aldcroft (ed.), *The Development of British Industry and Foreign Competition 1875-
1914*, University of Glasgow Social and Economic Studies, George Allen & Unwin (1968)
London.
David Bremner, *The Industries of Scotland — Their Rise, Progress and Present Condition*, 1869
Glasgow; Reprint (introduced by Butt and Donnachie), David & Charles, Newton Abbot, 1969.
Asa Briggs & John Savile (eds.), *Essays in Labour History, 1886-1923*, Macmillan (1971) London.
Keith Burgess, *The Challenge of Labour: Shaping British Society 1850-1930*, Croom Helm (1980)
London.
Tony Dickson (ed.), *Scottish Capitalism: Class, State and Nation from before the Union to the
Present*, Lawrence & Wishart (1980) London.
James Hamilton Muir, *Glasgow in 1901*, Hodge & Co. (1901) Edinburgh.
R. Harrison (ed.), *Independent Collier: Archetypal Proletarian Reconsidered*, Harvester (1978)
Brighton.
James Hinton, *The First Shop Stewards' Movement*, George Allen & Unwin (1973) London; 'The
Suppression of the "Forward" — a Note', in *Journal of the Scottish Labour Party History
Society*, No. 7, July 1973.
W. Kendall, *The Revolutionary Movement in Britain, 1900-21*, Weidenfeld & Nicolson (1969)
London.
Ian MacDougall (ed.), *Essays in Scottish Labour History*, John Donald (1978) Edinburgh.
Stuart Macintyre, *The Little Moscows*, Croom Helm (1980) London.
H. W. MacRosty, *The Trust Movement in British Industry*, Longmans (1907) London.
Joseph Melling, 'Clydeside Housing and the Evolution of State Rent Controls, 1900-1939', in
Melling (ed.), *Housing, Social Policy and the State*, Croom Helm (1980) London.

Joseph Melling, '"Non-Commissioned Officer" — British Employers and their Supervisory Workers, 1880-1920', *Social History*, Vol. 5, No. 2, May 1980, pp. 183-221.

Raphael Samuel, 'The Workshop of the world: steam power and hand technology in mid-Victorian Britain', *History Workshop* III (1977).

A. Slaven, *The Development of the West of Scotland, 1750-1960*, RKP (1975) London.

James D. Young, *The Rousing of the Scottish Working Class*, Croom Helm (1979) London.

Chapter 3   Crisis and the Division of Labour: Clydeside Shipbuilding in the Inter-War Period
Jim McGoldrick

Select Bibliography

The references noted in the chapter indicate the main sources of information, both primary and secondary. In giving a select bibliography, the latter are fairly straightforward as the works cited are all easily accessible. Primary sources, however, are not easily accessible but an indication of the main sources is included here.

Secondary Texts

1. K. Marx, *Capital*, Vol. 1 (London 1977).
   See especially Chs. 13-15 inclusive for his discussion of the labour process.
2. H. Braverman, *Labour and Monopoly Capital: the degradation of work in the 20th Century* (New York 1974).
3. C. Palloix, *The Labour Process from Fordism to Neo-Fordism* in the CSE Stage 1 pamphlet, *The Labour Process and Class Strategies* (London 1976).

These represent the core of recent theorising on the labour process; most other articles tend to address themselves to a debate with one or all of these.

4. E. Mandel, *Late Capitalism* (London 1975).
   This covers the analysis of capitalist crisis.
5. S. Pollard & P. Robertson, *The British Shipbuilding Industry 1870-1914* (Cambridge USA 1979).
6. A. Slaven, *The Development of the West of Scotland 1750-1960* (London 1975).
7. L. T. Jones, *Shipbuilding in Britain* (Cardiff 1957).

Primary Sources

1. *Glasgow Herald Trade Review* — an annual supplement with reports on Scottish industry in some detail as well as national and international situations. This is a good source of contemporary views on industrial problems. Held in *Mitchell Library*, Glasgow, from 1902.
2. Papers of the *Shipbuilders and Repairers National Association*, held in public record at the *National Maritime Museum*, Greenwich, London. This collection includes the Circulars of the *Shipbuilding Employers Federation* and the *Shipbuilding Conference* referred to in the text. There are other documents in the collection which refer to various aspects of the shipbuilding industry from Marketing to Technical Design. See L. A. Ritchie (1980), *Modern British Shipbuilding: a Guide to Historical Records* — Maritime Monographs and Reports, No. 48, National Maritime Museum, Greenwich, London.
3. *UCS Collection*. These are the papers of those firms included in the UCS Consortium. They are held by the Scottish Record Office in two archives: *John Brown and Co Ltd (UCS 1)* and *Alexander Stephen and Son Ltd (UCS 3)* are held in Glasgow University archives. The papers of *Fairfield Shipbuilding and Engineering Co (UCS 2)* are held in the Strathclyde Regional Archive in Glasgow City Chambers.
4. *Reports of the Boilermakers Society* held in the Society's head office in Newcastle. These date back to 1867 in a complete collection and in partial form back to 1834.
5. *Private Papers of Finlay Hart*. These are currently being catalogued by Clydebank District Library and will be available shortly.

Chapter 4 **The Vale of Leven 1914-1975: Changes in Working Class Organisation and Action**
Roddy Gallacher

P. Abercrombie & R. H. Mathew, *The Clyde Valley Regional Plan 1946* (Edinburgh 1948).

J. Agnew, *The Story of the Vale of Leven* (Gartocharn 1976).

S. Macintyre, Forms of Authority in the Vale of Leven 1900-1939, unpublished paper, CSE, Stirling, 1978.

S. Macintyre, *Little Moscows* (London 1980).

J. Neill, *Records and Reminiscences of Bonhill Parish*. First published in 1912, reprinted 1979.

J. D. Young, *The Rousing of the Scottish Working Class* (London 1979).

In addition to the above, considerable use was made of the following:
—conversations and taped interviews with people who were active in the inter-war and post-1945 labour movement;
—a number of strike documents and election pamphlets which were given or loaned by local people.

Chapter 5 **Occupational Stratification and the Sexual Division of Labour: Scotland since 1945**
Ian Watt

Section 1

Fraser of Allander Institute: *Quarterly Economic Commentary*.

A. Friedman, *Industry and Labour: Class Struggle at Work and Monopoly Capitalism* (London 1977).

Scottish Abstract of Statistics (Annually).

Scottish Trade Union Review (Quarterly).

Section 2

R. D. Barron & G. M. Norris, 'Sexual Divisions and the Dual Labour Market', in D. Barker & S. Allen (eds.), *Dependence and Exploitation in Work and Marriage* (London 1976).

I. Bruegel, 'Women as a Reserve Army of Labour', *Feminist Review*, No. 3, 1979.

M. Danson, 'The Industrial Structure and Labour Market Segregation: Urban and Regional Implications', Discussion Paper 32, *Urban and Regional Discussion Papers*, Glasgow University, 1980.

J. Firn, 'External Control and Regional Policy', in G. Brown (ed.), *The Red Paper on Scotland* (Edinburgh 1975).

N. Hood & S. Young, 'US Investment in Scotland — Aspects of the Branch Factory Syndrome', *Scottish Journal of Political Economy*, Vol. 23, 1976.

J. Rubery, 'Structured Labour Markets, Worker Organisation and Low Pay', *Cambridge Journal of Economics*, Vol. 2, 1978.

Section 3

R. Brown, 'Women as Employees: Some Comments on Research in Industrial Sociology', Barker & Allen (eds.), *op. cit.*

E. Garnsey, 'Women's Work and Theories of Class Stratification', *Sociology*, Vol. 12, 1978.

I. Watt, 'Linkages Between Industrial Radicalism and the Domestic Role Among Working Women', *Sociological Review*, Vol. 28, 1980.

Section 4

M. Blaxall & B. Reagan (eds.), *Women's Role in Economic Development* (Chicago 1976).

H. Braverman, *Labour and Monopoly Capitalism* (Monthly Review Press 1974).

C. Hakim, 'Occupational Segregation', *Research Paper No. 9*, DOE 1979.

S. Lewenhak, *Women and Trade Unions* (London 1977).

Chapter 6   The Scottish Labour Movement and the Offshore Oil Industry   Peter Wybrow

Primary Sources

Scottish Trade Union Congress, Reports of Annual Conferences, 1972, 1973, 1974, 1975, 1976.

Development of the Oil and Gas Resources of the United Kingdom, Reports to Parliament 1975, 1976, 1977, 1978, 1979, 1980; HMSO, London.

Offshore Safety, Report by the Burgoyne Committee, HMSO, London 1980, Cmnd. 7366.

Bob Middleton, 'North Sea Oil Action Committee — A Successful Pressure Group', Mimeo, 1977.

C. M. Mason (ed.), *The Effective Management of Resources* (London 1979).

Secondary Sources

Peter Kellner & Lord Crowther Hunt, *The Civil Servants: An Inquiry into Britain's Ruling Class* (London 1980).

Petter Nore & Terisa Turner, *Oil and Class Struggle* (London 1980).

K. Dam, *Oil Resources; Who Gets What, How?* (London 1976).

K. Middlemas, *Politics in Industrial Society* (London 1979).

Index